Humanitarianism & Media

New German Historical Perspectives

Series Editor: Paul Betts, St. Antony's College, University of Oxford

Established in 1987, this special St Antony's Series on New German Historical Perspectives showcases pioneering new work by leading German historians on a range of topics concerning the history of Modern Germany and Europe. Publications address pressing problems of political, economic, social and intellectual history informed by contemporary debates about German and European identity, providing fresh conceptual, international and transnational interpretations of the recent past.

Volume 1
Historical Concepts between Eastern and Western Europe
Edited by Manfred Hildermeier

Volume 2
Crises in European Integration: Challenges and Responses, 1945–2005
Edited by Ludger Kühnhardt

Volume 3
Work in a Modern Society: The German Historical Experience in Comparative Perspective
Edited by Jürgen Kocka

Volume 4
Popular Historiographies in the 19th and 20th Centuries: Cultural Meanings, Social Practices
Edited by Sylvia Paletschek

Volume 5
A Revolution of Perception? Consequences and Echoes of 1968
Edited by Ingrid Gilcher-Holtey

Volume 6
Anti-Liberal Europe: A Neglected Story of Europeanization
Edited by Dieter Gosewinkel

Volume 7
Poverty and Welfare in Modern German History
Edited by Lutz Raphael

Volume 8
Space and Spatiality in Modern German-Jewish History
Edited by Simone Lässig and Miriam Rürup

Volume 9
Humanitarianism & Media: 1900 to the Present
Edited by Johannes Paulmann

Humanitarianism & Media
1900 to the Present

Edited by
Johannes Paulmann

berghahn
NEW YORK · OXFORD
www.berghahnbooks.com

First published in 2019 by
Berghahn Books
www.berghahnbooks.com

© 2019, 2020 Johannes Paulmann
First paperback edition published in 2020

All rights reserved. Except for the quotation of short passages
for the purposes of criticism and review, no part of this book
may be reproduced in any form or by any means, electronic or
mechanical, including photocopying, recording, or any information
storage and retrieval system now known or to be invented,
without written permission of the publisher.

Library of Congress Cataloging-in-Publication Data
A C.I.P. cataloging record is available from the Library of Congress

British Library Cataloguing in Publication Data
A catalogue record for this book is available from the British Library

ISBN 978-1-78533-961-5 hardback
ISBN 978-1-78920-808-5 paperback
ISBN 978-1-78533-962-2 ebook

Contents

List of Figures   vii

Acknowledgements   ix

Humanitarianism and Media: Introduction to an Entangled History   1
Johannes Paulmann

I. Humanitarian Imagery

1. Promoting Distant Children in Need: Christian Imagery in
   the Late Nineteenth and Early Twentieth Centuries   41
   Katharina Stornig

2. 'Make the Situation Real to Us without Stressing the Horrors':
   Children, Photography and Humanitarianism in the Spanish
   Civil War   67
   Rose Holmes

3. Humanitarianism on the Screen: The ICRC Films, 1921–65   90
   Daniel Palmieri

4. 'People Who Once were Human Beings Like You and Me':
   Why Allied Atrocity Films of Liberated Nazi Concentration Camps
   in 1944–46 Maximized the Horror and Universalized the Victims   107
   Ulrike Weckel

5. The Polemics of Pity: British Photographs of Berlin, 1945–47   126
   Paul Betts

6. The Human Gaze: Photography after 1945   151
   Tobias Weidner

II. Humanitarian Media Regimes

7. On Fishing in Other People's Ponds: The Freedom from Hunger Campaign, International Fundraising and the Ethics of NGO Publicity   185
Heike Wieters

8. Advocacy Strategies of Western Humanitarian NGOs from the 1960s to the 1990s   201
Valérie Gorin

9. Humanitarianism and Revolution: Samed, the Palestine Red Crescent Society and the Work of Liberation   222
Ilana Feldman

10. Mediatization of Disasters and Humanitarian Aid in the Federal Republic of Germany   240
Patrick Merziger

11. NGOs, Celebrity Humanitarianism and the Media: Negotiating Conflicting Perceptions of Aid and Development during the 'Ethiopian Famine'   263
Matthias Kuhnert

12. The Audience of Distant Suffering and the Question of (In)Action   281
Maria Kyriakidou

Index   299

Figures

1.1 'Save us, for we perish.' 'Institution of the Holy Childhood' booklet, Pontifical Association of the Holy Childhood, 1856.   47

1.2 'Orphelins de la Sainte Enfance – Pékin'. Holy Childhood Association illustrated postcard.   50

1.3 'Das Negerkind', published with this front page 1912–39. St Petrus Claver Sodality.   51

1.4a and b 'Chine – Hongkong'. Holy Childhood Association illustrated postcard.   55

2.1 Walter M. Holmes, 'Nazi Bomb Kills Seventy Spanish Children', *Daily Worker*, 12 November 1936.   71

2.2 Cover, *Spain: An Appeal for the Work of The Society of Friends and The Save the Children International Union*, 1937.   73

2.3 Insert, *Spain: An Appeal for the Work of The Society of Friends and The Save the Children International Union*, 1937.   73

2.4 International Commission for the Assistance of Spanish Child Refugees pamphlet, ca. 1937.   77

2.5 'Saved from War's Terror'. NJC charity envelope, ca. 1938.   80

3.1. ICRC films by decade, 1920s–1960s   92

3.2 'Germany post-war 1946–1948. Distress, cold and hungry: famished old people.' Screenshot from the film *Helft Helfen,* 1948.   96

3.3 'Aid for Greek Civilians'. Screenshot from the film *Tous frères! (All Brothers!)*, 1952.   98

3.4 'Indochina War 1947–1954. Hanoï, camp for Vietnamese military prisoners. Visit of an ICRC delegate in the buildings for internees'. Screenshot from the film *Tous frères!,* 1952.   99

4.1 American prisoner of war Lt. Jack Taylor testifies at Mauthausen. American Army's liberation footage of Mauthausen, 1945. 109

4.2 Jewish medical doctor Hadassah (Ada) Bimko testifies at Bergen Belsen. British liberation footage from Bergen Belsen, shot by British Movietone, 1945. 110

4.3 Survivors at Bergen Belsen curse SS guards forced to carry corpses. British liberation footage from Bergen Belsen, shot by British Movietone, 1945. 111

4.4 Jewish prayer shawls taken from deportees at Auschwitz. Soviet footage of the liberation of Auschwitz, 1945. 114

5.1 Fresh milk on the dock, Gdansk, Poland, 1946. 129

5.2 Jewish DPs receiving food at Bindermichl UNRRA DP Camp in the U.S. Zone, Linz, Austria, date unknown (most likely 1946). 130

5.3 *Children of Europe* (Paris: UNESCO, 1949). 132

5.4 Leonard McCombe, 'Berlin', *Illustrated*, 22 September 1945. 134

5.5 Victor Gollancz, *Is it Nothing to You?* (London: Victor Gollancz/ Orion Publishing Group, 1945), cover. 138

5.6 Victor Gollancz, *In Darkest Germany: The Record of a Visit* (London: Victor Gollancz/Orion Publishing Group, 1947), image 14. 139

5.7 Victor Gollancz, *In Darkest Germany: The Record of a Visit* (London: Victor Gollancz/Orion Publishing Group, 1947), images 22–23. 140

5.8 Sargeant Wilkes, Berlin July 1945. 142

6.1 Robert Doisneau, 'L'enfant papillon', Saint-Denis, 1945. 168

6.2 Henri Cartier-Bresson, scene from a young pioneer camp near Moscow, 1954. 169

6.3 David Seymour, photograph from 'Children of Europe'. 170

8.1 City youth marching to protest world hunger, United Kingdom, May 1971. 205

8.2 Journalist Esther Rantzen in Oxfam's Baby Milk Campaign leaflet, 1983. 208

8.3 'March for the survival of Cambodia'. 211

Acknowledgements

The present volume originates from the Richard von Weizsäcker Fellowship I had the honour to hold at St Antony's College, Oxford, during the academic year 2014/15. My sincere thanks are due to the VolkswagenStiftung, which together with the Fritz Thyssen Stiftung and the Robert Bosch Stiftung financed this distinguished visiting professorship. The chance to be relieved of most duties at my home institution and contribute to the academic life at Oxford by giving a public lecture and organizing a conference proved a stimulating blend of intellectual leisure and academic obligations. The European Studies Centre (ESC) at St Antony's welcomed me warmly and also provided excellent working conditions. I am particularly grateful to Paul Betts, who was my host at the ESC and now has contributed a chapter of his own to the collection. I am indebted to Sarah Moran for her support and skilful planning of the events. Dorian Singh and other friends, old and new, made my sojourn enjoyable as well as memorable, also beyond the confines of 70 Woodstock Road.

I wish to thank the authors for their commitment to the volume and their understanding throughout the time it took to put it together. Thanks are also due to the anonymous reviewers whose critical comments were valuable in developing the book. At the Leibniz Institute of European History in Mainz, Joe Paul Kroll, Barbara Kunkel, Anna Katharina Pieper, Corinna Schattauer and Vanessa Wild helped to make my editorial task much easier. John Carter Wood skillfully constructed the index. Many thanks to all of them. The volume received its final touches in the environment of the LabEx EHNE 'Ecrire une histoire nouvelle de l'Europe' at Panthéon Sorbonne and Sorbonne Université. May it contribute to a better understanding of European history and its relations with the wider world – an aim that links the institutions that supported my efforts.

Mainz and Paris, October 2018

Humanitarianism and Media

Introduction to an Entangled History

Johannes Paulmann

'The media' are an essential feature of humanitarianism – and they have been ever since individuals or organizations began to undertake humanitarian action over long distances and across frontiers. A prerequisite for understanding why someone gives assistance to distant sufferers, media play a crucial role in providing information about other people's plight and setting public agendas. They bear witness and may serve those who are seeking to receive aid as a means to gain attention. They are also salient in representing and framing the bad fortune of some and the good deeds of others. Finally, media reports lead to action by those who learn about human beings in need; they evoke emotions and stir public debate. While the fundamental importance of media for humanitarianism is widely acknowledged, media and communication scholars have only recently started to refine and complicate our understanding of the role of media for relief, aid and humanitarianism. In academic and indeed public debate, scholars and pundits consequently often claim that their object of analysis was a 'first' and that something 'new' is happening right now. A lack of knowledge about historical precedents and continuities characterizes many publications, which seldom reach back to the period before the 1990s if they consider history at all. This is in part due to the relative novelty of the disciplines involved and the narrow focus on current issues. This said, exploring the history of humanitarianism as well as its relations to media is a comparatively new field of historiographical inquiry too. Moreover, those historians who specialize in these topics are only beginning to study the crucial relationship between humanitarianism and media in a more systematic way.

This volume reflects the complex interplay between the history of humanitarianism and media based on archival research and informed by theoretical debates.

It brings together historians, anthropologists, and media and communication scholars. Altogether, the case studies provide an overview reaching back more than a century. The story in fact starts before what has been called the 'Century of the Image'.[1] It begins in the nineteenth century, when Christian missionary publications created images of people in colonial territories and foreign countries whom they considered needy in spiritual as well as material respects.[2] It continues with the analysis of humanitarian imagery in photography and film during the period of the two World Wars covering atrocities, the work of aid agencies and particular visions of humanity. Further chapters investigate the media strategies of international organizations since the 1960s and television broadcasting and audience reactions to media reports of humanitarian crises in the present. While highlighting visual media, the studies presented here contextualize them in three ways. First, attention is paid to the interaction with textual forms and other cultural productions. Second, the historical studies focus on people and institutions who produce, use and distribute media images in specific circumstances for particular aims and purposes rather than engaging in a critique of the effects of the modern visual culture or studying images as actors in their own right.[3] Third, the contributions regard images only as one dimension of the media in a more general sense.

'Media' is indeed a broad term. Understood very widely, it also covers food parcels or money transfers as media of exchange and power relations between donors and recipients.[4] The present investigations follow a more limited definition as used in media and communication studies.[5] Media are (1) the *material forms* in which a content is presented and which carry different sign systems (textual, visual, audio and audiovisual), for example, an illustrated newspaper, a poster, a film or a commemorative plaque. In the sense of technologically based products, media thus form part of the history of technology. Media are (2) *organizations* that produce those material forms; they are, for example, broadcasting corporations, publishing and marketing companies, or humanitarian agencies themselves. Media as organizations have an institutional history and produce and publish in specific economic contexts. They include individual employees and representatives who work as journalists or public relations officers. Media comprise (3) an *institutionalized system* with legal and ethical norms, regulations, and standards that govern production, distribution and reception, and that form a structure with its own logic. All three aspects mentioned play a role in relation to humanitarianism, and when using the term 'media', we should keep in mind that it may refer to a product, a producer or a system of production, distribution and reception.

The volume reflects these various dimensions of media. Part I, 'Humanitarian Imagery', focuses primarily on media forms and their content, with a particular interest in visuals, since the late nineteenth century. Humanitarian actors and journalists have since used different technologies from printed texts, illustrations and photographic images to radio, cinematic films, television and internet media.[6] Although technological development has consecutively added new forms

Introduction

and thus opened different possibilities to communicate suffering and relief, it has not replaced 'older' media altogether. Indeed, a mixture of different media technologies characterized the twentieth century as much as it does the present media system.[7] At its best, a full historical analysis therefore encompasses the interplay between different forms, between text and image in books or magazines, in photos and captions, and on film. It investigates whether and how humanitarian imagery has changed since the end of the nineteenth century, assuming that specifically 'humanitarian' media forms actually existed.[8] Part II, 'Humanitarian Media Regimes', deals primarily with the actors in the field. Contributions focus on nongovernmental organizations (NGOs), newspaper companies, broadcasting corporations and audiences. By analysing who produced imagery under which conditions and for what purpose, the chapters also throw light on the evolving media system. They debate whether and how exactly the media have shaped and framed not only the processes and discourse of communication on humanitarian aid, but also the humanitarian agencies and their activities. The two parts of the book imply by no means a sharp separation of imagery and media regimes; rather, they stem from the particular focus of the authors' research. Indeed, all the different facets of 'the media' have a bearing on humanitarianism during the last century and a half.

Regarding the Pain of Others: Fatigue and Irony?

Since the 1990s, the relationship between humanitarian action and the communication of distant suffering has inspired some theories, abstract generalizations and speculative statements, as well as evidence-based research. Key works from media and communication scholars, anthropologists and sociologists provide a valuable starting point for historical inquiries, even if some of their hypotheses are to be questioned in the light of thorough empirical findings. Debates focus on the representation of distant suffering, on the effects of the imagery on donors and recipients of aid, and on the role of media as agents in the humanitarian field.

Susan Sontag's book *Regarding the Pain of Others* regularly serves as a reference point for inquiries into the representations of distant suffering and its effects.[9] The publication had its origins in the 2001 Oxford Amnesty Lecture, an event in a series that since the early 1990s has raised funds for Amnesty International and at the same time seeks to highlight the profile of human rights in the academic and wider communities.[10] It is thus in itself an example of the support given by intellectuals and scholars to organizations in their efforts to collect money and publicize their humanitarian cause more widely. In substance, Sontag explores photos of war victims by discussing issues such as the iconography of suffering, the double aspect of photos showing an 'objective' reality and a 'subjective' perspective, censorship and varying standards in the depiction of suffering, the phenomenon of voyeurism, and finally the memorial function of representing suffering.[11] Two arguments are worth highlighting here. First,

Sontag affirms that images of suffering are open to different interpretations; there is no direct connection between the representation of suffering and a feeling of pity sufficient to trigger humanitarian action.[12] Her case rests on war victims, a case where partisan perspectives are common by nature and different emotions – for example, a desire for revenge – may result from seeing photographs of mutilated bodies. For historians, context-specific interpretations and questions as to who uses photos for what purpose should be part of their everyday toolbox. Yet Sontag's point is worth remembering not only because humanitarian action often responds to suffering caused by war., but also because it is useful as an antidote against assuming unidirectional and universal effects set off by 'shocking' pictures and the impression they may make on scholars as individuals.

Second, when musing about the effects of the plethora of images shown of suffering, writers sometimes also refer to Sontag's essay on *Regarding the Pain of Others*. They quote her suggestion that the numerous visual campaigns that aid agencies run today actually numb viewers, who feel saturated and as a consequence fail to respond emotionally as well as in terms of donations.[13] Yet Sontag made a quite different point in 2003 when she discussed the possibility that shocking images might lose their impact on viewers. Indeed, she appears to retract her own position from the 1970s and now rejects the thesis she once vocally advocated by arguing that some images keep their force in terms of moving viewers.[14] Images of cruelty or suffering, according to Sontag, exemplify and reinforce existing notions. Sometimes they also evoke other, earlier images of sufferers; photographs taken during the Bosnian War in 1992 at the Omarska camp recalled images of the liberated concentration camps in 1945,[15] while images of suffering may play on Christian iconography and evoke the sufferings of Christian martyrs or even Jesus.[16] If the viewer is a 'believer' or has a prior disposition and the image fits an existing interpretative frame, it moves repeatedly no matter how often it appears on screen or paper. While Sontag considers empathy an unstable emotional reaction, she contends that it is the impotence to change anything, rather than the quantity of images, that leads to passivity. Yet the viewer remains passionate in terms of anger and frustration.[17] Based on Luc Boltanski's analysis, studies on audience research distinguish several forms of emotional commitment: denunciation (indignation and anger towards perpetrators of unjust suffering); sentiment (being touched by compassion and sympathy towards victims and benefactors); aesthetics (experiencing the sublime in the horror of suffering on display); shame (feeling conscious about one's own comfort and guilty of inaction); and powerlessness (feeling helpless through subjective awareness of the spectator's limits to prevent the suffering of others).[18] The argument worth highlighting is that by 2003, Sontag has come to consider the idea of 'compassion fatigue' together with that of the 'society of the spectacle' a very conventional criticism of modern society. In her opinion, these concepts universalize the viewing experience merely of a small elite living in the rich parts of the world; they are 'a cliché of the cosmopolitan discussion'.[19] To Sontag, keeping emotional distance to suffering is not a reaction that needs explanation;

rather, she considers it normal and a standard mode for individuals and collectives to keep fear or helplessness at bay.[20]

The discussion on the spectatorship of distant suffering has been advanced through the work of Lilie Chouliaraki, a professor of media and communications. In *Spectatorship of Suffering* (2006), Chouliaraki deals with the ethical role of the media by analysing how certain scenes of suffering are construed in television as capable of arousing the spectators' emotions, or alternatively being of no concern to Western viewers.[21] Rather than news production or audience reaction, Chouliaraki focuses on the choices made regarding the portrayal of sufferers on screen and how scenes of suffering are narrated. She distinguishes between 'adventure news' and 'emergency news' on the one hand, which displays suffering without pity, and 'ecstatic news' on the other, which links suffering to the identification of the viewers.[22] In general, she calls for a critical analysis of the reproduction of injustice, symbolic inequalities and representational hierarchies in the mediation of disasters and suffering. Her book is aimed at the conditions under which the media would be able to cultivate a disposition for care or, in other words 'an ideal identity for the spectator as a citizen of the world – a cosmo-politan'.[23] It claims that the dominant contemporary discourse is 'out of pace with our contemporary experience of suffering, which is thoroughly mediated'; therefore, to act in a compassionate manner – that is, in an on-the-spot manner – has become impossible. Instead, action is needed in the shape of pity that incorporates the dimension of distance. Cosmopolitan citizenship should therefore replace the dominant and by implication outdated ideal moral citizen modelled on the Good Samaritan.[24]

Chouliaraki moves between the critique of social theory and the empirical analysis of how contemporary television news portrays suffering and frames it narratively. However, acknowledging that public action has always been action at a distance, she identifies a new aspect in that the mass media have intensified the problem of distance through constantly confronting viewers with events that occur too far away from everyday life for Western audiences to feel that they can make a difference. Continuing her examination of the contemporary media display of suffering, Chouliaraki has recently published *The Ironic Spectator* (2013). Her key term describes 'an impure or ambivalent figure that stands, at once, as sceptical towards any moral appeal to solidarity action and, yet, open to doing something about those who suffer'.[25] The figure of the ironic spectator is clearly the opposite of the cosmopolitan who was the ideal of her 2006 book. The media conditions appear *not* to have moved towards a communicative structure that has the capacity 'to stage human vulnerability as an object of our empathy as well as of critical reflection and deliberation'. Chouliaraki wishes to advance a form of communication that employs narrative and visual resources in order to connect the feeling for the distant other with critical judgement as to why action on other people's suffering is necessary; sufferers themselves ought to have a voice in this. She argues for a 'theatricality of humanitarian communication' that places a solidarity of agonism at the centre –

that is, a connectivity between the other and us that creates collective action to change the conditions of suffering.[26]

This ideal shows a remarkable reliance on the notion of the 'theatre as a moral institution' (Friedrich Schiller), reaching back to eighteenth-century aesthetic ideals of a bourgeois elite and standing in stark contrast to Chouliaraki's analysis of the present state of humanitarian communication. According to Chouliaraki, the communication of solidarity has fundamentally shifted during the last three decades from 'solidarity as pity' to 'solidarity as irony'. A 'post-humanitarian' disposition oriented at the self has replaced the traditional humanitarian moral focus on the suffering of others. Expressing empathy by attending a charity concert or liking tweets by celebrities visiting refugee camps is more about the self than engaging with distant sufferers. 'Ironic solidarity', as Chouliaraki calls these activities, 'situates the pleasures of the self at the heart of moral action.' This is 'cool activism', which individualizes people and discourages commitment and political justification.[27] The emergence of the ironic disposition of simultaneous scepticism concerning the efficiency of aid and noncommitting activity is explained (based on secondary literature and theories) by changes in the humanitarian sphere since the 1980s: (1) The 'instrumentalization' of the aid and development field by the imperative of profitable performance.[28] As a consequence of the proliferation of nongovernmental and international organizations, the marketization of humanitarian practice has characterized the aid and development sector; branding and selling one's image are said to have become aims in themselves, distracting from real priorities in the Global South. (2) The retreat of the two grand narratives of solidarity, i.e. the solidarity of salvation and the solidarity of revolution. Both had been informed by universal norms of morality and have been replaced by a new morality of solidarity, which is anti-political because it adheres to an individualistic morality of 'a neoliberal lifestyle of "feel good" altruism' attempting to manage the present rather than striving for a better world.[29] (3) The 'technologization' of communication that has made the diffusion of this new morality possible, because the interactive use of the internet invites self-expression. It triggers a response without posing the question 'why we should act' and therefore leads to an absence of normative morality.[30] While the title of Chouliaraki's book places the spectator at the centre, the empirical analysis of appeals by humanitarian agencies, celebrity performances, aid concerts and television as well as social media news deals with the construction of solidarity and spectators in these various media forms. However, donors responding to appeals, humanitarian workers or indeed recipients of aid are absent as actors from the analysis; they appear only as 'Western audiences', 'the aid industry' or 'the Global South'. At least in their self-perception, none of these groups is likely to recognize themselves as 'ironic spectators'. The term leaves no space for sincere feelings or varying grades of commitment. It seems to be a judgement (and wishes to be one) as much as a heuristic or scholarly term. Instructive as Chouliaraki's empirical studies are for understanding the moral and political meaning of the communication of solidarity for suffering people, the conclusion of a fundamental shift in the relation between humanitarianism and the media is not fully convincing. There ought to be a more thorough investigation of the links with the contemporary history of society and international as well as national politics, and the theses put forward need scrutiny beyond the narrow focus on the Anglo-American sector of humanitarianism. At the same time, a longer historical perspective may help to question the significance of the perceived changes in the present.

Humanitarian Action: A Media Regime?

The observation that humanitarianism is inextricably linked to media reports of disasters and suffering has been expanded into the thesis of 'mediatization' of the aid and development sector. This claims that the media not only shape the ways in which human suffering and humanitarian action are communicated, but also that the media system today directly affects the work and activities of humanitarian agencies. These scholarly considerations reflect changes in the humanitarian sector that appear to have become central to the discussion in the 1980s and early 1990s. In 1993, the anthropologist Jonathan Benthall published *Disasters, Relief and the Media.* This book carefully investigates the relationship between relief agencies and the media, concentrating on Britain, but including comparison with French and American NGOs. It has benefited from the author's advisory role on a number of committees for Save the Children as well as numerous conversations with representatives from several NGOs, television stations, and the press. Benthall's aim is to understand better the emergence since the late 1960s of 'what may be called a media regime, to which the humanitarian agencies and politicians are increasingly having to adapt'.[31]

Benthall explicitly argues against simplified views of complicated issues. He acknowledges the crucial role of the media in the 'construction' of disasters for a Western audience and the pressure on governments and relief agencies to respond, particularly to those emergencies that make it into the headlines.[32] With government cuts and the end of the Cold War, demand for development and emergency funding has risen. The structural factor, however, effecting a larger role of the media is competition between NGOs that attempt to raise donations for themselves through increased media attention. Yet it is not simply about donations. All organizations that rely on government funds, but particularly international organizations like the United Nations (UN) agencies or the International Committee of the Red Cross, use media to spread information to the public, which in turn puts pressure on politicians to support aid and development. For Benthall, the growing importance of media is not an inescapable compulsion for aid agencies to conduct their business only in the way the media obliges them.

Rather, he describes various ways to cope with 'the dilemmas which face the agencies when fundraising priorities, developmental strategies and educational values do not harmonize'.[33]

With regard to limiting competition, a system of cooperation between major relief agencies and the broadcasting authorities has been in place in Britain since 1966; representatives meet in the Disasters Emergency Committee with the BBC and the Independent Television Commission to decide on and broadcast appeals by television and radio.[34] The system works discreetly behind closed doors, excludes all smaller organizations in favour of a few large ones, and ensures that television appeals remain mostly apolitical in character. The latter is easier in the case of natural disasters than in those regarded as manmade. According to Benthall, it also puts the agencies in a strong position with regard to the broadcasting authorities, so much so that it becomes difficult for them to resist moral pressure. The BBC, for example, on occasion had to insist on maintaining its editorial control – in other words, the humanitarian agencies exercise pressure on the media organization rather than vice versa.

Besides this form of regulating competition, Benthall analyses how the different character of humanitarian agencies results in different media relations.[35] For all of them, regular donors are essential and need to be cultivated beyond exceptional fundraising campaigns in the wake of major disasters. For religious charities such as Christian Aid or the Catholic Fund for Overseas Development, church and congregations connect them routinely with potential donors. Oxfam, on the other hand, originally had strong links with universities and students. Early on, it emphasized the need to develop poor people's resources and has been deemed left of centre in political terms, closely related to the readership of liberal newspapers like *The Guardian*. In the 1970s, its publicity played on feelings of responsibility and conscience, emphasizing guilt rather than compassion. Save the Children (UK) has an extensive branch network cultivating loyal supporters. In comparison with church-based organizations or Oxfam, its particular focus on children makes it easier to target a broader spectrum of opinion. Yet children easily suggest an apolitical imagery and impede arguments regarding the improvement of social systems rather than aid for individual children, opening up a potential gap between fundraising topics and field operations.[36] More generally, Benthall's analysis suggest the conclusion that the less focus there is on emergency relief and the more on rehabilitation and development, the greater the use of educational material and other media rather than advertisements in the mass media, television and press, or charity 'fun' events. Organizationally, development education is associated with public relations, not fundraising. Besides donations from the public, the collection of money also relies on sales in charity shops, payroll giving, corporate membership schemes, company sponsoring and legacies, as well as direct mailing.

Finally, Benthall points out that, at the time of writing in the early 1990s, there were NGOs for whom the media were of less relevance. The International Committee of the Red Cross (ICRC), for example, he saw in transition. It had been evolving from a 'pre-media' organization that relied on confidentiality and private communication with governments in order to successfully protect prisoners and casualties of war as well as political detainees, and to negotiate truces in internal conflicts, towards a humanitarian agency that has to justify how it spends the government funds it largely relies on. Moreover, the expansion of relief work by national Red Cross Societies, the proliferation of humanitarian NGOs and the blurring of conflicts (war between states, civil war and humanitarian intervention)[37] all make it imperative for the Geneva ICRC to explain its peculiar position to a larger public and therefore open up to the media. Two other organizations also seem at present not to have to pay much attention to the media. CARE and the Malteser International are both among the largest humanitarian organizations; they secure almost all of their funding from governments or have access to private wealth and can thus afford to ignore the competition for public support.

Compared to Benthall's differentiated analysis of contemporary changes during the 1980s and early 1990s, the field of Media and Communication Studies has discussed the relationship between aid and development agencies and the media in a more pointed manner. The issue of whether 'mediatization' is taking place first came up concerning politics – that is, the orientation of political activities in general to conform to the logic of the media.[38] More specifically, Patrick Donges distinguishes several levels: an increasingly mediated experience and perception of politics (micro-level), an adaption of organizational structure, resources and rules to media requirements (mid-level), an impact on behaviour, rules and norms in politics (mid- to macro-level), and finally the systemic orientation of political actors to a media logic.[39] Mediatization thus concerns policy, politics and polity. In 2007, Simon Cottle and David Nolan applied the mediatization thesis to the field of humanitarian aid. In what may be read as a pointed, if limited extrapolation of Benthall's questions from the early 1990s regarding the emergence of a media regime, they contend that the communication strategies of the major aid agencies to raise awareness, funds and support have 'assimilated to today's pervasive "media logic"', thereby being 'detracted from their principle remit of humanitarian provision'.[40] They base these claims empirically on semi-structured interviews with communication managers and media officers in Australia working in six leading international aid NGOs. However, the authors do not consider whether the data reflects the concerns and interests of the special departments as well as the tensions within the organizations rather than describing processes and actors in the humanitarian field, let alone its general structure.

Contrary to the common interpretation of mediatization, the journalism scholar Lutz Mükke turns the claim that the media directed the humanitarian organizations upside down. In his study on German news reports on Africa, he goes beyond merely asserting a 'symbiotic link' between aid agencies and foreign correspondents.[41] He ascribes a major role to humanitarian NGOs for the work of Western journalists in Africa, whom he describes as a kind of 'embedded journalists'. In terms of organization and logistics, the NGOs help correspondents with travel; they provide security, shelter and supplies, as well as local contacts. Individual correspondents do not have the financial and institutional means to go out on their own, so the argument goes, or have no easy access to crisis-torn regions. Furthermore, the content and information they gather is heavily influenced by the NGO through exaggerated briefings, event days like World Hunger Day or World Aids Day, celebrity involvement and free visual material. The aid industry is partially able to establish 'a monopoly on information and communication', Mükke concludes.[42] He bases his study on interviews with active and former German correspondents in Africa, all conducted in 2006. It is not too surprising that the results therefore read as the reverse of Cottle's and Nolan's arguments taken from NGO press officers. From these two contradictory perspectives, we may actually conclude that public relations and journalists serve as each other's counterparts rather than one governing the other.

The issue of a humanitarian media regime clearly merits further discussion that is more specific and openly framed. Has the manner in which human suffering and humanitarian relief is represented changed or has it shown continuities and perhaps cyclical repetitions? Has the establishment of PR departments and the work of press officers marked a significant departure, or is it more appropriate to speak of the professionalization of media relations rather than a process of 'mediatization'? How far has the lead in the interaction between media and humanitarian organizations changed, or has it not always been a cooperative, if sometimes tense or strained relationship? Finally, the general question of structural changes in the field induced by media logic appears so vague that it merely underlines other arguments or even borders on cultural criticism of contemporary issues. In terms of evidence, the analysis of disasters as media events, which describes the construction of emergencies calling for aid as a product of media attention, has a limited reach. It focuses on mass media and on exceptional cases, ascribing their prominence to media reporting.[43] This emphasis tends to ignore other factors that shape audiences and public action, such as cultural stereotypes, ideological forces tied to specific local, regional or national contexts of domestic politics, foreign policy and geopolitical interests.[44] All these questions and the general issues regarding the relationship between humanitarian agencies, the media and the public raised by Benthall during the early 1990s will benefit from further empirically based and historical analysis, lest we too easily declare the media to govern humanitarianism.

Humanitarian Imagery and Media Use: Historical Insights from the Late Nineteenth to the Early Twenty-First Century

The relationship between humanitarianism and media has only recently become a topic of historical inquiry, as has the whole field of the history of humanitarianism.[45] Heide Fehrenbach and Davide Rodogno have edited a stimulating collection of essays on *Humanitarian Photography*, which specifically investigates one particular medium and its use – that is, 'the mobilization of photography in the service of humanitarian initiatives across state borders'.[46] The volume moves the debate beyond fatigue, irony and mediatization by exploring how the medium emerged as part of the visual history of humanitarianism and how it has functioned in changing political, institutional and social contexts. With the economical application of new photographic and printing technologies in the 1890s (the convenient Kodak camera with film and the halftone printing method),[47] reformers, missionaries and journalists could produce images and transform episodes of human privation and suffering into reform campaigns. Photography thus played an important role in the emergence of a 'recognizable, if not unitary, "humanitarian imaginary"' around 1900.[48] Following visual conventions of ethnographic photography and resting on notions of scientific photography, the humanitarian images were (and are) at the same time evidence *and* rhetoric. Via the directness of their emotional address, the photos focus attention on suffering, which appears as unjust yet salutary and is isolated from political or social context: 'In this sense', Fehrenbach and Rodogno conclude, 'humanitarian imagery is *moral rhetoric* masquerading as visual evidence.'[49]

The historical studies in this recent volume and others demonstrate the power of photography as a medium, but also show that photography has been implicated in power relations, conflicts of interest and competing ideologies. Furthermore, they explain that humanitarian images function and take effect in the often-intertwined spheres of the domestic, the imperial and the international since the late nineteenth century.[50] The particular chronology of the use of photography presents humanitarian imagery as emerging out of missionary work before and around the First World War.[51] Yet it was not only part of moral campaigns, such as the relief of famine in India of 1876–78 and again in the late 1890s or the Congo Reform Association of 1903–13.[52] Humanitarian imagery also emerged in the context of a new mass culture and politics. It was therefore, so the argument of Kevin Rozario goes, a 'creation of a sensational mass culture' for consumers who wished to be entertained – a thesis that may sound familiar to readers of Chouliaraki's studies of more recent times and should be subjected to further scrutiny lest we too easily conflate context, content and audience reception.[53] Humanitarian photography expanded within various international organizations in the aftermath of the two World Wars. Examples studied are the Red Cross movement, the United Nations Relief and Rehabilitation Administration (UNRRA) and the World Health Organization.[54] These international organizations had the means to professionalize media work and collaborate with prominent photographic agencies. By the 1980s, a professional field had developed in which photographers received prizes for 'humanitarian' images and where those involved discussed the ethics of showing suffering, as well as the need for dialogue with recipients of aid.[55] In photography, so we may conclude from existing work, a defined field seems to have emerged over the course of more than a century from the first irregular use of the technology in humanitarian campaigns to today's professional image strategy of humanitarian organizations.

However, we need to investigate how the particular medium of photography and its epistemologies fit into the general history of humanitarianism and the media. What, for example, were key moments or basic elements of non-photographic imagery?[56] How did the various organizations from missionaries and international NGOs to governments and media organizations define and practise a 'humanitarian' use of media? Yet, the twentieth century is more than just a century of the image. We therefore need to pursue our inquiries beyond the analysis of the (visual) media products and the actors' self-perception, by seeing media also as organizations producing humanitarian images and as an institutionalized system with norms and regulations that govern distribution and reception. The immediate and wider historical contexts ought to be considered as well as historical developments, rather than focusing merely on what appears as new to contemporaries. We will thus gain a deeper insight into the humanitarian imagery and media use.

With regard to humanitarian imagery, this volume starts by correcting the predominant focus of available historical studies on the visualization of the vulnerable, suffering or mutilated human body.[57] Several case studies have analysed the portrayal of atrocities, genocide, famine or 'ideal victims' such as children or women, as well as the cultural, social or political notions connected with this kind of incident.[58] *Katharina Stornig* in her chapter revises prevailing ideas regarding the emergence of children in humanitarian imagery and specifies the effects of photography. Her scrutiny of Christian imagery in the late nineteenth and early twentieth centuries demonstrates that a complementary or alternative representational model existed and remained in use, as other chapters show; rather than physical suffering and pain, the images shared among Christian missionary communities presented moments of rescue and saved human beings.[59] Children were central to the humanitarian efforts from the mid nineteenth century and were well established in Christian publications before 1900.[60] Christian organizations, such as the Holy Childhood Association founded in France in 1843,[61] promoted a visual practice of child saving that relied on a clearly gendered European notion of childhood and established the young as innocents whose spiritual salvation and concomitant physical rescue was a Christian duty that at the same time benefited the saviour's soul. Promotional campaigns employed mass prints and artefacts before photographic reproductions appeared in the 1890s. The new technology did not change the imagery, as Stornig explains, but picture postcards served as 'visual exchange objects' and an effective and readily available medium for imagining a personal communication between European donors and non-European sponsored children.

After the First World War, when pictures of emaciated children from Central Europe and Russia attracted public attention,[62] these did not replace deserving and healthy children as objects of humanitarian efforts. In her study on photography in the Spanish Civil War, *Rose Holmes* explains that while the British popular press hardly showed children at all, the humanitarian agencies like the Friends' Service Committee did so in their publications and during lectures. Yet they considered it unacceptable to show the physical and emotional suffering of Spanish children. Instead, deserving children and the aid work for them figured prominently; the young in need usually appeared on their own without families in order to indicate their unstable existence. The Friends took this decision together with Save the Children International Union because they felt that shock images had lost their value and because they sought to avoid becoming part of leftist propaganda. Even the Trades Union Congress (TUC) followed this pattern because tensions with Catholic workers proved an obstacle for relief works and children were regarded as neutral objects of care. When in 1937 around 4,000 Basque children received temporary refuge in Britain, several agencies cooperated closely; the Basque Children's Committee of the National Joint Committee for Spanish Relief (NJC) brought together representatives from the TUC, the Labour Party, the Society of Friends, Save the Children, Spanish Medical Aid, and the Catholic Church. They took great care to represent these children as thoroughly screened, healthy and 'white' to allay fears voiced in the press that they might carry infectious diseases. Holmes concludes that the choice of imagery depends on various factors: contemporary judgements on taste, expediency and cost, religion, domestic politics and diplomacy. Those involved took the decision for a nonpolitical and reassuring visual narrative about deserving children consciously and without necessarily abandoning their politics regarding the Spanish Civil War or their religious motivation.

With cinematic films, a medium became available that was much more expensive to produce and required technical equipment and logistics, which made it less ready at hand than a photo camera. This may partially explain why the ICRC produced no films in the 1930s after it had commissioned several between 1921 and 1923, and only returned to the medium in the 1940s. Why then did the ICRC invest in productions at all? *Daniel Palmieri* sees the main reason in the necessity for the Swiss-based organization to position itself within the Red Cross movement. With the creation of the League of Red Cross Societies, in which national Red Cross societies organized from 1919 and that was backed foremost by the American Red Cross, there was a force with which to reckon politically.[63] This is a case not so much of the proliferation of aid agencies or of public fundraising, but, as it were, of intra-organizational rivalry. The ICRC sought to prove its value by depicting its continuing work after the end of the First World War with repatriated prisoners of war, refugees and civilians who were victims of the social and economic turmoil. The films were mainly aimed at a Swiss audience and delegates at Red Cross conferences. It seems that the negotiated agreement with the League in 1928 made this unnecessary, the need resurfacing only in the aftermath of the Second World War with new challenges coming from Red Cross societies in communist countries and accusations of an earlier lack of neutrality and impartiality towards fascist regimes. The content of the films focused on the humanitarian work done on behalf of the ICRC, with delegates, doctors and logistical operations emphasizing the male strength of the organization.[64] Victims did not figure prominently unless as beneficiaries; the one exception, a 1948 film with shocking scenes from postwar Germany, was not shown publicly because the ICRC regarded these as too disturbing and feared they would make the Committee appear too pro-German. The cinematic productions were, Palmieri concludes, more about the solidarity of the audience with the ICRC than with the victims, whose depiction often reflected hierarchies of civilization within Europe and colonial stereotypes. At the same time, they illustrate that horror images did not solely define 'humanitarian cinema', at least until the 1960s.

Yet atrocities were by no means absent from film and perhaps supplied the foil for the use of positive images by humanitarian organizations. *Ulrike Weckel* analyses one of the pivotal moments in the depiction of human suffering meant not to mobilize, but to moralize by its message of accusation and shame. The films made of liberated concentration camps in 1944–46 by the Western Allies need to be historicised, she asserts, to avoid misinterpreting their intentions and the particular image of the victims. Subsequent critics have reproached the films for supposedly perpetuating the dehumanization of the former inmates by failing to individualize them and not giving them a voice, instead making them appear as helpless, passive victims.[65] In fact, the survivors wanted the horror to be known, often re-enacted drills and were keen to demonstrate the worst camp conditions. With a view towards the intended German audience, maximizing the shock was a deliberate choice made by the filmmakers. The aim was to end the disbelief in the extent of the German crimes by 'shock pedagogy'. Weckel further refutes the suggestion that the films were anti-Semitic because they did not mention Jews other than in passing. Although the Western Allies thus failed to grasp the centrality of the Shoah, this was partially because they liberated camps predominately occupied by forced labourers and opponents of the regime. Yet more to the point is their intention to underline the victims' humanity by focusing on their dehumanization. Moreover, they attempted to counter the expectation on the part of German audiences that they would be accused of murdering the Jews. Undermining anti-Semitic attitudes seemed best achieved by speaking not about the Jewish 'race', but about 'political opponents' or victims from 'all over Europe'. In short, the films targeted a particular audience and deliberately showed crimes against humanity rather than particular segments of it or individuals. Scholars ought to carefully reconstruct contemporary intentions and context and avoid applying later knowledge or values.

In the aftermath of the Second World War, the images of victory over evil and inhuman perpetrators could change to images of pity and suffering. *Paul Betts* studies British photographs of defeated Germany after 1945 aimed at a British public, ranging from newspaper images to amateur army snapshots to photographs by humanitarian activists, such as London publisher Victor Gollancz.[66] The images that presented suffering German refugees and malnourished children rather than relief measures connected in the British public mind with the shocking images from the liberated Belsen concentration camp – and yet they seem to have affected attitudes towards Germans as perpetrators, transforming judgement into pity. Betts argues that the polemics of pity in the photographs and accompanying texts aimed, in fact, at the moral and civilizational standard the British claimed for themselves. The kind of humanitarian imagery thus created was very much self-reflective, appeared nonpolitical and emphasized the universal. It fitted not only with the notion Britain held of itself, but also sat comfortably alongside Cold War ideologies and served, in the case of Germany, Cold War alliances. Pity was therefore also polemical in a wider sense beyond the specific crisis – and it formed a new universalist sentiment that found expression in the postwar constellation.

Tobias Weidner analyses this moment in the visual representation of humanity, for which photography was crucial. It found prominent expression in the 1955 exhibition, *The Family of Man,* conceived by the photographer and curator Edward Steichen in collaboration with the Museum of Modern Art in New York and the United Nations Educational, Scientific and Cultural Organization (UNESCO) and seen by over nine million visitors. It aimed to show 'the essential one-ness of mankind throughout the world',[67] portraying peoples from across the globe in a kind of family album against the background of the excesses of inhumanity of the past decades and suspicions about the ideological character of the spoken as much as the written word. The exhibition exemplifies what Weidner proposes to call the 'human gaze' – a specific manner of visualizing humanity linked to a repertoire of assumptions about the 'authentic' potential of photography. He studies the popular diffusion and institutionalization of this vision, for which new photo agencies, particularly Magnum, were as decisive as museum curators, magazines or handbooks for amateur photographers. The basic visual patterns were the focus on humans, the themes of family, everyday life and leisure, as well as an interest in expressions of emotions and interaction (with the camera). The human gaze drew on French *photographie humaniste* of the interwar period and New Deal documentary photography. The experience of embedded war photographers affected the depiction of the darker sides of humanity in a reverse manner. Avoiding seemingly hopeless images of cruelty, representations of famine, revolt or even lynching were included, but were framed in a humanitarian narrative of prevailing human goodness. The photojournalism, especially in 1950s magazines, narrated human stories at a deliberate distance from politics. Steichen, for example, discarded the idea of explicitly invoking human rights because the topic had become, in his view, an 'international political football'.[68] In addition, this humanist vision constructed the 'concerned' photographer – committed, audacious, authentic and usually male. Contemporary and later critics such as Roland Barthes, Susan Sontag or Diane Arbus pointed out that this sentimental humanism stabilized social inequality and propagated the bourgeois nuclear family. It was immediately compatible with the Western ideology of a Christian and modernist character.[69] Nevertheless, this vision from the mid twentieth century continued in humanitarian imagery and even some photographers from the Global South adapted it. Similar to Christian imagery from the late nineteenth century, the repeated focus on rescue and the good deeds of humanitarian agencies, this unifying display of a shared humanity, has coexisted and seems to alternate with images intended to shock viewers. The emergence of humanitarian imagery in the twentieth century intertwined several threads reflecting different shades of humanity available for use according to political and economic interests in specific social and cultural circumstances.

After the Second World War, the founding of new organizations in the context of the UN such as the Food and Agricultural Organization (FAO), UNICEF or the World Food Programme required new negotiations at the international and national levels as media coverage of these agencies cut across boundaries. *Heike Wieters* analyses the conflicts over the legitimacy of international fundraising campaigns in the United States as some UN agencies, which governments were to finance directly, began to look for private resources. The problem emerged in the context of the *Freedom from Hunger* (FFH) campaign initiated by the FAO Director General Binay R. Sen (1898–1993), a former Indian Civil Service officer and diplomat. When he was unsuccessful in convincing governments to fund a World Food Congress in 1958, he appealed to NGOs all over the world to join a five-year campaign against hunger. The initiative unsettled the existing national arrangement in the United States. By the 1950s, most large American humanitarian agencies such as CARE, the American Friends Service Committee, the YMCA, Catholic Relief Services, Lutheran World Relief, the American Jewish Joint Distribution Committee, and Church World Service were members of the American Council of Voluntary Agencies for Foreign Service (ACVAFS). Founded in 1942, the umbrella organization had agreed on basic rules to promote best practices for public relations regarding unwanted soliciting and the decency and accuracy of slogans and pictures. It thereby also limited competition. The American Council protested against the direct contact the FAO sought in 1960 with the donor base of its member organizations. Eventually, the parties arrived at a mode of cooperation. This prescribed that international campaigns would include the national American NGOs as joint players that solicited donations under the FFH banner and used them in their own aid projects, while the FFH provided merely an administrative network and publicity hub. The case demonstrates how powerful private NGOs and new international organizations settled conflicts over the competing claims to access of relief organizations to the national public in the 1960s. The FFH proved an important step regarding cooperation across the national and international spheres. It confirmed the position of national organizations, which in addition benefited in terms of publicity, and it enabled the FAO to enlist support beyond governments from nongovernmental actors.

From the late nineteenth and early twentieth centuries, humanitarian organizations had applied some basic means in their campaigns to influence governments and other stakeholders. Besides discrete humanitarian diplomacy, particularly that practised by the ICRC, these had included winning support from celebrities in the arts, science and entertainment, fostering close relationships with journalists, and the diffusion of their causes and principles through various media. *Valérie Gorin* distinguishes two advocacy strategies, which evolved among Western humanitarian from the 1960s and established organizations of markedly different public characters and self-images. One she calls 'educational advocacy' as practised by the Save the Children Fund (SCF) and Oxfam in the United Kingdom, and the other 'political advocacy' as applied by Médecins Sans Frontières (MSF) in France. The decisive frame for the first strategy was British charity legislation that threatened the loss of charitable status for agencies spreading political propaganda. When SCF participated in the first FFH campaign, it feared that it might become too political. It therefore decided to concentrate on local rather than national activities to create awareness of the growing dangers from hunger and focused on the countries where it worked. The self-evaluation at the end of the campaign emphasized the commitment to an educational role. It prioritized addressing teachers, producing its own bulletin or specialized journals, and cooperating with voluntary youth agencies. Consequently, the SCF also participated in the second FAO (1967) campaign targeting experts and social leaders such as students, professors and business leaders. However, it declined to take part in the Fast for World Justice in 1972 because of what those responsible deemed militant public strategies. The example of Oxfam's involvement in the Baby Milk Campaign (1979–88) to end bottle-feeding in Third World countries demonstrates that the agenda set in UN special agencies strongly influenced advocacy campaigns in the 1970s and furthered the establishment by the NGO of a campaign unit in 1979 and a Public Affairs Unit in the 1980s.[70]

The second model of political advocacy had also emerged by the 1980s. Contrary to its own foundational myth of the experience in the Nigerian Civil War, the strategy of 'speaking out' and 'witnessing' pursued by MSF only evolved in stages and from experience after it was founded in 1971, particularly during the crises of the Vietnamese boat people (1978–79), a refugee crisis and famine in Cambodia (1979–80) and the Ethiopian famine (1984–85).[71] Prominent media appearances by one of its founders, Bernard Kouchner, and the blurring of lines between political operations and MSF's aid work in fact split the organization in 1979. Media issues again provoked divisions in the movement in the late 1980s when MSF developed its style of political advocacy in emergency settings, focusing on access and protection. Within the international aid community, the leading role played by MSF in publicizing and criticizing the political origins of the Ethiopian famine in 1984, and consequently leaving the country, led to wider debates about going public or alternatively negotiating behind closed doors. The line taken by MSF proved controversial and partially isolated it. The practical dilemmas of advocacy strategies, going public or not and how to balance emergency and educational goals have remained issues to the present day.

Elsewhere the line between charitable relief and political commitment could be drawn very differently from the way it was in Western metropoles. *Ilana Feldman* investigates Palestinian humanitarian activities during the 1970s – a case that moves the focus into a region outside Europe and looks at groups that occupied the dual position of aid providers and recipients. After being expelled from Jordan, two agencies of the Palestinian Liberation Organization (PLO) were active in Lebanon from 1970 to 1982: the Palestinian Martyrs Society (Samed), an economic institution running workshops in refugee camps, and the Palestinian Red Crescent Society (PRCS), which provided free health care and hospitals to Palestinian and Lebanese people. Both published journals to explain their mission to followers and to spread information on their work in the wider humanitarian field. Especially in later years, the journals included research articles on Palestinian economic, social and health conditions, and thus provided information and analysis for planners and activists. At the same time, they proclaimed and propagated the PLO, the Palestinian revolution and the institutions of that revolution – that is, they served political propaganda. Feldman places the activities at the intersection of humanitarianism and revolution. The PRCS journal highlighted that the humanitarian health work followed the principles of international humanitarian work. For example, it portrayed the Gaza hospital in Beirut as a place that worked impartially and as a centre of steadfastness stronger than tragedy, while interviews with patients stressed people's right to life and dignity. The magazine thereby claimed a place for the PRCS in the international humanitarian community and at the same time put forward claims for the Palestinian people among nation states. Conventional Western humanitarianism was not challenged, but was framed differently. Samed, on the other hand, defied humanitarianism through its aim of self-sufficiency in economic terms or, as Feldman puts it, by the efforts to break out of 'a life lived in relief'. The Samed magazine expanded the definition of the humanitarian clearly beyond relief. It rejected the hierarchies of assistance and of capitalist labour. Trying to transform people from objects of pity to subjects of solidarity, human beings appeared as the most valuable means of production as well as the revolutionary struggle. The notion of a full Palestinian subject also applied to women. The media work of Samed clearly highlighted the civil face of the Palestinian people. It addressed other Third World countries, as did the organization's practical projects of agricultural development in Africa. Samed and the PRCS positioned themselves in their press production in relation to both politics and humanitarianism. By emphasizing solidarity, one challenged the notion that relief as a mode of intervention creates hierarchies of 'victims' and 'relief agents', while the other proved that a political position does not prevent humanitarian actors from delivering aid in a neutral manner. With Feldman, we may conclude that both agencies in their journals shifted the political terrain of humanitarianism – a movement apparently not limited to Western actors such as MSF.

Contemporary observers and later scholars like to identify key moments of humanitarian action that they believe have changed relations with the media. In the later part of the twentieth century, the Nigerian Civil War (1967–70) and the pictures of suffering Biafran people has attracted interpretations of this kind. With regard to West Germany, *Patrick Merziger* contends that the images appearing in 1968 in the Western press and on TV showing extremely malnourished children with hunger oedema constituted a turning point in the media regime, because this was the first catastrophe in which media institutions took the leading role in the initiation of relief action.[72] From this perspective, the period from 1968 to 1985 constituted the heyday of media influence on humanitarian aid. Magazines such as *Stern* identified and 'constructed' disasters by emphasizing the suddenness of famine, for example, in 1973 in the Sahel. Merziger attributes great consequences to media reports. A prominent and well-known case was the BBC report by Michael Buerk on the famine in Ethiopia in 1984, which moved many viewers and affected fieldwork by making some agencies apparently shift their work from development to short-term relief. In addition, those aid agencies profited from public attention and donations who were willing to follow the media logic of decontextualized representation of suffering in camps, which was ideal for capturing shocking images on film. Yet, mediatization does not seem to have been an ever-intensifying process as Merziger sees politicization returning during the 1990s.

Archival sources show that the mediation of events was criticized at the very moment it occurred and from inside media organizations themselves as well as from existing NGOs, not to mention other public critics. Triggered by the huge success of Bob Geldof's Band Aid recording, when the musicians had managed to receive airtime against the rules, and the ensuing Live Aid concerts, those responsible at the BBC, for example, worried that the Corporation was not fulfilling its mission to inform and educate, but left matters to pop stars, acting as intermediaries.[73] *Matthias Kuhnert* studies the reaction by two British NGOs to the simplistic media accounts of the famine in Ethiopia and the public success of 'celebrity humanitarianism' during the 1980s. War on Want, associated with the Labour movement, and Christian Aid, founded by the British Council of Churches, were both most uncomfortable with the nonpolitical, stereotypical and paternalistic frame set by Buerk's report, spread widely by Band Aid and echoed by the press. They had been positing for some time a link between poverty, famine and political action. However, it proved to be very difficult to correct the media perception. In reaction, War on Want published leaflets, brochures and advertisements countering the narrative of a natural disaster by explaining the humanitarian disaster through a combination of factors from colonial agricultural practices, political and military strife in contemporary Ethiopia, and Cold War conflicts of interest. The leftist NGO used photographs that illustrated the development help for Ethiopian people to provide them with machinery, work and education. The frame deployed was one of solidarity with African partners rather than that of compassion for poor victims. These were attempts to counteract the images that dominated television and press, which probably managed to reassure those members of the public who already adhered to the perspective taken by War on Want.

Faced with the enormous financial success of Band Aid and the impossibility of changing public perception in general, the NGOs adapted and eventually tried to cooperate with Geldof's project. Despite corresponding reservations on its side, Band Aid also could not shun working with established charities because it depended on their expertise in identifying projects and indeed spending the money on specific projects. Christian Aid, along with others like Oxfam and Save the Children, tried and largely succeeded to convince Band Aid of the need to use its funds to support long-term projects of the kind that these NGOs pursued rather than short-term food deliveries, the ultimate recipient of which might even have been the military rather than the starving.[74] In the years following Band Aid, both War on Want and Christian Aid also adapted their own campaigns directing some of their fundraising efforts (if only a fraction) towards youth and pop magazines and recruiting celebrities. They are likely to have thereby reached a broader public than before, but also changed the perception held about them, possibly to the detriment of the analysis of humanitarian causes. Kuhnert's chapter corrects the widely held interpretation that NGOs willingly used simplistic messages about disasters in Africa in order to maximize their humanitarian 'business'. It also demonstrates that scholars need to analyse not just the images produced but also the institutional records reflecting the production process. In addition, considering more than one kind of media and their interaction – mass and quality press, broadcasting, publicity material and educational as well as scholarly publications – is necessary in order to grasp the role of the media as a changing system interacting with evolving humanitarianism.

The dimension that is most difficult to investigate, particularly from a historical point of view, is audience reaction, unless we simply take donation figures as a measure of successful campaigning. Media and communication scholars at least have the chance to conduct surveys and sample views.[75] Rather than conceptualizing reactions in terms of a general compassion-action model, *Maria Kyriakidou* maintains that audiences are locally situated actors in specific national, cultural and social contexts. Based on her study of the response of Greek audiences to telethons, she moves the discussion beyond the 'compassion fatigue' and 'denial' theses.[76] Telethons are televised fundraising events that last several hours or even days and ask audiences to pledge donations via telephone or the internet, or by participating in organized events throughout the country. They first appeared in the United States in the 1950s and later elsewhere for specific domestic charitable causes, whereas the collaboration with humanitarian aid organizations mostly began in the mid 1980s. The Greek focus group discussions reveal that the celebrities involved in the telethons make a bigger impression than the charitable cause; viewers engage with the media spectacle rather than with the suffering human beings. Kyriakidou further explores how members of the audience construct their moral agency vis-à-vis human suffering on television. One way to justify individual inaction is via a culture of mistrust that manifests itself in lacking trust in how the deliverers of aid will handle contributions. Moreover, mistrust is part of the broader political culture of Greece characterized by political cynicism and the placement of responsibilities with institutions rather than individual citizens. This culture is intertwined with a notion of powerlessness, in which Greece appears as the underdog, inferior to and a victim of the 'West'. In societal terms, this translates into small people versus powerful people, the rich at home and foreigners abroad. These notions, Kyriakidou concludes, form part of a broader sociological denial and help to explain the low level of charitable giving in Greece. Applying the hypothesis of her study to other cultures of humanitarianism redirects attention from the assumption of a direct relationship between the media texts and audience response to specific contemporary understandings of agency and public action – that is, to structures and processes very much at the centre of historical scholarship.

Towards an Entangled History of Humanitarianism and Media

The contributions to this volume demonstrate that the interplay between humanitarianism and media has always been complex. Thus, empirical historical analysis is squarely at odds with some of the wisdoms of current theoretical debates. If we analyse media not simply as images with a message, we can grasp the different shapes of media as material products carrying specific contents, as organizations with a history and economic interests, and as an institutional system with various actors who negotiate and apply norms and regulations for distribution and reception. Instead of emphatic declarations of the alleged novelty of the phenomena under study, it is necessary to thoroughly contextualize the relationship between humanitarianism and media, thereby opening it up for historical perspectives and explanations. As a consequence, theoretical concepts such as compassion fatigue or ironic spectatorship need to be taken with a grain of salt and applied in a more nuanced manner. It also becomes clear that humanitarian images as well as media and humanitarian organizations and systems were deeply implicated in power relations, conflicts of interests and competing ideologies during the course of the long twentieth century. In short, humanitarianism and media have an entangled history: entangled between them as well as intertwined with changing domestic, imperial and international spheres, to the evolution of which they also contributed.

Several essential conclusions emerge from the collection:

(1) *Patterns of humanitarian imagery:* the historical analyses have shown that, from the nineteenth century to the two decades following the Second World War, relief workers, missionaries, reformers, photographers and journalists developed a set of humanitarian imagery. It made up the visual and semantic web in existence until today, which we might call the Western humanitarian imaginary. Christian images, journals and campaigns strongly informed this development by the employment of mass prints and artefacts even before photographic reproductions.[77] Contrary to the scholarly focus on atrocities and suffering, the studies in this volume demonstrate that an alternative motif coexisted presenting *saved* human beings and their saviours. Probably more strongly gendered, the uplifting images have been in continuous use: as the narrative end of humanitarian action, as a visible and sometimes not visible foil to the plight

of people, and as a confirmation of the hope for a better world.[78] The use of both patterns varied throughout the twentieth century according to respective tastes, the availability of images, previous and simultaneous campaigns by others, and political expediency.

(2) *Professionalization of humanitarian imagery:* early humanitarian organizations may not yet all have had a public relations department, employed external agencies and used professional media analysis. Yet describing the existing media relations around the mid twentieth century as amateurish or intuitive and improvised underestimates the long experience of the philanthropic sector as well as the professionalism of the press, filmmakers and photographers.[79] It also tends to perpetuate the belittling of female expertise in this field compared to male professionalism. It further neglects the strategic communication of missionary societies, which reflected carefully about their internal and external media use and whose communication compares well with later twentieth-century NGOs.

(3) *The (non-)political character of humanitarian imagery:* misery and relief may have expressed themselves in seemingly apolitical representations of children and women. However, it would be too simple to equate an obvious message with the allegedly nonpolitical character of humanitarianism. British photographs of Germany, for example, demonstrate the reverse, in the change from images of perpetrators to those of suffering Germans in the aftermath of the Second World War.[80] The depiction of victims often presented hierarchies not only between those providing and those receiving aid, but also among the sufferers.[81] The films made by the Allied forces after the liberation of concentration camps in 1945 and the journals by the Palestinian humanitarian institutions during the 1970s show not only the involvement of those in need, but also ways of moralizing or revolutionizing asymmetrical relations.[82] Besides fundraising, humanitarian organizations such as Oxfam or the SCF also pursued 'educational advocacy' for the 'Third World', which was political in a wider sense and employed other channels than the mass media and advertising.[83] In addition, we should bear in mind that national laws regulated charitable fundraising. These regulations generally limited access to the charity market and restricted openly political campaigns even after liberalization measures.[84] The political character of humanitarianism in the media was therefore also a matter of negotiating what those involved regarded as political or nonpolitical.

(4) *The politics of aid and media:* negotiations and dealings within the aid polity, involving the growth of organizations in terms of size, number and outreach, and their relations amongst each other and with governments has certainly been a characteristic feature of the field since the first half of the twentieth century. Aid has therefore been political and this has affected media relations. Humanitarian organizations established their

own media culture and expertise, the instruments of which they used to create an imagined humanitarian community. The Red Cross movement of the interwar period was a case in point, directing media towards its own members to rally audiences behind its cause.[85] Organizations developed media relations based on expertise in fundraising and the spreading of information to potential donors, governments and the public at large. When international organizations arrived on the scene, particularly in the context of the UN, the established national actors defended their claim on the national public.[86] Today, social media may again be changing the politics of aid.[87] We can observe that even the ICRC, for a long time a very discreet humanitarian organization without the need or urge for public relations, is running a Twitter account and its president tweets from sites of humanitarian intervention that he occasionally visits.[88] What is even more significant is that, on the one hand, social media multiply the number of humanitarian advocates and make it easier for small groups and individuals, without much organizational and financial power, to quickly spread news about humanitarian emergencies. Yet, this pluralised capability to raise issues does not automatically entail a capacity to act by providing relief. Established aid organizations, on the other hand, which have that capacity, may counter the challenge of or indeed tie in with the pluralization of humanitarian advocacy by emphasizing their proper experience; trust therefore becomes an important element. Thus, social media may have made the humanitarian field more complex, but this may well benefit the expertise and experience of established organizations. If these organizations capitalize on their history, their professionalism and their experience, they may well emerge strengthened by the social media activities of others.

(5) *Mediatization and mediation of humanitarianism:* media relations of humanitarian organizations were far more complex than the almost exclusive focus of scholarship on the role of the illustrated mass press and television with their apparently simple messages of suffering would have it. Researching the institutional records of humanitarian agencies and media organizations allows historians to better understand the evolving relation between them. The practice in Britain of coordinating emergency appeals in broadcasting since the 1960s is but one example of a joint humanitarian media regime, which has endured in spite of occasional friction.[89] It also shows that media entrepreneurs and journalists seldom take over the reins.[90] 'Mediatization' conceived in the late 1990s as a linear process that – in its pointed form – supposedly makes humanitarian actors increasingly follow the logic of the media lacks analytical conviction in a field where the actors and the forms of representation have had an entangled history for more than a century. An alternative concept, sometimes regarded as complementary, is 'mediation'. This recognizes that media power is diffuse and understands mediation as 'a pro-

cess in which producers, subjects and audiences take part, and take part together'.[91] Roger Silverstone's term emphasizes the basic function of media to mediate between distant people and matters. In this social process, meanings are constructed, negotiated or contested. This involves ethical reflection on values, experience and expectations. Mediation is dialectic and uneven at the same time. It is dialectic as tensions may exist between producers, subjects and audiences, and as listeners and viewers engage in a creative manner with the products of mass communication. It is uneven because the power to work with, or against, the meanings that the media provide is, as Silverstone notes, unevenly distributed across and within societies.[92]

Drawing on the idea of mediation, which helps us to grasp the role of media in specific social, cultural, economic and political contexts and in periods of technologically changing mass communication,[93] we can identify characteristic features of the entangled history of humanitarianism and media from the late nineteenth century to the present day. The relationship has been based on *transformative* processes that resulted from the production, circulation and reception of humanitarian imagery, which constructed meanings of human suffering and humanitarian aid. It has not been a linear but a *multiple* history in which various actors in media and humanitarian organizations, but also outside of them, were involved. The history has been shaped throughout by *technological* changes where new technologies such as the Kodak camera or social media on the internet offered certain new means, but also became part of existing media systems with developed norms and regulations. As humanitarian mediation constructed and gave meanings to relations with distant others and established certain forms of conduct, it always had strong *ethical* implications. The very subject of humanitarianism affected media as much as media may have affected humanitarianism. Finally, manifold *asymmetric* relations have characterized an entangled history of tensions, negotiations and conflicts. The power of producing and questioning humanitarian imagery was distributed unequally within media systems, in the polity of humanitarian organizations and between the two. Asymmetries of access and power also existed in relation to domestic, national, imperial or international politics. Finally, humanitarianism at its very core harbours a fundamental asymmetry between beneficiaries and providers of succour. The kind of humanitarian imagery created and used by the media defined the needy as well as the humanitarian worker and partially determined their agency. For the period since the late nineteenth and early twentieth centuries, this has for the most part been a feature of the uneven relationship between European and Western societies on the one hand and large parts of the rest of the world on the other. An unequal world communication order braced this general asymmetry. A critical history of the entangled relationship of humanitarianism with media may perhaps help to challenge some of these asymmetries and strengthen those who advocate a new cosmopolitan consciousness recognizing the dignity and rights of others.

Introduction   25

Johannes Paulmann is Director at the Leibniz Institute of European History in Mainz. In 2014–15, he held the Richard von Weizsäcker Fellowship at St Antony's College, Oxford. His research interests cover European and International History. Among his publications is *The Mechanics of Internationalism: Culture, Society and Politics from the 1840s to the First World War* (coedited with Martin H. Geyer, 2001). He is joint Editor in Chief of *European History Online* (http:// www.ieg-ego.eu), a transnational history of Europe. His current research focuses on the history of humanitarianism, on which he recently published 'Conjunctures in the History of International Humanitarian Aid during the Twentieth Century', *Humanity* 4(2) (2013), 215–38, and edited *The Dilemmas of Humanitarian Aid in the Twentieth Century* (Oxford University Press, 2016).

Notes

1. G. Paul, *Das Jahrhundert der Bilder.* Vol. I: *1900 bis 1949,* vol. II: *1949 bis heute* (Göttingen: Vandenhoeck & Ruprecht, 2008). I am very grateful to Bernhard Gissibl for several helpful comments on earlier drafts of this chapter.
2. For a 'deep' history of humanitarianism placing the origins in the period from the sixteenth to the eighteenth centuries, cf. P. Stamatov, *The Origins of Global Humanitarianism: Religion, Empires, and Advocacy* (Cambridge: Cambridge University Press 2013), 8–11. Stamatov emphasizes 'issue entrepreneurs', the 'orchestration of organized support', particularly by religious actors and organizations, through existing institutions and networks, and the solidified practices in standardized and reproducible scripts of action. However, his work does not reflect on the role of media.
3. See A. Vowinckel, *Agenten der Bilder: Fotografisches Handeln im 20. Jahrhundert* (Göttingen: Wallstein Verlag, 2016), 7–30, 15, who uses the term 'Bildhandeln' (acting with images).
4. This extremely wide definition is used by J. Hörisch, *Der Sinn und die Sinne: Eine Geschichte der Medien* (Frankfurt am Main: Eichborn Verlag, 2001) (paperback ed.: *Eine Geschichte der Medien.* Frankfurt am Main: Suhrkamp, 2004).
5. Cf. U. Saxer, 'Der Forschungsgegenstand der Medienwissenschaft', in J.-L. Leonhard et al. (eds), *Medienwissenschaft: Ein Handbuch zur Entwicklung der Medien und Kommunikationsformen,* vol. 15.1 (Berlin: de Gruyter, 1999); and J.B. Thompson, *The Media and Modernity: A Social Theory of the Media* (Stanford: Stanford University Press, 1995), 26–31; H. Bonfadelli, O. Jarren and G. Siegert (eds), *Einführung in die Publizistikwissenschaft,* 3rd ed. (Bern: Haupt, 2010); and further discussions in M. Künzler et al. (eds), *Medien als Institutionen und Organisationen: Institutionalistische Ansätze in der Publizistik- und Kommunikationswissenschaft* (Baden-Baden: Nomos, 2013).
6. For an early use of photography by abolitionists, see M. Fox-Amato, 'An Abolitionist Daguerreotype, New York, 1850', in J.E. Hill and V.R. Schwartz (eds), *Getting the Picture: The Visual Culture of the News* (London: Bloomsbury, 2015), 22–25. Fox-Amato has a book under contract based on his dissertation, 'Exposing Humanity: Slavery, Antislavery, and Early Photography in America, 1839–1865', which highlights how photos were made and used by civil society activist and by (former) slaves; on consumer products and cultural objects as media in the anti-slavery campaign, see C. Midgley, 'Slave Sugar Boycotts, Female Activism and the Domestic Base of British Anti-slavery Culture', *Slavery and*

Abolition 17(3) (1996), 143–44; and M. Guyatt, 'The Wedgwood Slave Medallion: Values in Eighteenth-Century Design', *Journal of Design History* 13(2) (2000), 93–105. For the early usage of anti-slavery imagery in a different contexts, see also J. Lydon, 'Anti-slavery in Australia: Picturing the 1838 Myall Creek Massacre', *History Compass* 15(5) (2017). doi: 10.1111/hic3.12330.

7. For an overview, see A. Schildt, 'Das Jahrhundert der Massenmedien: Ansichten zu einer künftigen Geschichte der Öffentlichkeit', *Geschichte und Gesellschaft* 27(2) (2001), 177–206; J. Chapman, *Comparative Media History: An Introduction, 1789 to the Present* (Cambridge: Polity Press, 2005); and F. Bösch, *Mediengeschichte: Vom asiatischen Buchdruck bis zum Fernsehen* (Frankfurt am Main: Campus Verlag, 2011), 109–226.

8. Cf. M. Scott, 'What Makes News Humanitarian' (21 April 2017), retrieved 29 September 2018 from http://humanitarian-journalims.net/blog/what-makes-news-humanitarian.

9. S. Sontag, *Regarding the Pain of Others* (London: Penguin, 2004).

10. S. Shute and S. Hurley (eds), *On Human Rights: The Oxford Amnesty Lectures* (New York: Basic Books, 1993), vii.

11. Although Sontag's work is self-consciously essayistic rather than scholarly, scholars have repeatedly discussed and criticized her arguments. See, for example, Linfield, *The Cruel Radiance*, 3–31, at 13, who engages with her and other twentieth-century postmodern and poststructuralist critics sceptical of photography's 'victimization' of its objects and false claim to objectivity, and instead argues that emotion and feeling from viewing photos could enhance rather than undermine critical thinking.

12. Sontag, *Pain of Others*, 5–15. See the careful thoughts on the widely held notion of 'the power of images' by C. Brink, 'Überlegungen zum Zusammenhang von Fotografie und Emotionen', *Geschichte und Gesellschaft* 37(1) (2011), 104–29.

13. See, for example, the otherwise instructive essays by R. Hölzl, '"Mitleid" über große Distanz: Zur Fabrikation globaler Gefühle in Medien der katholischen Mission, 1890–1940', in R. Habermas and R. Hölzl (eds), *Mission global: Eine Verflechtungsgeschichte seit dem 19. Jahrhundert* (Cologne: Böhlau Verlag, 2014), 265–94, at 266; P. Balakian, 'Photography, Visual Culture, and the Armenian Genocide', in H. Fehrenbach and D. Rodogno (eds), *Humanitarian Photography: A History* (New York: Cambridge University Press, 2015), 89–114, at 109.

14. Sontag, *Pain of Others*, 72–80. For Sontag's earlier position, see S. Sontag, *On Photography* (New York: Farrar, Straus and Giroux, 1977), 19–21; and on the change of opinion, D. Campbell, 'The Myth of Compassion Fatigue' (2012), retrieved 9 August 2018 from https://www.david-campbell.org/wp-content/documents/DC_Myth_of_Compassion_Fatigue_Feb_2012.pdf.

15. For a similar argument relating to the Nigerian Civil War, cf. L. Heerten, '"A" as in Auschwitz, "B" as in Biafra: The Nigerian Civil War, Visual Narratives of Genocide, and the Fragmented Universalization of the Holocaust', in Fehrenbach and Rodogno, *Humanitarian Photography*, 249–74.

16. See, for example, F. Piana, 'Photography, Cinema, and the Quest for Influence: The International Committee of the Red Cross in the Wake of the First World War', in Fehrenbach and Rodogno, *Humanitarian Photography*, 140–64, at 153; K. Halttunnen, 'Humanitarianism and the Pornography of Pain in Anglo-American Culture', *American Historical Review* 100(2) (1995), 303–34, at 307.

17. Sontag, *Pain of Others*, 90–92.

18. For basic audience reactions with evidence from Swedish data, see B. Höijer, 'The Discourse of Global Compassion: The Audience and Media Reporting of Human Suffering',

Media, Culture & Society 24(4) (2004), 513–31; see also L. Boltanski, *Distant Suffering: Morality, Media, and Politics* (Cambridge: Cambridge University Press 1999), Part II, 'The Topics of Suffering' (first published as *La souffrance à distance: Morale humanitaire, médias et politique* (Paris: Métailié, 1993).

19. Sontag, *Pain of Others*, 97–101, at 99. Cf. S.D. Moeller, *Compassion Fatigue: How the Media Sell Disease, Famine, War and Death* (London: Routledge 1999), who criticizes the idea that the media industry, through market orientation, proliferation and sensationalism, supply a plethora of disaster images to viewers who, inured to the horrors, become mere apathetic spectators. Moeller's use of the term 'compassion fatigue' for various concerns of media critique make it an indiscriminate term of abuse.

20. Sontag, *Pain of Others*, 88–90.

21. L. Chouliaraki, *The Spectatorship of Suffering* (London: Sage, 2006), 7.

22. Under 'adventure news', she treats the shootings of two Americans in Indonesia, a boat accident in India and flooding in Bangladesh; under 'emergency news', which calls for immediate action, the rescuing of African refugees at Malta, a famine in Argentina and the sentencing to death by stoning of a Nigerian woman (all events reported in 2002–3). Chouliaraki does find some potential for pity in emergency news, as well as potential for action, on the condition that the scene of suffering is historicized (Chouliaraki, *Spectatorship*, 150). Her case for 'ecstatic news' is the 9/11 terrorist attack in New York.

23. Chouliaraki, *Spectatorship*, 2.

24. On the concept of cosmopolitanism as usefully adapted from the social sciences for historical research, cf. B. Gissibl and I. Löhr (eds), *Bessere Welten: Kosmopolitismus in den Geschichtswissenschaften* (Frankfurt am Main: Campus Verlag, 2017).

25. L. Chouliaraki, *The Ironic Spectator: Solidarity in the Age of Post-humanitarianism* (Cambridge: Polity Press, 2013), 2.

26. Ibid., 22, 52–53, 188–203. Underlying this critique is the concept of agonistics; see C. Mouffe, *Agonistics: Thinking the World Politically* (London: Verso, 2013).

27. Chouliaraki, *Ironic Spectator*, 4, 76–77.

28. Ibid., 5. The administrative knowledge produced in the discipline of Development Studies ultimately also legitimizes, so the further arguments, neoliberal governance of the sector and in the field, marginalizing the moral and political content of aid and development.

29. Ibid., 4, 9–15.

30. Ibid., 15–16.

31. J. Benthall, *Disasters, Relief and the Media* (London: I.B. Tauris, 1993), 2.

32. Ibid., 26–29, 36–40.

33. Ibid., 3.

34. Ibid., 42–55; see also A. Jones, 'The Disasters Emergency Committee (DEC) and the Humanitarian Industry in Britain, 1963–85', *Twentieth Century British History* 14(3) (2014), 264–85.

35. The following passage summarizes Benthall, *Disasters*, 56–76.

36. See also L. Malkki, 'Children, Humanity, and the Infantilization of Peace', in I. Feldman and M. Ticktin (eds), *In the Name of Humanity: The Government of Threat and Care* (Durham, NC: Duke University Press, 2010), 58–85.

37. On humanitarian intervention, see F. Klose (ed.), *The Emergence of Humanitarian Intervention: Ideas and Practice from the Nineteenth Century to the Present* (Cambridge: Cambridge University Press, 2016).

38. J.G. Blumler and D. Kavanagh, 'The Third Age of Political Communication: Influences and Features', *Political Communication* 16(3) (1999), 209–30; G. Mazzoleni and

W. Schulz, '"Mediatization" of Politics: A Challenge for Democracy?', *Political Communication* 16(3) (1999), 247–61; H.M. Kepplinger, 'Mediatization of Politics: Theory and Data', *Journal of Communication* 52(4) (2002), 972–86; W. Schulz, 'Reconstructing Mediatization as an Analytical Concept', *European Journal of Communication* 19(1) (2004), 87–101. Cf. also T. Meyer, *Mediokratie: Die Kolonisierung der Politik durch die Medien* (Frankfurt am Main: Suhrkamp Verlag, 2011); and A. Dörner, *Politainment: Politik in der medialen Erlebnisgesellschaft* (Frankfurt am Main: Suhrkamp Verlag, 2001).

39. P. Donges, 'Medialisierung der Politik – Vorschlag einer Differenzierung', in P. Rössler and F. Krotz (eds), *Mythen der Mediengesellschaft* (Konstanz: UVK-Verl.-Ges., 2005), 321–39; see also G. Vowe, 'Mediatisierung der Politik? Ein theoretischer Ansatz auf dem Prüfstand', *Publizistik* 51(4) (2006), 437–55. Cf. the all-encompassing 'meta-level' perspective by F. Krotz, 'Metaprozesse sozialen und kulturellen Wandels und die Medien', *Medien Journal* 27(1) (2003), 7–19. The reference to 'media logic' dates back to D.L. Altheide and R.P. Snow, *Media Logic* (Beverly Hills: Sage 1979), and D.L. Altheide and R.P. Snow, 'Towards a Theory of Mediation', *Communication Yearbook* 11 (1989), 194–223.

40. S. Cottle and D. Nolan, 'Global Humanitarianism and the Changing Aid-Media Field: "Everyone was Dying for Footage"', *Journalism Studies* 8(6) (2007), 862–78, at 862 and 863; cf. Patrick Merziger's chapter in the present volume.

41. L. Mükke, *'Journalisten der Finsternis': Akteure, Strukturen und Potenziale deutscher Afrika-Berichterstattung* (Cologne: Herbert von Halem Verlag, 2009), 256–91, at 264.

42. Ibid., 271.

43. On media events, see D. Dayan and E. Katz, *Media Events: The Live Broadcasting of History* (Cambridge, MA: Harvard University Press, 1992); E. Katz and T. Liebes, '"No More Peace'. How Disaster, Terror and War Have Upstaged Media Events', *International Journal of Communication* 1 (2007), 157–66; and N. Couldry, A. Hepp and F. Krotz (eds), *Media Events in a Global Age* (London: Routledge, 2010). For historical case studies, see F. Lenger and A. Nünning (eds), *Medienereignisse der Moderne* (Darmstadt: Wissenschaftliche Buchgesellschaft, 2008); C. Vogel, H. Schneider and H. Carl (eds), *Medienereignisse im 18. und 19. Jahrhundert: Beiträge einer interdisziplinären Tagung aus Anlass des 65. Geburtstages von Rolf Reichardt* (Munich: Oldenbourg Verlag, 2014). T. Scholz, *Distanziertes Mitleid: Mediale Bilder, Emotionen und Solidarität angesichts von Katastrophen* (Frankfurt am Main: Campus 2012) regards media events as a ritual instrument of social integration, starting his analysis with the images of the Lisbon earthquake in 1755.

44. See M. Kyriakidou, 'Rethinking Media Events in the Context of a Global Public Sphere: Exploring the Audience of Global Disasters in Greece', *Communications* 33(3) (2008), 273–91, 288.

45. See the recent works by M. Barnett, *Empire of Humanity: A History of Humanitarianism* (Ithaca: Cornell University Press, 2011); S. Salvatici, *Nel nome degli altri: Storia dell' umanitarismo internazionale* (Bologna: Il Mulino, 2015); J. Paulmann (ed.), *Dilemmas of Humanitarian Aid in the Twentieth Century* (Oxford: Oxford University Press, 2016); F. Klose and M. Thulin (eds), *Humanity: A History of European Concepts in Practice from the Sixteenth Century to the Present* (Göttingen: Vandenhoeck & Ruprecht, 2016); and the critical review of recent scholarship by E. Dal Lago and K. O'Sullivan, 'Introduction: Towards a New History of Humanitarianism', *Moving the Social – Journal of Social History and the History of Social Movements* 57 (2017), 5–20.

46. H. Fehrenbach and D. Rodogno, *Humanitarian Photography: A History* (New York: Cambridge University Press, 2015), 1.

47. See S. Sliwinski, 'The Childhood of Human Rights: The Kodak on the Congo', *Journal of Visual Culture* 5(3) (2006), 333–63; S. de Laat, 'Congo Free State, 1904: Humanitarian Photographs', in F. Klose et al. (eds), *Online Atlas on the History of Humanitarianism and Human Rights* (December 2015). Retrieved 9 August 2018 from http://hhr-atlas.ieg-mainz.de/articles/de_laat-congo.

48. Fehrenbach and Rodogno, *Humanitarian Photography*, 5–6.

49. Ibid., 6.

50. For the imperial and religious interplay from which humanitarianism emerged during the early modern period through to the nineteenth century, see Stamatov, *Origins*; and J. Paulmann, 'Humanitarianism and Empire', in J.M. MacKenzie (ed.), *The Encyclopaedia of Empire*, vol. II (Oxford: Wiley, 2016), 1112–23.

51. See K. Grant, 'Anti-slavery, Refugee Relief, and the Missionary Origins of Humanitarian Photography ca. 1900–1960', *History Compass* 15(5) (2017). doi: 10.1111/hic3.12383; cf. also J. Becker and K. Stornig (eds), *Menschen – Bilder – Eine Welt: Ordnungen von Vielfalt in der religiösen Publizistik um 1900* (Göttingen: Vandenhoeck & Ruprecht, 2018).

52. See H.D. Curtis, 'Picturing Pain: Evangelicals and the Politics of Pictorial Humanitarianism in an Imperial Age', in Fehrenbach and Rodogno, *Humanitarian Photography*, 22–46; C. Twomey, 'Framing Atrocity: Photography and Humanitarianism', in Fehrenbach and Rodogno, *Humanitarian Photography*, 47–63; K. Grant, 'The Limits of Exposure: Atrocity Photographs in the Congo Reform Campaign', in Fehrenbach and Rodogno, *Humanitarian Photography*, 64–88.

53. K. Rozario, '"Delicious Horrors": Mass Culture, the Red Cross, and the Appeal of Modern Humanitarianism', *American Quarterly* 55(3) (2003), 417–55, at 418–19; see also Halttunnen, 'Pornography of Pain', 303–34.

54. C. Reeves, 'Developing the Humanitarian Image in Late Nineteenth- and Early Twentieth- Century China', in Fehrenbach and Rodogno, *Humanitarian Photography*, 115–39; F. Piana, 'Photography, Cinema and the Quest for Influence: The International Committee of the Red Cross in the Wake of the First World War', in Fehrenbach and Rodogno, *Humanitarian Photography*, 140–64; and D. Rodogno and T. David, 'All the World Loves a Picture: The World Health Organization's Visual Politics, 1948–1973', in Fehrenbach and Rodogno, *Humanitarian Photography*, 223–48.

55. H. Lidchi, 'Finding the Right Image: British Development NGOs and the Regulation of Imagery', in Fehrenbach and Rodogno, *Humanitarian Photography*, 275–96; S. Nissinen, 'Dilemmas of Ethical Practice in the Production of Contemporary Humanitarian Photography', in Fehrenbach and Rodogno, *Humanitarian Photography*, 297–321.

56. See the review by Katharina Stornig in *Humanitarianism & Human Rights,* 1 April 2016. Retrieved 9 August 2018 from http://hhr.hypotheses.org//1321.

57. Cf. the chronology based on economic and political factors by J. Paulmann, 'Conjunctures in the History of International Humanitarian Aid during the Twentieth Century', *Humanity* 4(2) (2013), 215–38.

58. For children, see Malkki, 'Children'; and on 'ideal victims', see M. Breen-Smyth and S. Cooke, 'A Critical Approach: Violence, "Victims" and "Innocents"', in C. Kennedy-Pipe, G. Clubb and S. Mabon (eds) *Terrorism and Political Violence: The Evolution of Contemporary Insecurity* (London: Sage, 2015), 69–84.

59. For later usage, cf. G. Lingelbach, 'Das Bild des Bedürftigen und die Darstellung von Wohltätigkeit in den Werbemaßnahmen bundesrepublikanischer Wohltätigkeitsorganisationen', *Archiv für Kulturgeschichte* 89(2) (2008), 345–65.

60. Cf. H. Fehrenbach, 'Children and Other Civilians: Photography and the Politics of Humanitarian Image-Making', in Fehrenbach and Rodogno, *Humanitarian Photography*, 165–99, 167. Fehrenbach dates the photographic appearance of children first in social and familial groupings and pictured as suffering with mothers around 1900, followed by the lone suffering child after the First World War; see also V. Gorin, '"Millions of Children in Deadly Peril": Utilization des photographies d'enfants affamés par le Save the Children Fund pendant l'entre-deux-guerres', *Revue Suisse d'histoire – Itinera* 37 (2014), 95–112.

61. On the Holy Childhood Association, see also H. Harrison, '"A Penny for the Little Chinese": The French Holy Childhood Association in China, 1843–1951', *American Historical Review* 113(1) (2008), 72–92.

62. Fehrenbach, 'Children', 176–85; P.E. Veerman, *The Rights of the Child and the Changing Image of Childhood* (Dordrecht: Martinus Nijhoff, 1992), 88–91; C. Mulley, *The Woman Who Saved the Children: A Biography of Eglantyne Jebb, Founder of Save the Children* (Oxford: Oneworld Books, 2009), 239–41; and D. Marshall, 'Children's Rights and Children's Action in International Relief and Domestic Welfare: The Work of Herbert Hoover between 1914 and 1950', *Journal of the History of Childhood and Youth* 1(3) (2008), 351–88; see also E. Baughan, '"Every Citizen of Empire Implored to Save the Children!": Empire, Internationalism and the Save the Children Fund in Inter-war Britain', *Historical Research* 86(231) (2013), 116–37; E. Baughan, 'The Imperial War Relief Fund and the All British Appeal: Commonwealth, Conflict and Conservatism within the British Humanitarian Movement, 1920–1925', *Journal of Imperial and Commonwealth History* 40(5) (2012), 845–61; E. Baughan and J. Fiori, 'Towards a New Politics of Humanitarian Solidarity: Assessing the Contemporary Import of Dorothy Buxton's Vision for Save the Children', *Disasters* 39(2) (2015), 129–45.

63. See I. Herrmann, 'Décripter la concurrence humanitaire: Le conflit entre Croix-Rouge(s) après 1918', *Relations Internationales* 151 (2012), 91–192.

64. See Piana, 'Photography', 149–52, 158; for photos, see V. Gorin, 'Looking Back over 150 Years of Humanitarian Action: The Photographic Archives of the ICRC', *International Review of the Red Cross* 888 (2012), 1–31.

65. Cf. L. Malkki, 'Speechless Emissaries: Refugees, Humanitarianism and Dehistoricization', *Cultural Anthropology* 11(3) (1996), 377–404.

66. On Victor Gollancz and other humanitarian organization in occupied Germany, see also M. Frank, 'The New Morality: Victor Gollancz, "Save Europe Now" and the German Refugee Crisis, 1945–46', *Twentieth Century British History* 17(2) (2006), 230–56; M. Frank, 'Working for the Germans: British Voluntary Societies and the German Refugee Crisis, 1945–50', *Historical Research* 82(215) (2009), 157–75; and P. Weindling, '"For the Love of Christ": Strategies of International Catholic Relief and the Allied Occupation of Germany, 1945–1948', *Journal of Contemporary History* 43(3) (2008), 477–92.

67. E. Steichen (ed.), *The Family of Man* (New York: Museum of Modern Art, 1955), 4; for the controversy on exhibiting photojournalism in an art museum, see K. Gresh, 'An Era or Photographic Controversy: Edward Steichen at the MoMA', in Hill and Schwartz, *Getting the Picture*, 259–65.

68. K. Gresh, *Steichen: A Life in Photography* (New York: Harmony Books, 1963), 228.

69. Cf. J. Paulmann, 'Humanity – Humanitarian Reason – Imperial Humanitarianism: European Concepts in Practice', in Klose and Thulin, *Humanity*, 288–311, at 307–11.

70. On the campaign, see also T. Sasson, 'Milking the Third World? Humanitarianism, Capitalism, and the Moral Economy of the Nestlé Boycott', *American Historical Review* 121(4) (2016), 1196–224.

71. For the emergence of the MSF expert witness, see M. Givoni, 'Humanitarian Dilemmas, Concern for Others, and Care of the Self: The Case of Médecins Sans Frontières', in Paulmann, *Dilemmas*, 371–92.

72. The literature the Nigerian Civil War is large and growing, for other countries and actors, cf. E. Staunton, 'The Case of Biafra: Ireland and the Nigerian Civil War', *Irish Historical Studies* 31(124) (1999), 513–35; K. Waters, 'Influencing the Message: The Role of Catholic Missionaries in Media Coverage of the Nigerian Civil War', *Catholic Historical Review* 90(4) (2004), 697–718; M.-L. Desgrandchamps, 'Entre coopération et concurrence: CICR, Unicef et organisations religieuses au Biafra', *Relations internationales* 152(4) (2012), 51–62; R. Doron, 'Marketing Genocide: Biafran Propaganda Strategies during the Nigerian Civil War, 1967–70', *Journal of Genocide Research* 16(2–3) (2014), 227–46; L. Heerten and D. Moses, 'The Nigeria–Biafra War: Postcolonial Conflict and the Question of Genocide', *Journal of Genocide Research* 16(2–3) (2014), 169–203.

73. See S. Franks, *Reporting Disasters: Famine, Aid, Politics and the Media* (London: Hurst, 2013), 11–30.

74. For the debate over diversion of food aid, see S. Franks, 'Why Bob Geldof Has Got it Wrong', *British Journalism Review* 21 (2010), 51–56.

75. For a historical case study based on letters written by West German citizens to various government department on aid to Biafra, see F. Hannig, 'Mitleid mit Biafranern in Westdeutschland: Eine Historisierung von Empathie', *WerkstattGeschichte* 68 (2014), 65–67.

76. For the denial thesis, see S. Cohen, *States of Denial: Knowing about Atrocities and Suffering* (New York: John Wiley & Sons, 2001); and S. Cohen and I.B. Seu, 'Knowing Enough Not to Feel Too Much: Emotional Thinking about Human Rights Appeals', in M.P. Bradley and P. Petro (eds), *Truth Claims: Representations and Human Rights* (New Brunswick, NJ: Rutgers University Press, 2002), 187–204; I.B. Seu, '"Your Stomach Makes You Feel That You Don't Want to Know Anything about it": Desensitization, Defence Mechanisms and Rhetoric in Response to Human Rights Abuses', *Journal of Human Rights* 2(2) (2003), 183–96; I.B. Seu, '"Doing Denial": Audience Reaction to Human Rights Appeals', *Discourse & Society* 2(2) (2010), 438–57. For compassion fatigue, see above in this introduction.

77. See Katharina Stornig's chapter in the present volume.

78. See the chapters by Rose Holmes, Tobias Weidner and Ilana Feldman in the present volume. For the (in)visibility of human rights, cf. S. Linfield, *The Cruel Radiance: Photography and Political Violence* (Chicago: University of Chicago Press, 2010), 33, 37–39; and M.P. Bradley, *The World Reimagined: Americans and Human Rights in the Twentieth Century* (New York: Cambridge University Press, 2016).

79. For a debate on professionalism and varying national traditions of relief, see S. Salvatici, 'Professions of Humanitarianism: UNRRA Relief Officers in Post-War Europe', in Paulmann, *Dilemmas*, 236–59; and H. Fehrenbach, 'From Aid to Intimacy: The Humanitarian Origins and Media Culture of International Adoption', in Paulmann, *Dilemmas*, 206–33, at 211–16.

80. See Paul Betts' chapter in the present volume.

81. See Maria Kyriakidou's chapter in the present volume for notions of powerlessness with Greek audiences.

82. See the chapters by Ulrike Weckel and Ilana Feldman in the present volume.

83. See the chapters by Valerie Gorin and Matthias Kuhnert in the present volume.

84. Cf. S. Roddy, J.-M. Strange and B. Taithe, 'The Charity-Mongers of Modern Babylon: Bureaucracy, Scandal, and the Transformation of the Philanthropic Marketplace, c.1870–

1912', *Journal of British Studies* 54(1) (2015), 118–37; G. Lingelbach, 'Die Entwicklung des Spendenmarktes in der Bundesrepublik Deutschland: Von der staatlichen Regulierung zur medialen Lenkung', *Geschichte und Gesellschaft* 33(1) (2007), 127–57.

85. See the chapters by Daniel Palmieri and Ilana Feldman in the present volume.

86. See the chapter by Heike Wieters in the present volume.

87. For recent discussions of various effects of social media in media, communication and journalism studies, see M. Madianou, 'Humanitarian Campaigns in Social Media: Network Architecture and Polymedia Events', *Journalism Studies* 14(2) (2013), 249–66; M. Scott, 'Distant Suffering Online. The Unfortunate Irony of Cyber-utopian Narratives', *International Communication Gazette* 77(7) (2015), 637–53; G. Cooper and S. Cottle, 'Humanitarianism, Communications, and Change: Final Reflections', in G. Cooper and S. Cottle (eds), *Humanitarianism, Communications, and Change* (New York: Peter Lang, 2015), 251–64.

88. See https://twitter.com/ICRC and https://twitter.com/PMaurerICRC.

89. See Benthall, *Disasters*, 42–55.

90. See the chapters by Patrick Merziger and Matthias Kuhnert in the present volume.

91. R. Silverstone, *Media and Morality: On the Rise of the Mediapolis* (Cambridge: Polity Press, 2007), 38; see also N. Couldry, N. 'Mediatization or Mediation? Alternative Understandings of the Emergent Space of Digital Storytelling', *New Media & Society* 10(3) (2008), 373–91; A. Hepp, 'Mediatisierung und Kulturwandel: Kulturelle Kontextfelder und die Prägkräfte der Medien', in M. Hartmann and A. Hepp (eds), *Mediatisierung der Alltagswelt* (Wiesbaden: VS Verlag für Sozialwissenschaften, 2010), 65–84; and M. Hartmann, 'Mediatisierung als Mediation: Vom Normativen und Diskursen', in Hartmann and Hepp, *Mediatisierung der Alltagswelt*, 35–47.

92. R. Silverstone, 'Complicity and Collusion in the Mediation of Everyday Life', *New Literary History* 33(4) (2002), 761–80, at 762.

93. See M. Serelle, 'The Ethics of Mediation: Aspects of Media Criticism in Roger Silverstone's Works', *Matrizes* 10(2) (2016), 75–90.

Bibliography

Altheide, D.L., and R.P. Snow. *Media Logic*. Beverly Hills, CA: Sage, 1979.

———. 'Towards a Theory of Mediation'. *Communication Yearbook* 11 (1989), 194–223.

Balakian, P. 'Photography, Visual Culture, and the Armenian Genocide', in H. Fehrenbach and D. Rodogno (eds), *Humanitarian Photography: A History* (New York: Cambridge University Press, 2015), 89–114.

Barnett, M. *Empire of Humanity: A History of Humanitarianism*. Ithaca: Cornell University Press, 2011.

Baughan, E. 'The Imperial War Relief Fund and the All British Appeal: Commonwealth, Conflict and Conservatism within the British Humanitarian Movement, 1920–1925'. *Journal of Imperial and Commonwealth History* 40(5) (2012), 845–61.

———. '"Every Citizen of Empire Implored to Save the Children!" Empire, Internationalism and the Save the Children Fund in Inter-war Britain'. *Historical Research* 86(231) (2013), 116–37.

Baughan, E., and J. Fiori. 'Towards a New Politics of Humanitarian Solidarity: Assessing the Contemporary Import of Dorothy Buxton's Vision for Save the Children'. *Disasters* 39(2) (2015), 129–45.

Becker, J., and K. Stornig (eds). *Menschen – Bilder – Eine Welt: Ordnungen von Vielfalt in der religiösen Publizistik um 1900*. Göttingen: Vandenhoeck & Ruprecht, 2018.

Benthall, J. *Disasters, Relief and the Media*. London: I.B. Tauris, 1993.

Blumler, J.G., and D. Kavanagh. 'The Third Age of Political Communication: Influences and Features'. *Political Communication* 16(3) (1999), 209–30.

Boltanski, L. *Distant Suffering: Morality, Media, and Politics*. Cambridge: Cambridge University Press, 1999.

Bonfadelli, H., O. Jarren and G. Siegert (eds). *Einführung in die Publizistikwissenschaft*. Bern: Haupt, 2010.

Bösch, F. *Mediengeschichte: Vom asiatischen Buchdruck bis zum Fernsehen*. Frankfurt am Main: Campus Verlag, 2011.

Bösch, F. and Norbert Frei (eds). *Medialisierung und Demokratie im 20. Jahrhundert*. Göttingen: Wallstein, 2006.

Bradley, M.P. *The World Reimagined: Americans and Human Rights in the Twentieth Century*. New York: Cambridge University Press, 2016.

Breen-Smyth, M., and S. Cooke. 'A Critical Approach: Violence, "Victims" and "Innocents"', in C. Kennedy-Pipe, G. Clubb and S. Mabon (eds), *Terrorism and Political Violence: The Evolution of Contemporary Insecurity* (London: Sage, 2015), 69–84.

Brink, C. 'Überlegungen zum Zusammenhang von Fotografie und Emotionen'. *Geschichte und Gesellschaft* 37(1) (2011), 104–29.

Campbell, D. 'The Myth of Compassion Fatigue' (2012). Retrieved 9 August 2018 from https://www.david-campbell.org/wp-content/documents/DC_Myth_of_Compassion_Fatigue_Feb_2012.pdf.

Chapman, J. *Comparative Media History: An Introduction, 1789 to the Present*. Cambridge: Polity Press, 2005.

Chouliaraki, L. *The Spectatorship of Suffering*. London: Sage, 2006.

———. *The Ironic Spectator: Solidarity in the Age of Post-humanitarianism*. Cambridge: Polity Press, 2013.

Cohen, S. *States of Denial: Knowing about Atrocities and Suffering*. New York: John Wiley & Sons, 2001.

Cohen, S., and I.B. Seu. 'Knowing Enough Not to Feel Too Much: Emotional Thinking about Human Rights Appeals', in M.P. Bradley and P. Petro (eds), *Truth Claims: Representations and Human Rights* (New Brunswick, NJ: Rutgers University Press, 2002), 187–204.

Cooper, G., and S. Cottle, 'Humanitarianism, Communications, and Change: Final Reflections', in G. Cooper and S. Cottle (eds), *Humanitarianism, Communications, and Change* (New York: Peter Lang, 2015), 251–64.

Cottle, S., and D. Nolan. 'Global Humanitarianism and the Changing Aid-Media Field: "Everyone was Dying for Footage"'. *Journalism Studies* 8(6) (2007), 862–78.

Couldry, N. 'Mediatization or Mediation? Alternative Understandings of the Emergent Space of Digital Storytelling'. *New Media & Society* 10(3) (2008), 373–91.

Couldry, N., A. Hepp and F. Krotz (eds). *Media Events in a Global Age*. London: Routledge, 2010.

Curtis, H.D. 'Picturing Pain: Evangelicals and the Politics of Pictorial Humanitarianism in an Imperial Age', in H. Fehrenbach and D. Rodogno (eds), *Humanitarian Photography: A History* (New York: Cambridge University Press, 2015), 22–46.

Dal Lago, E., and K. O'Sullivan. 'Introduction: Towards a New History of Humanitarianism', *Moving the Social – Journal of Social History and the History of Social Movements* 57 (2017), 5–20.

Dayan, D., and E. Katz. *Media Events: The Live Broadcasting of History.* Cambridge, MA: Harvard University Press, 1992.

De Laat, S. 'Congo Free State, 1904: Humanitarian Photographs', in F. Klose et al. (eds), *Online Atlas on the History of Humanitarianism and Human Rights* (December 2015). Retrieved 9 August 2018 from http://hhr-atlas.ieg-mainz.de/articles/de_laat-congo.

Desgrandchamps, M.-L. 'Entre coopération et concurrence: CICR, Unicef et organisations religieuses au Biafra'. *Relations internationales* 152(4) (2012), 51–62.

Donges, P. 'Medialisierung der Politik – Vorschlag einer Differenzierung', in P. Rössler and F. Krotz (eds), *Mythen der Mediengesellschaft* (Konstanz: UVK-Verl.-Ges., 2005), 321–39.

Doron, R. 'Marketing Genocide: Biafran Propaganda Strategies during the Nigerian Civil War, 1967–70'. *Journal of Genocide Research* 16(2–3) (2014), 227–46.

Dörner, A. *Politainment: Politik in der medialen Erlebnisgesellschaft.* Frankfurt am Main: Suhrkamp Verlag, 2001.

Fehrenbach, H. 'Children and Other Civilians: Photography and the Politics of Humanitarian Image-Making', in H. Fehrenbach and D. Rodogno (eds), *Humanitarian Photography: A History* (New York: Cambridge University Press, 2015), 165–99.

———. 'From Aid to Intimacy: The Humanitarian Origins and Media Culture of International Adoption', in J. Paulmann (ed.), *Dilemmas of Humanitarian Aid in the Twentieth Century* (Oxford: Oxford University Press, 2016), 206–33.

Fehrenbach, H., and D. Rodogno. *Humanitarian Photography: A History.* New York: Cambridge University Press, 2015.

Fox-Amato, M. 'An Abolitionist Daguerreotype, New York, 1850', in J.E. Hill and V.R. Schwartz (eds), *Getting the Picture: The Visual Culture of the News* (London: Bloomsbury, 2015), 22–25.

Gissibl, B., and I. Löhr (eds). *Bessere Welten: Kosmopolitismus in den Geschichtswissenschaften.* Frankfurt am Main: Campus Verlag, 2017.

Givoni, M. 'Humanitarian Dilemmas, Concern for Others, and Care of the Self: The Case of Médecins sans Frontières', in J. Paulmann (ed.), *Dilemmas of Humanitarian Aid in the Twentieth Century* (Oxford: Oxford University Press, 2016), 371–92.

Gorin, V. 'Looking Back over 150 years of Humanitarian Action: The Photographic Archives of the ICRC'. *International Review of the Red Cross* 888 (2012), 1–31.

———. '"Millions of Children in Deadly Peril": Utilization des photographies d'enfants affamés par le Save the Children Fund pendant l'entre-deux-guerres'. *Revue Suisse d'histoire – Itinera* 37 (2014), 95–112.

Grant, K. 'The Limits of Exposure: Atrocity Photographs in the Congo Reform Campaign', in H. Fehrenbach and D. Rodogno (eds), *Humanitarian Photography: A History* (New York: Cambridge University Press, 2015), 64–88.

———. 'Anti-slavery, Refugee Relief, and the Missionary Origins of Humanitarian Photography ca. 1900–1960'. *History Compass* 15(5) (2017). doi: 10.1111/hic3.12383.

Gresh, K. *Steichen: A Life in Photography.* New York: Harmony Books, 1963.

———. 'An Era or Photographic Controversy: Edward Steichen at the MoMA', in J.E. Hill and V.R. Schwartz (eds), *Getting the Picture: The Visual Culture of the News* (London: Bloomsbury, 2015), 259–65.

Frank, M. 'The New Morality: Victor Gollancz, "Save Europe Now" and the German Refugee Crisis, 1945–46'. *Twentieth Century British History* 17(2) (2006), 230–56.

Frank, M. 'Working for the Germans: British Voluntary Societies and the German Refugee Crisis, 1945–50'. *Historical Research* 82(215) (2009), 157–75.

———. 'Why Bob Geldof has Got it Wrong'. *British Journalism Review* 21 (2010), 51–56.

————. *Reporting Disasters: Famine, Aid, Politics and the Media.* London: Hurst, 2013.

Guyatt, M. 'The Wedgwood Slave Medallion: Values in Eighteenth-Century Design'. *Journal of Design History* 13(2) (2000), 93–105.

Halttunnen, K. 'Humanitarianism and the Pornography of Pain in Anglo-American Culture'. *American Historical Review* 100(2) (1995), 303–34.

Hannig, F. 'Mitleid mit Biafranern in Westdeutschland: Eine Historisierung von Empathie', *WerkstattGeschichte* 68 (2014), 65–67.

Hartmann, M. 'Mediatisierung als Mediation: Vom Normativen und Diskursen', in M. Hartmann and A. Hepp (eds), *Mediatisierung der Alltagswelt* (Wiesbaden: VS Verlag für Sozialwissenschaften, 2010), 35–47.

Harrison, H. '"A Penny for the Little Chinese": The French Holy Childhood Association in China, 1843–1951'. *American Historical Review* 113(1) (2008), 72–92.

Heerten, L. '"A" as in Auschwitz, "B" as in Biafra: The Nigerian Civil War, Visual Narratives of Genocide, and the Fragmented Universalization of the Holocaust', in H. Fehrenbach and D. Rodogno (eds), *Humanitarian Photography: A History* (New York: Cambridge University Press, 2015), 249–74.

Heerten, L., and D. Moses. 'The Nigeria–Biafra War: Postcolonial Conflict and the Question of Genocide'. *Journal of Genocide Research* 16(2–3) (2014), 169–203.

Hepp, A. 'Mediatisierung und Kulturwandel: Kulturelle Kontextfelder und die Prägkräfte der Medien', in M. Hartmann and A. Hepp (eds), *Mediatisierung der Alltagswelt* (Wiesbaden: VS Verlag für Sozialwissenschaften, 2010), 65–84.

Herrmann, I. 'Décripter la concurrence humanitaire: Le conflit entre Croix-Rouge(s) après 1918'. *Relations Internationales* 151 (2012), 91–192.

Höijer, B. 'The Discourse of Global Compassion: The Audience and Media Reporting of Human Suffering'. *Media, Culture & Society* 24(4) (2004), 513–31.

Hölzl, R. '"Mitleid" über große Distanz: Zur Fabrikation globaler Gefühle in Medien der katholischen Mission, 1890–1940', in R. Habermas and R. Hölzl (eds), *Mission global: Eine Verflechtungsgeschichte seit dem 19. Jahrhundert* (Cologne: Böhlau Verlag, 2014), 265–294.

Hörisch, J. *Der Sinn und die Sinne: Eine Geschichte der Medien.* Frankfurt am Main: Eichborn Verlag, 2001.

Jones, A. 'The Disasters Emergency Committee (DEC) and the Humanitarian Industry in Britain, 1963–85'. *Twentieth Century British History* 14(3) (2014), 264–85.

Katz, E., and T. Liebes. '"No More Peace": How Disaster, Terror and War Have Upstaged Media Events'. *International Journal of Communication* 1 (2007), 157–66.

Kepplinger, H.M. 'Mediatization of Politics: Theory and Data'. *Journal of Communication* 52(4) (2002), 972–86.

Klose, F. (ed.). *The Emergence of Humanitarian Intervention: Ideas and Practice from the Nineteenth Century to the Present.* Cambridge: Cambridge University Press, 2016.

Klose, F., and M. Thulin (eds). *Humanity: A History of European Concepts in Practice from the Sixteenth Century to the Present.* Göttingen: Vandenhoeck & Ruprecht, 2016.

Krotz, F. 'Metaprozesse sozialen und kulturellen Wandels und die Medien'. *Medien Journal* 27(1) (2003), 7–19.

Künzler, M. et al. (eds). *Medien als Institutionen und Organisationen: Institutionalistische Ansätze in der Publizistik- und Kommunikationswissenschaft.* Baden-Baden: Nomos, 2013.

Kyriakidou, M. 'Rethinking Media Events in the Context of a Global Public Sphere: Exploring the Audience of Global Disasters in Greece'. *Communications* 33(3) (2008), 273–91.

Lenger, F., and A. Nünning (eds). *Medienereignisse der Moderne.* Darmstadt: Wissenschaftliche Buchgesellschaft, 2008.

Lidchi, H. 'Finding the Right Image: British Development NGOs and the Regulation of Imagery', in H. Fehrenbach and D. Rodogno (eds), *Humanitarian Photography: A History* (New York: Cambridge University Press, 2015), 175–296.

Linfield, S. *The Cruel Radiance: Photography and Political Violence.* Chicago: University of Chicago Press, 2010.

Lingelbach, G. 'Die Entwicklung des Spendenmarktes in der Bundesrepublik Deutschland: Von der staatlichen Regulierung zur medialen Lenkung'. *Geschichte und Gesellschaft* 33(1) (2007), 127–57.

———. 'Das Bild des Bedürftigen und die Darstellung von Wohltätigkeit in den Werbemaßnahmen bundesrepublikanischer Wohltätigkeitsorganisationen'. *Archiv für Kulturgeschichte* 89(2) (2008), 345–65.

Lydon, J. 'Anti-slavery in Australia: Picturing the 1838 Myall Creek Massacre'. *History Compass* 15(5) (2017). doi: 10.1111/hic3.12330.

Madianou, M. 'Humanitarian Campaigns in Social Media: Network Architecture and Polymedia Events'. *Journalism Studies* 14(2) (2013), 249–66.

Malkki, L. 'Speechless Emissaries: Refugees, Humanitarianism and Dehistoricization'. *Cultural Anthropology* 11(3) (1996), 377–404.

———. 'Children, Humanity, and the Infantilization of Peace' in I. Feldman and M. Ticktin (eds), *In the Name of Humanity: The Government of Threat and Care* (Durham, NC: Duke University Press, 2010), 58–85.

Marshall, D. 'Children's Rights and Children's Action in International Relief and Domestic Welfare: The Work of Herbert Hoover between 1914 and 1950'. *Journal of the History of Childhood and Youth* 1(3) (2008), 351–88.

Mazzoleni, G., and W. Schulz. '"Mediatization" of Politics: A Challenge for Democracy?'. *Political Communication* 16(3) (1999), 247–61.

Meyer, T. *Mediokratie: Die Kolonisierung der Politik durch die Medien.* Frankfurt am Main: Suhrkamp Verlag, 2011.

Midgley, C. 'Slave Sugar Boycotts, Female Activism and the Domestic Base of British Antislavery Culture'. *Slavery and Abolition* 17(3) (1996), 143–44.

Moeller, S.D. *Compassion Fatigue: How the Media Sell Disease, Famine, War and Death.* London: Routledge, 1999.

Mouffe, C. *Agonistics: Thinking the World Politically.* London: Verso, 2013.

Mükke, L. *'Journalisten der Finsternis': Akteure, Strukturen und Potenziale deutscher Afrika-Berichterstattung.* Cologne: Herbert von Halem Verlag, 2009.

Mulley, C. *The Woman Who Saved the Children: A Biography of Eglantyne Jebb, Founder of Save the Children.* Oxford: Oneworld Books, 2009.

Nissinen, S. 'Dilemmas of Ethical Practice in the Production of Contemporary Humanitarian Photography', in H. Fehrenbach and D. Rodogno (eds), *Humanitarian Photography: A History* (New York: Cambridge University Press, 2015), 297–321.

Paul, G. *Das Jahrhundert der Bilder.* Vol. I: *1900 bis 1949,* vol. II: *1949 bis heute.* Göttingen: Vandenhoeck & Ruprecht, 2008.

Paulmann, J. 'Conjunctures in the History of International Humanitarian Aid during the Twentieth Century'. *Humanity* 4(2) (2013), 215–38.

———. (ed.). *Dilemmas of Humanitarian Aid in the Twentieth Century.* Oxford: Oxford University Press, 2016.

———. 'Humanitarianism and Empire', in J.M. MacKenzie (ed.), *The Encyclopaedia of Empire* (Oxford: Wiley, 2016), 1112–23.

————. 'Humanity – Humanitarian Reason – Imperial Humanitarianism: European Concepts in Practice', in F. Klose and M. Thulin (eds), *Humanity: A History of European Concepts in Practice from the Sixteenth Century to the Present* (Göttingen: Vandenhoeck & Ruprecht, 2016) 288–311.

Piana, F. 'Photography, Cinema and the Quest for Influence: The International Committee of the Red Cross in the Wake of the First World War', in H. Fehrenbach and D. Rodogno (eds), *Humanitarian Photography: A History* (New York: Cambridge University Press, 2015), 140–64.

Reeves, C. 'Developing the Humanitarian Image in Late Nineteenth- and Early Twentieth-Century China', in H. Fehrenbach and D. Rodogno (eds), *Humanitarian Photography: A History* (New York: Cambridge University Press, 2015), 115–39.

Roddy, S., J.-M. Strange and B. Taithe. 'The Charity-Mongers of Modern Babylon: Bureaucracy, Scandal, and the Transformation of the Philanthropic Marketplace, c. 1870–1912'. *Journal of British Studies* 54(1) (2015), 118–37.

Rodogno, D., and T. David. 'All the World Loves a Picture: The World Health Organization's Visual Politics, 1948–1973', in H. Fehrenbach and D. Rodogno (eds), *Humanitarian Photography: A History* (New York: Cambridge University Press, 2015), 223–48.

Rozario, K. '"Delicious Horrors": Mass Culture, the Red Cross, and the Appeal of Modern Humanitarianism'. *American Quarterly* 55(3) (2003), 417–55.

Salvatici, S. *Nel nome degli altri: Storia dell'umanitarismo internazionale.* Bologna: Il Mulino, 2015.

————. 'Professions of Humanitarianism: UNRRA Relief Officers in Post-War Europe', in J. Paulmann (ed.), *Dilemmas of Humanitarian Aid in the Twentieth Century* (Oxford: Oxford University Press, 2016), 236–59.

Sasson, T. 'Milking the Third World? Humanitarianism, Capitalism, and the Moral Economy of the Nestlé Boycott'. *American Historical Review* 121(4) (2016), 1196–224.

Saxer, U. 'Der Forschungsgegenstand der Medienwissenschaft', in J.-L. Leonhard et al. (eds), *Medienwissenschaft: Ein Handbuch zur Entwicklung der Medien und Kommunikationsformen* (Berlin: de Gruyter, 1999), 1–15.

Schildt, A. 'Das Jahrhundert der Massenmedien: Ansichten zu einer künftigen Geschichte der Öffentlichkeit'. *Geschichte und Gesellschaft* 27(2) (2001), 177–206.

Scholz, T. *Distanziertes Mitleid: Mediale Bilder, Emotionen und Solidarität angesichts von Katastrophen.* Frankfurt am Main: Campus, 2012.

Schulz, W. 'Reconstructing Mediatization as an Analytical Concept'. *European Journal of Communication* 19(1) (2004), 87–101.

Scott, M. 'Distant Suffering Online: The Unfortunate Irony of Cyber-utopian Narratives'. *International Communication Gazette* 77(7) (2015), 637–53.

————. 'What Makes News Humanitarian' (21 April 2017). Retrieved 29 September 2018 from http://humanitarian-journalims.net/blog/what-makes-news-humanitarian.

Serelle, M. 'The Ethics of Mediation: Aspects of Media Criticism in Roger Silverstone's Works'. *Matrizes* 10(2) (2016), 75–90.

Seu, I.B. '"Your Stomach Makes You Feel That You Don't Want to Know Anything about it": Desensitization, Defence Mechanisms and Rhetoric in Response to Human Rights Abuses'. *Journal of Human Rights* 2(2) (2003), 183–96.

Seu, I.B. '"Doing Denial": Audience Reaction to Human Rights Appeals'. *Discourse & Society* 2(2) (2010), 438–57.

Shute, S., and S. Hurley (eds). *On Human Rights: The Oxford Amnesty Lectures 1993.* New York: Basic Books, 1993.

Silverstone, R. 'Complicity and Collusion in the Mediation of Everyday Life'. *New Literary History* 33(4) (2002), 761–80.

———. *Media and Morality: On the Rise of the Mediapolis*. Cambridge: Polity Press, 2007.

Sliwinski, S. 'The Childhood of Human Rights: The Kodak on the Congo'. *Journal of Visual Culture* 5(3) (2006), 333–63.

Sontag, S. *On Photography*. New York: Farrar, Straus and Giroux, 1977.

———. *Regarding the Pain of Others*. London: Penguin, 2004.

Stamatov, P. *The Origins of Global Humanitarianism: Religion, Empires, and Advocacy*. Cambridge: Cambridge University Press, 2013.

Staunton, E. 'The case of Biafra: Ireland and the Nigerian Civil War'. *Irish Historical Studies* 31(124) (1999), 513–35.

Steichen, E. (ed.). *The Family of Man*. New York: Museum of Modern Art, 1955.

Thompson, J.B. *The Media and Modernity: A Social Theory of the Media* (Stanford: Stanford University Press, 1995), 26–31.

Twomey, C. 'Framing Atrocity: Photography and Humanitarianism', in H. Fehrenbach and D. Rodogno (eds), *Humanitarian Photography: A History* (New York: Cambridge University Press, 2015), 47–63.

Veerman, P.E. *The Rights of the Child and the Changing Image of Childhood*. Dordrecht: Martinus Nijhoff, 1992.

Vogel, C., H. Schneider and H. Carl (eds). *Medienereignisse im 18. und 19. Jahrhundert: Beiträge einer interdisziplinären Tagung aus Anlass des 65. Geburtstages von Rolf Reichardt*. Munich: Oldenbourg Verlag, 2014.

Vowe, G. 'Mediatisierung der Politik? Ein theoretischer Ansatz auf dem Prüfstand'. *Publizistik* 51(4) (2006), 437–55.

Vowinckel, A. *Agenten der Bilder: Fotografisches Handeln im 20. Jahrhundert*. Göttingen: Wallstein Verlag, 2016.

Waters, K. 'Influencing the Message: The Role of Catholic Missionaries in Media Coverage of the Nigerian Civil War'. *Catholic Historical Review* 90(4) (2004), 697–718.

Weindling, P. '"For the Love of Christ": Strategies of International Catholic Relief and the Allied Occupation of Germany, 1945–1948'. *Journal of Contemporary History* 43(3) (2008), 477–92.

PART I
Humanitarian Imagery

1
Promoting Distant Children in Need

*Christian Imagery in the Late Nineteenth
and Early Twentieth Centuries*

Katharina Stornig

By now, the key place of children in contemporary humanitarian visual culture and the links to modern Western notions of childhood are well established.[1] Yet, we still know only little about the historical dimensions of this relationship. This is particularly the case for the Christian prehistory of humanitarianism and religious traditions of benevolent image making with the goal of mobilizing support for needy 'others' across large geographical distances. In a recent article, historian Heide Fehrenbach has proposed a chronology, according to which the symbolic figure of the child started to appear in humanitarian imagery around 1900.[2] According to her, while children featured mostly in social groupings, in families or with mothers during the first two decades of the twentieth century, it was only in connection with the famines in Central and Eastern Europe after the First World War that the image of the lone and suffering child evolved into a central trope in humanitarian visual culture.[3] However, while this is certainly an important finding with regard to a largely secular analytical framework, the following question emerges: what happens once we add religious traditions of institutionalized philanthropy and benevolent image making to the picture?

This chapter sets out to examine the historical relationship between images of children, the media and visual practices in the promotion and expansion of transnational aid by nineteenth-century Catholic charities. Arguing that children and notions of childhood were already central to European imaginations of aiding 'others' by the mid nineteenth century, the chapter pursues three goals.[4] First, approaching images as material objects, it attempts to demonstrate the key importance of child-centred images for organized giving across large geographical distances.[5] Pointing to the fact that images of children fulfilled important functions in fostering the communities of aid, the chapter particularly analyses when and how Catholic groups in Europe massively (re)produced, used and distributed them as tangible objects of exchange between donors, beneficiaries and philanthropic institutions. Second, drawing attention to the image contents, the chapter examines representational patterns in the promotional campaigns. In contrast to several studies pointing to the centrality of representations of bodily suffering and human pain in modern fundraising media,[6] the chapter argues that Christian image making was for a long time firmly embedded in a discourse on child saving. During the second half of the nineteenth century, this discourse had emerged powerfully and produced a distinct visual focus on supposed moments of rescue, adoption, relief and care.[7] Christian child saving, the chapter argues, not only contributed to modern notions of childhood, but also operated in a moral space of family, in which cultural representations and ideas of gendered parenthood, vulnerability and aid/care constituted key factors. Third, the chapter explores the great importance of the introduction of new visual technologies (i.e. photography) to institutionalized philanthropy. As will be shown, while the increasing use of photography did not bring about a caesura with regard to image contents and symbolic references to child saving, it did produce new meanings and initiated reconfigurations in the sphere of benevolent image making, because it enabled the emergence of new and individualized imaginations of relationships of aid and solidarity across large geographical distances. This was also due to the special quality of the relationship between a photographic image and its object, which has been theorized as indexical: photographs often enjoy(ed) a particular aura of authenticity,[8] for the photographic image, produced by the chemical reaction of light reflected from an object, displayed a unique and nondissolvable connection to the object photographed.[9] In the context of institutionalized philanthropy, photographs thus introduced a novel quality of 'humanitarian' witnessing in two ways: first, to the 'real' existence of distant needs and saving activities; and, second, as items that were literally moved between different parts of the world, they served to bridge distance and fostered real and imagined connections between donors and beneficiaries in different parts of the world. Images of distant children in need thus moved into Christian institutions, communities and households at a time when photography increasingly became an intrinsic part of family life and the relationship of familial love and care.

The Beginnings of Far-Off Child Saving and its Imagery

While some scholars have dated the beginnings of far-off child saving back to the onset of colonialism in the sixteenth century,[10] it was particularly from the 1830s to the 1860s that distant children moved more and more into the focus of social activists in Europe. In these decades, Christian philanthropists and missionaries in particular showed growing concern for the young in distant lands. They did so for two main reasons. First, Christian missionaries increasingly turned to children as key figures in evangelizing strategies. Given that, in the second half of the nineteenth century, the missionary school developed into a central site of evangelization, the young generation came to be seen as a vital resource to affect religious, social and political change.[11] Practically speaking, children were needed in order to fill missionary classrooms throughout the rapidly expanding missions all over Africa and Asia. Moreover, they were seen as a very promising group of 'heathen' peoples to be moulded and remade in the faith of Christianity.[12] This was likewise true for Catholic and Protestant groups, both of which, inspired by the steady development towards mass education in most Western countries, projected great hopes onto the young and promoted the education and upbringing of a new generation of non-European Christians. Often, this educational endeavour also met the interests of colonial states that placed the task into the hands of private religious bodies. Second, the expansion of international child saving in the mid nineteenth century both demonstrated the shifting social value of children in Western Europe and to a cultural (and scientific) understanding of childhood as an innocent, vulnerable and formative stage in human life that demanded the particular protection, assistance and guidance by adults, institutions and later the state.[13] In addition, the beginning of far-off child saving cannot be separated from domestic activism towards children in the middle decades of the nineteenth century. It was part and parcel of the philanthropic and (national) reform movements that had emerged in many Western countries in response to the social transformations (e.g. industrialization, population growth and disintegration of rural communities) of that time.

As several studies have shown, the 1830s and 1840s saw the beginnings of religious and secular initiatives focusing on poor, orphaned, abandoned, neglected and/or (morally) 'endangered' children in many Western countries. These initiatives fuelled child-centred philanthropic activism and, in the longer term, the development of modern (and national) systems of childcare, education and welfare policies.[14] Philanthropists and reformers (and soon also politicians and scientists) increasingly understood children as resources for social, religious and political change, and increasingly focused on the young in order to advance their respective projects. Christian conservatives, who tended to interpret social transformations as signs of spiritual crisis, in particular called for impulses towards religious revival in order to achieve social reform.[15] Thus, Christian charities all over Europe established numerous schools for the poor, children's homes or so-called *Rettungshäuser* in order to promote their religious educational programmes. For our context, it is important to note that these domestic efforts to improve and shape the lives of children were to some extent paralleled by the expansion of child-saving practices to geographically distant places. In the mid nineteenth century, several Protestant and Catholic initiatives publicly promoted the ransoming of child slaves in Africa, launched the beginning of transnational child sponsorship and encouraged the saving of abandoned children in various geographical settings. All of this initiated an unprecedented expansion of missionary childcare and education.[16] Inspired by domestic philanthropic efforts, these child-centred activities shaped and were shaped by both practical needs and a strong notion of childhood innocence, which became an important point of reference in Catholic circles. This is best shown by the example of the Holy Childhood Association, one of the earliest and largest transnational organizations dedicated exclusively to the saving of children since the mid nineteenth century.

The Holy Childhood Association was founded in 1843 by the Bishop of Lyon, Charles-Auguste-Marie-Joseph de Forbin-Janson (1785–1844).[17] Inspired by the missionary reports about child abandonment and infanticide in China that were widely circulated among the clergy in early nineteenth-century France and other European countries,[18] Forbin-Janson promoted the establishment of an institution, in which European Catholics (and particularly Catholic children) should promote the saving of Chinese children through their donations and intercessory prayers.[19] His understanding of saving was comprised of two aspects: while it meant the principal goal of religious salvation through baptism on the one hand, it related to physical rescue from abandonment or child murder on the other.[20] According to Forbin-Janson, Catholic agents in China should collect abandoned infants or buy unwanted babies from their parents, baptize them and raise the surviving children in Catholic orphanages. Besides, celebrating childhood as a special stage in human life and strongly promoting the claimed innocence of children as a source of spiritual power, he particularly invited Catholic children to come to the aid of those whom he introduced as their little 'heathen' brothers and sisters in foreign lands.[21] Interestingly enough, despite Forbin-Janson's death in 1844, his plan proved to be extremely successful. Due to the broad support of the clergy and laypeople, the mass use of print and artefacts, extensive travelling activity and promotional campaigns in the established Catholic media, the Holy Childhood Association soon expanded greatly: during the next three decades, the Association established branches throughout Catholic Europe and North America, and the donations rose enormously.[22]

For our context, it is important to note that, while the actual outlook of the Holy Childhood Association could differ across time and space, its promotional campaigns always focused on the symbolic figure of the poor, helpless, innocent, yet highly valuable 'heathen' child. In Europe, this child came to embody a moral demand, because it was constructed and transnationally promoted as lacking all local protection and being fully exposed to the arbitrary, cruel or even violent actions of 'heathen' adults and institutions. 'Heathen' children thus had to be saved by caring and loving Catholics. As stated earlier, the Association made productive use of different types of texts, such as booklets, leaflets, songbooks, annals and reports in order to circulate its ideas and mobilizing narratives. These texts were translated into several European languages and were distributed among adults and children by priests, nuns and lay activists (e.g. teachers). We may thus well assume that the appreciation of the image of this vulnerable yet highly valuable child, together with a shared moral judgement on the supposed actions of cruel or indifferent adults in 'heathen lands', forged what can be described as an imagined community of child savers.[23] In a passage that was endlessly repeated in diverse handbooks or leaflets, the Holy Childhood Association presented its goal as the task to:

> assist *unfortunate pagan children*, who daily perish by thousands and hundreds of thousands; to rescue them from a watery grave, or from the power of ferocious dogs and swine, to which unhappy lot the cruelty of their inhuman parents daily abandons them; to procure them the grace of Baptism, and if they survive, place them in charitable asylums.[24]

Similar wordings and imaginations feature in several promotional texts issued by the Association. To give but one example, a German booklet (1852) claimed that it was precisely in view of the 'hard destiny of these unhappy children . . . who are drowned by hundreds and hundreds of thousands in the sea or in rivers, or thrown to the dogs and swine' that Forbin-Janson was moved by compassion and decided to establish the Holy Childhood Association.[25] As these examples show, the authors created and reproduced a vision of vast misery in distant lands by putting forward the vivid imagination of a menace to young and innocent souls and bodies created by absent parents, dangerous waters and wild animals.

Given the frequent repetition of similar passages in fundraising texts, it comes as no surprise that key elements (massive misery, water, dogs or swine) also featured prominently in the Association's visual campaigns. Like many other Catholic groups and organizations at that time, it employed a broad range of images and illustrated objects with the goal of drumming up support. In so doing, it connected to a nineteenth-century visual practice in European Catholicism, which evolved around the distribution of cheaply produced and massively reproduced visual objects, such as medals, statues, postcards, collectors' cards and images of saints.[26] In the Holy Childhood Association, each member received a medal and a membership card, both of which featured child saving scenes. The Association produced and distributed a range of illustrated cards (showing, for instance, the infant Jesus, the Holy Family or founder Forbin-Janson) for promotional purposes. A statue of the infant Jesus, who was recognized as the Patron of the Association, formed part of all its major social and religious events.[27] Besides, the early promotional booklets already contained images that often referenced key elements of the founding narrative of the Association and featured visual links to the powerful ideas of the thread and saving of children. For instance, several images displayed tiny little bodies, which were often ethnically coded and were always depicted as left alone by their parents or native caretakers. Many illustrations referenced the theme of child abandonment as it was known through antique stories or biblical narratives and broadly addressed in Christian literature and art such as the story of Moses. In the media of the Holy Childhood Association, we find images showing little babies being rescued from drowning by religious child savers, being carried in baskets to priests or waiting to be collected on the doorstep of Catholic children's homes. Overall, in the imagery created, scenes of child saving and the adoption of children through Christian care workers prevailed over depictions of infantile endangerment and suffering.[28]

Figure 1.1 illustrates this impressively. It presents an image that was evidently reproduced in at least two promotional booklets issued by the Holy Childhood Association in North America (i.e. Canada) in 1856 and 1860, respectively.[29] The image gives great insight into the ways in which Catholic groups in the West presented and imagined child saving in distant China. The image shows a large number of tiny, naked little white bodies, who are presented as highly vulnerable and exposed to threats and suffering created by men and nature. Even though the image features only one baby who is virtually under attack, it presents what the Holy Childhood Association repeatedly presented as the myriad dangers (e.g. water, dogs or swine) faced by newborn babies who lacked the protection and even the sympathy of their parents. However, this impression of ubiquitous threat and infantile suffering is put into perspective by the visual presence of Catholic child savers, who are depicted as highly active: The image shows numerous priests and nuns, who not only collect and physically save the tiny bodies from drowning or abandonment, but also shelter them caringly in their arms or bless them. The great majority of babies could thus be imagined as saved by viewers, who certainly appreciated and valued the spiritual and material acts of child saving depicted. The whole setting clearly pointed to China, for several of the men carrying children and handing them over to the priests were ethnically coded through their dress, beards and bodies. Besides, the image also references a range of other themes central to the Holy Childhood Association, such as the infant Jesus (on top), the Holy Family (top left) and the Association's founder Forbin-Janson (the priest wearing the large cross and holding his arms wide open blessing the baby held up to him). All three elements were important to the visual (and textual) representation of the Association more generally.

Figure 1.1 can be seen as emblematic for the visual configuration of the most common type of image objects produced, disseminated and consumed in the Holy Childhood Association well into the twentieth century: its membership cards. As indicated earlier, from the outset, each regular supporter received two image objects, a medal and a membership card, both of which featured illustrations of child-saving scenes. These cards were personalized, for they contained space to record the name of the owner and the date of his or her reception into the Association. They were thus important objects of exchange that fulfilled specific functions in the peculiar spiritual economy of aid created. The membership cards functioned as mobile image objects connecting people: they were exchanged across borders and linked the supporters ideologically and physically to the Association that had produced and distributed them. We may well assume that the members shared a certain way or specific perspective of viewing and valuing them: owning or displaying such an illustrated card was a visible sign and statement of religious and philanthropic engagement for distant children. In other words, the owners of the cards could consider themselves active child savers who not only gave a small monthly amount for what they perceived as Chinese children in need, but also considered them on a daily basis in their prayers.[30]

Promoting Distant Children in Need 47

Figure 1.1. 'Save us, for we perish.' 'Institution of the Holy Childhood' booklet, Pontifical Association of the Holy Childhood, 1856. Public domain.

Thus, it is no surprise that actions of child saving featured prominently in these cards, even though the range of illustrations varied and contained both coloured and black-and-white lithographs.[31] For instance, an undated French card shows a priest with some Chinese boys and two men, one of whom is arriving at the group, carrying a pole with two baskets filled with infants at either end. Images of tiny babies being carried to children's homes in baskets became an important visual feature of the Holy Childhood Association that also appeared in later photographic material (see Figure 1.4). In turn, an Italian membership card shows a priest who, sitting at a desk, obviously seals the transfer of a child into Catholic custody by shaking hands with a Chinese man. This example may be seen as a reference to the notion of paternal rights and authority. However, the same picture also addressed the issue of (parental) childcare, for in the background, we see a priest and a nun, each carrying an infant in their arms.[32] A German membership card from 1871 likewise took up the theme of the transfer of Chinese children and their adoption into the custody of a Catholic institution:[33] again, the image displays several tiny naked bodies being carried in baskets and finding shelter in the arms of nuns and priests. The German card also prominently addressed the Catholic doctrine of baptism as a key act on the way to salvation, because it shows priests and nuns offering infants to God and cites a respective passage of the Gospel of John.[34]

In the Holy Childhood Association, the spiritual saving of as many children as possible continued to constitute an important theme well into the twentieth century. Indeed, child saving was promoted in quantitative terms right from the start. Many promotional booklets featured quantitative data on spiritual rescues.[35] Even though the Holy Childhood Association forcefully created the imagination of vast misery in China, at the same time it always saw to its supporters keeping track both of the sum necessary to save an individual child and of joint results. It thus introduced modes of fundraising that focused on the imagination of individualized savings: donors who fully financed the saving of a child were entitled to choose its sex and baptismal name, which would be forwarded to China by the workers of the Holy Childhood Association.[36] With that, the Holy Childhood Association transformed abstract acts of solidarity with geographically distant children through donations into individual and countable acts of saving, which scholars have described as a characteristic feature of modern humanitarianism more generally.[37] The first German promotional booklet of the Holy Childhood Association (1845) already claimed that 'according to the calculations of the missionaries, each member of our association, with his humble annual contribution, can save a soul a year'.[38] This again points to the great and, according to this imaginary, very concrete meaning that membership cards, illustrated with distant events of child saving, potentially acquired for owners. We may well assume that these cards even shaped their imagination of and desire to save distant children in need. To be sure, the function of images and the role of the visual in the formation and fostering of transnational relationships of aid still gained importance towards the end of the century, when the appropriation of photography and photographic technologies allowed new uses and functions of images and facilitated the visual reconfiguration of the fundraising media.[39]

The Reconfiguration of Benevolent Image Making through Photography

Mass-reproduced photographs started to enter the Christian media in significant numbers during the 1890s and thus at a time when many mission-supporting associations not only coexisted but also competed for donations. Despite the fact that most Christian fundraisers had in their possession growing collections of photos showing a great variety of subjects and people of all ages that missionaries had sent to Europe, they often chose to promote their concerns through images of children. This is true for not only child-centred organizations such as the Holy Childhood Association but also for several other Christian charities, which extensively drew on photographs of children in order to drum up support. In the context of missionary fundraising, this visual focus on children actually produced the development and international expansion of a distinct photographic genre, consisting of group portraits of children posing in front of the camera together with little blackboards featuring text messages (for example, greetings or thanksgiving) to donors in Europe.[40] The focus on children can also be observed in the Protestant context.[41] While in some missions, children were among the first subjects photographed, this trend obviously gained momentum after the Armenian massacres in the Ottoman Empire, where scholars have observed a 'missionary rivalry in post-1896 orphan relief'.[42] Indeed, photographs of children from Asia or Africa, often depicted on their own or under the care of Catholic priests or nuns and in isolation from parents or non-Christian adults, became a ubiquitous feature in the Christian fundraising media. By so doing, the visual politics and fundraising techniques of the missions also mirrored those of domestic charities, which likewise drew extensively on photography and photographic practices in order to raise support. As Lydia Murdoch has shown in her study on poor families and child welfare in nineteenth-century London, some philanthropists such as Thomas Bernardo (1845–1905) even established photographic studios in order to promote their children's homes.[43] Significantly, in the case of the Christian missions, it was not the physically suffering 'heathen child', but rather its healthy (and often baptized) counterpart that dominated image making in the name of transnational charity. Characteristically, children are depicted in a way that Western viewers would appreciate as nicely dressed, well supplied and responsibly cared for.

The children depicted usually featured a clean, covered and nurtured body, and they were either represented posing in ordered groups or engaging in those activities that Western audiences came to value as essential to 'proper' childhoods, such as play and school. Representations of children in Christian fundraising thus points to the universalization of a particular vision of childhood, which be-

Figure 1.2. 'Orphelins de la Sainte Enfance – Pékin'. Holy Childhood Association illustrated postcard. Author's collection.

came increasingly embedded in a discourse that, declaring the status of children as a benchmark of Western Christian civilization, also contributed to the conception of colonialism in terms of benevolence.[44] The Holy Childhood Association deliberately contrasted 'Christian' parental love in Europe with the actions of 'barbarian' fathers and mothers in China.[45] It usually represented the children on their own and visually disconnected from their parents, relatives and native society. Sometimes, texts explicitly introduced them as orphans.[46] Whether depicted at school, at play, in peer groups or together with religious care workers, the children appeared in a rather uniform way and somewhat detached from time or space. Their cultural or social background was visually eliminated. In the early twentieth century, Christian organizations typically resorted to an image of children as embodiments of saving and religious, social and cultural change. In this type of imagery, African or Asian children existed in the sole context of missionary work and Christian charity. Often they were depicted as universal objects of care and nourishment; for instance, being photographed in Western dress, the children were frequently pictured wearing the type of clothes that donors in Europe sent abroad in massive quantities. At times, captions explicitly referred to the donated dresses.[47] In contrast, it may be noted that editors generally drew on photographs of adults (or elderly people) when picturing persons of a non-Western cultural, religious or ethnic background.[48]

In that sense, the use of photographs of children in Christian fundraising media reminds us of what anthropologist Lisa Malkki has observed for contemporary humanitarian discourse. According to Malkki, children, rather than being introduced as social persons with histories of their own, often function as mere symbols of harmony, innocence and human goodness.[49] Already the portraits of children (re)produced and used by transnational Christian charities in the early twentieth century drew their appeal from the great emotional weight and symbolic power that modern Western societies have invested in children.[50] Figure 1.3

Figure 1.3. 'Das Negerkind', published with this front page 1912–39. St Petrus Claver Sodality. Courtesy of the St Petrus Claver Sodality.

illustrates this impressively. The image featured for many years on the cover of an international Catholic periodical entitled *The Negro Child*, which was launched by the Catholic St Petrus Claver Sodality in 1912 with the explicit goal to 'promote love for our poorest black brothers'.[51]

The St Petrus Claver Sodality was an international association founded by the Austrian countess Maria Teresia Ledóchowska (1863–1922) in the early 1890s. While the initiative had started as a cross-confessional movement against slavery and the slave trade in Africa, it soon developed into an extremely successful yet narrowly Catholic institution, which dedicated itself to raising funds for missionary work in Africa.[52] Ledóchowska, herself a prolific writer, speaker and promoter, saw the media as a prime means to mobilize charity and support for Africa and the Africans. After having established a printing press near Salzburg and gathering a group of supporters, she began to publishing huge numbers of illustrated booklets, journals, books, plays, books of sermons, etc. Coming from an aristocratic Polish family with links to the high clergy, Ledóchowska distributed her promotional material not only in all parts of Austro-Hungary, but also in Germany, Italy, Switzerland, France, Spain, England and the United States.[53] Importantly for us, her promotional campaigns likewise appealed to the construction of the innocent child slave in Africa, who had to be rescued from cruel and violent slave traders and indifferent adults by the joint efforts of a Catholic international. In that sense, Ledóchowska's activities centrally connected to earlier ideas and practices of child saving. To give but one example, in 1891, she appealed to the 'mothers of the civilized world' to come to the aid of African child slaves, promising that 'all you did for the miserable Negroes, God will reward on your own children'.[54] Appealing to a highly gendered and naturalized notion of maternal love, the Sodality invited particularly its female readers not only to love their biological children but also to embrace distant children in need and to take pity on them by donating money.[55] Again, while fundraising texts drew a picture of real and vast suffering on the African continent, the accompanying artwork largely consisted of photographs of children, who were first presented as a kind of universal symbol of human innocence and second in a way that Western Christian spectators could largely consider them saved.

This was also the case for the *The Negro Child*, which, by 1920, reached a total circulation of 110,000 copies, appearing six times a year not only in German but also in Italian, French, Polish, English, Czech, Slovakian and Hungarian.[56] Figure 1.3 shows the title page of the journal as it appeared on all issues up to 1930, with changes being made to form and background illustrations. Actually, the Sodality turned this image into some type of logo or brand, which was reproduced massively and appeared in different sizes, elaborations, formats and colouring in many media. In the first decades of the twentieth century, the image appeared in numerous publications issued by the St Petrus Claver Sodality, which, in turn, grew to one of the largest Catholic charities raising donations for Africa.[57] Detached from time, space, culture and society, the child pictured not only symbolized innocence, vulnerability, goodness and the Christian promise of salvation, but, with its big eyes gazing at the viewer, also demanded protection and support. This mode of representation did not require a voice, for it spoke powerfully to the great emotional load and symbolic power that children and child saving had become invested with.[58]

Yet, the meaning of mass-reproduced photographs of children was not limited to their power as symbols, but also relied closely on their (institutionalized) use. In the early twentieth century, they indeed became ubiquitous objects in the generation of transnational aid and the fostering of relationships of giving. In a similar fashion to the membership cards, photographs acquired meaning in a very practical sense as they were massively reproduced and became visual objects of exchange between donors, philanthropic institutions and beneficiaries. As such, they actively contributed to the fostering of donor relationships across large geographical distances. While such a social use of images had already started before the massive advent of photographs in nineteenth-century missionary contexts, it greatly expanded and took on some new meanings in later decades.[59] As compared with other types of images, photographs of children came to function as some sort of evidence for both the real existence of needy children and the visible effects of transnational charity. For instance, by then, most Christian fundraising institutions distributed photographically illustrated postcards or individualized certificates of baptisms or rescues as a reward for donations. Usually, picture cards referenced the core tasks of the respective institution in terms of the primary target groups and/or geographical focus of benevolence. In the case of the Holy Childhood Association, the visual programme frequently referenced the emotionally loaded nexus of child saving, China (or Asia more generally) and care work among supposedly abandoned or orphaned children.

Besides, the expansion of photographic technologies also allowed for some sort of novel documentary (and authenticating) use of images and the personalization of philanthropic image making more generally. For instance, in the first decades of the twentieth century, the journals of the St Petrus Claver Sodality regularly printed life stories of individual children who had apparently been rescued from the horrors of slavery by the joint efforts of missionaries and their supporting groups in Europe. Without a doubt, these life stories significantly gained credibility by the adding of photographic portraits claiming to show 'true images' of the respective children, who were usually introduced with their names and life stories.[60] Printed in the institutionalized context of the journals, these stories personalized collective aid and were moreover firmly embedded in fundraising endeavours, inasmuch as donors was given the opportunity to dedicate donations to the individuals they had encountered on the photographs.

Also, for the Holy Childhood Association, photographs became indispensable objects in the personalization of aid. This becomes most visible in the great expansion of transnational child sponsorship. While historians working on the development of secular child welfare in the twentieth century tend to qualify child sponsorship as a novel and market-oriented form of fundraising,[61] it must be noted that Christian associations had already promoted this type of media-based engagement for a long time. The Holy Childhood Association, which had provided donors from the outset with the possibility to choose the baptismal names of the children rescued with their money and to act as their imagined godparents, steadily expanded this practice during the 1920s and 1930s by the extensive use of new visual mass media. This can be seen most clearly in the production and distribution of so-called Christening cards among supporters, who could use them to actively initiate an act of child saving. In the twentieth century, donors could thereby select between merely financing the baptism of a child and contributing to what was called redemption or rescue (in French: *rachat*) and imagined as some sort of longer-term care by his or her full transfer into the social worlds of Catholic institutions (Figure 1.4). By introducing this distinction between the two ideas of spiritual rescue through baptism on the one hand and a more comprehensive rescue through the full change of living contexts on the other, the Holy Childhood Association also gradually secularized this practice. As we will see in what follows, the transnational exchange of photographs played a significant role in that process.

Due to the lack of sources, the reception of such images constitutes a very difficult topic. Yet, the available documents do allow us to assess the great importance that photographs acquired in the formation of transnational relationships of aid. The central archive of the Holy Childhood Association contains several letters by local representatives and individual donors, who, during the late 1920s and 1930s, requested to receive photographs of the children rescued with their money. In 1931, the head of the Austrian branch of the Association, Karl Drexler, not only ordered 5,000 copies of mass-produced images but also enquired about the possibility to receive individual photographs of the children rescued with donations from Austria.[62] In addition, the historical archives contain a collection of letters suggesting that individual donors were not only striving to get data (age, address, etc.) about the children rescued with their money, but were explicitly demanding to receive their photographs.[63] For instance, in 1932, the sisters Thérèse and Cécile Crépin from a small village near Lourdes wrote to the Holy Childhood Association and expressed their desire to finance the saving of six 'little Negroes'. Obviously, the sisters, who certainly were of a very young age themselves, had a very clear idea about which 'type' of children they aimed to save: according to their letter, they wished to save three girls and three boys from Madagascar who should ideally belong to an ethnic group known as the Betsimis-araka people.[64] Unfortunately, we are unable to assess whether the two girls from the Pyrenees knew about this ethnic group from the media issued by the Holy Childhood Association. However, the available documents do show that the girls imagined the African children as individuals: the sisters not only demanded to receive some information about whom they imagined as their African godchildren but also desired to receive their photographs.[65]

In the 1930s, the Holy Childhood Association indeed started to provide sponsors routinely with photographs of the children rescued with their money. However, while the sources available do not allow us to establish whether these

Promoting Distant Children in Need 55

Figures 1.4a and b. 'Chine – Hongkong'. Holy Childhood Association illustrated postcard. Author's collection.

photographs at the end consisted of mass-produced images or of individual photographs, they do point to the great meaning that respective imaginations and visual practices acquired at least for some child savers. In 1937, twelve-year old Simone Maurel from the surroundings of Toulouse wrote to the Holy Childhood Association,[66] stating that she deeply loved the little Chinese and regularly prayed for them. She desired to become the godmother of a baby girl in China, who was to be named Marie-Thérèse, a choice she explained by her great trust in St Thérèse of Lisieux. Yet, desiring that Marie-Thérèse also received a lasting souvenir of her 'petite marraine de France', Simone sent a postcard illustrated with her own photograph to the Association with the request to forward it on to China. Obviously, this never happened; instead, Simone's photograph, which shows her kneeling on a church bench on the day of her first communion, ended up in the archive. Yet, that way, the postcard allows us to gain a valuable insight into the workings of both a media-based Catholic culture of child saving and the powerful function of photographs being moved across space and thus bridging large geographical distances. Simone directed some lines to Marie-Thérèse on the back. For the twelve-year old girl in rural France, this photograph obviously constituted the most effective and accessible medium in order to communicate with the one whom she imagined and desired to be her little goddaughter in China.

Conclusion

Christian organizations, by extending religious ethics and social practices of charity to distant groups of people, belonged to the first actors who established long-term relationships of aid across large geographical distance. In doing so, they extensively drew on new media technologies and developed not only a practice but also a visual discourse of child saving. Considering the argument by scholar of media Lilie Chouliaraki, who has suggested analysing solidarity in late twentieth-century humanitarianism as an issue of communication,[67] we may acknowledge that it was particularly Christian charities that introduced visual dimensions and practices to this type of transnational communication, which turned out to be highly influential when it came to establishing moral imperatives towards distant children in need in the long run. This chapter has suggested that the activities of Christian organizations affected the wider history of transnational aid and philanthropy in two main respects. First, they promoted an influential imagery and visual practice of child saving, which, relying on modern notions of childhood and the growing social value of children in affective terms, established the young (and particularly infants) as needy innocents, symbols of humanity and human goodness, and thus prime objects of aid. Second, drawing extensively on visual technologies and moving image objects in fundraising, they institutionalized a specific use of visual technologies and promoted a representational dynamics, which both, without doubt, greatly influenced the professionalizing media work of the later religious and secular children's charities.

The chapter has pointed to the importance of taking the historical phenomenon of Christian child saving into account in all its ambivalences. As much as it provided religious satisfaction and produced a serious concern or honest engagement for distant children for the children's sake, the strident protection of the young, whether explicitly or not, contributed to the moral condemnation of distant adults and institutions. This, again, invites us to question particular ways of seeing, observing, valuing and feeling about this type of images as historically learned and symbolically stabilized cultural practices. The study of religious traditions of benevolent image making challenges established chronologies in the field of humanitarian visual culture, because it well pre-dates the mass production and usage of photographs on the part of secular charities in post-First World War contexts. Hence, exploring humanitarian imagery from the perspective of Christian social and charitable activism invites us to examine both image contents and certain uses of images in the name of benevolence under the conditions of advancing visual technologies as well as new developments in the field of (international) communication.[68] Seen from this angle, the introduction of photography in general and photographs of children in particular do not appear as caesura, let alone the beginning of humanitarian visual culture, but rather as an intrinsic part of what is best described as the complex history of benevolent image making.[69] Images of children and childhood were located at the core of this history at least since the middle third of the nineteenth century.

Katharina Stornig is Junior Professor of Cultural History at the University of Giessen. Her research interests include gender history, transnational history, the history of photography and the cultural history of aid and philanthropy. She is the author of *Sisters Crossing Boundaries. German Missionary Nuns in Colonial Togo and New Guinea, 1897–1960* (2013). Currently, she works on the history of transnational aid for children on which she has recently published 'Between Christian Solidarity and Human Solidarity: Humanity and the Mobilisation of Aid for Distant Children in Catholic Europe in the Long 19th Century', in Fabian Klose and Mirjam Thulin (eds), *Humanity: A History of European Concepts in Practice from the Sixteenth Century to the Present* (2016), 249–266 and 'Catholic Missionary Associations and the Saving of African Child Slaves in Nineteenth-Century Germany', *Atlantic Studies: Global Currents* 14(4) (2017), 519–42.

Notes

1. Scholars pointing out the great symbolic value of children have discussed the mobilizing potential of images of children critically. See, for instance, L. Malkki, 'Children, Humanity, and the Infantilization of Peace', in I. Feldman and M. Ticktin (eds), *In the Name of Humanity: The Government of Threat and Care* (Durham, NC: Duke University Press,

2010), 58–85; K. Manzo, 'Imagining Humanitarianism: NGO Identity and the Iconography of Childhood', *Antipode* 40(4) (2008), 632–57; W. McKenzie, 'Fresh Maimed Babies: The Uses of Innocence', *Transition* 65 (1995), 36–47; J. Bhaba, 'The Child – What Sort of Human?', *PMLA* 121(5) (2006), 1526–35, at 1527–28.

2. See H. Fehrenbach, 'Children and Other Civilians: Photography and the Politics of Humanitarian Image-Making', in H. Fehrenbach and D. Rodogno (eds), *Humanitarian Photography: A History* (Cambridge: Cambridge University Press, 2015), 165–99.

3. Fehrenbach, 'Children and Other Civilians', 167. A similar chronology is proposed by E. Baughan, '"Every Citizen of Empire Implored to Save the Children!" Empire, Internationalism and the Save the Children Fund in Inter-war Britain', *Historical Research* 86(231) (2013), 116–37; V. Gorin, '"Millions of Children in Deadly Peril": utilisation des photographies d'enfants affamés par le Save the Children Fund pendant l'entre-deux-guerres', *Revue Suisse d'histoire – Itinera* 37 (2014), 95–112; F. Kind-Kovács, 'Compassion for the Distant Other: Children's Hunger and Humanitarian Relief in Budapest in the Aftermath of WWI', in B. Althammer, L. Raphael and T. Stazic-Wendt (eds), *Rescuing the Vulnerable: Poverty, Welfare and Social Ties in Nineteenth- and Twentieth-Century Europe* (New York: Berghahn Books, 2016), 129–59.

4. This chapter is based on the analysis of religious fundraising media, as well as archival research in the Roman archives of the Pontifical Association of the Holy Childhood (POSI), the archives of the German Catholic charity mission e.V. based in Aachen and the Propaganda Fide Historical Archives (APF). I would particularly like to thank Johannes Paulmann, Anna Katharina Pieper, two anonymous reviewers and all the participants of the Richard von Weizsäcker Fellowship Conference held in June 2015 at St Antony's College, Oxford, for many perceptive comments and useful suggestions.

5. A material approach to images and particularly photographs is demanded by E. Edwards and J. Hart, 'Introduction: Photographs as Objects', in E. Edwards and J. Hart (eds), *Photographs Objects Histories: On the Materiality of Images* (New York: Routledge, 2004), 1–15.

6. A widely received theoretical discussion of this theme is provided by S. Sontag, *Regarding the Pain of Others* (New York: Farrar, Straus and Giroux, 2003). Moreover, see H. Fehrenbach and D. Rodogno, 'Introduction: The Morality of Sight', in H. Fehrenbach and D. Rodogno (eds), *Humanitarian Photography: A History* (Cambridge: Cambridge University Press, 2015), 1–21, 6f, 16; K. Grant, 'Christian Critics of Empire: Missionaries, Lantern Lectures, and the Congo Reform Campaign in Britain', *Journal of Imperial and Commonwealth History* 29(2) (2001), 27–58; K. Halttunen, 'Humanitarianism and the Pornography of Pain', *American Historical Review* 100(2) (1995), 303–34; R. Hölzl, '"Mitleid" über große Distanz: Zur Fabrikation globaler Gefühle in Medien der katholischen Mission (1890–1940)', in R. Habermas and R. Hölzl (eds), *Mission Global: Eine Verflechtungsgeschichte seit dem 19. Jahrhundert* (Cologne: Böhlau, 2014), 265–94; N. Maksudyan, 'Helden, Opfer, Ikonen: Massenmobilisierung und osmanische Kinder während des Ersten Weltkriegs', in J. Angelow (ed.), *Der Erste Weltkrieg auf dem Balkan* (Berlin: Be.bra, 2011), 161–73; S. Sliwinski, 'The Childhood of Human Rights: The Kodak in the Congo', *Journal of Visual Culture* 5(3) (2006), 333–63, at 340–42; T.J. Thompson, *Light on Darkness? Missionary Photography of Africa in the Nineteenth and Early Twentieth Century* (Grand Rapids, MI: William B. Eerdmans, 2012), 165–206. On the key function of depictions of suffering in humanitarian contexts in general, see A. Wilson and R. D. Brown (eds), *Humanitarianism and Suffering: The Mobilization of Empathy* (Cambridge: Cambridge University Press, 2009).

7. Indeed, it was only in the 1920s that images of sick and starving children entered Christian visual discourse significantly. The reasons for this still demand further research. However, it can be assumed that media coverage of major humanitarian events (famines, refugee crises in the aftermath of the Armenian genocide, etc.), the emergence of new humanitarian actors and growing competition between aid institutions introduced new visual styles and viewing habits.

8. Richard Howells has emphasized this for historical photographs by stating that owning a photograph 'was like owning a little piece of reality itself'. R. Howells, *Visual Culture* (Malden, MA: Blackwell Publishers, 2013), 153. The potential of photographs as indexical image objects connecting people and fostering (individualized) relationships of giving is emphasized in K. Stornig, 'Authentifizierung kultureller Begegnungen durch Fotografie: Über die Verwendung von Fotos als Spuren in der transnationalen Spendenwerbung im 19. Jahrhundert', *Saeculum. Jahrbuch für Universalgeschichte* 66(2) (2016), 207–28, at 214–19.

9. See J. Jäger, *Fotografie und Geschichte* (Frankfurt am Main: Campus, 2009), 12f. Most famously, Roland Barthes has characterized the photograph as 'literally an emanation of the referent'. R. Barthes, *Camera Lucida: Reflections on Photography* (London: Vintage Books, 2000), 80.

10. See D. Marshall, 'International Child Saving', in P. Fass (ed.), *The Routledge History of Childhood in the Western World* (London: Taylor & Francis, 2015), 469–90, at 469.

11. Felicity Jensz has aptly referred to nineteenth-century Christian visions of missionary schools as the 'nursery of the church'. See F. Jensz, 'The Cultural, Didactic, and Physical Space of Mission Schools in the 19th Century', *Österreichische Zeitschrift für Geschichtswissenschaften* 24(2) (2013), 70–91, at 70. The importance of children and notions of childhood to nineteenth-century missionary visions have stressed in K. Vallgårda, *Imperial Childhoods and Christian Mission: Education and Emotions in South India and Denmark* (Basingstoke: Palgrave Macmillan, 2015), 2; H. Morrison and M.C. Martin (eds), *Creating Religious Childhoods in Anglo-World and British Colonial Contexts, 1800–1950* (London: Routledge, 2017).

12. See R. Alsheimer, *Zwischen Sklaverei und christlicher Ethnogenese: Die vorkoloniale Missionierung der Ewe in Westafrika (1847–ca. 1890)* (Münster: Waxmann, 2007), 59–64.

13. See E. Hermsen, *Faktor Religion: Geschichte der Kindheit vom Mittelalter bis zur Gegenwart* (Cologne: Böhlau, 2006), 139–45.

14. For instance, see H. Cunningham, *Children and Childhood in Western Society since 1500* (Harlow: Longman, 1995), 134–62; I. Jablonka, 'Social Welfare in the Western World and the Rights of Children', in P. Fass (ed.), *The Routledge History of Childhood in the Western World* (London: Taylor & Francis, 2015), 380–99; F.-M. Konrad, 'Sollen die Kinder der Armen erzogen werden? Über einige ideengeschichtliche Hintergründe der öffentlichen Kleinkinderziehung in der ersten Hälfte des 19. Jahrhunderts', in S. Hering and W. Schröer (eds), *Sorge um die Kinder. Beiträge zur Geschichte von Kindheit, Kindergarten und Kinderfürsorge* (Weinheim: Juventa, 2008), 25–38; J. Marten, *Childhood and Child Welfare in the Progressive Era: A Brief History with Documents* (Boston: Bedford, 2005), 172–75; L. Murdoch, 'From Barrack Schools to Family Cottages: Creating Domestic Space for Late Victorian Poor Children', in J. Lawrence and P. Starkey (eds), *Child Welfare and Social Action in the Nineteenth and Twentieth Centuries: International Perspectives* (Liverpool: Liverpool University Press, 2001), 147–73; B. Sandin, 'Education', in C. Heywood (ed.), *A Cultural History of Childhood and Family in the Age of Empire* (London: Bloomsbury, 2014), 91–110.

15. R. Dickinson, *The Politics of Child Welfare from the Empire to the Federal Republic* (Cambridge, MA: Harvard University Press, 1996), 12. In addition, see A, Przyrembel, 'Der Missionar Johann Hinrich Wichern, die Sünde und das unabänderliche Elend der städtischen Unterschichten um 1855', *Werkstatt Geschichte* 57 (2011), 53–67.

16. See H. Harrison, '"A Penny for the Little Chinese": The French Holy Childhood Association in China, 1843–1951', *American Historical Review* 113(1) (2008), 72–92; Jensz, 'The Cultural, Didactic, and Physical Space', 73f; K. Stornig, 'Figli della Chiesa. Riscatti e globalizzazione del welfare cattolico (1840–1914)', *Genesis. Rivista della Società Italiana delle Storiche* 14(1) (2015), 55–83.

17. On the history of the Association from its foundation in France to its expansion in Europe, see S. Heywood, 'Missionary Children: The French Holy Childhood Association in European Context, 1843–1914', *European History Quarterly* 45(3) (2015), 446–66.

18. The early promotional literature issued by the Holy Childhood Association often claimed to cite reports allegedly penned by eyewitnesses 'who had themselves visited China and carefully explored the state of the country'. See Der Verein der Heiligen Kindheit (ed.), *Der Verein der Heiligen Kindheit: Kurze Darstellung seiner Entstehung und seines Zweckes, nebst Berichten über seine Wirksamkeit bis zum Jahre 1851* (Aachen: Verlag der Cremerschen Buchhandlung, 1852), 10.

19. The Holy Childhood Association was also inspired by the international expansion of the so-called Society for the Propagation of the Faith, a lay organization that was founded in 1822 with the goal of raising funds and support for the Catholic missions. The international entanglement of Catholic philanthropic and missionary organizations is discussed in V. Viaene, 'Nineteenth Century Catholic Internationalism and its Predecessors', in A. Green and V. Viaene (eds), *Religious Internationals in the Modern World: Globalization and Faith Communities since 1750* (Basingstoke: Palgrave Macmillan, 2012), 82–110, 92f.

20. Der Verein der Heiligen Kindheit (ed.), *Der Verein der Heiligen Kindheit: Geschichte seines Entstehens, seines Wachsthums und gegenwärtigen Bestandes* (Mainz: Kirchheim, Schott and Thielmann, 1845), 1.

21. The mobilization of Catholic children in Europe in the Holy Childhood Association is discussed by K. Stornig, '"Armes Kindlein in der Ferne, – Wie machst du das Herz mir schwer!" Kindermissionsvereine und die religiösen Verflechtungen des Helfens in Deutschland, Europa und der Welt, 1843–1920', *Themenportal Europäische Geschichte* (2015). Retrieved 15 August 2018 from http://www.europa.clio-online.de/2015/Article=741.

22. Until 1900, it established branches in, for example, France, Germany, Austria-Hungary, Switzerland, Luxembourg, the Netherlands, Belgium, Italy, Malta, Spain, Portugal, Great Britain, the United States and Canada. During the first sixty years of its existence, the total income of the Holy Childhood Association had been rising from 13,885146 Francs in 1843–63 to 69,788411 Francs in 1883–1903. See B. Arens, *Die katholischen Missionsvereine: Darstellung ihres Werdens und Wirkens ihrer Satzungen und Vorrechte* (Freiburg: Herder & Co, 1922), 74.

23. Anderson's concept is indeed useful here, for it points to the great importance of print and shared mediated imaginations in the formation of large communities. See B. Anderson, *Imagined Communities: Reflections on the Origin and Spread of Nationalism* (London: Verso, 2006), 4–7 and 37–46. The importance of shared symbols in community building is emphasized by A. Cohen, *The Symbolic Construction of Community* (London: Tavistock, 1985), 11–21.

24. 'Institution of the Holy Childhood', leaflet, 1856, original publication held by the Seminary of Quebec, Retrieved 15 August 2018 from https://archive.org/details/cihm_06605, 2 (emphasis in original).

25. Der Verein, *Der Verein der Heiligen Kindheit: Kurze Darstellung*, 5.

26. Since the medals, illustrated cards and statues were largely produced in Paris and sent to the various branches for distribution, the exchange of these image objects can be traced in the correspondence. Hence, we know that medals and cards were popular items among the supporters of the Association. See, for instance, the respective correspondence between the German branch and the international center of the Association in Paris: 'Demandes d'images et de médailles (1859–1950)', in POSI Série E Lettres des Directeurs nationaux, 6 and 'Demandes d'images et de médailles (1868–1950)', in POSI Série F Correspondance administrative, 12.

27. As much can be taken from the numerous reports about special feasts or church services that were published in the periodical of the Association.

28. Such images can be found frequently in the Holy Childhood Association's publications. For instance, see the artwork to various promotional texts: 'Documentation sur l'Œuvre', in POSI Série A Règlements et statuts – Généralités, 3. A French engraving from 1848/49 showing baskets and naked babies is also discussed in Harrison, '"A Penny"', 74f.

29. See 'Institution of the Holy Childhood', 1856, retrieved 18 August 2018 from https://archive.org/details/cihm_06605; and, 'Institution of the Holy Childhood for the Redemption of the Children of Infidels', booklet 1860, original publication held by the Bibliothèque nationale du Québec, retrieved 18 August 2018 from https://archive.org/details/cihm_94187, 2.

30. According to the statutes, each member was committed to giving a small monthly contribution and to saying a daily prayer for themselves and the 'heathen children'.

31. This is at least the case for the sample of membership cards available in archives or antiquarians.

32. While the collection of the general archives of the Association in Rome contains some cards and medals, nowadays both can be easily purchased in antiquarian bookstores on the internet. Consequently, an internet research easily provides an insight into the ways in which European child savers imagined the work of the Association in China.

33. See 'Material für Mitgliederbetreuung', in Historical Archives of the International Catholic Missionary Organization missio e.V. A – 850.

34. The text said: 'If one is not reborn of the water and the Holy Spirit he cannot enter the kingdom of God.'

35. Such data contained both information about the total of salvations (baptisms), statistics of incoming donations and national rankings. For instance, a North American booklet from 1856 indicated 216,404 saved children for the current year compared to 192,000 in the year before. See 'Institution of the Holy Childhood', leaflet, 2.

36. In view of the expansion of the geographical scope of child saving, donors could also choose whether a child should be saved in China or in Africa. The lists of donations kept in the central archive of the Holy Childhood Association show that, first, donors made use of this offer and, second, their name choices indeed played a role in the administrative process. See POSI Série E Lettres des Directeurs nationaux, 2 Allemagne (1850–1923).

37. See M. Barnett, 'Humanitarianism Transformed', *Perspectives on Politics* 3(4) (2005), 723–40, at 724.

38. Der Verein, *Der Verein der Heiligen Kindheit: Geschichte seines Entstehens*, 13.

39. The imperative to include technological aspects to the analysis of writing practices is emphasized by C. Zimmermann and M. Schreiber, 'Introduction: Towards a New Perspective on Journalism and Technology', in M. Schreiber and C. Zimmermann (eds), *Journalism and Technological Change: Historical Perspectives, Contemporary Trends* (Frankfurt am Main: Campus, 2014), 9–29, at 9.

40. See A. Eckl, 'Ora et labora: Katholische Missionsfotografie aus den afrikanischen Kolonien', in M. Bechhaus-Gerst and S. Gieseke (eds), *Koloniale und postkoloniale Konstruktionen von Afrika und Menschen afrikanischer Herkunft in der deutschen Alltagskultur* (Frankfurt am Main: Peter Lang, 2006), 231–50, at 240f.

41. See Stornig, 'Authentifizierung'; F. Jensz, 'Hope and Pity: Depictions of Children in Five Decades of the Evangelisch-Lutherisches Missionsblatt, 1860–1910', in J. Becker und K. Stornig (eds), *Menschen – Bilder – Eine Welt. Ordnungen von Vielfalt in der religiösen Publizistik um 1900* (Göttingen: Vandenhoeck & Ruprecht, 2018), 259–81.

42. See N. Maksudyan, *Orphans and Destitute Children in the Late Ottoman Empire* (Syracuse: Syracuse University Press, 2014), 119f.

43. Murdoch has pointed to the great number of 'melodramatic images' that originated from Bernardo's studio. These staged images of children, who were specifically dressed up in order to visualize destitution and rescue, were massively reproduced and used in fundraising throughout the United Kingdom. See L. Murdoch, *Imagined Orphans: Poor Families, Child Welfare, and Contested Citizenship in London* (New Brunswick, NJ: Rutgers University Press, 2006), 12–15 and 32–42.

44. See Vallgårda, *Imperial Childhoods and Christian Mission,* 6f.

45. Der Verein der Heiligen Kindheit, (ed.), *Der Verein der heiligen Kindheit* (Vienna: Mechitharisten-Buchdruckerei, 1855), 42.

46. The emotional appeal of this notion in nineteenth-century charity has been stressed by Murdoch, *Imagined Orphans,* 12–42.

47. For instance, see 'Happy Little Negroes in New Dress Received from European Benefactors', *Das Negerkind* (1912), 121.

48. See K. Stornig, 'Globalisierte Körper: Repräsentationen der Welt und ihrer BewohnerInnen auf der vatikanischen Missionsausstellung (1925)', in L. Ratschiller and S. Weichlein (eds), *Der schwarze Körper als Missionsgebiet: Medizin, Ethnologie, Theologie in Afrika und Europa 1880–1960* (Vienna: Böhlau, 2015), 123–52, at 141f.

49. See Malkki, 'Children', 60.

50. See P. Fass, 'Children and Globalization', *Journal of Social History* 36(4) (2003), 963–77, at 964. Sociologist Viviana Zelizer has examined the emergence of what she calls the priceless child in the nineteenth century. According to her, the social value of children profoundly changed between 1870 and 1930, for they had come to stand apart from the economy and to be valued in terms of adult pleasure and affect. See V.A. Zelizer, *Pricing the Priceless Child: The Changing Social Value of Children* (New York: Basic Books, 1985), 7–15.

51. See *Das Negerkind* (1912), 1.

52. Several recent studies have discussed Catholic antislavery activism that was in the making since the late 1880s. See A. Ribi Forclaz, *Humanitarian Imperialism: The Politics of Antislavery Activism 1880–1940* (Oxford: Oxford University Press, 2015), 14–45.

53. In 1912, the *Echo from Africa* was published in nine languages. See Letter from Maria Teresia Ledóchowska to Congregation for the Propagation of the Faith, 21 February 1913, and the answer from 18 March 1913, APF N.S. Vol. 527, 375 and 377.

54. See *Echo aus Afrika* 3(2) (1891), 16.

55. For instance, a short piece on 'universal maternal love' in one of the journals of the Sodality opened as follows: 'A truly loving mother's heart does not limit its care to the closest family circle. The deeper it loves the own happy swarm of children, the deeper it will feel for the suffering of other children and take pity on their needs'; 'Allumfassende Mutterliebe', *Das Negerkind* 21 (1914), 118.

56. See Letter from Maria Teresia Ledóchowska to the Congregation for the Propagation of the Faith, 12 April 1919, APF N.S. Vol. 620, 47–51, 47f.

57. As much can be taken from the fact that the Sodality was publicly lauded for its 'work of propaganda' in the framework of the universal missionary exhibition held in the Vatican in 1925. See 'Die Hilfswerke für die Missionen, *Weltschau des Katholizismus* 2 (1925), 54–58, at 58.

58. See Fass, 'Children and Globalization', 964.

59. A good example is the case of the Protestant Norddeutsche Missionsgesellschaft that had already been using photographs of children in order to individualize donor relationships between northern Germany and West Africa in the late 1860s. See Stornig, 'Authentifizierung', 212–19.

60. For instance, in 1911, the Sodality published the story of a boy in Tansania named Robert, who was kidnapped on the streets of Bagamoyo by an Arab slave trader. However, hearing the church bells, young Robert was able to escape and found shelter at a missionary station. The account, penned by the Bishop in Bagamoyo, was published together with a photograph showing a poorly dressed boy looking anxiously in the camera and captioned by 'Robert (true image)'. See X. Vogt, 'Wie ein kleiner Schwarzer durch das Läuten der Glocken aus der Sklaverei befreit wurde', *Kleine Afrika Bibliothek* 17 (1911), 5–8.

61. See Baughan, '"Every Citizen"', 131.

62. See Letter from Karl Drexler to Eugene Merio, 23 March 1931, POSI Série E 12 Autriche Lettres du Mgr. Drexler (1926–38).

63. See POSI Série F5 Correspondance et envois de fonds pour le rachat d'enfants chinois, avec demandes de photographies (1933–39).

64. See Letter from Thérèse and Cécile Crépin to the Holy Childhood Association Paris, 27 January 1932, POSI Série F5 Correspondance et envois de fonds pour le rachat d'enfants chinois, avec demandes de photographies (1933–39), Les Phot.

65. Significantly, the girls also asked for the addresses of the children, for they intended to send little presents (clothes) to Madagascar. See ibid.

66. Série F Correspondance administrative, 5. See Letter from Simone Maurel to the Holy Childhood Association Paris, 11 January 1937, POSI Série F5 Correspondance et envois de fonds pour le rachat d'enfants chinois, avec demandes de photographies (1933–39), Les Phot.

67. L. Chouliaraki, *The Ironic Spectator: Solidarity in the Age of Post-Humanitarianism* (Cambridge: Polity Press, 2013), 2–4.

68. See M. Barnett, *Empire of Humanity: A History of Humanitarianism* (Ithaca: Cornell University Press, 2011), 51.

69. A similar approach has been pursued by Sharon Sliwinski, who starts her analysis of the relationship between images and moral judgements in modern history with paintings of the Lisbon earthquake in 1755, which she sees as 'one of the first mass media events'. See S. Sliwinski, *Human Rights in Camera* (Chicago: University of Chicago Press, 2011), 35–47; quotation: S. Sliwinski, 'The Aesthetics of Human Rights', *Culture, Theory & Critique* 50(1) (2009), 23–39, at 23.

Bibliography

Alsheimer, R. *Zwischen Sklaverei und christlicher Ethnogenese: Die vorkoloniale Missionierung der Ewe in Westafrika (1847–ca. 1890)*. Münster: Waxmann, 2007.

Anderson, B. *Imagined Communities: Reflections on the Origin and Spread of Nationalism*. London: Verso, 2006.

Arens, B. *Die katholischen Missionsvereine: Darstellung ihres Werdens und Wirkens ihrer Satzungen und Vorrechte*. Freiburg: Herder & Co, 1922.

Barnett, M. 'Humanitarianism Transformed'. *Perspectives on Politics* 3(4) (2005), 723–40.

———. *Empire of Humanity: A History of Humanitarianism*. Ithaca: Cornell University Press, 2011.

Barthes, R. *Camera Lucida: Reflections on Photography*. London: Vintage Books, 2000.

Baughan, E. '"Every Citizen of Empire Implored to Save the Children!" Empire, Internationalism and the Save the Children Fund in Inter-war Britain'. *Historical Research* 86(231) (2013), 116–37.

Bhaba, J. 'The Child: What Sort of Human?'. *PMLA* 121(5) (2006), 1526–35.

Chouliaraki, L. *The Ironic Spectator: Solidarity in the Age of Post-humanitarianism*. Cambridge: Polity Press, 2013.

Cohen, A. *The Symbolic Construction of Community*. London: Tavistock, 1985.

Cunningham, H. *Children and Childhood in Western Society since 1500*. Harlow: Longman, 1995.

Dickinson, R. *The Politics of Child Welfare from the Empire to the Federal Republic*. Cambridge, MA: Harvard University Press, 1996.

Eckl, A. 'Ora et labora: Katholische Missionsfotografie aus den afrikanischen Kolonien', in M. Bechhaus-Gerst and S. Gieseke (eds), *Koloniale und postkoloniale Konstruktionen von Afrika und Menschen afrikanischer Herkunft in der deutschen Alltagskultur* (Frankfurt am Main: Peter Lang, 2006), 231–50.

Edwards, E., and J. Hart. 'Introduction: Photographs as Objects', in E. Edwards and J. Hart (eds), *Phonographs Objects Histories: On the Materiality of Images* (New York: Routledge, 2004), 1–15.

Fass, P. 'Children and Globalization'. *Journal of Social History* 36(4) (2003), 963–77.

Fehrenbach, H. 'Children and Other Civilians: Photography and the Politics of Humanitarian Image-Making', in H. Fehrenbach and D. Rodogno (eds), *Humanitarian Photography: A History* (Cambridge: Cambridge University Press, 2015), 165–99.

Fehrenbach, H., and D. Rodogno. 'Introduction: The Morality of Sight', in H. Fehrenbach and D. Rodogno (eds), *Humanitarian Photography: A History* (Cambridge: Cambridge University Press, 2015), 1–21.

Gorin, V. '"Millions of Children in Deadly Peril": utilisation des photographies d'enfants affamés par le Save the Children Fund pendant l'entre-deux-guerres'. *Revue Suisse d'histoire – Itinera* 37 (2014), 95–112.

Grant, K. 'Christian Critics of Empire: Missionaries, Lantern Lectures, and the Congo Reform Campaign in Britain'. *Journal of Imperial and Commonwealth History* 29(2) (2001), 27–58.

Halttunen, K. 'Humanitarianism and the Pornography of Pain'. *American Historical Review* 100(2) (1995), 303–34.

Harrison, H. '"A Penny for the Little Chinese": The French Holy Childhood Association in China, 1843–1951'. *American Historical Review* 113(1) (2008), 72–92.

Hermsen, R. *Faktor Religion: Geschichte der Kindheit vom Mittelalter bis zur Gegenwart.* Cologne: Böhlau, 2006.

Heywood, S. 'Missionary Children: The French Holy Childhood Association in European Context, 1843–1914', *European History Quarterly* 45(3) (2015), 446–66.

Hölzl, R. '"Mitleid" über große Distanz: Zur Fabrikation globaler Gefühle in Medien der katholischen Mission (1890–1940)', in R. Habermas and R. Hölzl (eds), *Mission Global: Eine Verflechtungsgeschichte seit dem 19. Jahrhundert* (Cologne: Böhlau, 2014), 265–94.

Howells, R. *Visual Culture.* Malden, MA: Blackwell, 2013.

Jablonka, I. 'Social Welfare in the Western World and the Rights of Children', in P. Fass (ed.), *The Routledge History of Childhood in the Western World* (London: Taylor & Francis, 2015), 380–99.

Jäger, J. *Fotografie und Geschichte.* Frankfurt am Main: Campus, 2009.

Jensz, F. 'The Cultural, Didactic, and Physical Space of Mission Schools in the 19th Century'. Österreichische Zeitschrift für Geschichtswissenschaften 24(2) 2013, 70–91.

———. 'Hope and Pity: Depictions of Children in Five Decades of the Evangelisch-Lutherisches Missionsblatt, 1860–1910', in J. Becker and K. Stornig (eds), *Menschen – Bilder – Eine Welt. Ordnungen von Vielfalt in der religiösen Publizistik um 1900* (Göttingen: Vandenhoeck & Ruprecht 2018), 259–81.

Kind-Kovács, F. 'Compassion for the Distant Other: Children's Hunger and Humanitarian Relief in Budapest in the Aftermath of WWI', in B. Althammer, L. Raphael and T. Stazic-Wendt (eds), *Rescuing the Vulnerable: Poverty, Welfare and Social Ties in Nineteenth- and Twentieth-Century Europe* (New York: Berghahn Books, 2016), 129–59.

Konrad, F.-M. 'Sollen die Kinder der Armen erzogen werden? Über einige ideengeschichtliche Hintergründe der öffentlichen Kleinkinderziehung in der ersten Hälfte des 19. Jahrhunderts', in S. Hering and W. Schröer (eds), *Sorge um die Kinder: Beiträge zur Geschichte von Kindheit, Kindergarten und Kinderfürsorge* (Weinheim: Juventa, 2008), 25–38.

Maksudyan, N. 'Helden, Opfer, Ikonen: Massenmobilisierung und osmanische Kinder während des Ersten Weltkriegs', in J. Angelow (ed.), *Der Erste Weltkrieg auf dem Balkan* (Berlin: Be.bra, 2011), 161–73.

———. *Orphans and Destitute Children in the Late Ottoman Empire.* Syracuse: Syracuse University Press, 2014.

Malkki, L. 'Children, Humanity, and the Infantilization of Peace', in I. Feldman and M. Ticktin (eds), *In the Name of Humanity: The Government of Threat and Care* (Durham, NC: Duke University Press, 2010), 58–85.

Manzo, K. 'Imagining Humanitarianism: NGO Identity and the Iconography of Childhood'. *Antipode* 40(4) (2008), 632–57.

Marshall, D. 'International Child Saving', in P. Fass (ed.), *The Routledge History of Childhood in the Western World* (London: Taylor & Francis, 2015), 469–90.

Marten, J. *Childhood and Child Welfare in the Progressive Era: A Brief History with Documents.* Boston: Bedford, 2005.

McKenzie, W. 'Fresh Maimed Babies: The Uses of Innocence'. *Transition* 65 (1995), 36–47.

Morrison, H., and M.C. Martin (eds). *Creating Religious Childhoods in Anglo-World and British Colonial Contexts, 1800–1950.* London: Routledge, 2017.

Murdoch, L. 'From Barrack Schools to Family Cottages: Creating Domestic Space for Late Victorian Poor Children', in J. Lawrence and P. Starkey (eds), *Child Welfare and Social Action in the Nineteenth and Twentieth Centuries: International Perspectives* (Liverpool: Liverpool University Press, 2001), 147–73.

————. *Imagined Orphans: Poor Families, Child Welfare, and Contested Citizenship in London.* New Brunswick, NJ: Rutgers University Press, 2006.

Przyrembel, A. 'Der Missionar Johann Hinrich Wichern, die Sünde und das unabänderliche Elend der städtischen Unterschichten um 1855'. *Werkstatt Geschichte* 57 (2011), 53–67.

Ribi Forclaz, A. *Humanitarian Imperialism: The Politics of Anti-slavery Activism 1880–1940.* Oxford: Oxford University Press, 2015.

Sandin, B. 'Education', in C. Heywood (ed.), *A Cultural History of Childhood and Family in the Age of Empire* (London: Bloomsbury, 2014), 91–110.

Sliwinski, S. 'The Childhood of Human Rights: The Kodak in the Congo'. *Journal of Visual Culture* 5(3) (2006), 333–63.

————. 'The Aesthetics of Human Rights'. *Culture, Theory & Critique* 50(1) (2009), 23–39.

————. *Human Rights in Camera.* Chicago: University of Chicago Press, 2011.

Sontag, S. *Regarding the Pain of Others.* New York: Farrar, Straus and Giroux, 2003.

Stornig, K. '"Armes Kindlein in der Ferne, – Wie machst du das Herz mir schwer!" Kindermissionsvereine und die religiösen Verflechtungen des Helfens in Deutschland, Europa und der Welt, 1843–1920'. *Themenportal Europäische Geschichte* (2015). Retrieved 15 August 2018 from http://www.europa.clio-online.de/2015/Article=741.

————. 'Figli della Chiesa. Riscatti e globalizzazione del welfare cattolico (1840–1914)'. *Genesis. Rivista della Società Italiana delle Storiche* 14(1) (2015), 55–83.

————. 'Globalisierte Körper: Repräsentationen der Welt und ihrer BewohnerInnen auf der vatikanischen Missionsausstellung (1925)', in L. Ratschiller and S. Weichlein (eds), *Der schwarze Körper als Missionsgebiet: Medizin, Ethnologie, Theologie in Afrika und Europa 1880–1960* (Vienna: Böhlau, 2015), 123–52.

————. 'Authentifizierung kultureller Begegnungen durch Fotografie: Über die Verwendung von Fotos als Spuren in der transnationalen Spendenwerbung im 19. Jahrhundert'. *Saeculum. Jahrbuch für Universalgeschichte* 66(2) (2016), 207–28.

Thompson, T.J. *Light on Darkness? Missionary Photography of Africa in the Nineteenth and Early Twentieth Century.* Grand Rapids, MI: William B. Eerdmans, 2012.

Vallgårda, K. *Imperial Childhoods and Christian Mission: Education and Emotions in South India and Denmark.* Basingstoke: Palgrave Macmillan, 2015.

Verein der Heiligen Kindheit (ed.). *Der Verein der Heiligen Kindheit: Geschichte seines Entstehens, seines Wachsthums und gegenwärtigen Bestandes.* Mainz: Kirchheim, Schott and Thielmann, 1845.

————. *Der Verein der Heiligen Kindheit: Kurze Darstellung seiner Entstehung und seines Zweckes, nebst Berichten über seine Wirksamkeit bis zum Jahre 1851.* Aachen: Verlag der Cremerschen Buchhandlung, 1852.

————. *Der Verein der heiligen Kindheit.* Vienna: Mechitharisten-Buchdruckerei, 1855.

Viaene, V. 'Nineteenth Century Catholic Internationalism and its Predecessors', in A. Green and V. Viaene (eds), *Religious Internationals in the Modern World: Globalization and Faith Communities since 1750* (Basingstoke: Palgrave Macmillan, 2012), 82–110.

Wilson, A., and R.D. Brown (eds). *Humanitarianism and Suffering: The Mobilization of Empathy.* Cambridge: Cambridge University Press, 2009.

Zelizer, V.A. *Pricing the Priceless Child: The Changing Social Value of Children.* New York: Basic Books, 1985.

Zimmermann, C., and M. Schreiber. 'Introduction: Towards a New Perspective on Journalism and Technology', in M. Schreiber and C. Zimmermann (eds), *Journalism and Technological Change: Historical Perspectives, Contemporary Trends* (Frankfurt am Main: Campus, 2014), 9–29.

2

'Make the Situation Real to Us without Stressing the Horrors'

Children, Photography and Humanitarianism in the Spanish Civil War

Rose Holmes

In 2007, the rediscovery of the 'Mexican Suitcase' containing previously lost negatives of three Spanish Civil War photographers, Robert Capa, David 'Chim' Seymour and Gerda Taro, became an international media sensation and a successful touring exhibition, renewing a public interest in the photography of the Spanish Civil War and reinforcing certain narratives about the representation of the conflict. The exhibition was reviewed as giving poignant insight into the social consequence of war, and much was made of the role of the photojournalists.[1] The Spanish Civil War has long been regarded as the crucible of photojournalism, summarized by Susan Sontag's famous assertion that the Spanish Civil War was 'the first war to be witnessed ("covered") in the modern sense'.[2] In the thick of the action and enabled by new handheld cameras to become (often partisan) participants in conflict, photographers in Spain heralded a new era in photographic technology and reception. In more recent analysis, the 'authors' of photographs have been increasingly recognized as artists and, in the case of war photographers, become part of a heroic narrative around the mythic and intrepid photojournalist.[3]

This narrative has been based almost entirely on analyses of press photography, and relatively little attention has been paid to the humanitarian photography of the conflict. As this volume establishes, disentangling the media representation of humanitarian activity can offer insight into material and cultural attitudes around aid, especially when that aid is targeted at 'others'. In Britain, the Spanish

Civil War created an intense level of public political action on behalf of another country. Nearly all this aid work was grassroots in origin, deeply political in motivation and took place on the Republican side of the conflict. This in itself proved a departure from previous humanitarian work that had tended to be carried out based on the principle of political neutrality. Historians of Britain's civic response to the Spanish Civil War have disagreed about the character of British humanitarian support for Spain, but have agreed that popular interest in, and awareness of, the conflict was high and that Spain galvanized support across political divides.[4]

In this chapter I analyse humanitarian photographs and publicity pamphlets produced by the Quaker Society of Friends, the Save the Children International Union, the Trades Union Congress, the Co-operative, the International Commission and the National Joint Committee for Spanish Relief, and compare them with the press photography of the conflict. The most striking and immediate contrast is that the humanitarian agencies focused almost exclusively on images of children. This was a conscious decision and was deliberately decided upon as a marketing strategy by the humanitarian agencies that, with the exception of the Trades Union Congress (TUC), were mostly led and staffed by women, to raise awareness of their cause by evoking public sympathy. My argument is that the way in which Spanish children were represented by these groups was consciously done to create a reassuring image of them, in contrast to photographs of starving children from foreign lands that had been used since the First World War by British humanitarian organizations to raise funds. In fact, they represented more closely pre-1914 images of 'deserving', healthy children.[5]

Humanitarian photography, I will show in this chapter, developed alongside other forms of photographic representation (press, artistic and advertising), but differed in several ways – crucially in the selection and dissemination of images. Those taking and distributing humanitarian photographs constantly negotiated a position that would maximize the public sympathy for their work, while keeping within the limits of political expediency and public taste. Images of children became the focus for this work in a way that both echoed the history of Christian missionary activity and foreshadowed the professionalized postwar humanitarianism of UNESCO. I use committee minutes, publications, memoirs and letters of those involved in humanitarian work in Spain alongside analysis of the images they selected to build a picture of the choices and compromises involved in relief work.

Choosing Humanitarian Imagery

British humanitarian groups had been using images of children to raise funds – and awareness of suffering at home and overseas – since the mid nineteenth century. As Heide Fehrenbach has established, the chronology of humanitarian photography can be tied closely to Western imperialism and particularly to the influence of Christian missionaries in reform campaigning.[6] While nineteenth-century humanitarian activists would show shocking images of wounded or starving children, they were just as, if not more, likely to show images of a child being cared for by its mother or a Christian missionary, or groups of children playing, or children looking smart on their way to church.[7] Indeed, as Katharina Stornig has shown in the previous chapter, the act of child-saving by priests, nurses or missionaries was widely represented in Christian missionary imagery from the 1830s. Early humanitarian visual endeavours as represented in British publications can broadly be categorized as 'domesticating the Empire': making foreign children seem familiar and deserving of care to the British public.

This strategy changed radically after the First World War, influenced by the early campaigning of the Save the Children Fund (SCF), which was established in 1919 in response to the famine in Germany and Austria that resulted from the British blockade. A conscious decision was made by SCF cofounders and sisters Eglantyne Jebb and Dorothy Buxton to focus aid on children, as they saw child starvation as a particularly barbaric continuation of the war.[8] The use of a controversial image of a naked and emaciated Austrian baby on the front of an SCF pamphlet called *A Starving Baby and Our Blockade Has Caused This* brought a criminal prosecution for Jebb and a great deal of publicity and sympathy for her campaign. This marked a turning point for British humanitarian photography. Throughout the 1920s, as British aid workers sought to raise funds and awareness for humanitarian work in Russia, China and the Balkans, children were increasingly shown starving and naked as innocent civilian victims of conflict in deliberately shocking photographs.

The photographs taken and deployed were shaped by what was technologically possible, socially plausible and politically intended. This was the age of the Leica and the Brownie. The affordable and portable cameras, which made it possible for Taro, Chim and Capa to take such intimate documentary photographs, were also available to amateur photographers.[9] In this, those taking and selecting the photographs to use were dependent on the visual literacy of the British public. *Picture Post* was a popular publication and cinema, crucially, was a leisure activity enjoyed across class and social lines.[10] With the simultaneous rise of both cinema and the popular national daily press, mass-produced images became a central part of cultural life in Britain, meaning that the public could now be relied upon to respond to a visual campaign.

Deciding on the parameters of the socially plausible was a much thornier issue, and it is in this delicate balance that the significance of a focus on children becomes clear. Showing the suffering of children has long been a powerful tool for those working for humanitarian or pacifist ends, and children occupy a significant place in the history of the iconography of humanitarian intervention. The uses of particular images of children have been controversial, but also groundbreaking. Many of the iconic twentieth-century images of war have been of children, especially those associated with anti-war campaigns. Susie Linfield attributes this impact to the particular social role of children as 'the purest victims', whose suffering presents a more compelling moral call to arms to viewers than images of adults who have, by implication, more agency in their own suffering.[11] In Spain, as in all humanitarian crises, the way activists negotiated the representation of children can reveal much about the particular political and social climate in which they were operating. Fundamentally, the choice of image can reveal a tactical compromise between the needs of those suffering and the requirements of public taste.

British press photographs of the Spanish Civil War scarcely featured children with the images that showed children tending to be in the context of a mass of refugees.[12] While most newspapers would describe atrocities in detail, they would only publish pictures of wounded or killed adults. A significant exception to this was the *Daily Worker* showing photographs of children killed in the Getafe bombing in November 1936 (see Figure 2.1). The editors of the *Daily Worker* found it necessary to write a lengthy piece justifying their decision to publish the images, which were contrasted with an image of an English girl playing happily in a sunny garden. Publishing the pictures of the dead children was above all a political gesture by the editors of the left-wing newspaper, which took the risk of upsetting public sensibilities by showing the images, and wanted to draw attention to the civilian consequences of fascist aggression. The *Daily Worker* was in favour of Britain's involvement in an armed response to Franco, and mobilized pictures of dead children in part to rouse the public in support of this. The publication of this controversial page clearly established that, in this conflict, showing photographs of dead or injured children was to declare your organization as left wing.

Humanitarian agencies, operating on the principle of political neutrality, chose to represent children in a very different way. The children in the Spain photographs are seen alone or in groups, mostly unmediated by the presence of mothers, nurses or aid workers. We assume these caring figures are behind the camera, that those taking the pictures are adults who care, who are trying. Many of the aid workers in Spain were women, which perhaps influenced the development of this implied photographic maternal connection. The viewers are an imagined community of those who *would* care for that child or those children. In this assumed relationship, children are implicitly understood as an innocent group – more innocent than adults – who also have the potential to be saved, that is, to be changed according to the values of those doing the saving. If it is recognized that those children come from families (as the British doctors who would select those who were to be saved wrote), the families are good, clean and loving.[13] But mostly the families are absent. The children's bodies are whole and wholesome, as yet inviolate by the war from which they need to be saved. The absence of family members or nurses implies that their existence is fragile, unstable and impermanent. Being received into the moral space of the British family is what will save them.

Ultimately, the photographs of Spanish civilians produced, procured or purchased, and then disseminated by British humanitarian workers, were a tentative plea to the public conscience. They had to be. Showing the full extent of the physical and emotional suffering of Spanish children was, for reasons of

'Make the Situation Real to Us without Stressing the Horrors' 71

Figure 2.1. Walter M. Holmes, 'Nazi Bomb Kills Seventy Spanish Children', *Daily Worker*, 12 November 1936. Reproduced by courtesy of the TUC Archive, Modern Records Centre, University of Warwick.

taste, diplomacy, expedience and cost, deemed by humanitarian workers to be unacceptable.

The Humanitarian Imagery of Deserving Children

The first British humanitarian work in Spain was a joint project in Barcelona in October 1936 between the Quaker Friends' Service Committee (FSC) and the Save the Children International Union (SCIU). It was intended to provide food relief to refugees entering Barcelona and was led by Alfred and Norma Jacob, who were enthusiastic yet inexperienced relief workers. The Jacobs were a young, dynamic and politically engaged couple and, in correspondence, one senses a certain reluctance to entrust them with the politically sensitive task of heading FSC work. In a 1989 interview, Norma Jacob recalled that she and Alfred were asked to resign their membership of the Labour Party before being allowed to work in Spain.[14] The Spanish-speaking Jacobs were, nonetheless, so clearly the most suitable candidates that in November 1936, they moved to Barcelona, the city with the greatest refugee crisis, and began to establish relief operations. Children were not initially considered to be the main focus for relief work. Indeed, workers were reluctant to give milk exclusively to children when adults were also in need of help.[15] This attitude was rapidly altered by both the FSC's working relationship with SCIU and from the relationship with local Spanish aid organizations that tended to prioritize children, including Ayuda Infantil, Pro-Infancia Obreza and the International Red Committee. Alfred Jacob outlined the political rationale for the FSC/SCIU work in a letter in December 1936:

> Our effort is simply to do the works of peace in the midst of war . . . We have begun with the children, because no one regards children as Reds or Anti-Reds, and they can be fed and clothed without in the least helping the progress of the war. Moreover, by mobilising masses of opinion on behalf of the children we cut across barriers of party and creed both outside Spain and inside.[16]

Correspondence between relief workers on the ground and directors in Britain referred from the outset to the need for publicity to help with direct appeals in Britain.[17] Publicity materials containing photographs were rapidly produced, using photolithographic reproduction that was nearly as cheap as mimeographing for publicity leaflets.[18] The most widely circulated leaflet was entitled *Spain: An Appeal for the Children* and had five photographs, all of children being fed and cared for, and gave financial targets for fundraising on the basis of direct costs (see Figures 2.2 and 2.3). The focus of the photographs was on the work done rather than the need for the work. Repeated appeals for documentary evidence were sent from Friends House, the central offices of British Quakers, to the Barcelona workers. In a characteristic and revealing request, Fred Tritton wrote in 1937: 'We want everything we can get to make the situation real to us *without stressing the horrors.*'[19]

'Make the Situation Real to Us without Stressing the Horrors' 73

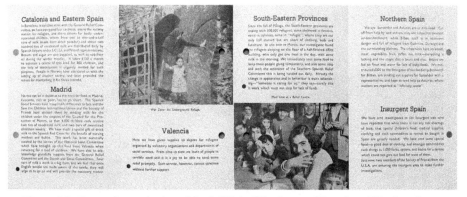

Figure 2.2. Cover, *Spain: An Appeal for the Work of The Society of Friends and The Save the Children International Union*, 1937. Friends House Archives, © Religious Society of Friends (Quakers) in Britain.

Figure 2.3. Insert, *Spain: An Appeal for the Work of The Society of Friends and The Save the Children International Union*, 1937. Friends House Archives, © Religious Society of Friends (Quakers) in Britain.

This reluctance to dwell on the horrors had two motivations. First, photographs of naked and starving children from foreign countries had been used widely in humanitarian campaigns in Britain since the Boer War. British people knew what a starving child looked like and it was felt that the images had lost sympathy-eliciting shock value and instead put viewers off donating. While the Quaker workers drew on the history of these Christian campaigns, they wanted to position the work in Spain differently. Second, in keeping with the official strategy of political neutrality, the Quaker/Save the Children leaflets had to differentiate themselves from the propaganda of the Left, most significantly the controversial photographs shown in the *Daily Worker*.

This imagery was consciously sought. Alfred Jacob wrote that 'it is difficult to get pictures of children arriving because they generally arrive at night, but I shall keep after the ministry of Propaganda, who promised us some'.[20] A subsequent letter enclosing the prints stated:

> The 24 pictures I enclose were done by the Propaganda Dept. and are worthy of careful study. They are all taken in the Stadium of the Exhibition grounds . . . Some of them I have chosen for the children's faces – perhaps you will feel it worthwhile to use one child as a sort of emblem for this work – a poster, say, with 'This child needs *your* help'.[21]

In addition to getting photographs directly from the Republican propaganda ministry, humanitarian workers also took some of their own photographs. Alfred Cope, an American Friends Service Committee (AFSC) volunteer who arrived in Spain with his wife, Ruth, in the summer of 1938 to take over responsibility for the accounts of the Murcia team, also took charge of obtaining and sending photographic negatives to the FSC and AFSC head offices. He took some of the images himself and was clear about their use, writing: 'List of negatives . . . to be used in helping find funds and gifts in kind for the Spanish Child Feeding Mission.'[22] Alfred and his American colleague Esther Farquhar also commissioned photographs on at least one occasion when they paid William Finley $150 to take pictures of the child feeding centres that had been established in Barcelona and Murcia.[23]

To raise funds for their work, humanitarian workers showed photographs and gave lectures at fundraising events across Britain. These events often raised huge sums of money. Leah Manning, the Member of Parliament and campaigner for Spain, recalled: 'it was quite common to raise £1,000 at a meeting, besides plates full of rings, bracelets, brooches, watches and jewellery of all kinds'.[24] Francesca Wilson, an experienced relief worker who had previously worked to alleviate famine in Russia in the early 1920s, wrote in her 1944 memoir about the way in which she gathered information and fundraised. Wilson was a journalist and reporter of humanitarian events, who had been working as a history teacher at Edgbaston Church of England Girl's College when she asked the Quakers if she could to go to Spain to undertake some publicity work in the spring of 1937.[25] Horrified by the appalling conditions she saw in Murcia, she requisitioned a lorryload of supplies from the FSC distribution centre in Valencia and set up a feeding centre that within days fed 2,000–3,000 children a day. At the request of the FSC in London, the AFSC took over the running of Wilson's Murcia operations while she returned to Birmingham to raise funds and awareness. Having held several public fundraisers, Wilson returned in August 1937 with 'hundreds of pounds to spend as I liked', which she used to set up ten sewing workshops.[26] She then visited the colonies of children at Rubí, which had been set up by British public subscription, bringing back glowing reports of the children's progress. She also brought back quantities of publicity material, including photographs, which were widely circulated among Aid Spain networks and also used as slides at fundraising meetings in Birmingham. Wilson additionally wrote several newspaper articles about the situation in Spain from a personal perspective.[27]

Wilson's autobiography includes several of the photographs she used as publicity material. The images of clothed and cared-for Spanish children are directly contrasted with those Wilson had previously used of Russian children from 1922, who are pictured naked and alone, although eating from a bowl of soup. Wilson writes in a caption on the subsequent page: 'The Spanish Republic took special care of their children during the Civil War and the Catalan Government reached a particularly high standard.'[28] For Wilson, who was working closely with Spanish colleagues and sympathetic to the Republican cause, showing images of children being cared for not only raised awareness, but was also a way of demonstrating to the British public the civilised and deserving nature of the Spanish children.

Prominent figures were called upon to use their contacts with the national press to publish appeals. Joan Mary Fry, well known for her work with allotments in Britain, wrote to the editor of *The Times* to ask for publicity in 1936.[29] Her request was presumably not successful, as *The Times* printed notably little about child refugees of the Spanish Civil War. Articles on Spain tended to be from the perspective of British foreign policy decisions and were focused on the Empire, especially the Middle East. The newspaper that consistently provided a voice for humanitarian agencies was the *Manchester Guardian*. It regularly published articles and letters emphasizing the importance of caring for refugees and published contact details for relief agencies.[30] Headlines tended to evoke clear pleas for support, for example: 'Ambulance in Spain: People's Urgent Need of Food, Clothing and Medical Supplies'.[31] Notably, images of children tended not to be shown even alongside articles expressing the importance of caring for them.

The reluctance to show images of injured or distressed children was also manifested in the representation of British children during this period, and journalists would often reflect openly in their copy about whether the use of certain images pushed the boundaries of public sensibility too far. In the *Daily Express* in 1937, a photograph of a three-year-old girl named Muriel Purser with a black eye was used to illustrate a short article about the prosecution of her mother for child cruelty.[32] The article begins with a brief reference to the photograph, making it clear that, while it was recognized that the publication was sensitive, the editors felt that drawing attention to the issue was important. The article ends with a reference to the National Society for the Prevention of Cruelty to Children (NSPCC), drawing the reader's attention to the growing problem of child cruelty. Newspapers were clearly aware of the sensitivity around photographs of children and also that readers could be motivated to action by the emotive impact of such imagery.

Commentators, too, recognized both the impact of photography and the limits of public taste. Virginia Woolf wrote extensively about photography in *Three Guineas,* saying that for her, photographs outlined the horror of the Spanish conflict in the most straightforward terms possible. Woolf reflected at length on the emotional impact of photographs of trauma, writing: 'When we look at those photographs some fusion takes place within us; however different the education, the traditions behind us, our sensations are the same; and they are violent.'[33] She opted not to reproduce any of the photographs that had affected her in her book, perhaps uncertain about how they would be received.

The humanitarian representation of Spanish children in Britain by the Quakers and the SCIU used reassuring, domestic images that were at odds with previous humanitarian photography that had tended towards shocking pictures of starving children. They were also at odds with mainstream press photography that tended to focus on adults, particularly soldiers. Both departures were a conscious political decision by the humanitarian agencies involved, which operated on the basis of political neutrality. But what of the humanitarian organizations that were not politically neutral? After all, the main instigator of British support for Spain was the various organizations of the Left, in particular the TUC. Notably, the Left tended to focus on raising funds for the International Brigades and the medical support of combatants, and paid relatively little attention to the civilians caught up in the conflict. However, the TUC did have clear policies on support for refugees and civilians, produced a significant amount of publicity material and was the main organization involved in coordinating the group migration of Basque children in 1937.

The TUC response to the Spanish Civil War has been characterized by its leading chronicler as fragmented and anxious to differentiate itself from Communism.[34] The TUC initially supported the *Milk for Spain* Fund led by the Co-operative, and distributed leaflets showing children being fed and asking for more funds so this could continue.[35] From the outset, the TUC's humanitarian campaigning followed the pattern set by the Quakers/SCIU of showing healthy children and asking for funds so that these children could continue being fed.

Religion at times proved a stumbling block in Labour's response to conflict in Spain. Tom Buchanan has documented the tensions exposed between the British Labour movement and some sections of its Catholic working-class membership, whose feelings of marginalization were amplified when it came to disagreements over choosing an appropriate response to the Spanish Civil War.[36] Saving children (who Linfield positions as 'the purest victims')[37] could be seen as a compromise that allowed groups to acknowledge the tragic human consequences of conflict by taking decisive action, while stopping short of any action that could influence the outcome of the conflict. Certainly, the Catholic representatives of the TUC were much more active in the (avowedly politically neutral and interagency) Basque Children's Committee than in any other aspects of support for Spain.

Bring 'Pure-Washed' Refugee Children to Britain

A significant exception to the carefully chosen, politically neutral and reassuring images of children presented by even overtly political humanitarian projects such as the TUC was the International Commission (see Figure 2.4). By October

Figure 2.4. International Commission for the Assistance of Spanish Child Refugees pamphlet, ca. 1937. Friends House Archives, © Religious Society of Friends (Quakers) in Britain.

1937, a new wave of refugees from Santander streamed towards Barcelona. Barcelona aid workers tried to anticipate their need, sending a lorryload of milk to meet them on the road, but the sheer numbers meant that private charity could no longer provide sufficient support. The Republican government set up several subsidized canteens, but the shortfall was obvious. The Quaker relief worker Edith Pye's response was to establish the International Commission for the Care of Spanish Refugees (IC). Pye was well acquainted with the mechanisms of international governance, having been an executive member of the Women's International League for Peace and Freedom (WILPF) and the WILPF representative on the League of Nations Women's Advisory Committee.[38] The purpose of the IC was to create a space where European governments could donate money to aid Spanish civilians without the risk of breaching their self-imposed nonintervention treaties. Pye liaised with the British Foreign Office, which pledged to donate £10,000 to a neutral, international Committee if Pye could persuade other governments to do the same. Viscount Cranborne, the Under-Secretary of State for Foreign Affairs, authorized the donation and served as joint Vice-President of the IC.[39]

Using the personal connections she had built over thirty years of international relief work, Pye established a central committee based in Geneva under the chairmanship of Judge Michael Hansson of Norway. The first meeting was held in December 1937.[40] Edith Pye personally wrote to prominent figures including Eamonn de Valera and Jawaharlal Nehru to solicit donations, as well as working with other committee members (who were all seasoned aid workers or League of Nations internationalists) to request funds from governments. The money flooded in. The British government eventually donated a total of £25,000 plus goods in kind. Part of the success of the IC's fundraising was the pledge that money donated by a government would be spent on goods produced within that country. Norway's contribution, for example, was largely spent on the fish-oil supplements for which Norway was the largest and cheapest producer. In total, the IC raised and spent over £500,000 between December 1937 and April 1940.[41] It was the only British humanitarian organization that used images of starving children in its publicity. Photographs in pamphlets tended to be either of starving children or pictures of goods or food sent, reflecting the practical material concern of the Commission. Significantly, these pamphlets were intended for the attention of civil servants, international relief agencies and politicians rather than for the general public.

American humanitarian organizations, even those affiliated with British projects, also worked very differently. In the United States, it was felt by relief workers that images of starving children *were* needed to shock the public into taking an interest in Spain. John F. Reich, the director of the American Friends Service Committee's Spanish Child Feeding Mission, repeatedly asked his British colleagues for more harrowing images, such as in this letter of 1939: 'I am quite anxious to secure photographs of current activities. Please send me pictures of undernourished children, such as appears on the back of your last folder. I have simply nothing of the sort.'[42] This letter both gives a sense of the extensive interagency cooperation that underpinned British humanitarian support for Spain and hints at the growing international nature of humanitarian relief during this period. Sharing funds and resources to efficiently manage particular projects or campaigns became, in the interwar period, the backbone of practical humanitarian intervention.

In May 1937, almost 4,000 Basque children arrived in Britain from Spain. Their evacuation had been organized entirely by the same voluntary agencies that had, for the previous year, been showing the British public photographs of healthy, wholesome Spanish children. This is not tangential. While the voluntary agencies had not planned their representation of Spanish children around putative immigration, the unprecedented temporary immigration of these children was legitimized by the careful representation that had been created by the voluntary agencies. We see a shift to direct campaigning focused on supporting the Basque children in Britain, accompanied by a revised yet consistent photographic representation.

The idea of evacuating children abroad had been in circulation since December 1936. It was immensely unpopular with relief workers on the ground in Spain, who objected on the principle it was not cost-effective and might prove psychologically damaging to the children.[43] Nevertheless, in a lengthy correspondence between London and Barcelona, relief workers were eventually convinced on the basis that the publicity and public sympathy engendered by the 'rescue' of the children would prompt a boom in donations, which could then be used to develop relief work in Spain.[44] The publicity around the humanitarian work of the TUC, the Salvation Army, the Society of Friends, SCIU and nearly all other humanitarian organizations interested in Spain became focused on supporting the Basque children in Britain.

The evacuation of the children was organized by the National Joint Committee for Spanish Relief (NJC), an interagency humanitarian coalition that included such diverse figures as the Tory MP the Duchess of Atholl and the Communist leader Isabel Brown.[45] On 5 May 1937, the Basque Children's Committee was set up as a subdivision of the NJC with two TUC representatives (one place later given to the Labour Party), one each from the Society of Friends, Save the Children, Spanish Medical Aid and the Catholic Church, and three non-affiliated officials.[46] After repeated petitioning, the British Foreign Office agreed to allow the Basque children into Britain, provided that the NJC would meet the entire financial cost of their upkeep (including a ten-shilling guarantee per child) and that the stay of the children would only be temporary. The Home Office stipulated the children should be cared for in group settings rather than private homes, mainly due to fears over the possibility the children could carry infectious diseases.[47]

Leah Manning and Edith Pye were sent by the NJC to Bilbao to work with the Basque government and the Spanish aid organization Asistencia Social to arrange for the evacuation of the children to England.[48] The first 2,000 children

Figure 2.5. 'Saved from War's Terror'. NJC charity envelope, ca. 1938. Reproduced courtesy of the TUC archive Modern Records Centre, University of Warwick.

were due to travel in the summer of 1937, with the rest to follow a few months later. A Ministry of Health proviso was that the children should be screened for infectious diseases before selection for the voyage.[49] There was real fear expressed in several newspapers, most notably *The Times,* that the Spanish children would bring infectious disease into Britain.[50] This was also linked to interwar concerns about the health of the poor in Britain; public anxiety over health was by no means restricted to foreign children.[51] Still, the voluntary agencies had to convince the government and the public that the Basque children were clean and healthy. To this end, the NJC sent two British doctors to screen all the children before they could board the boat to Britain.

The delegated doctors, Dr Audrey Russell and Dr Richard Ellis, were both employed and sent by the FSC. Ellis was an assistant physician for children's diseases at Guy's Hospital in London. During his time in Spain, he became so convinced of the physical and psychological damage to children of being involved in modern warfare that he later wrote that 'total war as it affects the child may be considered as an infectious disease'.[52] Russell was an experienced nutritionist and puericulture expert based at University College Hospital in London who had worked in the East End and with the FSC and International Commission in Barcelona.

The physical bodies of the refugee children were scrutinized intently and were the object of debate for and against their migration. After medically screening the children with the extensive support of Asistencia Social medical professionals (who kept detailed records on the health of each child), Russell and Ellis recommended unequivocally that all 4,000 children should be taken to Britain at once. *The Lancet* and the *British Medical Journal* between them published four detailed articles on the Basque children (two by Ellis and Russell from Spain and two from doctors based in England) and two lengthy letters on the subject from Pye and Russell between May 1937 and December 1938.[53] Ellis and Russell's articles stressed the 'whiteness' of the Spanish children: 'Many have light brown or even red hair, a few are blue-eyed, and very few could be described as swarthy. Their facial colouring would usually pass for that of a sunburnt English child.'[54] The positive nature and self-help approach of the Spanish family units were also praised in the medical articles: 'The women showed admirable courage and spirit and a scene of intense activity centred around a running brook in the station yard, where children were being vigorously scrubbed, brushed, and combed, and in a few hours the whole yard was gay with newly washed garments drying in the sun.'[55] The bodies of children were shown as pure-washed in fresh Spanish spring water and only contaminated with the 'infectious disease' of war.

The reception of the Basque children in Britain was mixed. Press coverage focused on the children as a group rather than as individuals. The *Manchester Guardian* printed a series of articles emphasizing the importance of caring for the children and reviews of the music concerts at which the children performed to raise funds for their support.[56] Most other newspapers published photographs showing the arrival of the children on board the *SS Habana* as it docked at Southampton, but carried few further reports.[57] The *Daily Mail* quickly took a critical line, emphasizing the dangerous nature of the children with a series of articles in the summer of 1937 outlining the alleged poor behaviour of the 'Bad Basque Boys'.[58]

Meanwhile, the Basque Children's Committee encouraged charities, private individuals and communities to form small colonies to care for groups of children. The Catholic Church (which took financial and administrative responsibility for the care of 1,200 of the children at a cost that ran at approximately £500–600 a week) and the Salvation Army (which cared for 400–500 of the children) took primary responsibility for establishing group homes.[59] Smaller regional committees established hundreds of small homes or 'colonies' nationwide. To fund this, all sorts of campaigns were organized, including 'adoption', with people encouraged to befriend particular children and offer financial and emotional support.[60] This was all to be short-lived. Amid some anxiety over their safety, the majority of the children returned to Spain during late 1937 and 1938, although around 400 whose families could not be located remained.[61] These remaining *niños/niñas* were joined in Britain only a few months later by the first arrivals from the *Kindertransports* – immigration this time of 10,000 unaccompanied children fleeing from fascism in Germany and Austria.

Conclusion

This chapter has outlined the parameters of a visual correspondence between voluntary agencies, the British public and Spanish children. Photographs that were mostly curated by women aid workers and that focused almost exclusively on children represented a significant departure from press photography and, capitalizing on the boom in visual literacy, had more in common with emerging documentary photography. As Johannes Paulmann discusses in the Introduction to this volume, the logic or sentiment around the relationship of a society to the sufferings of others should not be assumed to be either linear or generalized. Nonetheless, humanitarian photographs used of Spanish children are able to tell us something about what humanitarian workers assumed about the sentiments and visual literacy of the British public. The period between the two world wars had seen considerable developments in the technology available to humanitarian workers seeking to chart the suffering of others, and a shift in the sensibilities involved in portraying such suffering.[62] Readily available amateur photographs were, by the late 1930s, viewed by a public that relied on photographic images to tell stories, provide entertainment and sell products.

The self-awareness with which the British humanitarian workers in Spain navigated the need to record the suffering of Spanish children belies a particular conception of childhood, identified by Liisa Malkki and others, in which children serve as universal representations of human innocence and goodness.[63] Malkki describes the visual representation of children as 'ritual and affective', in its attempts to evoke a global humanity.[64] The photographs of Spanish children used by humanitarian workers to raise funds and awareness were an amalgamation of the new techniques of documenting human suffering with an eye to reform and the old humanitarian tradition of using images of cared-for foreign children to alert British public sympathy. On the one hand, as Alfred Jacob recognized, photographs of children were a part of trying to configure a politically neutral international space. On the other hand, they were a marketing decision. Showing children being cared for made the children appear familiar and emphasized the success of the financial investment being made in protecting them.

The outcome was the creation of a consciously nonpolitical and reassuring visual narrative, where Spanish children were usually presented as healthy and happy in order to legitimize their support by the voluntary intervention of the British public, in the absence of significant governmental humanitarian support. Saving 'deserving' children was presented to the public as a morally unambiguous intervention that could, by implication, also serve to reformulate and repair the fratricidal European family. In a political climate where humanitarian aid could breach international treaties and influence matters of state, presenting subjects of aid as healthy, cared for, children served the duel function of legitimizing aid to the British public while tiptoeing around the hazards of international diplomacy. In a manifestation of the sensitivity around refugee migration into Britain, the images of and writings about the Basque refugee children show an extra emphasis on care, community and cleanliness, while the images of the children who were to be left in Spain could, at times, show suffering and abandonment.

After the Second World War, both journalistic and humanitarian visual projects became enveloped in a formalized international apparatus that had its origins in the interwar period. In 1948, David 'Chim' Seymour was commissioned by the United Nations Educational, Scientific and Cultural Organization (UNESCO) to produce the photographs for its *Children of Europe* pamphlet.[65] After the destabilizing influence of fascism, UNESCO was concerned with a fundamental international reconfiguration of commonality.[66] Chim's photographs showed children emaciated but defiant, wounded but playing, lost yet searching. The black-and-white images appeared in the pamphlet alongside *Letter to a Grown-Up,* text written from a child's point of view that gave facts about the effect of war on children and asked for reconstruction work to continue.

For UNESCO, photographs had the potential to contribute to the reconfiguration of the European family. Tara Zahra and others have written about the substantial postwar efforts to heal European trauma through caring for children.[67] But the reassuring way in which children were represented in *Children of Europe* should not be seen as a distinctively postwar iconography. Chim's photographs in Spain had concentrated on fighters, property and conflict; his extraordinary images were very different from those taken by humanitarian workers seeking to raise awareness and funds to support civilians affected by the Civil War. The compromises and renegotiations made by humanitarian workers in selecting images to use in their publicity were rooted in their time and place. Photographs of cared-for, not-suffering children demonstrated that those children deserved saving and that there was a European family future to save them for.

Rose Holmes is a postdoctoral researcher at Birkbeck, University of London, and is working on a project on the history of global trafficking. She is currently writing on histories of transnational child migration. She previously completed a PhD in History at the University of Sussex, and her thesis was entitled, 'A Moral Business: The Work of British Quakers with Refugees from Fascism, 1933–1939'. Her research interests focus on the histories of welfare, poverty and humanitarianism, especially in Britain and Europe in the 1920s and 1930s.

Notes

1. See H. Cotter, 'Images of War, Finally Unpacked', *New York Times* (23 September 2010); A. Budick, 'The Mexican Suitcase, the International Center for Photography, New York', *Financial Times* (6 October 2010); S. O'Hagan, 'Robert Capa and Gerda Taro: Love in a Time of War', *The Observer* (13 May 2012). See also the documentary film about the discovery of the negatives: T. Ziff (dir.), *The Mexican Suitcase* (2011).
2. S. Sontag, 'Looking at War: Photography's View of Devastation and Death', *New Yorker* (9 September 2002).
3. M. Rosler, 'In, around and afterthoughts on documentary photography', in M. Rosler (ed.), *Decoys and Disruptions: Selected Writings 1975–2001* (Cambridge, MA: MIT Press, 2004), 151–206; J. Stallabrass, *Memory of Fire: Images of War and the War of Images* (Brighton: Photoworks, 2013); D. Crimp, 'The Museum's Old/The Library's New Subject', in R.

Bolton (ed.), *The Contest of Meaning: Critical Histories of Photography* (Cambridge, MA: MIT Press, 1986), 3–14.

4. See F. Mendlesohn, *Quaker Relief Work in the Spanish Civil War* (Lewiston: Edgar Mellen Press, 2002); J. Fyrth, *The Signal was Spain: The Aid Spain Movement in Britain 1936–39* (London: Lawrence & Wishart, 1993); T. Buchanan, "A Far Away Country of Which We Know Nothing'? Perceptions of Spain and its Civil War in Britain, 1931–1939', *Twentieth Century British History* 4(1) (1993), 1–24; T. Buchanan, *The Spanish Civil War and the British Labour Movement* (Cambridge: Cambridge University Press, 1991).

5. The most well-known (and controversial) images being reproduced in Emily Hobhouse's book and her distribution at public meetings of images of the emaciated child Lizzie Van Zyl, who died in Bloemfontein camp in South Africa in 1902. See E. Hobhouse, *The Brunt of War and Where it Fell* (London: Methuen, 1902). See also M. Godby, 'Confronting Horror: Emily Hobhouse and the Concentration Camp Photographs of the South African War', *Kronos* 32 (2006), 34–48.

6. H. Fehrenbach, 'Children and Other Civilians: Photography and the Politics of Humanitarian Image-Making', in H. Fehrenbach and D. Rodogno (eds), *Humanitarian Photography: A History* (New York: Cambridge University Press, 2015), 165–99.

7. See Katharina Stornig's chapter in this volume.

8. For further discussion of Jebb and Buxton's motivations, see P.E. Veerman, *The Rights of the Child and the Changing Image of Childhood* (Dordrecht: Martinus Nijhoff, 1992), 88–91.

9. The most comprehensive guide on the rise and cultural weight of amateur photography is E. Edwards, *The Camera as Historian: Amateur Photographers and Historical Imagination* (Durham, NC: Duke University Press, 2012).

10. C. Langhamer, *Women's Leisure in England, 1920–1960* (Manchester: Manchester University Press, 2000), 58–63.

11. S. Linfield, *The Cruel Radiance: Photography and Political Violence* (Chicago: Chicago University Press, 2010), 130–31.

12. See C. Brothers, *War and Photography: A Cultural History* (London: Routledge, 2007), 141–60.

13. See the 'Bring 'Pure-Washed' Refugee Children to Britain' section of this chapter for more discussion of this.

14. Interview with Karen Lee, by Norma Jacob, 31 March 1989, AFSC archives. Quoted in A. Jackson, *British Women and the Spanish Civil War* (London: Routledge, 2002), 116.

15. Correspondence. Alfred Jacob and various London contacts, spring 1937, Friends House Archive, Euston, London (hereinafter FHA). FSC/R/SP/1/1. Folder 1, Box 1. Letters to/from Barcelona.

16. Letter, Alfred Jacob to Judith Corcoran [of the British Youth Peace Assembly], 8 December 1936, FHA FSC/R/SP/1/1, folder: 1, Box 1. Letters to/from Barcelona.

17. For example: Letter, from A. Jacob to Edith Pye, 28 November 1936, FHA FSC/R/SP/1/1, folder: 1, Box 1. Letters to/from Barcelona.

18. Dorothy Thompson, who worked at Friends House in London, had found out about the technique from American colleagues after being impressed by the quality of their leaflets. Letter, John F. Reich to Dorothy Thompson, 6 October 1937, FHA FSC/R/SP/2/1.

19. Letter, Fred Tritton to A. Jacob, 24 March 1937, FHA FSC/R/SP/1/5, Folder 5, Box 1. Letters to/from Barcelona. Emphasis added.

20. A. Jacob to F. Tritton, 29 November 1936. FHA FSC/R/SP/1/1. Folder 1, Box 1. Letters to/from Barcelona.

21. Letter, from A. Jacob to F. Tritton, 5 December 1936, FHA FSC/R/SP/1/1, Folder 1, Box 1, Letters to/from Barcelona. Emphasis in original.

22. Letter, from A. Cope to J. F. Reich, 22 November 1938, FHA AFSC Reports, FSC/R/SP/2/1. Folder 2, Box 1, Letters to/from Barcelona. Alfred Cope would later cause controversy when he described to a reporter how Franco's troops had seized goods intended for civilian relief. His comments were taken as evidence of partisan relief work. See *New York Times* (9 June 1939).

23. William Finley was not a humanitarian worker, at least not in any official capacity. It is unclear whether he was in Spain as a journalist/photographer or in a private capacity. See Letter from J.F. Reich to D. Thompson, 23 September 1938, FHA FSC/R/SP/2/1, Folder 2, Box 1, Letters to/from Barcelona.

24. L. Manning, *A Life for Education: An Autobiography* (London: Victor Gollancz, 1970), 120.

25. For the most detailed account of Francesca Wilson's life and work, see S.L. Roberts, 'Place, Life Histories and the Politics of Relief: Episodes in the Life of Francesca Wilson, Humanitarian Educator Activist', PhD dissertation (Birmingham: University of Birmingham, 2010).

26. F.M. Wilson, *In the Margins of Chaos: Recollections of Relief Work in and between Three Wars* (London: John Murray, 1944), 190.

27. Articles from this period include F.M. Wilson, 'The Women of Madrid: Dancing in the Food Queues', *Manchester Guardian* (4 May 1937); F.M. Wilson, 'Social Work in War-Time Spain: Impressions of a Relief Worker', *Manchester Guardian* (15 April 1938); F.M. Wilson, 'A Farm Colony in Spain', *The Friend* (2 September 1938); F.M. Wilson, 'Spaniards in Exile: The Civilian Camp at Argelès', *Manchester Guardian* (9 May 1939).

28. Wilson, *In the Margins of Chaos,* 176.

29. Letter, J.M. Fry to *The Times,* 11 November 1936, FHA FSC/R/SP/5, Box 5. Reports.

30. 'Funds for Spanish Relief', *Manchester Guardian* (19 October 1936).

31. *Manchester Guardian,* 28 December 1936.

32. 'It *Can* Happen Here', *Daily Express* (10 December 1937). Emphasis in original.

33. V. Woolf, *Three Guineas* (London: Hogarth Press, 1938), 96.

34. Buchanan, *Spanish Civil War,* 33–36.

35. Leaflet, 'Milk for Spain' fund: second appeal. July 1938. Trades Union Congress Archive, University of Warwick (hereinafter TUC). Document 292/946/17a/56. Spanish Rebellion – Documents 1938.

36. Buchanan, *Spanish Civil War,* 167–95.

37. S. Linfield, *The Cruel Radiance: Photography and Political Violence* (Chicago: University of Chicago Press, 2010), 130–31.

38. A longstanding member of the executive and various other committees, Pye was also the League of Nations Women's Advisory Committee member from 1930. See Minutes, 'Executive Committee Minutes 1930', London School of Economics WILPF archives. WILPF 1–6. Executive Committee Minutes.

39. National Archives, Kew. T161/932 Treasury. 10 December 1937–11 February 1939. Contribution by H.M. Government to the International Commission for the assistance of Child Refugees.

40. *Revue Internationale de la Croix-Rouge et Bulletin International des Sociétés de la Croix-Rouge 22.* 1940, 474.

41. International Commission Pamphlet, c. 1937, FHA FSC/R/SP/5, Spain Publicity 1936–37.

42. Letter, from J.F. Reich to D. Thomson, 30 March 1939. FHA FSC/R/SP/2/1. Relief Workers' Correspondence.

43. Letter, from A. Jacob to F. Tritton, 13 January 1937. FHA FSC/R/SP/1/1. Letters to/from Barcelona.

44. Correspondence, A. Jacob and F. Tritton. FHA FSC/SP/1-5. Files on Spain.

45. The Members of Parliament involved being the Duchess of Atholl; Eleanor Rathbone; David Grenfell; Wilfrid Roberts and John Macnamara. The organizations represented by the National Joint Committee were: the Society of Friends; the Save the Children Fund; the Spanish Medical Aid Committee; the Scottish Ambulance Unit; the Spanish Women's Committee for help to Spain; the Women's Committee against War and Fascism; and the Spanish Youth Food Ship Committee. Booklet, TUC, February 1937. Document 292/946/18b/26. National Joint Committee for Spanish Relief.

46. Buchanan, *Spanish Civil War*, 163.

47. For more details on the Home Office stipulations, see D. Legarreta, *The Guernica Generation: Basque Refugee Children of the Spanish Civil War* (Nevada: University of Nevada Press, 1984), 100–5.

48. Leah Manning provides a detailed account of this in her autobiography. See Manning, *A Life for Education*, 112–40.

49. This proviso was expressed in a letter dated 18 May 1937 from the Home Secretary Sir John Simon to the MP Wilfrid Roberts (who was a leader of the NJC). Contents of the letter reported in 'Minutes of Executive Committee Meeting', document 292/946/39/107, Basque Children's Committee: Minutes and Documents 1937–39.

50. It is notable that medical supervision, quarantine and risk of infectious disease from the Basque children are mentioned frequently in articles, including 'Care of Spanish War Victims', *The Times* (14 May 1937); 'Basque Children for England', *The Times* (22 May 1937); 'Basque Refugee Children: Lords on Health Precautions', *The Times* (26 May 1937).

51. I. Zweiniger-Bargielowska, 'Raising a Nation of "Good Animals": The New Health Society and Health Education Campaigns in Interwar Britain', *Social History of Medicine* 20(1) (2007), 73–89.

52. R.W.B. Ellis, 'Effects of War on Child Health', *British Medical Journal* 1(4544) (1948), 239–45. See also R.[W.B.] Ellis, 'Women and Children Last', *New Statesman and Nation* (1939).

53. A.E. Russell, 'Children in Catalonia' (Correspondence), *The Lancet* (1938), 1437; E. Pye, 'Refugees in Catalonia' (Correspondence), *The Lancet* (1938), 339–40; R.W.B. Ellis and A.E. Russell, 'Four Thousand Basque Children', *The Lancet* (1937), 1303–4; R.W.B. Ellis and A.E Russell, 'The Refugees in Catalonia', *The Lancet* (1937), 929–38; R. Taylor, 'Typhoid Fever in the Basque Refugee Camp', *British Medical Journal* 2(4006) (1937), 760–61; and H.C.M. Williams, 'The Arrival of the Basque Children at the Port of Southampton', *British Medical Journal* 1(3988) (1937), 1209–10.

54. Ellis and Russell, 'Four Thousand Basque Children', 1303–4.

55. Ellis and Russell, 'The Refugees in Catalonia', 929–38.

56. See, e.g., 'The Basque Children at Watermillock', *Manchester Guardian* (12 December 1938); 'Basque Children in Wales: An "Adoption" Scheme', *Manchester Guardian* (9 January 1939); 'Basque Children: Concert Tour in Lake District', *Manchester Guardian* (24 January 1939).

57. For an example of the type of photograph of the *SS Habana* used by the British press, see 'Arrival of Refugee Basque Children at Southampton', *The Times* (24 May 1937).

58. The headlines are indicative of the tone of the articles and are as follows: 'Basque Children Stampede', *Daily Mail* (21 June 1937); 'Child Refugees Attack Nuns', *Daily Mail* (30 June 1937); 'Basque Boys May Be Sent Back', *Daily Mail* (27 July 1937); 'Bad Basque Boys to Be Sent Back', *Daily Mail* (29 July 1937); 'Basque Boys Chase Cook', *Daily Mail* (30 July 1937); 'Mystery Rick Fire in Basque Camp', *Daily Mail* (9 August 1937); 'More Bad Basque Boys', *Daily Mail* (27 August 1937).

59. See Canon Craven's reports to the Basque Children's Committee in Executive Committee minutes, including 'Basque Children's Committee, Minutes of Executive Committee', 1 October 1937, TUC, document 292C/946/2/111. For more details on the care of the children, consult the informative book by A. Bell, *Only for Three Months: The Basque Children in Exile* (Norwich: Mousehold Press, 1996).

60. Leaflet, '4,000 Children Saved', 1937, TUC, document 292/946/18a/65, Basque Children's Committee, Spanish Situation – Pamphlets, leaflets, etc., 1936–37.

61. The children (or *niños/niñas*, as they call themselves) who remained retained a sense of their origins into adulthood. There is an active 'Basque Children of '37 Association', which has a website at http://www.basquechildren.org (accessed 22 August 2018).

62. M. Olivier, 'George Eastman's Modern Stone-Age Family: Snapshot Photography and the Brownie', *Technology and Culture* 48(1) (2007), 1–19.

63. L. Malkki, 'Children, Humanity, and the Infantilization of Peace', in I. Feldman and M. Ticktin (eds), *In the Name of Humanity: The Government of Threat and Care* (Durham, NC: Duke University Press, 2010), 58–85.

64. ibid., 58.

65. Photos, 'Children of Europe', by David Seymour, 1949, publication No. 403 of the United Nations Educational, Scientific and Cultural Organization, France: UNESCO Paris.

66. For UNESCO's original remit, see J. Huxley, *UNESCO: Its Purpose and Philosophy* (Washington DC: Preparatory Commission of UNESCO, 1946). There has been an increasing body of research on UNESCO in recent years. For a comprehensive analysis of its history and identity, see P. Betts, 'Humanity's New Heritage: UNESCO and the Rewriting of World History', *Past and Present* 228 (2015), 249–85; A. Rehling, 'Universalismen und Partikularismen im Widerstreit: Zur Genese des UNESCO-Welterbes', *Zeithistorische Forschungen* 8(3) (2011), 414–36; and for the context of the global commons, see A. Rehling, '"Kulturen unter Artenschutz?" Vom Schutz der Kulturschätze als Gemeinsames Erbe der Menschheit zur Erhaltung kultureller Vielfalt', *European History Yearbook* 15 (2013), 109–37.

67. T. Zahra, *The Lost Children: Reconstructing Europe's Families after World War II* (Cambridge, MA: Harvard University Press, 2011).

Bibliography

Bell, A. *Only for Three Months: The Basque Children in Exile*. Norwich: Mousehold Press, 1996.

Betts, P. 'Humanity's New Heritage: UNESCO and the Rewriting of World History'. *Past and Present* 228 (2015), 249–85.

Brothers, C. *War and Photography: A Cultural History.* London: Routledge, 2007.

Buchanan, T. *The Spanish Civil War and the British Labour Movement.* Cambridge: Cambridge University Press, 1991.

———. '"A Far Away Country of Which We Know Nothing"? Perceptions of Spain and its Civil War in Britain, 1931–1939'. *Twentieth Century British History* 4(1) (1993), 1–24.

Budick, A. 'The Mexican Suitcase, the International Center for Photography, New York'. *Financial Times* (6 October 2010).

Crimp, D. 'The Museum's Old/The Library's New Subject', in R. Bolton (ed.), *The Contest of Meaning: Critical Histories of Photography* (Cambridge, MA: MIT Press, 1986), 3–14.

Edwards, E. *The Camera as Historian: Amateur Photographers and Historical Imagination.* Durham, NC: Duke University Press, 2012.

Fehrenbach, H. 'Children and Other Civilians: Photography and the Politics of Humanitarian Image-Making', in H. Fehrenbach and D. Rodogno (eds), *Humanitarian Photography: A History* (New York: Cambridge University Press, 2015), 165–99.

Fyrth, J. *The Signal was Spain: The Aid Spain Movement in Britain 1936–39.* London: Lawrence & Wishart, 1993.

Godby, M. 'Confronting Horror: Emily Hobhouse and the Concentration Camp Photographs of the South African War'. *Kronos* 32 (2006), 34–48.

Hobhouse, E. *The Brunt of War and Where it Fell.* London: Methuen, 1902.

Huxley, J. *UNESCO: Its Purpose and Philosophy.* Washington DC: Preparatory Commission of UNESCO, 1946.

Jackson, A. *British Women and the Spanish Civil War.* London: Routledge, 2002.

Langhamer, C. *Women's Leisure in England, 1920–1960.* Manchester: Manchester University Press, 2000.

Legarreta, D. *The Guernica Generation: Basque Refugee Children of the Spanish Civil War.* Nevada: University of Nevada Press, 1984.

Linfield, S. *The Cruel Radiance: Photography and Political Violence.* Chicago: University of Chicago Press, 2010.

Malkki, L. 'Children, Humanity, and the Infantilization of Peace', in I. Feldman and M. Ticktin (eds), *In the Name of Humanity: The Government of Threat and Care* (Durham, NC: Duke University Press, 2010), 58–85.

Manning, L. *A Life for Education: An Autobiography.* London: Victor Gollancz, 1970.

Mendlesohn, F. *Quaker Relief Work in the Spanish Civil War.* Lewiston: Edgar Mellen Press, 2002.

Olivier, M. 'George Eastman's Modern Stone-Age Family: Snapshot Photography and the Brownie'. *Technology and Culture* 48(1) (2007), 1–19.

Rehling, A. 'Universalismen und Partikularismen im Widerstreit: Zur Genese des UNESCO-Welterbes'. *Zeithistorische Forschungen* 8(3) (2011), 414–36.

Rehling, A. '"Kulturen unter Artenschutz?" Vom Schutz der Kulturschätze als Gemeinsames Erbe der Menschheit zur Erhaltung kultureller Vielfalt'. *European History Yearbook* 15 (2013), 109–37.

Roberts, S.L. 'Place, Life Histories and the Politics of Relief: Episodes in the Life of Francesca Wilson, Humanitarian Educator Activist'. PhD thesis. Birmingham: University of Birmingham, 2010.

Rosler, M. 'In, around and Afterthoughts on Documentary Photography', in M. Rosler (ed.), *Decoys and Disruptions: Selected Writings 1975–2001* (Cambridge, MA: MIT Press, 2004), 151–206.

Stallabrass, J. *Memory of Fire: Images of War and the War of Images.* Brighton: Photoworks, 2013.

Veerman, P.E. *The Rights of the Child and the Changing Image of Childhood.* Dordrecht: Martinus Nijhoff, 1992.

Wilson, F.M. *In the Margins of Chaos: Recollections of Relief Work in and between Three Wars.* London: John Murray, 1944.

Woolf, V. *Three Guineas.* London: Hogarth Press, 1938.

Zahra, T. *The Lost Children: Reconstructing Europe's Families after World War II.* Cambridge, MA: Harvard University Press, 2011.

Zweiniger-Bargielowska, I. 'Raising a Nation of "Good Animals": The New Health Society and Health Education Campaigns in Interwar Britain'. *Social History of Medicine* 20(1) (2007), 73–89.

3

Humanitarianism on the Screen

The ICRC Films, 1921–65

Daniel Palmieri

So far, very little has been written on the history of the International Committee of the Red Cross (ICRC) humanitarian cinema. The scarce literature mostly focuses on either the ICRC movies of 1920s,[1] when the organization started to use cinema as a tool for its humanitarian propaganda, or the films produced around the time of the Second World War.[2] This relative lack of interest is due not to a lack of material: several dozen films have been produced by the ICRC since 1921 and, with the development of new technologies (video, digital cameras), this number has grown exponentially since the 1980s. Overall, since the beginning of the twentieth century, the ICRC has produced more than 6,500 films in all formats and lengths. On most of them, there is some information, however scant, in the ICRC Archives. So this lack of scholarly interest seems more linked to the difficulty of grasping this specific activity and understanding the policy and the justification that lay behind it, as the ICRC films prove to be both varied and out of step with their times. For instance, while the 1930s were a rich period for cinema, including propaganda, the ICRC seems to have lost interest in this very popular medium, although it had used it during the previous decade and would use it again in the Second World War and beyond.

The lack of an explicit cinematographic strategy on the part of the ICRC or the impossibility today to retrace through archives its 'own media culture' at that time[3] might explain why the (so far) few works on this topic focus either on a very limited period or on one particular film. Moreover, the weak, all-encompassing and contested definition of what exactly the concept of 'humanitarian cinema'[4] means is an additional element explaining the lack of a general overview on ICRC film production, added to the fact that this terminology is sometimes contested by the filmmakers themselves.[5] Therefore, if researchers get together to trace the birth of the 'humanitarian cinema' during the First World War or its immediate aftermath,[6] they seem to have given up on a more precise description of what this cinematographic genre exactly covers, simply supposing that it exists per se. It is the same problem as with the concept of 'humanitarianism': only a few scholars have tried to decipher the different facets of this used and often misused term.[7]

Using as an example the ICRC, the oldest 'humanitarian' organization still active, this chapter will define humanitarianism as the work of outside parties – who are nonreligious and civilian – providing transnational assistance to victims of armed violence or of its direct consequences. Although transnational assistance provided by the same parties in situations of natural disaster, including epidemics and famines, can also fall under this definition, this chapter will only analyse responses to armed conflict. 'Humanitarian cinema', then, is composed of films documenting this foreign aid. This analysis on the ICRC humanitarian cinema – the first ever made on an extensive period – will cover the years from 1921 to 1965. The first chronological boundary explains itself by the fact that no ICRC films were made before the 1920s. The second boundary is imposed by the closure to the public of the ICRC records after 1965 and hence by the impossibility to document films after this date.[8]

But, first, it is important to bear in mind that a great paradox lies at the core of humanitarian cinema: it is supposed, in the case of the ICRC, to depict war and its victims not in a fictional or elusive form, but realistically, in order to show to the public the horrors of violence and how deeply those affected by armed conflicts suffer and need help. But as a result of fear, disgust, fatigue or indifference, people do not necessarily want to see this violence and pain. And yet humanitarian work relies on public support. If the public does not empathize with what the ICRC does for victims of war, it gets no political or financial support and cannot carry out its work. In other words, the ICRC humanitarian cinema was, between the 1920s and the 1960s, at the forefront of efforts to rally public support, even if the topic itself is not particularly inspiring or attractive. While producing its films, the ICRC will always have to handle this contradiction. The chapter also examines what tactics the Geneva institution used to confront this problem and what the aims were for the films it made. The analysis will show that the ICRC's final objective was as much political as humanitarian.

The ICRC Films Production

Between 1921 and 1965, the ICRC produced thirty-eight films to be screened in public.[9] They were not evenly spread across this timespan, but rather clustered in four periods, as shown in the table below: sixteen films were produced between 1921 and 1923, seven in the Second World War and its aftermath, five in the 1950s and ten in the 1960s. No films were made in the 1930s. Their duration

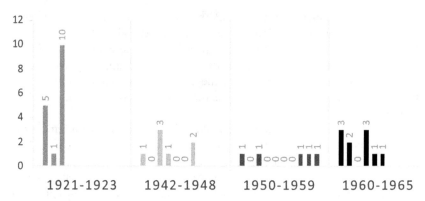

Figure 3.1. ICRC films by decade, 1920s–1960s.

ranges from one to 37 minutes. Most of them are in black and white. Colour film began to be used only in the 1960s.[10]

Not all thirty-eight films may be qualified as humanitarian films according our definition. For instance, in 1959 and 1963, several clearly historical and commemorative films were produced for the anniversaries of the Battle of Solferino in June 1859,[11] and the founding of the Red Cross, in 1863. A further two films – *Ein Soldat wird vermisst* (*A Soldier is Missing*) and *Prisonnier de guerre . . .* (*Prisoner of War*) – both produced during the Second World War do not qualify because although they deal with humanitarian issues in wartime, they are not real documentaries, but semi-fictional movies that also used actors. Thus, thirty-two true humanitarian films were produced during the period. They cover all the main ICRC operations during thirty-four years of activities except the Spanish Civil War (1936–39), the Sino-Japanese War (1937–45) and the Italian-Ethiopian War (1935–36).[12]

The content of these films was not necessarily novel. Of the sixteen films produced between 1921 and 1923, ten focused on the ICRC's humanitarian work during the Greco-Turkish War (1919–22). A number of these films borrowed content from one another. The film entitled *le CICR à Genève: ses activités d'après guerre* (*The ICRC in Geneva: Its Post-war Activities*, 1923) covered all operations in the immediate postwar period, like the repatriation of prisoners of war, the fight against typhus or the assistance to Russian refugees. It reused shots from the four films produced in 1921. Likewise, the 1961 version of the film *Le rapatriement des Coréens du Japon en République démocratique de Corée* (*The Repatriation of the Koreans from Japan to the Democratic Republic of Korea*) is a condensed version of the 1960 film. However, all the productions of the 1940s and 1950s are original.

The conditions in which the films were produced are often not clear, due to a lack of documentation in the archives. This is especially the case for the first releases of the 1920s.[13] It seems that it was the ICRC that commissioned the films and either sent professionals to bring back footage or instructed its delegates (representatives) in the field to collect material about their activities. For two films made in Poland in 1921 on the fight against the typhus epidemic, it is known that the ICRC delegate Victor Gloor himself took the initiative to produce these documentaries.[14] In some cases, the filmmakers were at the same time ICRC delegates, as with both films on the Congo in 1960.

Generally, many of the films were produced by professional directors.[15] For instance, the nine films about the Greco-Turkish War were shot by Joseph Hepp (1897–1968), a Hungarian cinematographer who spent his career in Greece. Others, like Jean Brocher (1899–1979) or Kurt Früh (1915–79), were famous Swiss filmmakers. Not all of them worked on location or in the field. Charles-George Duvanel (1906–75), for example, produced three films in Geneva in the 1950s by combining newsreels with footage brought back by ICRC delegates. Duvanel was also in charge of translating the commentary and making copies of the films.

The documentaries were commonly translated into several languages, most often from French into English, German, Spanish and occasionally Italian. In the silent films of the 1920s, the title cards were in French and/or English. These bilingual indications imply that, from the beginning, the ICRC documentaries were supposed to be distributed internationally. In fact, the distribution took a number of forms. Most often, the ICRC films were shown in cinemas and later on television. The principal audience was Swiss; this explains why the documentaries were translated into German and Italian, which alongside French are the national languages in Switzerland. For the screenings in cinemas, the ICRC collaborated with Swiss and foreign distributors (including such famous names as Pathé, RKO and Twentieth Century Fox) to project the films in cinemas – typically in the news portion of the programme.[16] From the beginning of 1960s, the ICRC documentaries were broadcasted on TV only.[17]

The films were also shown at ICRC delegations, Swiss embassies and Swiss cultural associations around the world. Copies of *Inter Arma Caritas,* produced in 1948, were screened in southern Africa, but we have no record of who watched them. In addition, the National Red Cross and Red Crescent Societies were encouraged to buy ICRC films[18] when they were not simply given copies.

The ICRC documentaries were expensive to produce. No information on the first productions is available in the ICRC documentation. But the films produced in 1942 (*Le drapeau de l'humanité – The Flag of Humanity*) and 1944 (*Une voie reste ouverte! – One Way Remains Open!*) cost 15,000[19] and 24,000 Swiss francs respectively,[20] which represented, at that time, huge amounts for the ICRC. More than 50,000 Swiss francs were spent on the 1948 production of *Inter Arma Caritas* – four times the ICRC's initial communication budget for the entire year.[21] The costs of these productions may explain why more films were not made in the analysed period and why none were produced in the 1930s: there was no money for such luxuries at that time. Moreover, to produce a documentary was always a loss-making operation for the ICRC, which was never able to recoup the money it had invested in its films.[22]

The Use of Documentaries by the ICRC

Nevertheless, the belief at the ICRC was that films, whatever the cost, were important and necessary because they fed the propaganda (i.e. communication) activities of the Geneva institution. In fact, they served a dual purpose. First, they were quite useful to attract donations. The ICRC was conscious of the importance to show itself publicly to capture the attention of potential donors. So, in the 1950s, it made a point of releasing its films before its annual fundraising drive in Switzerland each September. During the Second World War, the films were meant to raise the funds needed to keep operations running. This is why they highlighted the work for prisoners of war, which was one of the ICRC's core activities. The films on Yemen, Nepal, Palestine and the Congo were used to meet unexpected financing needs for the humanitarian operations in these countries. That said, by analysing the ICRC budgetary structure, it appears that the private fundraising via cinema remained a very marginal way of obtaining funds. Using its reputation, especially in Switzerland, the institution preferred to adopt a door-to-door strategy in relation to firms or individuals, and then to governments. In fact, the main purpose for producing films was to position the ICRC politically within the Red Cross Movement. Political motives often influenced when films were made, and on more than one occasion, the films saved the ICRC from falling by the wayside.

The political motives are clear for the films of the early 1920s. At the time, the ICRC was being overshadowed by the newly founded League of Red Cross Societies (created in 1919). Even if the ICRC had shown its ability and importance during the Great War, by assisting thousands of prisoners of war (and by being recognized for this work by the award of the 1917 Nobel Peace Prize), the League saw the Geneva institution as a relic that no longer had a humanitarian role to play after the war, and wanted to take its place. Organized by Allied countries and being at first only constituted by the Red Crosses of the five major victorious powers (France, the United States, the United Kingdom, Italy and Japan), the League considered that it was the organization best able to face new challenges created by the new (and peaceful) world order, such as the fight against epidemics and venereal diseases, and the promotion of hygiene. So the already sexagenarian ICRC had to prove its worth (and its modernity) for the postwar period, which rapidly appeared to be as violent as the past, especially in Eastern Europe (the Polish-Soviet war, the uprising in Silesia and the Hungarian Bolshevik revolution). One way of doing this was by showing that, though the First World War was over, its consequences persisted. Thus, the ICRC asked its foreign delegations to send footage of their work with refugees, repatriated prisoners of war and civilians who were victims of political, economic and social turmoil directly linked to the war. These films were screened in 1921 at the 10th International Conference of the Red Cross.[23] There, it was decided that the ICRC should continue to exist as an operative body and to carry out its original mandate. The films also proved that the ICRC was not nearly as outdated as it was thought, because it could make use of the modern technology of cinema. Along the same lines, the film entitled *Le CICR à Genève* was produced in view of the 11th International Conference in 1923.[24] It was perfectly placed to defend once more the ICRC's activities at a time when the dispute with the League had not yet been settled.[25]

Just after the Second World War, the ICRC again faced a challenger, this time in the form of Red Cross Societies in communist countries, which questioned its past role during the Second World War and also its present role in the Red Cross Movement. During the 17th International Conference of the Red Cross in 1948, the ICRC was accused of lack of neutrality and impartiality for not having denounced the Nazi and fascist crimes, and for not having done enough to protect some categories of war victims, for instance, captured partisans. The ICRC's response was to present *Inter Arma Caritas,* a medium-length film offering a large panorama of the intervention of the institution during the Second World War.[26] A second documentary – *Helft Helfen (That They May Live Again,* 1948) – was also produced for the 17th International Conference, but it was not screened on this occasion for the reasons detailed below. Later, communist critics, especially from the USSR, of the ICRC condemned its nondenunciation of some 'war crimes' perpetrated by the Western powers, and at first by the United States, during armed conflicts such as the Korean War. In response to this ongoing dispute, the ICRC prepared several films showing its huge involvement for victims of recent or still-active armed conflicts. These documentaries were presented for the 18th and 19th International Conferences of the Red Cross in 1952 and 1957.[27]

The strong connection between the films' production and the necessity for the ICRC to defend itself against the verbal attacks from other parts of the Red Cross Movement could also explain, besides real financial problems, the lack of documentaries produced at the end of the 1920s and during the 1930s. One may wonder if due to the (provisional) end of its antagonism with the League and the strengthening of its position as a humanitarian institution, the ICRC no longer saw cause to use film as a means of asserting itself with regard to other members of the Red Cross. In fact, since 1925, the ICRC regained confidence in its 'fight' with the League, which was losing momentum. The ICRC also gained the support of the National Red Cross Societies that agreed to take part in the 12th International Conference of the Red Cross (Bern, 1925). This conference, which was boycotted by the League, clearly confirmed the ICRC as a full member of the Red Cross family. The situation quietened down with the agreement negotiated in 1928 between both institutions. This text clarified and shared out the respective roles of the League and the ICRC in times of peace and in times of war.

A Special Film: *Helft Helfen* (1948)

The films used to politically defend the ICRC had a distinctive structure. Generally, they were retrospectives on the ICRC's work in the period since the last

International Conference. Their primary purpose was to just show how involved the ICRC had been in past conflicts and just how valuable its wartime work was. There was one exception: *Helft Helfen,* produced in 1948.[28] Under the disguise of a universally applicable commentary, the film showed the activities still being carried out in postwar Germany, and especially in East and West Berlin, and called for financing to continue this humanitarian assistance. In fact, the main donors, Swiss and Irish Mutual Aid Funds, had decided at the end of 1946 to stop funding these activities for Germany. Thus, the ICRC had to find other resources to continue a huge assistance and medical programme for the German civilian population. The initiative to produce a documentary was made by Hans Meyer, the chief of the ICRC delegation in Berlin, and was supported by the headquarters in Geneva. Meyer rapidly obtained the support of the newly formed Deutsche Film-Aktiengesellschaft (DEFA),[29] which offered the ICRC material and professional technical staff for this film as a way of thanking it for its humanitarian mission in Germany.[30] Shooting took place during the winter of 1947–48 in and around Berlin,[31] and the film was completed in May 1948. The documentary shows the tragic situation of the civilian German population confronted with hunger, cold and tuberculosis, with a particular focus on children; it again takes up some *topoi* of the imagery describing the city.[32] The film also shows the activities of the ICRC, in partnership with National Red Crosses or German welfare institutions, to alleviate these pains. The film alternates happy sequences (chil-

Figure 3.2. 'Germany post-war 1946–1948. Distress, cold and hungry: famished old people'. Screenshot from the film *Helft Helfen,* 1948. V-P-HIST-03280-28, © ICRC archives (ARR).

dren during a meal) with very crude images (half-naked women suffering from tuberculosis). It ends on terrifying shots of undernourished and crying newborn babies, with a comment asking the audience to help (hence its title in German).

Even though the film is really emblematic of human suffering, its reception by the ICRC was reticent.[33] The headquarters found the images too shocking to be shown to a wider public. The documentary was also perceived as too pro-German, even if its comments pointed to the general suffering of all civilian populations affected by the consequences of the war. For the ICRC, it appeared difficult to 'sell' these films abroad to a wide audience. Consequently, the documentary was never broadcast. If *Helft Helfen* was supposed at first to be screened during the 17th International Conference of the Red Cross, it eventually lost its place to *Inter Arma Caritas* – a documentary also produced in 1948, but one more politically correct in the ICRC's eyes.

Besides its perhaps too pro-German point of view, other reasons contributed to the failure of *Helft Helfen*. The fact that the film was offered by the DEFA, at that time in Soviet hands, was certainly a drawback for the ICRC governance, which was defiant in the face of communism. Far from considering this partnership with a production company in the Soviet Zone of Occupation in Germany as an advantage in trying to build closer links with the Eastern Bloc, the ICRC headquarters was wary of being instrumentalized by a foreign government that, at the same time, was very critical of the institution.[34] The ICRC was certainly also annoyed by the messages delivered by the documentary, especially those making references to the past, showing that a population in distress could make bad choices that, in turn, could have repercussions on the whole of humanity. And because the film was shot in Germany, this reference was quite explicit and still fresh in the collective memory. The fact that naked and skinny bodies were shown was a bothersome element too, because these images were a reminder of other naked and skinny bodies found after the liberation of the concentration camps. But the most annoying thing was certainly the nationality of the victims presented by *Helft Helfen*,[35] not only because German victims – even children – were not attractive enough to arouse empathy in the postwar world,[36] but also because, by showing the fate of the populations in Germany, the ICRC could be accused of taking the perpetrators' side. This last point begs the question of how the victims were portrayed in the ICRC films.

The Representation of Victims in the ICRC Films

By focusing so intensively on the victims, *Helft Helfen* was not typical of the ICRC cinematographic productions. It is noteworthy that, in the ICRC films from the period 1921–65, victims were generally underrepresented in comparison to the humanitarian work carried out on their behalf. Certainly, this intention must be qualified for the documentaries of the 1920s, where the beneficiaries of the ICRC assistance were more present. But in this case, the victims were not imme-

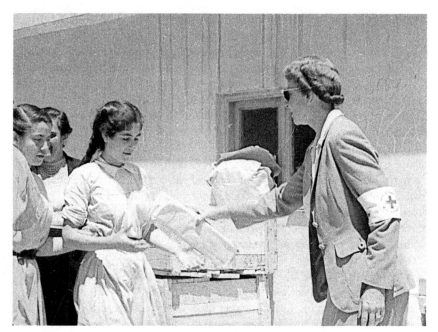

Figure 3.3. 'Aid for Greek Civilians'. Screenshot from the film *Tous frères!* (*All Brothers!*), 1952. V-P-HIST-00902-05, © ICRC.

diately recognizable on the images, and it is often only the title cards that help to identify the people depicted as victims of war or of its consequences. Generally, victims depicted in the ICRC documentaries were relegated to the background and seemed to exist only inasmuch as the Geneva institution or other humanitarian organizations were coming to their aid. This underrepresentation could be explained by the fact that humanitarian work and workers had to be featured prominently, to the detriment of victims, so that the audience would understand what the ICRC was and what it did, and to forge a sense of solidarity primarily between the audience and the ICRC rather than the audience and those suffering as a consequence of wars.[37]

Furthermore, war victims were sometimes totally ignored altogether, for instance, in the film *S.O.S. Congo* (1960). If the camera follows a wounded soldier, he is not an African, but a UN peacekeeper. The African victims were passed over, even though they were the primary aid recipients during this huge operation directed by the ICRC. What is more, the Congolese were broadly reduced to postcard or outright colonial stereotypes – for instance, in the same documentary, a group of white doctors taking a rest while drinking and smoking are served by a black boy in uniform.

The viewpoint of some of the filmmakers on the victims is also problematic. For instance, the footage showing the ICRC's work in Indochina and in Algeria in *Tous frères!* (1952) and *Car le sang coule encore !* (1958) was recorded by the cinema service of the French army. The portrayal of the victims and the ICRC's assistance was necessarily skewed because the filmmakers were on one side of the conflict and focused on the (good) collaboration between the ICRC delegates and the French authorities. The victims were represented in a submissive position – for instance, the captured Vietminh in *Tous frères!* sitting on the ground for lunch, while the delegate and the military authorities are standing, looking at the captives.

These images also served as a vehicle for a political representation of the victims, based again on the supremacy, including from its military side, of white people over indigenous people. Even when the filmmakers were neutral (i.e. Swiss), it did not preclude them from having preconceived notions. The ICRC's sometimes paternalistic view of victims was echoed in film images and comments,[38] most often regarding non-Europeans. All the usual clichés about Africans or Asians may be found in the ICRC documentaries. Although the main message was that the ICRC went wherever there is suffering in the world, the films also seemed to depict once again the superior white man on his humanitarian mission to civilize victims still living in their 'natural state'. Since it has long been an institution exclusively composed of Western Europeans (especially Swiss), the ICRC was imbued with racial stereotypes. This racist make-believe is not only linked to the period 1921–65, but also goes back to the origins of

Figure 3.4. 'Indochina War 1947–1954. Hanoï, camp for Vietnamese military prisoners. Visit of an ICRC delegate in the buildings for internees'. Screenshot from the film *Tous frères!,* 1952. V-P-INDO-N-00009-06, © ICRC.

the ICRC.[39] This portrayal changed perceptibly only in the mid 1960s with the arrival of a new generation of (young) ICRC delegates and under the influence of Third World theories. Henceforth, the focus would be placed on victims and their suffering, as in the films produced on the ICRC activities in Yemen.[40]

Conclusion

In conclusion, the ICRC's humanitarian films for the period 1921–65 are not so much documentaries of victims' suffering as a kind of 'anthropological' account of those trying to end the suffering. This is why the films focus on the helpers rather than the helped. Furthermore, the political and economic motivations behind many of these films were just as important as the humanitarian aims, if not more so. This explains why the victims and their hardships and suffering were often absent. The only film that showed raw suffering, *Helft Helfen,* was to be rejected by the ICRC.

Thus, we come full circle to the paradox of not showing the public the ills they do not or no longer want to see. For forty years, the ICRC handled this contradiction by glossing over the victims and sparing viewers the discomfort of seeing images of war that were too horrible. The films tried to put viewers in the shoes not of the people enduring the suffering, but of those coming to their aid. In so doing, the ICRC sought to promote financial and moral solidarity with its work. This was possible quite simply because humanitarian cinema followed and relied on the wider cinematic trends.

But all this was set to change with the arrival of television and live coverage. Television would, in many ways, strip away the filters that had previously sugar-coated victims' plight and broadcast the horrors of war in near-real time right into viewers' living rooms. The ICRC, forced to reinvent its cinema, would fall into the trap of going to the opposite extreme, this time overrepresenting the victims of armed violence. This new face of the ICRC humanitarian cinema is particularly visible in the documentaries shot during the Nigerian Civil War (1967–70): dead bodies, malnourished corpses and dying children are shown openly. If a particular focus was now put on victims' suffering, this does not mean that the ICRC's documentaries made after 1965 fulfilled only a humanitarian objective. In fact, the Nigeria-Biafra war opened a new era of critics about the work carried out by the ICRC during the conflict.[41] Thus, the institution has perhaps been tempted, once again, to justify its policy by using cinema. The only noticeable modification compared to the previous films of the 1921–65 period would lie in a change of emphasis. If during the 1920s, 1940s or 1950s the main argument was to show how useful the ICRC was for the victims of armed conflicts, the documentaries from the 1960s reversed the discourse by emphasizing how much the victims – now omnipresent on the images – needed the Geneva institution. This trend is closely linked to the increasing and more permanent presence of the ICRC in war contexts. Moreover, the major humanitarian crises of the late 1960s and early 1970s (starting with the Nigerian Civil War) have accustomed the public to the focus on victims; victims also became a central element in humanitarian communication, as well as in humanitarian fundraising. In competition with new emerging and proactive nongovernmental organizations (NGOs) (for instance, Médecins Sans Frontières), the ICRC has also had to adapt itself to these newly established challenging 'marketing' strategies. Promoting the victims' proximity was the final outcome of this change of paradigm in the humanitarian environment.

Daniel Palmieri is Historical Research Officer at the ICRC. His research interests cover humanitarian history. He recently edited *The Minutes from Meetings of the International Prisoners-of-War Agency* (2014). He is also one of the curators of the exhibition 'Humanizing War ? ICRC – 150 Years of Humanitarian Action', which was presented at the Mémorial de Caen.

Appendix 1: List of ICRC Films, 1921–65 (Original Titles)

CICR: rapatriement des prisonniers de guerre (1921)*
CICR : rapatriement des prisonniers de guerre (via Stettin et Narva) (1921)
Les réfugiés russes de Constantinople (1921)*
La lutte contre le typhus : l'activité du CICR en Pologne (1921)*
La lutte contre le typhus : l'activité du CICR et action de secours en faveur des enfants hongrois à Budapest (1921)*
La guerre gréco-turque. Grèce 1923 (1923)
La guerre gréco-turque : mission Reding (1923)
La guerre gréco-turque : rapatriement des internés civils turcs (1923)
La guerre gréco-turque : action de secours en faveur des réfugiés grecs (1923)
Le CICR à Genève : ses activités d'après-guerre (1923)*
Le drapeau de l'Humanité (1942)
Une voie reste ouverte (1944)
Ein Soldat wird vermisst (1944)
Deutsche Kriegsgefangenen in einem Arbeitslager in Kanada (1944)
Prisonnier de guerre . . . (1945)
Helft helfen (1948)
Inter Arma Caritas (1948)*
Les errants de Palestine (1950)
Tous frères ! (1952)*
Croix-Rouge par-delà les frontières (1957)*
Car le sang coule encore ! (1958)
Soferino (1959)
Opération Congo (1960)
S.O.S Congo (1960)
Le rapatriement des Coréens du Japon en République démocratique populaire de Corée (1960)
Le rapatriement des Coréens du Japon en République démocratique populaire de Corée (1961)
Action Népal (1961)

Inauguration du monument Henry-Dunant (1963)
Croix-Rouge sur fond blanc (1963)
Lancement du M/S Henry-Dunant (1963)
Yémen, terre de souffrance (1964)
Visite d'un camp au Cambodge (1965)
* Films shown during the International Conferences of the Red Cross.

Appendix 2: ICRC 'Humanitarian' Films, by Director/*Cameraman*

Augusta Lindberg and Nils Asttur: 2 (1921)
M. Semenoff: 1 (1921)
W. Lenczewsky and Béla Heltai: 2 (1921)
Joseph Hepp: 9 (1923)
Jean Brocher: 1 (1923)
Kurt Früh and Gertrud Spoerri (ICRC); *Adrien Porchet*: 1 (1942)
Kurt Früh and Adolf Forter; *Hans Zickendraht*: 1 (1944)
Karl von Barany; *Bruno Timm* and *Fernand Reymond*: 1 (1948)
Fernand Reymond and Frédéric Siordet (ICRC); *Fernand Reymond* and *Adrien Porchet*: 1 (1948)
Charles-Georges Duvanel; *Arnold Blanc*: 1 (1950)
Charles-Georges Duvanel: 2 (1952, 1958)
François Bardet and Jean-Louis Roy: 1 (1957)
Georges Kuhne (ICRC), Pierre Molteni and Raymond Bech; *Roger Bovard*: 2 (1960)
Jürg Baër (ICRC); *Roger du Pasquier* (ICRC): 1 (1961)
Jean-Paul Faure and Jérôme Santandrea (ICRC): 1 (1964)
Not known: 5 (1923, 1944, 1960, 1961, 1965)

Notes

1. See, for instance, L. Straumann, *L'humanitaire mis en scène : La cinématographie du CICR des années 1920* (Geneva: CICR, 2000); E. Natale, 'Quand l'humanitaire commençait à faire son cinéma : les films du CICR des années 1920', *International Review of the Red Cross* 854 (2004), 415–37; F. Piana, 'Photography, Cinema, and the Quest for Influence: The International Committee of the Red Cross in the Wake of the First World War', in H. Fehrenbach and D. Rodogno (eds), *Humanitarian Photography: A History* (New York: Cambridge University Press, 2015), 140–64.
2. M. Cornu, *Le Comité international de la Croix-Rouge et le cinéma au lendemain de la Seconde Guerre mondiale* (Lausanne: Université de Lausanne, 2006); M. Meier and D. Palmieri, 'Les équivoques du cinéma humanitaire : L'exemple D'*Helft Helfen* (1948)', in C. Delporte et al. (eds), *La guerre après la guerre : Images et constructions des imaginaires dans l'Europe du XXe siècle* (Paris: Nouveau Monde Éditions, 2009), 65–79; I. Herrmann and S. Maulini, 'Un nouveau cinéma muet? Décrypter les non-dits d'*Inter Arma Caritas*', *Revue du Ciné-club universitaire* (2015), hors-série, Geneva: University of Geneva, 11–14; M. Meier, 'Note sur *Une voie reste ouverte*', in *Revue du Ciné-club universitaire* (2015), hors-série, Geneva: University of Geneva, 15–19.

3. See the Introduction to this volume by Johannes Paulmann.
4. This deficiency is generally linked to the absence of a clear definition of the term 'humanitarian'.
5. The French Canadian films director Catherine Hébert, for instance, insists on the dissymmetrical position, including in the so-called 'humanitarian films' or 'human rights films', between the filmmaker and the subject who is filmed, and on the fact that filming victims of war could sometimes have a negative effect by simply reinforcing their victimhood; C. Hébert, 'The Other Side of the Country: Filming the Human Experience of War', in D. Mazurana, K. Jacobsen and L. Andrews Gale (eds), *Research Methods in Conflict Settings: A View from below* (Cambridge: Cambridge University Press, 2013), 27–55.
6. B. Cabannes, *The Great War and the Origins of Humanitarianism, 1918–1924* (Cambridge: Cambridge University Press, 2014), 312.
7. See, for instance, J. Paulmann, 'The Dilemmas of Humanitarian Aid: Historical Perspectives', in Johannes Paulmann (ed.), *Dilemmas of the Humanitarian Aid in the Twentieth Century* (Oxford: Oxford University Press, 2016), 1–31.
8. The ICRC archives for the period 1966–75 were opened to the public in June 2015, just after the writing of this chapter.
9. See Appendix 1. The author thanks Marina Meier, ICRC film archivist, for the information she provided.
10. These films are *Action Népal* (*Nepal Action,* 1961) and *Yémen, terre de souffrance* (*Yemen, Land of Suffering,* 1964).
11. The Battle of Solferino may be considered the founding event for the ICRC and, more generally, for the Red Cross Movement. In *Un souvenir de Solferino* (1862), which he wrote after assisting soldiers wounded in Solferino, Henry Dunant proposed the creation of national, permanent and civilian societies for helping the military wounded, regardless of their nationality, as well as an international treaty protecting the work of these societies. To examine these two proposals (which would clear the way for the National Societies of the Red Cross, the Red Crescent and the Geneva Conventions), Dunant and four other Geneva citizens created the ICRC.
12. The ICRC films archives own a film on the Red Cross/ICRC action during the Italian-Ethiopian war, which was not, however, produced by the ICRC. No films were produced by the ICRC during the Spanish Civil War and the Sino-Japanese War. The reason is certainly a lack of opportunity and money.
13. Piana, 'Photography, Cinema, and the Quest for Influence', 147.
14. Cornu, *Le Comité international de la Croix-Rouge et le cinéma*, 22.
15. See Appendix 2.
16. In Switzerland, especially during the Second World War, there was a legal obligation to show newsreels (*Ciné-Journal Suisse*) in each cinema; Letter, from the chief editor of the *Ciné-Journal Suisse* to the ICRC President, 12 August 1943, Archives of the International Committee (ACICR), B G 58/807 III.
17. Cornu, *Le Comité international de la Croix-Rouge et le cinéma*, 31.
18. This is precisely the case for the film *Inter Arma Caritas,* which was requested by several Red Cross Societies; Letter, from Georges Dunand to the National Societies of the Red Cross, Red Crescent and Red Lion with Sun, 1 October 1948, ACICR, B G 58/821. Some films were also requested for private projections for schools or churches.
19. Letter, from Central-Film AG Zurich to the ICRC, 6 September 1943, ACICR, B G 58/808/IV.

20. It took also two years to produce this documentary: ACICR, B AG 58/808/VI.
21. ACICR, B G 58/809/VII. Conversely, the production *Car le sang coule encore !* (*Blood is Still Being Shed!,* 1958) needed 'only' 10 per cent of the 1958 ICRC budget for the publications, information and documentation sector; *Rapport d'activité 1958.* 1959. Geneva: CICR, 68.
22. For instance, the film *Une voie reste ouverte* brought in a revenue of 5,500 Swiss francs, that is to say less than a quarter of its total costs; ACICR, B AG 58/808/IV.
23. See *Dixième Conférence internationale de la Croix-Rouge tenue à Genève du 30 mars au 7 avril. Compte rendu.* 1921. Geneva: ICRC, 235–36. The International Conferences of the Red Cross gather representatives of the recognized National Red Cross and Red Crescent Societies and representatives of the states that have ratified the Geneva Conventions.
24. Cornu, *Le comité international de la Croix-Rouge et le cinéma,* 22.
25. A modus vivendi between both organizations was found in 1928. On the ICRC–League 'conflict', see I. Herrmann, 'Décrypter la concurrence humanitaire: le conflit entre Croix-Rouge(s) après 1918', *Relations internationales* 151 (2012), 91–102.
26. This film was screened three times during the 17th International Conference of the Red Cross, in its French, English and Spanish versions: ACICR, A PV, séance du Bureau du 11 août 1948 à 9h30. Significant financial resources were invested in this documentary, leading to overspending. Two Swiss distributors (Columbus Film, Condor Film) agreed to distribute *Inter Arma Caritas* internationally: ACICR, A PV, séance du Bureau du jeudi 9 septembre 1948 à 9h30.
27. The films were *Tous frères!* (*All Brothers*) and *Croix-Rouge par-delà les frontières* (*Red Cross beyond Frontiers*).
28. For more information on this film, see Meier and Palmieri, 'Les équivoques du cinéma humanitaire'.
29. Being the first film production company in postwar Germany, DEFA had been created in 1946 in the Soviet Zone of Occupation and became the official state-owned film studio when the GDR was founded in 1949.
30. The Director was Karl (Carl) von Barany and the camera operator was Bruno Timm.
31. During the same period, the Italian director Roberto Rossellini was shooting his film *Germania, anno zero.*
32. See the chapter by Paul Betts in this volume.
33. ACICR, A PV, séance du Bureau du mercredi 31 mars 1948 à 9h30. See also Meier and Palmieri, 'Les équivoques du cinéma humanitaire', 72–74.
34. For instance, the USSR (and the others European communist states) boycotted the 17th International Conference of the Red Cross held in Stockholm in 1948 – the first conference organised after the Second World War – because the ICRC was one of the organizers. The USSR accused the ICRC of not having denounced the 'fascist crimes' and the violations of the Geneva and The Hague Conventions committed by Nazi Germany; *Dix-septième Conférence internationale de la Croix-Rouge. Compte rendu.* Stockholm: Boktryckeriet P.A Nordstedt & Söner, 1952, 31.
35. On a similar debate in Britain on German victims, see M. Frank, 'The New Morality: Victor Gollancz, "Save Europe Now" and the German Refugee Crisis, 1945–46', *Twentieth Century British History* 17(2) (2006), 230–56; M. Frank, 'Working for the Germans: British Voluntary Societies and the German Refugee Crisis, 1945–50', *Historical Research* 82(215) (2009), 157–75; J.-D. Steinert, 'Food and the Food Crisis in Post-War Germany, 1945–1948: British Policy and the Role of British NGOs', in J. Flemming and F. Trent-

mann (eds), *Food and Conflict in Europe in the Age of the Two World Wars* (Basingstoke: Palgrave Macmillan, 2006), 266–88.

36. On how the ICRC confronted the lack of empathy for German victims, see D. Palmieri and F. Kahn Mohammad, 'Des morts et des nus: le regard du CICR sur la malnutrition extrême (1940–1950)', in R. Dickason (ed.), *Mémoires croisées autour des deux guerres mondiales* (Paris: Mares & Martin, 2012), 85–104.

37. The same applies to the ICRC published photos, which generally show ICRC delegates at work and/or the ICRC logo.

38. The two ICRC films on Congo (*S.O.S Congo* and *Opération Congo,* both 1960) are symptomatic of this kind of perception.

39. See, for instance, some articles published in the *Bulletin international de la Croix-Rouge,* a periodical edited by the ICRC since 1869. It emphasized the lack of civilizational standards in certain cultures (Africa and China), which prevented them from respecting the humanitarian principles of the Red Cross. Other peoples, like the Turks, were criticized for their supposedly atavistic cruelty, especially against Christians. On this topic, see I. Herrmann and D. Palmieri, 'Humanitaire et massacres : l'exemple du CICR (1904–1995)', in J. Sémelin, C. Andrieu and S. Gensburger (eds), *La résistance aux génocides : de la pluralité des actes de sauvetage* (Paris: Presses de Sciences Po, 2008), 235–45.

40. For instance, *Yémen, terre de souffrance,* 1964.

41. See T. Hentsch, *Face au blocus : La Croix-Rouge internationale dans le Nigéria en guerre (1967–1970).* Geneva: Institut Universitaire des Hautes Etudes internationales, 1973.

Bibliography

Cabannes, B. *The Great War and the Origins of Humanitarianism, 1918–1924.* Cambridge: Cambridge University Press, 2014.

Cornu, M. *Le Comité international de la Croix-Rouge et le cinéma au lendemain de la Seconde Guerre mondiale.* Lausanne: Université de Lausanne, 2006.

Frank, M. 'The New Morality: Victor Gollancz, "Save Europe Now" and the German Refugee Crisis, 1945–46'. *Twentieth Century British History* 17(2) (2006), 230–56.

———. 'Working for the Germans: British Voluntary Societies and the German Refugee Crisis, 1945–50'. *Historical Research* 82(215) (2009), 157–75.

Hébert, C. 'The Other Side of the Country: Filming the Human Experience of War', in D. Mazurana, K. Jacobsen and L. Andrews Gale (eds), *Research Methods in Conflict Settings: A View from below* (Cambridge: Cambridge University Press, 2013), 27–55.

Hentsch, T. *Face au blocus: La Croix-Rouge internationale dans le Nigéria en guerre (1967–1970).* Geneva: Institut Universitaire des Hautes Etudes internationales, 1973.

Herrmann, I. 'Décrypter la concurrence humanitaire: le conflit entre Croix-Rouge(s) après 1918'. *Relations internationales* 151 (2012), 91–102.

Herrmann, I., and S. Maulini. 'Un nouveau cinéma muet? Décrypter les non-dits d'*Inter Arma Caritas*'. *Revue du Ciné-club universitaire* (2015), hors-série, Geneva: University of Geneva, 11–14.

Herrmann, I., and D. Palmieri. 'Humanitaire et massacres: l'exemple du CICR (1904–1995)', in J. Sémelin, C. Andrieu and S. Gensburger (eds), *La résistance aux génocides: de la pluralité des actes de sauvetage* (Paris: Presses de Sciences Po, 2008), 235–45.

Meier, M. 'Note sur *Une voie reste ouverte*'. *Revue du Ciné-club universitaire* (2015), hors-série, Geneva: University of Geneva, 15–19.

Meier, M., and D. Palmieri. 'Les équivoques du cinéma humanitaire: L'exemple D'*Helft Helfen* (1948)', in C. Delporte et al. (eds), *La guerre après la guerre: Images et constructions des imaginaires dans l'Europe du XXe siècle* (Paris: Nouveau Monde Éditions, 2009), 65–79.

Natale, E. 'Quand l'humanitaire commençait à faire son cinéma : les films du CICR des années 1920'. *International Review of the Red Cross* 854 (2004), 415–37.

Palmieri, D., and F. Kahn Mohammad. 'Des morts et des nus : le regard du CICR sur la malnutrition extrême (1940–1950)', in R. Dickason (ed.), *Mémoires croisées autour des deux guerres mondiales* (Paris: Mares & Martin, 2012), 85–104.

Paulmann, J. 'The Dilemmas of Humanitarian Aid: Historical Perspectives', in Johannes Paulmann (ed.), *Dilemmas of the Humanitarian Aid in the Twentieth Century* (Oxford: Oxford University Press, 2016), 1–31.

Piana, F. 'Photography, Cinema, and the Quest for Influence: The International Committee of the Red Cross in the Wake of the First World War', in H. Fehrenbach and D. Rodogno (eds), *Humanitarian Photography: A History* (New York: Cambridge University Press, 2015), 140–64.

Steinert, J.-D. 'Food and the Food Crisis in Post-War Germany, 1945–1948: British Policy and the Role of British NGOs', in J. Flemming and F. Trentmann (eds), *Food and Conflict in Europe in the Age of the Two World Wars* (Basingstoke: Palgrave Macmillan, 2006), 266–88.

Straumann, L. *L'humanitaire mis en scène : La cinématographie du CICR des années 1920*. Geneva: CICR, 2000.

4

'People Who Once were Human Beings Like You and Me'

Why Allied Atrocity Films of Liberated
Nazi Concentration Camps in 1944–46
Maximized the Horror and Universalized the Victims

Ulrike Weckel

Using film footage of victims to enlighten the public about German crimes against humanity after the liberation of concentration camps seems a matter of course. Before that, the Western world knew, and could have known, about Nazi Germany's systematic enslavement and mass murder of Jews and other groups only from words written or spoken by witnesses. But many had preferred not to believe the witnesses, to assume they were exaggerating or at least not to take their warnings seriously enough to take action (or even consider what that might mean). All the more, then, did the sensory impressions overwhelm Western Allied troops when they came across a much larger number of camps than expected in which conditions were much worse than imagined.[1] The films (and photographs) army cameramen shot in the camps were intended to convey eyewitnesses' shock to the rest of the world and decisively end any remaining disbelief or indifference. Thus, these images not only informed their viewers; they also carried a moral message. In contrast to usual interpretations of humanitarian pictures showing 'victims', the primary message of these images was not that the pitiful survivors depicted needed immediate help; before all else, they carried an indictment and aroused shame. They indicted all who had participated in genocide, mistreatment and organized neglect, and they shamed those who had condoned these crimes, especially when they had lived next to camps and now claimed not to have known about them.[2] But they also had the potential – as far as viewers were open to such a reading – to shame the Allied nations who had come too late to prevent the worst and all who had disbelieved or downplayed witnesses' earlier reports.

The Allied documentaries compiled from this liberation footage, which moralized – implicitly through imagery or explicitly through narration – at the time when they were shown, have themselves come under moralizing criticism in the last thirty years. In this chapter, I want to respond to two prevalent reproaches. The first is that images of heaps of naked corpses, emaciated bodies, shaved heads and inmates hovering on the edge between life and death, often referred to as 'walking skeletons', perpetuate the dehumanization to which those depicted had been subjected. The Allied atrocity films, which themselves pile horror on top of horror according to critics, fail to identify or individualize those they portray; they do not 'give the victims a voice'. On the contrary, they expose them as passive, helpless and stripped of their humanity.[3] The second reproach is that the narration in none of these films describes the mass murder of Jews as the Nazis' central crime.[4] If they mention Jews at all, then it is only in the course of listing victimized groups, thereby ignoring the singularity of the Nazis' attempted annihilation of the Jewish 'race', as the Nazis put it. Both claims raise important issues, to be sure, but – as is often the case with moralizing arguments – both fail to understand the historical situation in which these films were compiled and intended to affect their different audiences. In what follows, therefore, I will historicize the Allied atrocity films of 1944–46 in response to these two issues discussed by the later-born.

Maximizing the Horror

It is true that the Allied atrocity films pile horror upon horror.[5] Though they differ from one another more than their later critics are aware, they are all full of gruesome examples of the effects of humiliation and dehumanization. Yet, this is what the filmmakers deliberately chose to do. They focused on these effects because most viewers at the time were not yet aware of the extent of Nazi brutality and some had even doubted reports of it. Several films show similar dreadful scenes at different locations, suggesting that horrendous crimes had been perpetrated in all of these places indiscriminately. As the American prosecutor at Nuremberg, who introduced the film *Nazi Concentration Camps* to the courtroom, phrased it: 'This film . . . represents in a brief and unforgettable form an explanation of what the words "concentration camp" imply.'[6] At this early stage, the intention in screening atrocity films was to get people to grasp the scope of what had happened and not to differentiate – among different camps, different phases of persecution or the different fates of victims. And, in order to show audiences the extent to which German perpetrators had degraded and dehumanized their victims, filmmakers deliberately portrayed the worst effects of this dehumanization so as not to risk downplaying the conditions that the liberators of camps had discovered in them. This decision of the filmmakers was in accord with the dope sheets that cameramen sent back with their footage to explain what it showed.[7] In them, they noted that their pictures could not reveal the full horror: the stench, which many described as even worse than what they saw, was not recordable, as were the sounds, since combat cameramen hardly ever carried sound equipment.

This leads us to ask about the kinds of footage from which filmmakers could choose. Literally 'giving a voice to the victims' was indeed difficult without sound. And the few statements from liberated inmates, recorded on synchronous sound film, which they apparently had prepared and about which later critics seem not to know, might not satisfy those critics' need for representations of 'victims' agency' (see Figures 4.1 and 4.2).[8] More powerful in this respect is a long sequence of burials at Bergen Belsen, also filmed with sound by a British newsreel crew, in which one can hear and see survivors cursing the SS guards who were forced to drag typhus-ridden corpses to mass graves with their bare hands. Clips from this material, however, only made it into the British film *German Concentration Camps Factual Survey*, which was not finished at the time.[9] The narration planned for the sequence was: 'The faces of the bystanders showed just a little of the hate that Germany has inspired – and some of the anguish too'[10] (see Figure 4.3). We can only speculate about whether other filmmakers had access to that

Figure 4.1. American prisoner of war Lt. Jack Taylor testifies at Mauthausen. American Army's liberation footage of Mauthausen, 1945. Accessed at the US Holocaust Memorial Museum, courtesy of National Archives & Records Administration.

Figure 4.2. Jewish medical doctor Hadassah (Ada) Bimko testifies at Bergen Belsen. British liberation footage from Bergen Belsen, shot by British Movietone, 1945. Photo: © IWM, still from film A70 514/97.

newsreel footage and, perhaps, decided against using it because they did not want to create the impression that unruly former concentration camp inmates now sought revenge. It is certain, though, that filmmakers did not prioritize footage that showed survivors in such active roles.

It is also true that at least Western Allied cameramen were not committed to noting victims' names or finding out about their stories. Apparently, the conditions they discovered in the camps gave them other priorities. The abundance of corpses seems to have been more important to them, and that was easier to document on film than the fates of individuals. Moreover, it was precisely inmates' individuality that appeared to have been wiped out. It is not surprising, then, that liberators, feeling estranged from or even disgusted by this 'strange simian throng, who crowded to the barbed wire fences', as one of them phrased his impression,[11] did not think to ask for and record individuals' stories. The strategy of Soviet filmmakers differed in this respect. Already since the end of 1941, when they had filmed the evidence of German war crimes against Russian civilians and prisoners of war in reconquered Soviet territory, it had been their habit to search out family members, preferably elderly mothers or grandmothers, of those killed; they took them to the crime scenes and had them identify and bewail their dead for the camera.[12] This emotional filmic representation was supported by a com-

Figure 4.3. Survivors at Bergen Belsen curse SS guards forced to carry corpses. British liberation footage from Bergen Belsen, shot by British Movietone, 1945. Photo: © IWM, still from film A70 514/98.

mentary that claimed that the Soviet people ('we') would not forgive or forget such barbarous crimes. Another device to mobilize outrage and the population's support for the costly war effort was that a film's narrator would give the names of victims that the camera singled out from larger groups of bodies as emblematic of the wider Soviet suffering.[13] While the strategy of showing mourning family members could no longer be followed when the Red Army's cameramen got to Majdanek and Auschwitz, the Soviet films on the liberations of these two death camps still attempted to present victims as individuals with names, families, home towns and professions.[14]

The main subject matter of atrocity films was German crimes against humanity or, more precisely, the results of those crimes that Allied troops had found on their advance towards and into Germany. This is why in internal memos the films were often labelled 'atrocity film' – they were not intended to memorialize the victims of the Holocaust. Films that did seek to do that were made later, and they seem to have shaped the expectations of later-born critics of the original Allied atrocity films. Since there was no Nazi footage documenting Germans in the act of committing their crimes, which the Allies could have seized and released as definitive proof,[15] images of victims in camps abandoned by the SS were the next best thing. Whenever the Allies did get hold of SS guards, as in Bergen-Belsen, they exposed them to the camera, and the resulting footage was included in all of the atrocity films.[16]

Only in a few liberated camps did army film units stay longer than a day or two. In Bergen-Belsen, in particular, British cameramen took the time to film the clean-up efforts and aiding survivors: medical help; the installation of showers; the burning of lice-infested barracks; survivors choosing from among clothes confiscated from Germans; and children receiving a nourishing meal followed by a piece of chocolate, singing with a kindergarten teacher and playing with toys. In the unfinished film *German Concentration Camps Factual Survey,* these hopeful scenes are set in brutal contrast to others showing dead and dying inmates for whom rescue had come too late. Had it been completed and screened around the time of the first anniversary of VE Day as planned, it would have been the only Allied film to arrange its footage into a story rather than stringing together horrific sights, one more disturbing than the next, as an exercise in the pedagogy of shock.[17] The film starts with excerpts from German newsreels showing the Nazis gaining popular support and power, then tries to explain the function of concentration camps for the Nazi regime and tells how British soldiers entering the pretty village of Belsen in April 1945 noticed a terrible smell and, step by step, discovered the catastrophe in the camp. Viewers are taken by the hand cinematically and guided through the camp as they look over the shoulders of British soldiers and rescue workers. In its second half, the film places Bergen-Belsen in amongst eleven other camps, beginning with a relatively mild labour camp, proceeding to larger and larger concentration camps and, finally, coming to the extermination camps in Poland. The film was supposed to conclude with footage of Germans who had been forced to visit a camp near their town right after its liberation. Accordingly, the film was intended to tell a didactic story of the 'journey' the Germans had embarked on when they applauded Hitler and that ended with their shameful confrontation with the consequences of their previous behaviour[18] – a confrontation that the viewing of such atrocity films by other Germans, who were not so located, was meant to replace.

Although Germans were the most important target group of the atrocity films and this influenced the type of film produced, we must consider one further aspect of the maximization of horror. Part of the discomfort we feel when watching atrocity footage today stems from the fact that the dead and the apathetic survivors, many of them naked and in extreme misery, seemed to have no chance to object to being filmed.[19] Critics of the films therefore often represent themselves as the victims' advocates. However, this role is entirely self-appointed. As far as I have seen, there is no evidence from the time of liberation that survivors protested against or expressed unease with the documentation of their misery.[20] On the contrary, they often volunteered to re-enact SS torture procedures for Allied visitors and cameramen.[21] In several memoirs, survivors tell how SS men had fuelled their despair by saying that even if they survived, nobody would ever believe their testimony.[22] The Nazis had counted on their unprecedented crimes exceeding human imagination, and liberated prisoners were eager to prove to liberators that camp conditions had been much worse before their arrival. Former concentration camp inmates who, as POWs in British custody, saw an atrocity film complained that it did not document inmates' suffering when the camp was in operation.[23] One such critic suggested replacing the film's musical score with the screams of people being tortured.[24] And, finally, some freed concentration camp inmates later went to the cinema to watch an atrocity film. The screenings of *Die Todesmühlen,* the 20-minute-long American atrocity film, produced for German audiences and shown all over the American zone of occupation for one week in early 1946, were particularly well attended in venues close to Displaced Persons (DP) camps.[25] Also, the fact that a Yiddish narration was produced suggests that there was a demand.

Universalizing the Victims

The allegation made by critics that none of the Allied atrocity films represents the extermination of European Jewry as the Nazi regime's central crime or represents Jews as a special, particularly numerous victim group is also correct. Yet, it would be rash to suspect Allied filmmakers of anti-Semitism. To be sure, each Allied nation had its anti-Semites, some of whom were part of the government, and other government members were careful not to act in ways that would play into the hands of anti-Semites or make themselves appear in their eyes to be 'Jew-lovers'. There may have been a thin line between the fear of mobilizing anti-Semitism and anti-Semitism itself. However, answering the question why the British, Americans, French and Soviets did not stress Jewish victimhood in their atrocity films needs historical investigation.

The allegation may well be correct in the Soviet case. We know today that Red Army cameramen[26] filmed scenes at Majdanek and Auschwitz that unambiguously showed that victims were Jewish; among them was a shot of heaped prayer shawls in an Auschwitz barrack in which the SS had sorted and stacked everything they had taken from deportees (see Figure 4.4).[27] In the end, almost none of this footage made it into any of the Soviet films and when it did, the clip was cut in a way that obscured the victims' Jewishness.[28] This editing was probably motivated by anti-Semitism, which was on the rise again in 1945 and would soon prompt thousands of Jews who had survived the Holocaust in the Soviet Union to flee, some of them to the American Zone of Occupation in Germany. The narrations of the three Soviet films dealing with Nazi camps in Eastern Europe that were screened in the West speak of 'victims from all occupied countries of Europe' and list most of these countries, stressing that the Red Army had liberated their imprisoned citizens. Two of these films mention Jews once as among the many nationalities.[29] Named victims are also identified by their nationality or their city of residence – for example, 'Dr. Bruno Sigismund Fischer, specialist of neurology from Prague'.[30] A viewer might guess from his name that he was Jewish; however, what the film stresses here is that Fischer and three other

Figure 4.4. Jewish prayer shawls taken from deportees at Auschwitz. Soviet footage of the liberation of Auschwitz, 1945. Courtesy of the Russian State Documentary Film and Photo Archive (RGAKFD).

named survivors, all filmed in striped uniforms, were members of Europe's intelligentsia. The narrations of the films that the Soviets had already screened to their own population before the end of the war both 'Russified' or, more generally, 'Slavized' victims and individualized them in an effort to stir up their audiences emotionally and mobilize them behind the war effort, with its high casualties, despite the widespread unpopularity of the Soviet regime conducting the war.[31]

Jews do not figure more prominently among the victims in the Western Allies' films. The narrations of these films also speak of victims from all across Europe, and most also list victims by nationality at some point.[32] I refer to the seven films that were screened to German audiences at the time and produced with those audiences,[33] or the trial of German war criminals, in mind. Four of the seven do not mention Jews at all.[34] The other three mention them only in passing. Twice Jews are referred to together with Lutherans and Catholics, suggesting that Jews should be thought of as a religious group. The unfinished British film planned to introduce Jewish victims when commenting on the mass graves at Bergen-Belsen: 'We shall never know who they were or from what homes they were torn. Whether they were Catholics, Lutherans, or Jews, we only know they were born, they suffered and died in agony in Belsen camp. And so they lie, Jews, Lutherans and Catholics – indistinguishable cheek-to-cheek in a common grave.' One might take this to suggest that all three groups were persecuted for their faith and with equal ruthlessness, but that would be inaccurate. Another reading, however, is that religious distinctions disappear with death or, possibly, were already erased in this case by shared subjection to Nazi persecution. The second time Jews are explicitly mentioned is in *Die Todesmühlen* in which they are referred to as a religious group when considering survivors as such: 'Members of all European nations, Russians, Poles, Frenchmen, Belgians, Yugoslavians, Germans, Czechs; members of all faiths, Protestants, Catholics, Jews; thousands who had suffered unspeakably . . . celebrated the day of liberation.' However, later in the film, when considering the Nazis' reasons for persecution, Jews are listed as a nationality: 'They [the dead] were murdered because they would hold fast to their religion, their faith, others because they did not want to become Nazis, because they were Russians, Poles, Belgians, Frenchmen, Czechs or Jews, because they had been denounced by their own neighbors.' The reason for this dual classification may have been that survivors were supposed to be repatriated, and Jewish survivors, unlike Russians, Czechs and Poles, had no state to which they could return.[35] But too little is known about the composition of the narration to do more than suggest.[36] However, more often than they differentiate victim groups, as in the previous quotations, narrators describe inmates as 'political prisoners' or 'fighters against National Socialism', and they regularly mention that these included Germans. But before we consider the possible didactic purposes of marginalizing Jewish victims as such and stressing political opposition, we should consider which camps the Western Allies liberated and whom they found there.

The Red Army liberated the Majdanek and Auschwitz extermination camps in Poland. Here Jews were the majority of the hundreds of thousands of dead and of the several hundred survivors that the SS had left behind when evacuating the stronger inmates westwards. However, the Western Allied troops who did not encounter any extermination camps discovered Jewish prisoners only in some of the larger camps within the German Reich in which the SS had dumped the survivors of their evacuation transports from the East, especially Buchenwald and Bergen-Belsen.[37] The latter was the only camp liberated by the Western Allies in which Jews were the majority of the inmate population at the time of liberation.[38] Thus, much of the footage in their atrocity films did indeed show camps in which no or hardly any Jews had been liberated, but mostly Russian and Polish forced labourers in small work camps and subcamps, and mostly political opponents of the Nazi regime in concentration camps. When listing victims' nationalities in their narrations, filmmakers may have simply repeated what liberators had found in extant camp registration lists or what survivors had told them. A bigger picture of the Nazi crimes still had to be put together. Visually, it is true that Jews do not appear as such. But in retrospect, it is hard to tell whether it would have been possible for Western cameramen to shoot footage showing – by stars on prisoners' uniforms, for example – that victims were Jews and persecuted as such. Either way, the images that predominate are of crowds of indistinguishable, miserable creatures who barely look human any longer, but, rather, like a species of their own. Thus, the films' narrators regularly remind viewers that the depicted subjects are human beings. '[M]any years of debasing imprisonment broke these people in body and soul, degraded them to animals', the narrator of *Todesmühlen* remarks. 'And yet, they once were human beings like you and me.'[39]

Reaffirming victims' humanity underscored the scandal of their dehumanization and at the same time reconnected them to film viewers, the vast majority of whom were Gentile. After years of insufficient international concern for the people interned in Nazi camps, filmmakers seem to have felt a need to mobilize viewers' empathy by stressing that they too could have been targeted. Therefore, most narrations mentioned German victims. The producers of *British Movietone News* used the same device for their British viewers, getting them to envision how they could have ended up in similar circumstances. In the episode *Atrocities – The Evidence,* the narrator comments during a shot of the last Belsen commandant, the coarse-looking Josef Kramer: 'And the SS commandant – a thing called Kramer – you may have seen its photograph in the papers. If the Hun had invaded Britain, *this* might have had [the] power to torture and to starve any one of us. Yes, such atrocities might have been inflicted on the people of these islands. They *were* inflicted on the people in Belsen. Thousands upon thousands perished.'[40]

When we bear in mind that the Western Allies produced most of their atrocity films in order to confront postwar Germans with Nazi crimes, they appear in a new light. Mentioning Jewish victims merely in passing and stressing political opposition as the cause for incarceration in a concentration camp conveyed a multilayered message to German audiences. First, Germans expected the Western Allies to accuse them of attempting to annihilate the Jews. Since 1944, Nazi propaganda had stopped denying Allied charges of the mass murder of Jews in Eastern Europe and had begun its attempt to turn German citizens into accomplices by letting them know just enough.[41] In order to induce them to fight to the very end, a propaganda of fear warned Germans that the Allies' revenge would be cruel. Accordingly, by not addressing the mass murder of Jews in particular, atrocity films bypassed Germans' expectations and avoided making the reproach against which many might have immunized themselves. (By the way, my study of reception clearly shows that German viewers identified the victims depicted in these films as Jews despite filmmakers' lack of explicitness.) And, second, the characterization of camp inmates as 'political prisoners' and 'fighters against National Socialism' also took German viewers' expected responses into account. Along with the claim 'not to have known', the Allies constantly heard the excuse that it had been impossible to oppose the Nazi regime. Often, it seems, the same person made both pleas, which led to the sarcastic recommendation of some occupiers to make up one's mind about which of the two contradictory pleas one wanted to make.[42] Narrators' claims that Germans had been among those who opposed the regime undermined the credibility of both excuses.

A closer look at the reasons that Western Allied filmmakers may have had in 1945 for not making more than passing reference to Jews shows that, rather than being anti-Semitic, they were trying to undermine the anti-Semitism of contemporary German audiences. By not stressing what the Germans already knew and were probably ashamed of, filmmakers avoided making exactly the accusation that Germans were awaiting and were prepared to reject. That the decision not to highlight Jewish victimhood might have been far-sighted is suggested by a survey that the American Office of War Information's Surveys Unit conducted of 821 German prisoners of war (POWs) in July 1945 in order to measure the effects of their viewing of an atrocity film.[43] In this anonymous survey, two groups of approximately the same size were matched in terms of education, age and branch of military service. Each respondent was asked to state whether or not he had trusted in 'the Führer' until the end of the war. In one group everybody had watched the film *KZ*; in the other, nobody had.[44] One of the questions was intended to reveal whether watching the atrocity film had reduced a viewer's anti-Semitism. The POWs were asked which of the following three statements they agreed with in general: (a) 'The measures taken against the Jews were in no way justified'; (b) 'Hitler went too far in his handling of the Jews, but something had to be done to keep them in bounds'; or (c) 'The Jews got what they deserved from Hitler'. A relatively small number of respondents (twenty) agreed with (c). What is striking is that sixteen of these had recently seen *KZ*, and of them thirteen had declared that they had had faith in Hitler until the war's end.[45] One interpretation of this result is that among formerly avid supporters of National Socialism, Allied confrontation with the Jewish victims of German crimes provoked defiant declarations of loyalty to the regime's anti-Semitic ideology in order to express their unyieldingness to what they considered to be Allied propaganda.

Yet, the Western Allies' reluctance to represent Jews as the central victim group seems to have been motivated not just by strategic considerations of Germans' reception. Each Allied nation had its own reasons for not stressing the victimization of Jews specifically. The British were particularly concerned not to use Nazi concepts, in this case their categorization of Jews as a 'race'. With their concept of 'citoyens', the French meant to transcend national-ethnic allegiances, such as being Jewish. And the Americans focused on individuals and the rights of individuals, not on their membership in collectives. Preoccupied in this way, they failed to realize that Jews had been subjected to persecution specifically as a 'race', that most had had their citizenships revoked before they were murdered and that their human rights as individuals did not secure their protection since there was no authority, like a 'human-wide' state, to secure it. Humans need, as Hannah Arendt put it, 'the right to have rights', a right that is only granted by being a member of a political community.[46]

And yet, universalizing as such is not anti-Semitic. Moreover, in 1945, it could have been intended as an intelligent strategy against anti-Semitism. However, the consequence was a failure to grasp or – for different reasons – a refusal to stress the centrality of the Shoah. Alternatively, maybe the Western Allies had failed to grasp the special targeting of Jews and thus their atrocity films did not pay special attention to Jewish victims. That, in turn, may have had the unintended but fortuitous consequence of not triggering the 'allergic' reaction of contemporary German audiences to having the fate of the Jews brought up yet again.

To conclude, historizing the Allies' atrocity films reveals that the suspicions of later-born critics that cameramen and filmmakers were insensitive to victims' dignity (or, at least, were not as sensitive as they – the critics themselves – are) or acted out of anti-Semitism in universalizing the Nazis' victims are unfounded. Both charges should be reconfigured, and then considered, as questions. First, do we still need to show these by now well-known images, which do indeed reproduce the dehumanization of their subjects (and if we do, then to whom and why)? Second, how should the narration of such footage explain Nazi crimes so as not to oversimplify a complex phenomenon? After all, historians have studied it intensively since 1945, when the original narrations were written.

Ulrike Weckel is Professor for History in the Media and in the Public at the Justus Liebig University in Gießen. Her research interests include the postwar dealings with the Nazi past, film history, reception studies and the gender history of the European Enlightenment. Among her recent publications are *Beschämende Bilder: Deutsche Reaktionen auf alliierte Dokumentarfilme über befreite Konzentrationslager* (2012); 'Shamed by Nazi Crimes: The First Step towards Germans' Reeducation or a Catalyst for Their Wish to Forget?', in Stephanie Bird et al. (eds), *Reverberations of Nazi Violence in Germany and Beyond: Disturbing Pasts* (2016) and 'Watching the Accused Watch the Results of Nazi Crimes: Observers' Reports on the Atrocity Film Screenings in the Belsen, Nuremberg, and Eichmann Trials', *London Review of International Law* (2018). She is *WerkstattGeschichte*'s film review editor (http://www.werkstattgeschichte.de).

Notes

1. R.H. Abzug, *Inside the Vicious Heart: Americans and the Liberation of Nazi Concentration Camps* (New York: Oxford University Press, 1985); B. Flanagan and D. Bloxham (eds), *Remembering Belsen: Eyewitnesses Record the Liberation* (London: Valentine Mitchell, 2005). More liberators' recollections are available online through the Visual History Archive of the USC Shoah Foundation.
2. For the argument in detail, see my book: U. Weckel, *Beschämende Bilder: Deutsche Reaktionen auf alliierte Dokumentarfilme über befreite Konzentrationslager* (Stuttgart: Franz Steiner, 2012); for a summary, see U. Weckel, 'Shamed by Nazi Crimes: The First Step towards Germans' Reeducation or a Catalyst for Their Wish to Forget?', in S. Bird et al. (eds), *Reverberations of Nazi Violence in Germany and Beyond: Disturbing Pasts* (London: Bloomsbury Academics, 2016), 33–46.
3. S.L. Carruthers, 'Compulsory Viewing: Concentration Camp Film and German Re-education', *Millennium: Journal of International Studies* 30(3) (2001), 733–59, at 742; B.J. Hahn, *Umerziehung durch Dokumentarfilm? Ein Instrument amerikanischer Kulturpolitik im Nachkriegsdeutschland (1945–1953)* (Münster: LIT Verlag, 1997), 108f.; S. Kramer,

'Nacktheit in Holocaust-Fotos und -Filmen', in S. Kramer (ed.), *Die Shoah im Bild* (Munich: edition text + kritik, 2003), 225–48; C.J. Picart and J.G. McKahan, 'Visualizing the Holocaust in Gothic Terms: The Ideology of U.S. Signal Corps Cinematography', in C.J. Picart (ed.), *The Holocaust Film Soucebook* (Westport: Praeger, 2004), 2 vols, 508–15.

4. D. Culbert, 'American Film Policy in the Re-education of Germany and Her Allies after World War II', in N. Pronay and K. Wilson (eds), *The Political Re-education of Germany and Her Allies after World War II* (London: Croom Helm, 1985), 173–95, at 180; D.E. Lipstadt, *Beyond Belief: The American Press and the Coming of the Holocaust 1933–1945* (New York: Free Press, 1986), 250–63; T. Kushner, *The Holocaust and the Liberal Imagination: A Social and Cultural History* (Oxford: Blackwell, 1994), 205–25; T. Kushner, 'The Memory of Belsen', in J. Reilly et al. (eds), *Belsen in History and Memory* (London: Cass, 1997), 181–205, at 187–89; J. Reilly, *Belsen: The Liberation of the Concentration Camp* (London: Routledge, 1998), 77; L. Douglas, *The Memory of Judgment. Making Law and History in the Trials of the Holocaust* (New Haven: Yale University Press, 2001), 11–37; Carruthers, 'Compulsory Viewing', 744–47; D. Bloxham, *Genocide on Trial: War Crimes Trials and the Formation of Holocaust History and Memory* (Oxford: Oxford University Press, 2001), 81f.; J.K. Olick, *In the House of the Hangman: The Agonies of German Defeat, 1943–1949* (Chicago: University of Chicago Press, 2005), 102; C.S. Goldstein, *Capturing the German Eye: American Visual Propaganda in Occupied Germany* (Chicago: University of Chicago Press, 2009), 55. In relation to the Soviet films, see S. Liebman, 'Documenting the Liberation of the Camps: The Case of Aleksander Ford's *Vernichtungslager Majdanek–Cmentarzysko Europy* (1944)', in D. Herzog (ed.), *Lessons and Legacies VII: The Holocaust in International Perspective* (Evanston: Northwestern University Press, 2006), 333–51; J. Hicks, 'From Atrocity to Action: How Soviet Cinema Initiated the Holocaust Film: Imagining the Unimaginable in a Soviet Context', in S. Bardgett et al. (eds), *Justice, Politics and Memory in Europe after the Second World War: Landscapes after the Battle* (London: Valentine Mitchell, 2011), 249–66; J. Hicks, *First Films of the Holocaust: Soviet Cinema and the Genocide of the Jews, 1938–1946* (Pittsburgh: University of Pittsburgh Press, 2012), 157–210.

5. I have analysed all of the Allied atrocity films that were screened (or, in one case, supposed to be screened) in Germany in 1945–46: *Atrocities – The Evidence* (*British Movietone News* No. 830); *KZ* (*Welt im Film* No. 5), German version of *Atrocities Found in German Camps*, produced by the U.S. Office of War (OWI); *Maidanek* and *Auschwitz (Oświęcim)*, both produced by the Central Studio for Documentary Film in Moscow; *Les camps de la mort*, produced by the French newsreel production company Actualités Françaises; *Belsen Camp Evidence*, produced for the British prosecution at the Belsen trial; *Nazi Concentration Camps*, produced for the American prosecution at the Nuremberg trial; *Kinodokumenty o zverstvakh nemetsko-fashistskikh zakhvatchikov* (*Filmdocuments of Atrocities Committed by the German-Fascist Invaders*), produced for the Soviet prosecution at Nuremberg; *Deutschland Erwache*, produced by the U.S. Ministry of War; *Die Todesmühlen*, produced by the Office of Military Government for Germany, U.S. (OMGUS); and *German Concentration Camps Factual Survey*, produced by the British Ministry of Information (MOI), which remained unfinished. In addition to these films, footage of camps' liberations was included in various American, British and French newsreels.

6. *Trial of the Major War Criminals before the International Military Tribunal. Nuremberg 14 November 1945–1 October 1946*, 42 volumes, Nuremberg 1947–1949, vol. 2, 264.

7. H. Caven, 'Horror in Our Time: Images of the Concentration Camps in the British Media, 1945', *Historical Journal of Film, Radio and Television*, 21(3) (2001), 205–53,

at 207f, 222f; T. Haggith, 'Filming the Liberation of Bergen-Belsen and its Impact on the Understanding of the Holocaust', *Holocaust Studies. A Journal of Culture and History* 12(1/2) (2005), 89–122.

8. *Nazi Concentration Camps* contains statements from both Lt. Jack Taylor, an American prisoner of war liberated at Mauthausen, and Hadassah (Ada) Bimko, a female doctor liberated at Bergen-Belsen.

9. This film, produced at MOI under the direction of Sidney Bernstein, was supposed to run for about 80 minutes and was the most carefully considered, sophisticated Allied atrocity film. It is not altogether clear why the project was dropped shortly before it was completed. It is certain, though, that in the autumn of 1945, British occupation policy in Germany prioritized reconstruction over re-education because of the poor economic conditions in their zone. Political Intelligence therefore let Bernstein know that there was no hurry to complete the film since it would not be screened before the difficulties of the coming winter were solved. A 55-minute fragment of the film was rediscovered in the 1980s and released under the title *Memory of the Camps*. A team at the Imperial War Museum in London completed and restored the film in 2014. For the story of the film, see Weckel, *Beschämende Bilder*, 130–150; K. Gladstone, 'Separate Intentions: The Allied Screening of Concentration Camp Documentaries in Defeated Germany in 1945–46: *Death Mills* and *Memory of the Camps*', in T. Haggith and J. Newman (eds), *Holocaust and the Moving Image: Representation in Film and Television since 1933* (London: Wallflower, 2005), 50–64, at 60; T. Haggith, 'The 1945 Documentary *German Concentration Camps Factual Survey* and the 70th Anniversary of the Liberation of the Camps', *The Holocaust in History and Memory* 7 (2014), 181–97; and the documentary *Night Will Fall* (United Kingdom, 2014, dir. A. Singer).

10. Proposed Line of Commentary for Film on Concentration Camps. Imperial War Museum, London (IWM), Film Archive, F3080, 3.

11. D. Sington, *Belsen Uncovered* (London: Duckworth, 1964), 16. This expression has often been quoted; only seldom, however, has the rest of what Sington said been: 'the half-credulous cheers of these almost lost men, of these clowns in their terrible motley, who had once been Polish officers, land-workers in the Ukraine, Budapest doctors, and students in France, impelled a stronger emotion, and I had to fight back my tears'.

12. Hicks, *First Films*, 44–78.

13. E.g. commenting on dead civilians in the town of Rostow: 'This is the family of Prof. Rojdetstvensky, tortured. Young Vitia Golovlev, murdered for refusing to give up her pigeon. The wife of the engineer Gordeev, raped, then shot.' *Filmdocuments of Atrocities Committed by the German-Fascist Invaders*, English subtitles. According to Jeremy Hicks, the corpse that a Soviet cameraman filmed with a live pigeon on it had been a sixteen-year-old male member of the resistance, which used carrier pigeons. By omitting the political context, 'Vitia' appears to have been the victim of pure German sadism and a symbol of childlike innocence; Hicks, *First Films*, 51–54.

14. In *Majdanek*, the camera pans over passports: 'Passports of the murder victims: Poles, Russians, Dutch, Frenchmen, Czechs, Serbs, Norwegians, Danes, Greeks: Fontenau, Homère, French, a farmworker, 20 years old; Bruno Cariac, Italian, a preschool teacher; Petrus Josef Jansen, Dutch, electrician, 20 years old; Konstantin Sanikopulos and his sister, Greeks; Irina Leonora Peters, a Polish woman from the town of Radom, 32 years old.' In *Auschwitz (Oświęcim)*, the commentary on the camp's hospital runs: 'The Hungarian Spaul and the Frenchman Valdi were inoculated with leprosy artificially by German doctors. The young Benkel from Hungary had shared his bread ration with his starving

neighbour. For doing so he received a shot in the head from his tormentors.' (The translations from the films' dubbed German are mine.)

15. According to Budd Schulberg, the OSS unit that assembled film footage for the Nuremberg trial eagerly searched for such filmic documentations of Nazi crimes. However, his claim that captured SS men had revealed an underground hiding place, but that Schulberg's crew only arrived as the incriminating films were being set on fire and could only watch them go up in flames is not credible. In old age, Schulberg recounted this adventurous story in several interviews, e.g. in Christian Delage's documentary *Nuremberg: The Nazis Facing Their Crimes* (F 2006).

16. See U. Weckel, '(Ohn)mächtige Wut auf die Täter: Männliches und weibliches KZ-Personal vor den Kameras alliierter Befreier', *Historische Anthropologie* 18(2) (2010), 232–46.

17. Bernstein's team noted in their draft of the film's commentary that it was their intention 'to let the picture tell its own story' and to 'avoid overloading the film with commentary so that the audience may have time to think, and absorb what is hoped will be a dreadful lesson'; Proposed Line of Commentary, front page. Memos show that Bernstein had wanted to give German viewers, for whose re-education the film was made, an even more comprehensive story of the concentration camps, including the involvement of German companies and biographies of SS personnel. However, the necessary footage was not available.

18. The scripted narration was: 'This was the end of the journey they had so confidently begun in 1933. Twelve years? No – in terms of barbarity and brutality they had travelled backwards for twelve thousand years. Unless the world learns the lesson these pictures teach, night will fall. But by God's grace we who live will learn.' Proposed Line of Commentary, 14.

19. Cornelia Brink employs the term 'Fotografien-wider-Willen' (photographs-against-somebody's-will), which the media scholar Susanne Regener coined, and discusses the consequences of the lack of consent for research. C. Brink, 'Vor aller Augen: Fotografien-wider-Willen in der Geschichtsschreibung', *WerkstattGeschichte* 47 (2007), 61–74.

20. Susan Sontag, too, assumes that in general, 'it is victims' interest that their suffering is represented'. S. Sontag, *Regarding the Pain of Others* (New York: Farrar, Straus and Giroux, 2003), 112.

21. Disturbingly realistic is a scene from Breendonck included in *Nazi Concentration Camps*; in *Deutschland erwache* and *Todesmühlen,* instruments of torture are shown to the camera.

22. See, for example, P. Levi, *Survival in Auschwitz: The Nazi Assault on Humanity,* trans. Stuart Woolf (New York: Simon & Schuster, 1996), 60.

23. Some POWs seem to not have understood that the footage only showed camps at the moment of liberation. For example: 'In my opinion the film does not give a complete picture of what was really going on inside KZs. It ought to have shown not only the instruments of tortures but also how the inmates endured them, phase by phase.' Hans O., cited in: Excerpts from Ps/W letters showing the reaction to the German concentration camp atrocities film during the first week of showing (Camp 379), 20 July 1945, 5, the National Archives, Kew (TNA): FO 939/72.

24. 'One prisoner, who had been in a concentration camp himself, suggested that the incidental music might be replaced with the screams of the women and groans of the men being tortured so that others could hear what he had heard daily. Explained to him that this would make it a "faked" film.' Cinema Diary – 306 P/W Camp, Subject: Atrocity Film, 28 July 1945, TNA: FO 939/72.

25. A few days after the screenings of *Todesmühlen* had started in Bavaria, local American intelligence telegrammed to its headquarters that theatres were filled to capacity, adding: 'One movie in district inhabited by DP's had queues for several hours.' As the intelligence summary report a week later summed it up: 'The audiences in many of the theatres were made up primarily of working class people and DPs.' Telegram Hart to Powell and Kinard, 29 January 1946, NARA: RG 260/OMGUS, ICD, MPB, Box 290, Folder: Film Atrocity; Atrocity Film in Bavaria, in Information Control, Intelligence Summary (ICIS) No. 30, 9 February 1946, NARA: RG 260/OMGUS, ICD, MPB, Box 281, Folder: Film, Intelligence Reports.

26. Several of them were Jews. See D. Shneer, *Through Soviet Jewish Eye:. Photography, War, and the Holocaust* (New Brunswick: Rutgers University Press, 2011).

27. Hicks, *First Films,* 171–85, image 177; V. Pozner, A. Sumpf and V. Voisin, 'Que faire des images soviètiques de la Shoah?', *1895. Revue d'histoire du cinéma* 76 (2015), 9–41, at 30, image 33.

28. Hicks, *First Films,* 62–63, at 69.

29. In *Auschwitz (Oświęcim),* earlier photographs of deportees, discovered following the liberation of the camp, are commented upon as follows: 'This is how they looked when they arrived here from all parts of Europe! Poles, Czechs, Hungarians, Jews, Frenchmen, Serbs, Romanians, Belgians.' (This is my translation from the German-dubbed version of the film.) This listing of nationalities is repeated in the *Filmdocuments of Atrocities,* which the Soviet prosecutors presented at the Nuremberg trial.

30. *Auschwitz (Oświęcim).*

31. Hicks, *First Films,* 67, 182.

32. In his recent book, the film scholar John J. Michalczyk falsely claims that 'the British and American footage . . . did not distinguish the ethnicity of the victims'. Unfortunately, this is not the only case in which his publication is out of step with the current state of research. J. Michalczyk, *End of the Holocaust: Allied Documentaries, Nuremberg and the Liberation of the Concentration Camps* (London: Bloomsbury, 2014), 37.

33. Listed in footnote 5.

34. These are the episode *Atrocities – The Evidence* from *British Movietone News, KZ, Deutschland erwache* and *Les camps de la mort.*

35. The British government in particular had no interest in supporting the idea of thinking of Jews as a nation that might now want to found a nation-state in Palestine. See B. Wasserstein, *Britain and the Jews of Europe 1939–1945* (Oxford: Oxford University Press, 1979).

36. Its author was Oskar Seidlin, a Jewish emigre to the United States who had interrupted his university career teaching German literature and language after the United States had entered the war in order to join the Army's Intelligence Division. In Europe, he worked for the secret, black-propaganda radio station 1212, which broadcast into Nazi Germany through the facilities of Radio Luxembourg. H. Burger. 1977. *Der Frühling war es wert: Erinnerungen* (Munich: C. Bertelsmann Verlag), 259; on Seidlin, see also the entry in *Lexikon deutsch-jüdischer Autoren,* 19 vols (Berlin: De Gruyter, 2012), 212–18.

37. J. Bridgman, *The End of the Holocaust: The Liberation of the Camps* (Portland: Areopagitica Press, 1990); D. Stone, *The Liberation of the Camps: The End of the Holocaust and its Aftermath* (New Haven: Yale University Press, 2015).

38. E. Kolb, *Bergen Belsen: Geschichte des 'Aufenthaltslagers' 1943–1945* (Hanover: Verlag für Literatur und Zeitgeschehen, 1962); Reilly, *Belsen.*

39. Later, the narrator repeats: 'That once were human beings, God's children.' And in *KZ* we find the commentary: 'These once were human beings.' These translations from the original German films are mine.

40. The newsreel was produced for a British audience, but this one episode was also shown to Germans, at least in two towns in the British zone, as early as May 1945. Weckel, *Beschämende Bilder*, 364–90.

41. See P. Longerich, *'Davon haben wir nichts gewusst!': Die Deutschen und die Judenverfolgung 1933–1945* (Munich: Siedler, 2006).

42. See e.g. Bassfreund quoted in Stone, *Liberation*, 25f. The notorious contradiction also made it into the feature film *Judgment at Nuremberg* of 1961, when Judge Haywood (Spencer Tracy) points out to the German servant couple, with the telling name 'Halber-stadt' (alluding to 'half of the town'), that their second justification, not to have been able to do anything about concentration camps, does not make sense if their first, not to have known of their existence, is true.

43. OWI Surveys Unit, Report No. 140: German Prisoners' Reactions to a Film on Atrocites, 26 July 1945, NARA: RG 260/OMGUS, ICD, MPB, Box 290, Folder Film Atrocity.

44. A total of 26 per cent of the group who had been confronted with the atrocity film had stated that they had trusted Hitler until the end, in contrast to 15 per cent of the other group, of whom another 7 per cent refused to answer the question (something that only 3 per cent of the first group did).

45. For a more detailed interpretation of this survey, see Weckel, *Beschämende Bilder*, 281f.

46. See, in particular, H. Arendt, *The Origins of Totalitarianism*, 2nd ed. (New York: Meridian Books, 1958), 290–302 ('The Perplexities of the Rights of Men').

Bibliography

Abzug, R.H. *Inside the Vicious Heart: Americans and the Liberation of Nazi Concentration Camps*. New York: Oxford University Press, 1985.

Arendt, H. *The Origins of Totalitarianism*. New York: Meridian Books, 1958.

Bloxham, D. *Genocide on Trial: War Crimes Trials and the Formation of Holocaust History and Memory*. Oxford: Oxford University Press, 2001.

Bridgman, J. *The End of the Holocaust: The Liberation of the Camps*. Portland: Areopagitica Press, 1990.

Brink, C. 'Vor aller Augen: Fotografien-wider-Willen in der Geschichtsschreibung'. *Werkstatt-Geschichte* 47 (2007), 61–74.

Burger, H. *Der Frühling war es wert: Erinnerungen*. Munich: C. Bertelsmann Verlag, 1977.

Carruthers, S.L. 'Compulsory Viewing: Concentration Camp Film and German Re-education'. *Millennium. Journal of International Studies* 30(3) (2001), 733–59.

Caven, H. 'Horror in Our Time: Images of the Concentration Camps in the British Media, 1945'. *Historical Journal of Film, Radio and Television* 21(3) (2001), 205–53.

Culbert, D. 'American Film Policy in the Re-education of Germany and Her Allies after World War II', in N. Pronay and K. Wilson (eds), *The Political Re-education of Germany and Her Allies after World War II* (London: Croom Helm, 1985), 173–95.

Douglas, L. *The Memory of Judgment: Making Law and History in the Trials of the Holocaust*. New Haven: Yale University Press, 2001.

Flanagan, B., and D. Bloxham (eds). *Remembering Belsen: Eyewitnesses Record the Liberation*. London: Valentine Mitchell, 2005.

Gladstone, K. 'Separate Intentions: The Allied Screening of Concentration Camp Documentaries in Defeated Germany in 1945–46: *Death Mills* and *Memory of the Camps*', in T. Haggith and J. Newman (eds), *Holocaust and the Moving Image: Representation in Film and Television since 1933* (London: Wallflower, 2005), 50–64.

Goldstein, C.S. *Capturing the German Eye: American Visual Propaganda in Occupied Germany*. Chicago: University of Chicago Press, 2009.

Haggith, T. 'Filming the Liberation of Bergen-Belsen and its Impact on the Understanding of the Holocaust'. *Holocaust Studies: A Journal of Culture and History* 12(1/2) (2005), 89–122.

———. 'The 1945 Documentary *German Concentration Camps Factual Survey* and the 70th Anniversary of the Liberation of the Camps'. *The Holocaust in History and Memory* 7 (2014), 181–97.

Hahn, B.J. *Umerziehung durch Dokumentarfilm? Ein Instrument amerikanischer Kulturpolitik im Nachkriegsdeutschland (1945–1953)*. Münster: LIT Verlag, 1997.

Hicks, J. 'From Atrocity to Action: How Soviet Cinema Initiated the Holocaust Film. Imagining the Unimaginable in a Soviet Context' in S. Bardgett et al. (eds), *Justice, Politics and Memory in Europe after the Second World War: Landscapes after the Battle* (London: Valentine Mitchell, 2011), 249–66.

———. *First Films of the Holocaust: Soviet Cinema and the Genocide of the Jews, 1938–1946*. Pittsburgh: University of Pittsburgh Press, 2012.

Kolb, E. *Bergen Belsen: Geschichte des 'Aufenthaltslagers' 1943–1945*. Hanover: Verlag für Literatur und Zeitgeschehen, 1962.

Kramer, S. 'Nacktheit in Holocaust-Fotos und -Filmen', in S. Kramer (ed.), *Die Shoah im Bild* (Munich: edition text + kritik, 2003), 225–48.

Kushner, T. *The Holocaust and the Liberal Imagination: A Social and Cultural History*. Oxford: Blackwell, 1994.

———. 'The Memory of Belsen', in J. Reilly et al. (eds), *Belsen in History and Memory* (London: Cass, 1997), 181–205.

Levi, P. *Survival in Auschwitz: The Nazi Assault on Humanity*, trans. Stuart Woolf. New York: Simon & Schuster, 1996.

Lexikon deutsch-jüdischer Autoren. Berlin: De Gruyter, 2012.

Liebman, S. 'Documenting the Liberation of the Camps: The Case of Aleksander Ford's *Vernichtungslager Majdanek–Cmentarzysko Europy* (1944)', in D. Herzog (ed.), *Lessons and Legacies VII: The Holocaust in International Perspective* (Evanston: Northwestern University Press, 2006), 333–51.

Lipstadt, D.E. *Beyond Belief: The American Press and the Coming of the Holocaust 1933–1945*. New York: Free Press, 1986.

Longerich, P. *'Davon haben wir nichts gewusst!': Die Deutschen und die Judenverfolgung 1933–1945*. Munich: Siedler, 2006.

Michalczyk, J. *End of the Holocaust: Allied Documentaries, Nuremberg and the Liberation of the Concentration Camps*. London: Bloomsbury, 2014.

Olick, J.K. *In the House of the Hangman: The Agonies of German Defeat, 1943–1949*. Chicago: University of Chicago Press, 2005.

Picart, C.J., and J.G. McKahan. 'Visualizing the Holocaust in Gothic Terms: The Ideology of U.S. Signal Corps Cinematography', in C.J. Picart (ed.), *The Holocaust Film Sourcebook* (Westport: Praeger, 2004), 508–15.

Pozner, V., A. Sumpf and V. Voisin. 'Que faire des images soviètiques de la Shoah?'. *1895. Revue d'histoire du cinéma* 76 (2015), 9–41.

Reilly, J. *Belsen: The Liberation of the Concentration Camp.* London: Routledge, 1998.

Shneer, D. *Through Soviet Jewish Eye: Photography, War, and the Holocaust.* New Brunswick: Rutgers University Press, 2011.

Sington, D. *Belsen Uncovered.* London: Duckworth, 1964.

Sontag, S. *Regarding the Pain of Others.* New York: Farrar, Straus and Giroux, 2003.

Stone, D. *The Liberation of the Camps: The End of the Holocaust and its Aftermath.* New Haven: Yale University Press, 2015.

Wasserstein, B. *Britain and the Jews of Europe 1939–1945.* Oxford: Oxford University Press, 1979.

Weckel, U. '(Ohn)mächtige Wut auf die Täter: Männliches und weibliches KZ-Personal vor den Kameras alliierter Befreier'. *Historische Anthropologie* 18(2) (2010), 232–46.

———. *Beschämende Bilder: Deutsche Reaktionen auf alliierte Dokumentarfilme über befreite Konzentrationslager.* Stuttgart: Franz Steiner, 2012.

———. 'Shamed by Nazi Crimes: The First Step towards Germans' Reeducation or a Catalyst for Their Wish to Forget?', in S. Bird et al. (eds), *Reverberations of Nazi Violence in Germany and Beyond: Disturbing Pasts* (London: Bloomsbury Academics, 2016), 33–46.

5

The Polemics of Pity

British Photographs of Berlin, 1945–47

Paul Betts

The relationship between humanitarianism and photography was forged in the nineteenth century and has been an intimate one ever since. In fact, the term 'humanitarian' first emerged in 1844, just five years after the invention of photography.[1] And perhaps it is hardly coincidental that the birth of the Red Cross and the breakthrough of photography occurred roughly at the same time.[2] For almost a century and a half, humanitarians have used photography to draw attention to and publicize human suffering, much of which is associated with the effects of war, dislocation and poverty. Whilst such humanitarian photography may have originated in the nineteenth century, it exploded in the wake of the First World War as a means of politicizing injustice and atrocity, with the aim of mobilizing popular support in the name of various international moral causes and social reform.[3] However, less attention has been paid to how this humanitarian photographic sensibility was revived and refashioned after the Second World War.

This chapter explores photography as a forgotten dimension of British–German relations in and just after 1945. The immediate aftermath of war was a period of dramatic transformation, and photographs from the period register these shifts in political and moral attitude. In what follows, I would like to concentrate on a few British photographs of defeated Germany in 1945 aimed at a British public, ranging from newspaper images to amateur army snapshots to photographs by humanitarian activists, such as London publicist Victor Gollancz. While certainly a victor's view of the defeated enemy, these British pictures – and ensuing broad public discussion about them – reflected a surprising attitude towards their German charges that carried wide implications for the historical development of a humanitarian sensibility. Revealing is not only the speed with which British images of hard-fought victory over German perpetrators turned to expressions of pity towards the vanquished, a sentiment that distinguished British representations of Germans from their American counterparts; also notable is that the British public discourse about German suffering in the British Zone of Occupied Germany – as evidenced in both print and photographs – was bound up with broader discussions about the very meaning of British civilization at the time. British photographs of defeated Germany were often used (and even sensationalized) to enlist moral and material support from a war-weary and quite antipathetic British public towards Germans living under British control. The polemics of pity thus pivoted on depicting defeated Germans in a seemingly apolitical manner in order to highlight the universal quality of suffering civilians, especially children, and to help build more fraternal relations with their former enemies on the ground. In this sense, these shifts of photographic representations reflected changing British attitudes towards Germany and Germans in a new Cold War setting of Western political alliance and moral reconstruction.

Allied Photography at the End of the War

It is worth recalling that most of the initial pictures of defeated Germany were taken by the Allied victors. The link between the media and the war was a direct one for the Allies: no less than 558 writers, reporters, photographers and cameramen were embedded in the Allied invading forces, and were recruited precisely to chronicle military triumph.[4] By contrast, the Third Reich prohibited images of material destruction and social chaos in the endgame of the war, whilst the Soviet occupiers required all Germans to turn in their cameras to the authorities. The result was that Germans were rarely the ones who took photos of their own decimated country in the immediate aftermath of war. The few who did, such as August Sander, Friedrich Seidenstücker and Willi Saeger, tended to focus on destroyed cityscapes and ruined statues as allegories of the fate of the country and its citizens more generally.[5] By the early 1950s, there was a brisk trade in the photographic imagery of blasted German cities on the commercial market, as 'before and after' so-called ruin-books of German cities (especially Berlin, Cologne and Hamburg) became a bestselling genre.[6] Sebald's claim that postwar German writers wilfully ignored the destruction of war found little correspondence in photography, yet the early postwar photographs (and visual memories of the period) were literally framed by the Allies.[7]

Allied photographers have left a dramatic visual archive of war action, and most of the first photos of defeated Germany unsurprisingly concerned the taking of German prisoners of war. For their part, the Soviets had been documenting Nazi atrocities with their cameras since 1941, yet their wartime focus on the horrors of German misdeeds was replaced by celebratory pictures of conquest and heroism – the seizure of the Reichstag and the Reichskanzlei were favorite photographic trophies.[8] Whilst there was some initial Allied sympathy towards captured German soldiers in 1944 and early 1945, especially among the British, such compassion duly evaporated with the shock and horror resulting from the liberation of the concentration camps. Allied soldiers documented and photographed Bergen-Belsen, Dachau and Buchenwald in great detail, after which these images were splashed across the national media in both the United States and the United Kingdom. American antipathy towards Germans under occupation could be seen in the imagery of defeated former enemies, especially evident in Signal Corps pictures of a clear black-and-white moral world of perpetrators and victims. American troops commonly forced Germans to confront their heinous misdeeds, even to the point of compelling them to hold corpses (in staged photographs) as punishment for their sins, with the hope of provoking a show of remorse.[9] Margaret Bourke-White's *Dear Fatherland, Rest Quietly* is a famous example of this genre of using the camera to cast judgement on the German people, depicting concentration camp victims, destroyed cities, shameless looting, corpses strewn in the streets and even the moral scourge of fraternization. These American photographs reflected a distinct physical and moral separation between occupiers and occupied. The careful filming of the Nuremberg trials (where much of the camera work honed in on defendant reactions to the atrocity films shown in the courtroom) was inspired by the same spirit of retribution and coerced contrition.[10]

However, there were other actors on the ground in 1945 who appeared less judgemental in their attitude towards German survivors. For instance, humanitarian fieldworkers working for the United Nations Relief and Rehabilitation Agency (UNRRA) were frontline witnesses of destitute Europe, and often kept diaries and photographic accounts of Displaced Persons (DPs) and war victims eking out lives amid the ruins. UNRRA was created in 1943 to help with the 'return of prisoners and exiles to their homes', and gained support from forty-four nations. The agency was engaged in food distribution, medical care, locating missing people, overseeing refugee centres and repatriating children, and many fieldworkers enthused about the agency's effort to help create a 'a true world community with new social systems and international relations'.[11] A number of soldiers-turned-photographers at UNRRA documented what they saw while working for the agency, most famously the American *Magnum* photographers Arthur Rothstein in China and John Vachon in Poland. In Vachon's letters from Poland to his family back in the United States, he vividly chronicled the problems of the camps and provided shocking pictures of devastated Warsaw that included destroyed buildings, devastated urban life and forlorn children, all represented with great sympathy and compassion towards these survivors, as seen in Figure 5.1.[12] This dovetailed with the photographic work of other groups working with UNRRA, such as a number of Jewish relief groups who photographed life in DP camps, including the activities of hospital clinics, food distributions, vocational training programmes and the transport of people to Palestine.[13]

Figure 5.1. Fresh milk on the dock, Gdansk, Poland, 1946. Photo by John Vachon. Courtesy of UNRRA/4459, United Nations Archives and Record Management.

That said, UNRRA photos were polemic in their own way. Where the experience of many DPs in these camps was one of disorder, despair and conflict, UNRRA photos depicted an orderly world of functioning camps and well-organized refugee repatriation. Pain and suffering were rarely shown; instead, the stress was on positive moments of refugee life – eating, working, children playing and boarding ships or trains to go back home,[14] as noted in Figure 5.2. In part this was done to justify the good work (and spiralling costs) of such a sprawling international humanitarian undertaking, but also to present a story of progress to other refugees languishing in these relief and rehabilitation camps so as to help overcome the exhaustion and demoralization of what was called at the time 'DP apathy' or even 'Belsenitis'.[15] UNRRA photographers were under clear instructions to portray the UN relief mission in a good light, what Vachon cynically called 'UNRRA's angle'.[16] UNRRA's apparent universal relief programme also betrayed political limits: there was to be no provision to help Germans, but rather only the 'victims of Nazi persecution'; if victims happened to be of German nationality, only the 'victims of Nazi terror' qualified for relief.[17] The massive humanitarian crisis across Europe at the end of 1945, intensified by huge influx of German refugees from the East, prompted some UNRRA officials to suggest the

Figure 5.2. Jewish DPs receiving food at Bindermichl UNRRA DP Camp in the U.S. Zone, Linz, Austria, date unknown (most likely 1946). Photo by Lepore. United States Holocaust Memorial Museum, courtesy of National Archives and Records Administration, College Park, MD, 111-SC–234939, CC0 1.0 Universal.

need to attend to Germans on the ground too.[18] The justification for a broader scope of humanitarian relief was the focus on children. A number of articles in international social work journals discussing UNRRA's work saw aid to children as a test case of human rights. Even so, aid was only extended to the lands formerly occupied by Nazi Germany; Germans themselves were excluded from any notions of humanitarian assistance or human rights discourse.[19]

The Visual Language of Pity

What is puzzling is that this visual ideology that separated the suffering into deserving and undeserving existed alongside the advent of a new universal morality after the war, one that culminated with the Universal Declaration of Human Rights in 1948. Photography served as a key broker of this new universal morality, and several landmark photography shows are commonly trotted out as manifestations of this new sensibility. One of the first photobooks after the war was the anonymous *KZ: Bilderbericht aus fünf Konzentrationslagern*, put together by the American Information Unit in 1945 to document the horrors of the Nazi period.[20] Conveying compassion for war victims was central to the creation of the *Magnum* agency in 1947 by various war veterans (among them Robert Capa, David Seymour and Leonard Freed), whose express aim was reporting on conflict and strife in the world. A UNESCO photobook produced two years after the war, the 1947 *The Book of Needs,* shifted the tone by focusing on children, education and reconstruction.[21] A similar spirit could be seen in UNESCO's 1949 *Children of Europe* book, with photos by David 'Chim' Seymour. While the suffering child became a visual staple after the First World War as a rallying cry of humanitarian assistance, ranging from the British 'Save the Children' Fund through the Spanish Civil War,[22] such imagery was revived as moral compass after 1945. In *Children of Europe,* Europe's orphans were depicted as victims of war against ruined European landscapes, irrespective of background or nationality, and as such helped create a new inclusive European sensibility (Figure 5.3).[23] Such sentiment found supreme expression in the 1955 blockbuster show *The Family of Man,* conceived by Edward Steichen in collaboration with the Museum of Modern Art in New York and the United Nations Educational, Scientific and Cultural Organization (UNESCO) in Paris; this was the most popular international photography exposition of all time, seen by over nine million people in thirty-eight countries. It aimed to show what Steichen called 'the essential oneness of mankind throughout the world',[24] portraying peoples from across the world in a kind of intimate family album of postfascist humanity.[25]

So how did this postwar photography go from accentuating disdain and difference towards German survivors to universal inclusivity in several short years? The easy answer is that things changed dramatically in those years, as the main experience moved from war to peace, from combat to occupation to Cold War alliance with West Germany. However, this still does not tell much about how this change of sensibility took place. In order to try to answer this question, I will analyse a few British photographs of defeated Germany in 1945 to trace these changes. The broader point is that this new universalist sentiment was hardly a given in 1945 either in politics or photography, but had to be constructed from scratch like everything else after the war; this forgotten chapter of British photography, I would argue, contributed to the moral breakthrough of this revived humanitarian universalism after the Second World War.

By the second half of 1945, British photographers were parting company from their American counterparts, and offered surprisingly sympathetic press towards the Germans. This could be seen in outlets such as the *Daily Herald,* the Labour Party's mass-circulation newspaper, and *News Chronicle,* a liberal daily.[26] Like the American Signal Corps, most of the British photographers were War Office photographers working within the Army Film and Photography Unit (AFPU), and those who shot photographs for British illustrated magazines after the ceasefire usually had been AFPU photographers during the war.[27] However, their attitude was often different. Eyewitness reports from journalists on special assignment were invariably struck by the humanitarian crisis afflicting the 'homeless hordes' across Germany. A number of reports circulated of the deplorable

Figure 5.3. *Children of Europe* (Paris: UNESCO, 1949). Photo by David Seymour. © Magnum Photos.

conditions of Germans in the British Zone of Occupation living in squalor, malnourished and badly suffering from illness and disease. A 1945 *News Chronicle* piece reported Berlin's shocking spectacle of 'the dead and dying and starving flotsam left by the tide of human misery that reaches Berlin', concluding that 'these excesses, wreaked only on the women and children of Germany, on families of the modest means of shopkeepers or small farmers, cannot be allowed to continue'.[28] Another article conveyed the words of well-known British philosopher J.B. Priestley, who happened to be in Berlin to promote Anglo-Russian understanding. After spending the whole day touring hostels and camps teeming with starving children, Priestley surmised: 'What I have seen and heard from responsible relief workers on the spot shocks the conscience – and it would upset the conscience of anyone in England could they visit Berlin and see for themselves. These children are guiltless – yet they are the ones who are paying the heaviest part of the price for Germany's guilt.'[29]

In a *Picture Post* article in September 1945 entitled 'Report on Chaos', journalist Lorna Hay and photographer Haywood Magee published a story on the 2.1 million displaced persons in Germany. They reported that their diet consisted of 1,000 calories a day, compared to British rations at 2,000 calories a day, and U.S. Army rations at 3,500 calories a day. They grimly concluded that:

> German misery this winter will be on a scale unknown in Europe since the Middle Ages. It may be that those who have not seen the beginning of this misery will not be impressed. They may say: 'The Germans deserve it. Why should we worry?' Maybe they do deserve it. But do our armies of occupation deserve to be set down in such a country, or to be asked to face the consequences of the breakdown of civilised life among a population of 90,000,000?[30]

Other newspaper pictures depicted the chaos of checkpoints and train stations, lorries full of refugees, scavengers on the road, refugees huddled in 'ragged camp' in a 'gallery of misery', as noted in Figure 5.4. The style was still quite distant, but there was a discernible sense of compassion present too.[31]

The difficult moral issue of expressing compassion towards former enemies was neatly captured by one *Daily Herald* journalist:

> Today I have seen thousands of German civilians – old men and women and children of all ages – reduced to the depths of misery and suffering that the Nazis inflicted on others during their beastly reign. I didn't like it. It gave me no satisfaction, although for years I have hoped that the Germans would reap from the seeds they had sown.

What is more, the victims were described as ordinary people, 'most of whom are peasants, working families and the lower-middle class, the least deserving of the suffering, humiliation and starvation – are pushed from place to place, their condition getting rapidly worse every day'. For this journalist, the plight of Germans was nothing less than a test of British values and the very fibre of British civilization:

> This is the aftermath of war, raising problems more difficult to solve than almost any that existed during it. But if we are to prove to the German race, that our methods, our civilisation, our creed were right and theirs wrong, and if we are to keep faith with those who died, were maimed and suffered intolerable hardship, then these problems have got to be solved and have got to be solved quickly.[32]

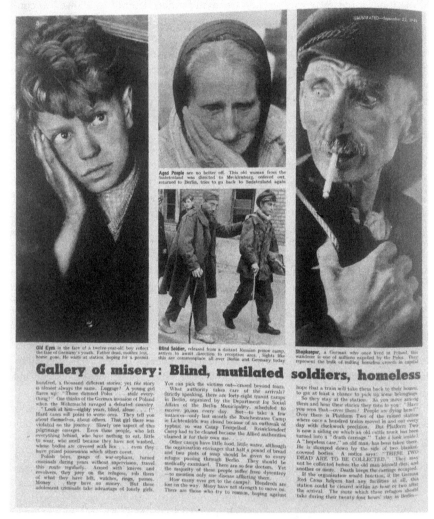

Figure 5.4. Leonard McCombe, 'Berlin', *Illustrated*, 22 September 1945.

Such sentiments reflected a growing British sensibility about seeing suffering in universal terms visited upon all Europeans.

These disturbing photographs in *The Times* and the *News Chronicle* spurred broader discussion in the British press, as the issue of pity began to surface that autumn. Another *Picture Post* article on the problems of occupation asserted: 'This article is not intended to arouse pity for the Germans. The Germans don't need pity . . . The Germans need food, houses, work.'[33] Even so, this language of compassion and pity began to suffuse the debate. In another *Picture Post* article entitled 'Wanted: A New Policy for Germany', Labour Party MP Maurice

Edelmann wrote that he was tired of the 'you brought it upon yourselves' argument, countering: 'Those arguments, while being true, do not take into account that we should treat fellow human beings, not by Nazi standards, but by the standards of Christian civilization; and that self-interest, quite apart from common humanity, demands that we prevent the Germans from suffering the disastrous epidemics which accompany famine and know no frontiers.'[34] Other politicians expressed similar views. The well-known MP Richard Crossman argued in a *New Statesman and Nation* piece in 1945 that the situation in Germany was deteriorating badly, yet the matter went far beyond maladministration, the flood of refugees, expulsions and Russian noncooperation. The fate of Europe hung in the balance and aid to Germany was the first step towards European reconstruction. In Crossman's view, the crisis was not just:

> [A] matter of conscience and humanity. There are other peoples of Europe starving or near starvation who, where pity is concerned, no doubt have a priority. But this creation of economic chaos and famine will be disastrous, not merely to Germans, but to all Europe. The plight of Hitler's victims from Holland to Jugoslavia can only be made ten times worse by what is happening in Germany.[35]

Gollancz's Germany

It was at this point that the brash London publicist Victor Gollancz entered the fray. Gollancz was a prominent London publisher and used the profits from his successful Left Book Club in the 1930s to peddle his own strong views on postwar problems. In the 1930s, he published a series of pamphlets chronicling Nazi terror, such as Dudley Leigh Aman Marley's *The Brown Book of the Hitler Terror and the Burning of the Reichstag* (1933), Hensley Henson's *The Yellow Spot* (1936), which recorded the cruelties inflicted on Jews in Germany, and *Let My People Go: Some Practical Proposals for Dealing with Hitler's Massacres of the Jews and an Appeal to the British Public* (1943), which attempted to incite public opinion about the plight of Polish Jews. But in 1945 he changed tack, expressing concern about how the 'Nazi spirit' was insidiously infecting the victors, evidenced in what he saw as callous British attitudes towards the expulsions of ethnic Germans from Czechoslovakia and Poland, as well as the parlous fate of Germans in the British sector. During the war, Gollancz had bravely written a book attacking Vansittart and so-called 'Vansittartism'. In particular, he was outraged by Lord Robert Vansittart's infamous and bestselling *Black Book: Germans Past and Present,* which was originally a series of radio talks aired by the BBC in December 1940. Vansittart had been Under-Secretary at the Foreign Office in the 1930s and then Chief Diplomatic Advisor to the British Government between 1938 and 1941. He argued that Germans were nothing but a 'race of hooligans' that 'from the dawn of history has been predatory and bellicose', and his booklet sold over a million copies in the first few months of its publication. Gollancz was particularly exercised about the way that British politicians and the press whipped up emotions and hatred towards the Germans, and wanted to pursue a policy of peace and fair postwar settlement for all concerned, in the name of socialism.[36]

Gollancz first waded into controversy with his April 1945 pamphlet *What Buchenwald Really Means,* in which he wanted to remind British readers that some Germans were not guilty and even had acted heroically, and thus any charges of collective guilt – as peddled by the outraged press following the liberation of the camps – were ill-judged and vindictive. If that were not enough, Gollancz went on to castigate Britons for doing nothing to save Jews, which provoked a good deal of hate mail in response.[37] In fact, he finished the *Buchenwald* book by saying: 'This Judeo-Christian tradition is our inner citadel. We have been fighting to preserve it for our children: are we now to surrender it in the very moment of victory?'[38]

Gollancz became increasingly outraged by the harrowing press reports from the British Zone of Occupation, and used pamphlets and photos to argue for the better treatment of Germans. He started with a letter to the *News Chronicle* in August 1945, in which he lamented the emergence of a dangerous 'new morality' that regarded mercy and pity as 'not merely irrelevant, but positively disgraceful'.[39] What was needed, he continued, was 'to turn our backs on the whole evil tradition of self-interest and self-righteousness in international affairs' and 'to feed our starving neighbours'.[40] For Gollancz, Britons must work to alleviate suffering in Europe regardless of nationality. His letter, signed by the likes of Bishop George Bell, Gilbert Murray and Eleanor Rathbone, asserted that: 'It is not in accordance with the traditions of this country to allow children – even the children of ex-enemies – to starve.'[41] He ratcheted up the rhetoric still further in his 1946 pamphlet *Leaving Them to Their Own Fate: The Ethics of Starvation.* He felt compelled to write out of a 'mounting sense of shame' and recounted newspaper coverage in the *Daily Herald* and *The Observer* about German workers 'collapsing from hunger', and brazenly accused the English of 'starving the German people', especially in and around Hamburg.[42] He added: 'And we are starving them, not deliberately in the sense that we definitely want them to die, but willfully in the sense that we prefer their death to our inconvenience.'[43] Gollancz cited reports about low food intake, malnutrition and infant mortality rate, and was angered that discussion to cut German calories to 1,000 a day was accompanied by increased British rations. For him, any talk of putting Germany at the end of the food queue 'is simply to deny the whole western faith of the respect for personality', and British assistance should be motivated by a moral 'obligation dictated by general principles and common humanity', not least because UNRRA barred aid to German civilians. In his eyes, Germany's unconditional surrender made this a supreme moral issue of *noblesse oblige* for Britain. As he put it: 'Germans were required to place themselves utterly in our hands ... If that does not impose a special obligation on a nation that calls itself civilised, then what does?'[44] Accordingly, Britain's 'special obligation' was the duty of the 'liberal or Christian conqueror to his enemy'; at issue was nothing less than 'the preservation of western values'.[45] To add weight to the argument, Gollancz published Bishop Bell's

If Thine Enemy Hunger in 1946, which argued that British enmity towards its former enemies only undermined Christian principles. For Gollancz, 'civilized humanity' thus began with forgiveness and inclusiveness towards the Germans.[46]

Gollancz took up the broader moral dimension of the poor treatment of Germans inside the British Zone of Occupaion even more pointedly in his 1947 book *Our Threatened Values,* which sold over 50,000 copies and went through three reprints in the first month of publication.[47] Here he again cited extracts from a speech made by Field Marshal Viscount Montgomery, in which the Field Marshal was reported to have said: '"The German food-cuts have come to stay ... We will keep them at 1000 calories (Britons get 2800). They gave the inmates of Belsen only 800." These words reveal – they could not have revealed more clearly if they had been spoken for the purpose – the moral crisis with which western civilisation is faced.'[48] Gollancz went on to say:

> This deprecation of mercy and pity, this denial of the gentleness which the distinguishing mark of Judeo-Christian liberalism, is becoming, indeed, a positive mania: there is hardly a politician, hardly a newspaper whether of the study or the gutter, that doesn't succumb to it ... I might mention, if this were the place, the element of hypocrisy in our whole procedure: for to starve the Germans, and do to them some of the very things which Hitler did to others, seems an odd background for re-education.[49]

Given the positive support from readers, Gollancz launched his 'Save Europe Now' scheme in late 1945, which asked members of the British public voluntarily to cut their rations so as to help feed needy German children. His plea garnered surprisingly large popular appeal. By this time, the German refugee crisis was the dominant issue in the daily press and especially in the illustrated print media, and public figures like philosopher J.B. Priestley and President of the Liberal Party and BBC Governor Violet Bonham Carter supported aid for Germany. Minister of Education Ellen Wilkinson went so far as to say that Gollancz's 'Save Europe Now' was 'carrying on in the Dunkirk spirit'.[50] Some MPs supported the campaign strictly out of national interest, arguing that starvation in Europe might lead to disease and epidemics that could affect British troops. But on the whole, the 'Save Europe Now' initiative was conceived in a spirit to 'foster and encourage reconciliation between ordinary people in Britain and elsewhere and the peoples of ex-enemy countries, especially Germany'.[51] On the ground, 'Save Europe Now' worked closely with the German Protestant relief organization Evangelisches Hilfswerk and other international agencies in Germany such as Caritas, Arbeiterwohlfahrt, the German Red Cross, the Swedish Red Cross, Don Suisse and the American Friends Service. The charity sent a large number of parcels of rationed food donated by British families, which were distributed by Red Cross relief teams. Moreover, 'Save Europe Now' took the initiative to organize the first international conference on youth problems (in September 1948 in Bad Fredeburg), which led to the establishment of the German Standing Committee on Youth Problems.[52] By the end of 1948, over 35,000 parcels had been sent to the Continent, half of which were dispatched to Germany, whose 'spiritual and psychological importance have been far greater than their calorie value'.[53] In North Rhine-Westphalia, 'Save Europe Now' even helped alleviate a dangerous shortage of penicillin, leading to the treatment of some 2,500 patients.[54] Thus, feeding Germans properly in the British Zone of Occupation – however difficult this was to countenance after the war – was seen as the very marker of British civilization.

However, it was the photographic element of Gollancz's campaign that was most striking. In late 1945, Gollancz rushed out a pamphlet before Christmas to make an appeal for relief for German expellee children, called *Is it Nothing to You?* He was scandalized that the British Minister of Food, Sir Ben Smith, had announced that Britain's rations were to be increased before Christmas, in crass contrast to the harrowing situation in the British Zone of Occupation in Germany.[55] To drive home the point, Gollancz's book featured images of emaciated German expellee children in hospital beds languishing in pain and hunger, photographs that he took himself. The cover – featuring a starving German child – was a moral exhortation aimed to British readers to show sympathy towards their former enemies (Figure 5.5).

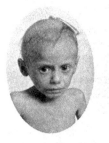

Figure 5.5. Victor Gollancz, *Is it Nothing to You?* (London: Victor Gollancz/Orion Publishing Group, 1945), cover. All attempts to trace the copyright holder for this image were unsuccessful.

Such imagery was not new, recalling as it did the 1919 poster by British 'Save the Children Fund' founder Eglantyne Jebb, 'A Starving Child'. This poster famously sought to draw British attention to the plight of Viennese children suffering from the consequences of the Allied blockade during the First World War. What distinguished Jebb's crusade was that it focused on directing humanitarian aid towards former enemies in the wake of war;[56] Jebb focused on children as a means of building goodwill among former enemy nations, including sending food supplies to help Russian children in aftermath of the 1921 famine. Gollancz's imagery broke from the new genre of humanitarian relief films after the First World War produced by the League of Nations and the International Red Cross as well as the photographic documentation by international agencies of relief assistance during the Spanish

Civil War.[57] In these International Red Cross films, the footage of emaciated Germans was never shown to the public; in fact, ICRC films tended to focus on the relief given, that is, the positive image of the Red Cross. Suffering was not the subject of media attention in this instance. Gollancz consciously took a different tack and put images of civilian suffering at the heart of his call to humanitarian action. In this sense, his imagery recalled images used to publicize the wartime campaign to assist starving children, as noted in Mabel Thérèse Bonney's 1943 photobook *Europe's Children,* which became an overnight sensation.[58] But of course the main reference was to the mass-produced imagery of starved Holocaust survivors spread across the newspapers of the West following the liberation of the camps, and here Gollancz was trying to extend the story of humanitarian neglect and cruelty across the 1945 divide and to invert the perpetrator–victim distinction. To this end, his report of his 1946 visit to Germany, *In Darkest Germany,* also included harrowing photos of squalid living conditions and malnourished children, with the aim of showing that Germany was not recovering from the war (Figure 5.6).[59]

Gollancz also included no less than twenty-four pages of dilapidated children's footwear to dramatize poor care in the British Zone of Occupation (Figure 5.7). He often appeared in the photos himself as a kind of solemn witness. Some have argued that his main motive behind the book and pictures was to call attention to the expense and difficulty of administering the zone, so as to hand it

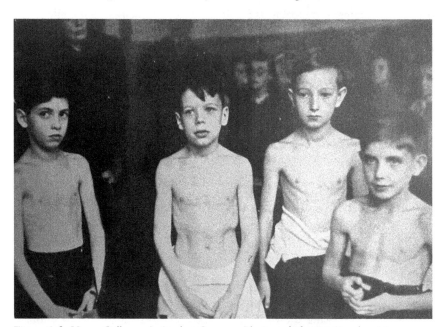

Figure 5.6. Victor Gollancz, *In Darkest Germany: The Record of a Visit* (London: Victor Gollancz/Orion Publishing Group, 1947), image 14. All attempts to trace the copyright holder for this image were unsuccessful.

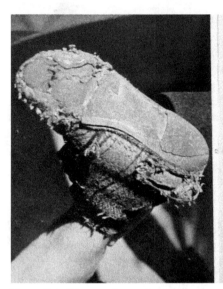 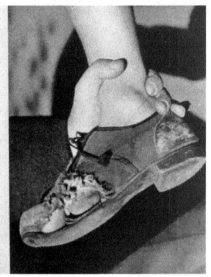

Figure 5.7. Victor Gollancz, *In Darkest Germany: The Record of a Visit* (London: Victor Gollancz/Orion Publishing Group, 1947), images 22–23. All attempts to trace the copyright holder for this image were unsuccessful.

over to the Germans as quickly as possible.[60] After all, there were initially fewer than 100 British public health officials in an area comprising around 22 million people.[61] Whatever the case, these were shocking images all the same. What made them so unusual was the way in which they sought to provoke shame and pity in a war-weary British public unaccustomed to sympathy towards the Germans. Like Jebb's 'Save the Children' Fund after the First World War, Gollancz's campaign was directed towards former enemies in the wake of war.[62] But where Jebb was arrested for her poster on the grounds of public indecency, Gollancz's own scandalous photographs found a supportive audience, especially among the churches, for humanitarian aid towards Britain's former enemy.

Towards a Visual Humanitarian Universalism

Renewed photographic interest in close-ups of beaten and forlorn ex-enemies after 1945 was also significant in revealing relations on the ground. Such proximity marked the end of the war and brought with it the possibility of interpersonal contact once the fighting was over. The dawning of twentieth-century warfare characterized by a new distance between weapon, target and enemy combatant not only radically changed the imagery of war, but also undermined the ability to 'experience feelings of common humanity with people fifteen miles beyond or five miles beneath'.[63] *Magnum* photographers were committed to humanizing warfare in the name of empathy and common humanity. The stress on children in much postwar photography was no coincidence, as war orphans were featured as innocent victims of misfortune, symbols of hope and need.[64] Those sympathetic to the plight of Germans often used refugee children as a means of eliciting sympathy, and Gollancz was not shy in using this strategy in his publications.

Such aesthetics of pity also challenged another key issue on the ground in the immediate postwar period, namely nonfraternization. We may recall that Allied policy imposed strict nonfraternization measures between their troops and local Germans after the war. Nonfraternization policies in both the U.S. and British zones were motivated by concerns relating to health and hygiene, given the outbreak of disease at the end of the war; the same problems dogged UNRRA as well.[65] Yet such policies were also a moral imperative, to the extent that 'nonfratting' was constructed as a means of distancing the victors and vanquished socially as part of moral reconstruction. However, such distancing policies were in stark contrast to the situation in France and the Netherlands, where fraternization with local residents was acceptable and even encouraged.[66] For their part, local Germans sometimes favoured anti-fraternization too, for various reasons, ranging from racism (especially if African-American soldiers were involved) to anti-Allied leftist resistance.[67] Even so, Gollancz denounced British nonfraternization policies precisely because they undermined the very values for which the Allies were supposedly fighting the war. In his characteristically polemic manner, he asserted:

> The horror of non-fraternisation was that having fought the war for human brotherhood we made a studied policy of outraging it . . . for these policies for which we have been jointly or solely responsible – annexations, expulsions, spoliation, economic enslavement, non-fraternisation and starvation – are more in the spirit of the Hitler we fought than in that of the western liberalism for which we fought him.[68]

His views were not isolated. The problems and political costs of nonfraternization were widely discussed in the British press and sometimes compared negatively to more lenient Soviet policies.[69] Over time, the tone of the British Zone photographs changed too. The more strident military photography that initially demarcated the occupying forces from their German charges softened by the late 1940s, as the British occupying forces began to get used to living in Germany and with Germans.[70] With the stabilization of the situation, photographers increasingly turned to everyday life and civilian reconstruction, and the heroism of the so-called 'rubble women', or *Trümmerfrauen,* became a favorite theme of British photographers. What was new was that British photographs now featured Germans alongside Britons in occupied Germany. This overcoming of social distance was part of the increasing relaxation of the once-stern nonfraternization policies and could be noted in new photography of German women and children (Figure 5.8), often in interaction with Allies, which went a long way towards 'humanizing' the former enemy by the late 1940s.[71] To be sure, such changed views also carried a Cold War political message in both the American and British zones. As

Figure 5.8 Sargeant Wilkes, Berlin, July 1945. Photo: © Imperial War Museum (BU 8670).

Stefan Ludwig Hoffmann notes, this 'new humanitarian sentiment' in Western Allied photography of postwar Berlin reflected a larger interest in bringing about the 'rapid transition from punitive occupation to political alignment'.[72]

In Gollancz's case, a renewed British civilizing mission began with feeding and forgiving the Germans. And while his 'Save Europe Now' movement was short-lived, it did mark an important shift of sensibility. His campaign to visualize the 'pain of others' was an effort to forge a new way of seeing Britain's ex-enemy, and his scandalous propaganda photographs played a key role in this campaign. Like the nineteenth-century abolition crusades, Gollancz's polemics were designed to forge a new community of emotion and engagement from a distance, in an attempt to turn Nazis back into Germans. What made his campaign distinctive was that he strove to use the plight of former belligerents to enact a new British sensibility of humanitarian universalism framed by Judeo-Christian values.[73]

In this way, Gollancz's humanitarian media campaign helped resuscitate a liberal language of moral universalism after 1945. It is well known that there was a renewed faith in universalism as a reaction against fascism, and in particular against Nazi theories of irreconcilable national difference, racial antagonism and the assumption that political violence was the real driver of global affairs. This was evident in the Universal Declaration of Human Rights as well as in the founding of the United Nations and its spin-off agencies like UNESCO, which was committed to a one-world 'world civilization' ideal. Photography played a key mediating function in lending visual expression to these dreams, and was closely aligned to the human rights cause internationally. Indeed, UNESCO's particular brand of cultural universalism managed to outlive most of the other forms of post-1945 political universalism as one of the last defenders of a secular ideal of humanity beyond Cold War antagonism and the ideologies of difference. Gollancz's media campaign played a vital role in making such views palatable to a British audience, precisely because it was couched in notions of 'Judeo-Christian' civilization.

In Gollancz's case, this moral universalism was based on quite idealistic views (both rhetorically and visually) of former enemies. No wonder then that Gollancz's polemic compassion was extremely controversial at the time. He was severely criticized in the both British Jewish community and the right-wing press as unpatriotic, arrogant and anti-Jewish, and many felt that his moralizing was excessive and inappropriate immediately after the war.[74] Officials from the Public Health Branch of the British military government claimed that Gollancz exaggerated the level of German malnourishment.[75] Others too were alarmed by such English pro-German sentimentality. The Polish poet Czeslaw Milosz remarked to a British visitor in 1945 that: 'I don't understand your people . . . You have hearts, yes, but do you think with them?'[76] Gollancz's views unsurprisingly met with great adulation in Germany at the time; in 1950, he was hailed at an official gathering at the Opera House in Nuremberg by the mayor as a 'modern Nathan the Wise' who 'never preached hatred and revenge against the German people, although you know too well the nameless atrocities committed by a loathsome minority of our people'. In 1953, he was given the Order of Merit by the German Ambassador as the first non-German recipient of the award,[77] and in 1960, he was bestowed with the Peace Prize of the German Book Trade for his work with 'Save Europe Now'. No less than Konrad Adenauer, the Federal Republic's first Chancellor, acknowledged that 'Germany owes Victor Gollancz a great debt of gratitude, a debt which is all the greater in view of his Jewish descent'.[78] No doubt there was an air of moral self-righteousness ever-present in Gollancz's press crusade, but it did lead to seeing Germans differently, and spurred great popular interest and support, often in league with Christian charity groups. In the end, this broader British press campaign was a particularly British understanding of idealized British–German relations, motivated above all by the better management (and quick handover) of the British Zone of Occupation in north Germany.

What made British views of the Germans so unique is that they turned the criticism on themselves as occupiers, to the extent that they saw the proper treatment of Germans in the British Zone of Occupation as the very marker and test case of British civilization itself. And even if it was often motivated by Christian principles, it was the care of the bodies (not souls) that spurred calls for action. Viewed in hindsight, it may be true, as Susan Sontag observed, that such 'concerned' photography 'has done at least as much to deaden conscience as arouse it'.[79] But this long-forgotten moment of early postwar British photography of Germany and Germans recalls a time when a post-1945 humanitarian conscience was still contentious and in short supply, and nonetheless aimed to include ex-Nazis in a new moral universe of common humanity so soon after the fighting had ended.[80] If anything, it can be argued that such sentiment was a call for British moral leadership in Europe and was shaped by a renewed mission to lend the British occupation of Germany a higher Christian purpose in the aftermath of war.[81] However, such idealism did not last long, as it soon gave way to Cold War exigencies; over time, the visual strategy of scandalizing poverty and misery – especially among children – became a staple of international relief organizations, such as UNICEF and the World Health Organization, one in which atrocity itself was redefined in terms of hunger and unmet material needs. This episode of British humanitarian photography towards former enemies helped create the conditions for its moral breakthrough, diverse application and subsequent widespread diffusion.

Paul Betts is Professor of Modern European History at St Antony's College, Oxford. Before that, he taught at the University of Sussex (2000–12) and the University of North Carolina at Charlotte (1996–99). He is the author of several books and numerous articles on twentieth-century German history. His most recent book, *Within Walls: Private Life in the German Democratic Republic,* was published in 2010 and received the Fraenkel Prize for Contemporary History from the Wiener Library. Among the essay collections he has edited are *The Ethics of Seeing: Photography and 20th Century German History,* with J. Evans and S.-L. Hoffmann (2017); *Science, Religion and Communism in Cold War Europe,* with S.A. Smith (2016); and *Heritage in the Modern World* (2015), with C. Ross. He was Joint Editor of *German History* (2003–9) and serves on the Editorial Board for *Past & Present.* He is currently researching a book on comparative ideas of civilization in postfascist Europe.

Notes

1. M.W. Marien, *Photography: A Cultural History* (Upper Saddle River: Laurence King Publishers, 2006), 1–23.
2. N. Bouvier and M. Mercier, *Focus on Humanity: A Century of Photography* (Geneva: Skira, 1995), 7–8.

3. H. Fehrenbach and D. Rodogno, 'Introduction: The Morality of Sight: Humanitarian Photography in History', in H. Fehrenbach and D. Rodogno (eds), *Humanitarian Photography: A History* (Cambridge: Cambridge University Press, 2015), 1–21.

4. P. Knightley, *The First Casualty* (London: Quartet Books, 1978), 322, quoted in M. Caiger-Smith, 'The Face of the Enemy', in M. Caiger-Smith (ed.), *The Face of the Enemy: British Photographers in Germany, 1944–1952* (Berlin: Dirk Nischen, 1988), 5–26, at 9.

5. S.-L. Hoffmann, 'Gazing at Ruins: German Defeat as Visual Experience', *Journal of Modern European History* 9(3) (2011), 328–50, at 340–41; and L. Derenthal, *Bilder der Trümmer- und Aufbaujahre: Fotografie im sich teilenden Deutschland* (Marburg: Jonas Verlag, 1999).

6. T. Allbeson, 'Ruins, Reconstruction and Representation: Photography and the City in Postwar Western Europe, 1945–1958', PhD dissertation (Durham: University of Durham, 2012).

7. W.G. Sebald, *On the Natural History of Destruction*, trans. Anthea Bell (London: Modern Library, 2004).

8. D. Shneer, *Through Soviet Jewish Eyes: Photography, War and the Holocaust* (New Brunswick: Rutgers University Press, 2011).

9. D. Barnouw, *Germany 1945: Views of War and Violence* (Bloomington: Indiana University Press, 1996), 25 and related images on 14, 23, 30, 31.

10. K. Reynolds, 'That Justice Be Seen: The American Prosecution's use of Film at the Nuremberg International Military Tribunal', PhD dissertation (Brighton: University of Sussex 2010); and U. Weckel, *Beschämende Bilder: Deutsche Reaktionen auf alliierte Dokumentarfilme ueber befreite Konzentrationslager* (Stuttgart: Franz Steiner 2012).

11. S.T. Pettiss, *After the Shooting Stopped* (Victoria, BC: Trafford Publishing, 2004), 7.

12. A. Vachon (ed.), *Poland 1946: The Photographs and Letters of John Vachon* (Washington DC: Smithsonian, 1995).

13. E. Nooter, 'Displaced Persons from Bergen-Belsen: The JDC Photographic Archives', *History of Photography* 23(4) (1999), 331–40.

14. S. Salvatici, 'Sights of Benevolence: UNRRA's Recipients Portrayed', in H. Fehrenbach and D. Rodogno (eds), *Humanitarian Photography: A History* (Cambridge: Cambridge University Press, 2015), 200–22.

15. P. Weindling, '"Belsenitis": Liberating Belsen, its Hospitals, UNRRA, and the Selection for Re-emigration, 1945–1948', *Science in Context* 19(3) (2006), 401–18.

16. Vachon, *Poland 1946*, 53.

17. G.D. Cohen, 'Between Relief and Politics: Refugee Humanitarianism in Occupied Germany, 1945–1946', *Journal of Contemporary History* 43(3) (2008), 437–49.

18. W. Arnold-Forster, 'UNRRA's Work for Displaced Persons in Germany', *International Affairs* 22(1) (1946), 1–13. See also L. Humbert, '"When Most Relief Workers Had Never Heard of Freud": UNRRA in the French Zone of Occupation in Germany, 1945–1947', in S. Barkhof and A.K. Smith (eds), *War and Displacement in the 20th Century* (Abingdon: Routledge, 2014), 199–223.

19. M. Branscombe, 'The Children of the United Nations: UNRRA's Responsibility for Social Welfare', *Social Service Review* 19(3) (1945), 310–23.

20. *KZ: Bilderbericht aus fünf Konzentrationslagern*. Amerikanisches Kriegsinformationsamt, April 1945 (no other publishing information). Such documentary humanist photography could be seen elsewhere in Europe as well, with the Dutch leading the way in documenting the occupation. The most influential was the clandestine wartime underground group, De Ondergedoken Camera, whose work culminated in the 1947 book *Amsterdam tijdens*

den hongerwinter (*Amsterdam during the Hunger Winter*) about the last year of war and deprivation; M. Parr and G. Badger, *The Photobook: A History* (London: Phaidon, 2004), 188.

21. D. Seymour, *The Book of Needs* (Paris: UNESCO, 1947).

22. See Rose Holmes' chapter in this volume; and H. Fehrenbach, 'Children and Other Civilians: Photography and the Politics of Humanitarian Image-Making', in Fehrenbach and Rodogno, *Humanitarian Photography*, 165–99, at 167.

23. D. Seymour, *Children of Europe* (Paris: UNESCO, 1949).

24. E. Steichen (ed.), *The Family of Man* (New York: Museum of Modern Art, 1955), 4. See also Tobias Weidner's chapter in this volume.

25. Significantly, some of the images from *Children of Europe* were included in the 1955 *The Family of Man* show, which also often focused on children. *The Family of Man* exhibition inspired the production of other photobooks that similarly featured depoliticized images of everyday life, such as J.-P. Charbonnier, *Chemins de la vie* (Monte-Carlo: editions du Cap, 1957).

26. *Picture Post* reporter Macdonald Hastings: 'All the suffering, all the evil, all the horror that this man and his breed brought down on the world seems suddenly remote and unconvincing. The enemy is just a grey-faced wretch with his hands up, his uniform in rags, and his weary eyes fixed fearfully on your gun. Right down inside, you almost want to let the fellow go.' M. Hastings, 'Prisoners Face to Face', *Picture Post* (1944), as quoted in Caiger-Smith, 'Face of the Enemy',10.

27. Caiger-Smith, 'Face of the Enemy', 7.

28. N. Clark, '25,000 Seek Food Every Day at the Gates of Berlin', *News Chronicle* 1 (24 August 1945), 4.

29. N. Clark, 'Plea for German Children: Theirs Not the Guilt, Says JB Priestley', *News Chronicle* (12 September 1945), 1.

30. L. Hay and H. Magee, 'Report on Chaos', *Picture Post* 28(10) (1945), 7–13, at 9.

31. Interestingly, the next week's issue (15 September) featured a profile of UNRRA by the same team of journalists and photographers, discussing its daunting mission and difficulties related to relatively little local military administrative support. But as was typical of UNRRA photos in general, the pictures showed UNRRA agents doing good work in this Polish refugee camp, distributing food and requisitioning clothes – and in this case, no Germans were depicted. L. Hay and H. Magee, 'Can UNRRA Relieve the Chaos in Europe?', *Picture Post* 28(11) (1945), 16–19.

32. C. Bray, 'Retribution. It falls on Women and Children', *Daily Herald* (24 August 1945), 2.

33. S. Jacobson, 'Europe Cannot Afford this Germany", *Picture Post* (8 September 1945), quoted in Caiger-Smith, 'Face of the Enemy', 21.

34. *Picture Post,* 1 December 1945, cited in Barnouw, *Germany 1945,* 152.

35. R.H.S. Crossman, 'Why Germany Matters', *New Statesman and Nation* (22 September 1945), 188.

36. V. Gollancz, *Shall Our Children Live or Die? A Reply to Lord Vansittart on the German Problem* (London: Victor Gollancz, 1945).

37. R.D. Edwards, *Victor Gollancz: A Biography* (London: Victor Gollancz, 1987), 404–5.

38. V. Gollancz, *What Buchenwald Really Means* (London: V. Gollancz, 1945), 16.

39. Quoted in M. Frank, 'The New Morality: Victor Gollancz, "Save Europe Now" and the German Refugee Crisis, 1945–1946', *Twentieth Century British History* 17(2) (2006), 230–56, at 238.

40. V. Gollancz, 'In Germany Now', *News Chronicle* (27 August 1945), 2.
41. 'Tragedy over Europe', *News Chronicle*, 12 September 1945, 2.
42. V. Gollancz, *Leaving Them to Their Own Fate: The Ethics of Starvation* (London: Victor Gollancz, 1946), 1, 21.
43. Ibid., 1.
44. Ibid., 30–32.
45. Ibid., 34, 43.
46. Barnouw, *Germany 1945*, 151.
47. Edwards, *Victor Gollancz*, 425.
48. V. Gollancz, *Our Threatened Values* (London: Victor Gollancz, 1946), 7.
49. Ibid., 8, 23, 29.
50. Gollancz, *Leaving*, 11.
51. Frank, 'New Morality', 242–47.
52. M. Kelber, 'Patterns of Relief Work in Germany', in *The Year Book of World Affairs 1951* (London: Stevens and Sons, 1951), 158–82.
53. *Save Europe Now, 1945–1948: Three Years' Work* (London: Victor Gollancz, 1948), 9, 5.
54. J. Farquharson, '"Emotional But Influential": Victor Gollancz, Richard Stokes and the British Zone of Germany, 1945–9', *Journal of Contemporary History* 22(3) (1987), 501–19, at 512.
55. V. Gollancz, *Is it Nothing to You?* (London: Victor Gollancz, 1945), 2–3.
56. S. Roberts, 'Exhibiting Children at Risk: Child Art, International Exhibitions and Save the Children Fund in Vienna, 1919–1923', *Paedagogica Historica* 45(1/2) (2009), 171–90.
57. See the chapters by Daniel Palmieri and Rose Holmes in this volume.
58. M.T. Bonney, *Europe's Children* (New York: Plantin, 1943). For discussion, see Fehrenbach, 'Children and Other Civilians', 177–87.
59. V. Gollancz, *In Darkest Germany: The Record of a Visit* (London: Victor Gollancz, 1947).
60. B. Shepherd, *The Long Road Home: The Aftermath of the Second World War* (London: Anchor, 2012), 253.
61. J. Reinisch, *The Perils of Peace* (Oxford: Oxford University Press, 2013), 153.
62. Roberts, 'Exhibiting Children at Risk', 171–90.
63. G. Best, *War and Law since 1945* (Oxford: Oxford University Press, 1994), 53.
64. T. Allbeson, 'Photographic Diplomacy in the Postwar World", *Modern Intellectual History* (2015), 1–33.
65. L. Haushofer, '"The Contaminating Agent": UNRRA, Displaced Persons, and Venereal Disease in Germany, 1945–1947', *American Journal of Public Health* 100(6) (2010), 993–1003.
66. P. Knauth, 'Fraternization: The Words Takes on a Brand-New Meaning in Germany', *LIFE* (2 July 1945); and his *Germany in Defeat* (New York: Knopf, 1946). See also E.F. Ziemke, *The US Army and the Occupation of Germany 1944–1946* (Washington DC: Center of Military History, U.S. Army, 1975 [1946]).
67. P. Biddiscombe, 'Dangerous Liaisons: The Anti-fraternization Movement in the US Occupation Zones of Germany and Austria, 1945–1948', *Journal of Social History* 34(3) (2001), 611–47; and R. Knight, 'National Construction Work and Hierarchies of Empathy in Postwar Austria', *Journal of Contemporary History* 49(3) (2014), 491–513.
68. Gollancz, *Threatened*, 116, 155, 156.
69. L.O. Mosley, *Report from Germany* (London: Victor Gollancz, 1945), 124–25.
70. Caiger-Smith, 'Face of the Enemy', 21.

148 Paul Betts

71. G. Gronefeld, *Frauen in Berlin, 1945–1947* (Berlin: Nishen, 1984).
72. Hoffmann, 'Gazing', 347.
73. L. Malkki, 'Children, Humanity and the Infantilization of Peace', in I. Feldman and M. Ticktin (eds), *In the Name of Humanity: The Government of Threat and Care* (Durham, NC: Duke University Press, 2010), 58–85.
74. Edwards, *Victor Gollancz*, 548, 623.
75. Farquharson, '"Emotional But Influential"', 508.
76. Quoted in Frank, 'New Morality', 254.
77. Edwards, *Victor Gollancz*, 458–62.
78. K. Adenauer, *Memoirs, 1945–1953* (London: Weidenfeld & Nicolson, 1966), 60.
79. S. Sontag, *On Photography* (New York: Farrar & Strauss, 1977), 21.
80. P. Betts, 'Universalism and its Discontents: Humanity as a Twentieth-Century Concept', in M. Thulin and F. Klose (eds), *Humanity: A History of European Concepts in Practice from the Sixteenth Century to the Present* (Göttingen: Vandenhoeck & Ruprecht, 2016), 51–70.
81. F. Graham-Dixon, *The Allied Occupation of Germany: The Refugee Crisis, Denazification and the Path to Reconstruction* (London: I.B. Tauris, 2013).

Bibliography

Adenauer, K. *Memoirs, 1945–1953.* London: Weidenfeld & Nicolson, 1966.
Allbeson, T. 'Ruins, Reconstruction and Representation: Photography and the City in Postwar Western Europe, 1945–1958'. PhD dissertation. Durham: University of Durham, 2012.
———. 'Photographic Diplomacy in the Postwar World'. *Modern Intellectual History* (2015), 1–33.
Arnold-Forster, W. 'UNRRA's Work for Displaced Persons in Germany'. *International Affairs* 22(1) (1946), 1–13.
Barnouw, D. *Germany 1945: Views of War and Violence.* Bloomington: Indiana University Press, 1996.
Best, G. *War and Law since 1945.* Oxford: Oxford University Press, 1994.
Betts, P. 'Universalism and its Discontents: Humanity as a Twentieth-Century Concept', in M. Thulin and F. Klose (eds), *Humanity: A History of European Concepts in Practice from the Sixteenth Century to the Present* (Göttingen: Vandenhoeck & Ruprecht, 2016), 51–70.
Biddiscombe, P. 'Dangerous Liaisons: The Anti-fraternization Movement in the US Occupation Zones of Germany and Austria, 1945–1948'. *Journal of Social History* 34(3) (2001), 611–47.
Bonney, M.T. *Europe's Children.* New York: Plantin, 1943.
Bouvier, N., and M. Mercier. *Focus on Humanity: A Century of Photography.* Geneva: Skira, 1995.
Branscombe, M. 'The Children of the United Nations: UNRRA's Responsibility for Social Welfare'. *Social Service Review* 19(3) (1945), 310–23.
Caiger-Smith, M. 'The Face of the Enemy', in M. Caiger-Smith (ed.), *The Face of the Enemy: British Photographers in Germany, 1944–1952* (Berlin: Dirk Nischen, 1988), 5–26.
Cohen, G.D. 'Between Relief and Politics: Refugee Humanitarianism in Occupied Germany, 1945–1946'. *Journal of Contemporary History* 43(3) (2008), 437–49.
Derenthal, L. *Bilder der Trümmer- und Aufbaujahre: Fotografie im sich teilenden Deutschland.* Marburg: Jonas Verlag, 1999.

Edwards, R.D. *Victor Gollancz: A Biography*. London: Victor Gollancz, 1987.

Farquharson, J. '"Emotional But Influential": Victor Gollancz, Richard Stokes and the British Zone of Germany, 1945–9'. *Journal of Contemporary History* 22(3) (1987), 501–19.

Fehrenbach, H. 'Children and Other Civilians: Photography and the Politics of Humanitarian Image-Making', in H. Fehrenbach and D. Rodogno (eds), *Humanitarian Photography: A History* (Cambridge: Cambridge University Press, 2015), 165–99.

Fehrenbach, H., and D. Rodogno. 'Introduction: The Morality of Sight', in H. Fehrenbach and D. Rodogno (eds), *Humanitarian Photography, A History* (Cambridge: Cambridge University Press, 2015), 1–21.

Frank, M. 'The New Morality: Victor Gollancz, "Save Europe Now" and the German Refugee Crisis, 1945–1946'. *Twentieth Century British History* 17(2) (2006), 230–56.

Gollancz, V. *Is it Nothing to You?* London: Victor Gollancz, 1945.

———. *Shall Our Children Live or Die? A Reply to Lord Vansittart on the German Problem*. London: Victor Gollancz, 1945.

———. *What Buchenwald Really Means*. London: Victor Gollancz, 1945.

———. *Leaving Them to Their Own Fate: The Ethics of Starvation*. London: Victor Gollancz. 1946.

———. *Our Threatened Values*. London: Victor Gollancz, 1946.

———. *In Darkest Germany: The Record of a Visit*. London: Victor Gollancz, 1947.

Graham-Dixon, F. *The Allied Occupation of Germany: The Refugee Crisis, Denazification and the Path to Reconstruction*. London: I.B. Tauris, 2013.

Gronefeld, G. *Frauen in Berlin, 1945–1947*. Berlin: Nishen, 1984.

Haushofer, L. '"The Contaminating Agent": UNRRA, Displaced Persons, and Venereal Disease in Germany, 1945–1947'. *American Journal of Public Health* 100(6) (2010), 993–1003.

Hoffmann, S.-L. 'Gazing at Ruins: German Defeat as Visual Experience'. *Journal of Modern European History* 9(3) (2011), 328–50.

Humbert, L. '"When Most Relief Workers Had Never Heard of Freud": UNRRA in the French Zone of Occupation in Germany, 1945–1947', in S. Barkhof and A.K. Smith (eds), *War and Displacement in the 20ᵗʰ Century* (Abingdon: Routledge, 2014), 199–223.

Kelber, M. 'Patterns of Relief Work in Germany', in *The Year Book of World Affairs 1951* (London: Stevens and Sons, 1951), 158–82.

Knight, R. 'National Construction Work and Hierarchies of Empathy in Postwar Austria'. *Journal of Contemporary History* 49(3) (2014), 491–513.

Knightley, P. *The First Casualty*. London: Quartet Books, 1978.

Malkki, L. 'Children, Humanity and the Infantilization of Peace', in I. Feldman and M. Ticktin (eds), *In the Name of Humanity: The Government of Threat and Care* (Durham, NC: Duke University Press, 2010), 58–85.

Marien, M.W. *Photography: A Cultural History*. Upper Saddle River: Laurence King Publishers, 2006.

Mosley, L.O. *Report from Germany*. London: Victor Gollancz, 1945.

Nooter, E. 'Displaced Persons from Bergen-Belsen: The JDC Photographic Archives'. *History of Photography* 23(4) (1999), 331–40.

Parr, M., and G. Badger. *The Photobook: A History*. London: Phaidon, 2004.

Pettiss, S.T. *After the Shooting Stopped*. Victoria, BC: Trafford Publishing, 2004.

Reinisch, J. *The Perils of Peace*. Oxford: Oxford University Press, 2013.

Reynolds, K. 'That Justice Be Seen: The American Prosecution's use of Film at the Nuremberg International Military Tribunal'. PhD dissertation. Brighton: University of Sussex, 2010.

Roberts, S. 'Exhibiting Children at Risk: Child Art, International Exhibitions and Save the Children Fund in Vienna, 1919–1923', in *Paedagogica Historica* 45(1/2) (2009), 171–90.

Salvatici, S. 'Sights of Benevolence: UNRRA's Recipients Portrayed', in H. Fehrenbach and D. Rodogno (eds), *Humanitarian Photography: A History* (Cambridge: Cambridge University Press, 2015), 200–22.

Sebald, W.G. *On the Natural History of Destruction,* trans. Anthea Bell. London: Modern Library, 2004.

Seymour, D. *The Book of Needs.* Paris: UNESCO, 1947.

———. *Children of Europe.* Paris: UNESCO, 1949.

Shepherd, B. *The Long Road Home: The Aftermath of the Second World War.* London: Anchor, 2012.

Shneer, D. *Through Soviet Jewish Eyes: Photography, War and the Holocaust.* New Brunswick: Rutgers University Press, 2011.

Sontag, S. *On Photography.* New York: Farrar & Strauss, 1977.

Steichen, E. (ed.). *The Family of Man.* New York: Museum of Modern Art, 1955.

Vachon, A. (ed.). *Poland 1946: The Photographs and Letters of John Vachon.* Washington DC: Smithsonian, 1995.

Weckel, U. *Beschämende Bilder: Deutsche Reaktionen auf alliierte Dokumentarfilme ueber befreite Konzentrationslager.* Stuttgart: Franz Steiner, 2012.

Weindling, P. '"Belsenitis": Liberating Belsen, its Hospitals, UNRRA, and the Selection for Re-emigration, 1945–1948'. *Science in Context* 19(3) (2006), 401–18.

Ziemke, E.F. *The US Army and the Occupation of Germany 1944–1946.* Washington DC: Center of Military History, U.S. Army, 1975 [1946].

6

The Human Gaze

Photography after 1945

Tobias Weidner

In late 1943, the American magazine *Popular Photography* published an article on William Rogers, Jr., the Democrat elected to Congress that year.[1] In the article, Rogers praised the extent of photographic opportunities in Washington DC, but also explained his urge to avoid the usual pictures – like those all the visitors to the capital took. Rogers stated he did not 'give a darn about arty pictures', but also did not want to focus on 'the buildings' because his photography was about 'the men and women'. He wanted 'to catch people on the fly – as they really are' and 'rather take pictures of the Washingtonians going about their daily life'. Doing this, he claimed to 'go considerably below the surface', exploring 'the human element'. The author of the article, Robert Eichberg, concluded that Roger's interest 'in *people* rather than in *things*' was hard to categorize: 'The serious student of photography would be hard put to classify him, for he is neither a modernist, a pictorialist, nor an impressionist.' He then proposed to classify Rogers as 'a member of a new school of photography: the humanist'.[2]

Rogers, the 'Congressman with a camera', hardly occurs in histories of photography. His career as a politician also did not last long. He left Congress in May 1944 to return to the army. Later, the son of the (unequally more famous) humourist Will Rogers mainly turned to entertainment.[3] The article in *Popular Photography* claimed he was a friend of Edward Weston, the cofounder of the influential San Francisco group of photographers called 'f/64'. But unlike Weston, he never built up a notable reputation as a photographer. Nevertheless, the article was an early and remarkable reflection on developments in photography that gained importance after the Second World War.

As the example of Will Rogers shows, the photographic interest in humanity after the Second World War went well beyond prominent photographers like Henri Cartier-Bresson, Robert Capa or Robert Doisneau, to whom a humanist approach is frequently ascribed. This interest is of relevance for the general cultural history of the postwar period because it was connected to a broader change in the way humanity was perceived through the media. Recent research has carved out a multilayered discourse on humanity for the time after 1945. Many of the new and comprehensive studies on human rights[4] and humanitarian aid[5] give important insights into debates on *humanité, Menschlichkeit,* human rights and humanitarianism, but also *Humanismus.*[6] Although the terms could vary in meaning, they frequently became mixed in public debates and influenced each other in a characteristic way, even across linguistic boundaries. Common lexical definitions of humanity encompass the collective of humankind, the concern about the humanitarian improvement of its life, the act of being humane and human nature in general.[7] At least below the philosophical and theoretical *Höhenkamm*[8] semantics of humanity, humanitarianism and humanism constituted an intertwined web of meanings in actual use.[9] This makes it difficult to offer a general hypothesis on clearly distinguishable diachronic change in the broader semantic field of humanity after 1945 beyond its mere omnipresence. Nevertheless, it is rewarding to take a closer look at another striking shift from (written and spoken) language to visual media, especially photography.[10] My hypothesis is that photography was crucial for a novel perspective on (and interpretations of) humanity in the specific postwar constellation. Influential groups of photographers picked up elements from older photographic 'schools' and were backed up by developments in the media that also dated back to the interwar years, especially the triumph of illustrated magazines like *Life.* The postwar period then brought together decidedly humanist enterprises in photography as much as systematic reflections on the universal potentials of photography in its relation to humanity. It was the time of diffusion and institutionalization of what I propose to call the *Human Gaze* – a specific way of visualizing humanity closely linked to a repertoire of assumptions about the potential of photography.[11] The rise of this 'Gaze' followed on from the experience of the Nazi era and the Second World War: the excesses of inhumanity and general suspicions about the ideological character of the spoken as much as the written word.[12] Already before the war had ended, various authors claimed an outstanding role for photography in the postwar era. Ansel Adams – to cite one of the most famous photographers of the time – stated in a 1944 edition of the *American Annual of Photography* 'that the highest function of post-war photography will be to relate the world of nature to the world of man, and man to men in the fullest meaning of the terms'.[13]

I will concentrate on a selection of examples from the 1940s to the 1960s to present a repertoire of characteristic features of the 'Gaze'. I will try to show which photographic traditions the pioneers of that approach adopted, what the resulting photographic representations of humanity actually looked like and how they were produced technically. I will then examine how the 'Gaze' gained currency in various fields along with different institutional settings in a process of popularization, asking for structural conditions of its success and means of diffusion. Finally, I will highlight decided countermovements and critiques of 'photographic humanism' since the mid 1950s, but will also give examples of its striking persistence throughout the rest of the century.

Humanist Traditions

Many aspects Eichberg identified in Roger's photography in the example from 1943 may seem reminiscent of the French *photographie humaniste*. However, Eichberg's reflections also revealed that even well-informed experts in photography considered a distinctly humanist photography something novel. So what was new about the postwar-humanist approach and which traditions did it draw from?

The *photographie humaniste* is well researched. The work of some photographers usually related to this 'movement' by historians and other scholars today dates back to the first half of the twentieth century. If you take a focus on human beings and their commonalities as the central criterion for a humanist movement in photography, it is easy to identify it in many fields, e.g. in the street photography of the interwar years. Some early French street photographers became famous for their images of Paris: an early example to think of is Brassaï; another artist who may be considered an important precursor of the humanist approach, Eugène Atget, was even active at the end of the nineteenth century.[14]

If you take newer studies on American documentary photography of the New Deal era at their word, the major photographic projects of the Farm Security Administration (FSA) programme also contained a humanist dimension. It has been convincingly argued that already photographers 'from Hine to the FSA' had 'used humanism as a strategy to promote reform'.[15] For example, Dorothea Lange was (and still is) defined as the 'supreme humanist' in the FSA programme.[16] In retrospect, this older documentary tradition was also incorporated into explicit humanist efforts in photography and fits in very well.[17]

Notwithstanding these traditions, I would argue that strikingly many photographers consciously became humanists or started reflecting on the universal potentials of photography after (or by the end of) the Second World War.[18] An important sign of this qualitative shift was the reorientation and founding of new photo agencies directly after the war. For example, in Paris, prominent exponents of the *photographie humaniste* collectively joined the agency *Rapho* reopened in 1945.[19] In April 1947, *Magnum Photos* was founded – probably the most important institutionalization of humanist photographic approaches in the twentieth century. Edward Steichen even called the agency 'a miniature United Nations of photographers'. Their humanist vision upheld 'values of liberty, equality and dignity' that strikingly resembled the Universal Declaration of Human Rights from 1948.[20] The agency significantly contributed to the omnipresence humanist approaches gained in photojournalism until the 1960s and its extensive popularization.[21]

From a broader perspective, there is evidence for a direct link between such efforts and the experience of many pivotal photographers as embedded war photographers. Ansel Adams' emphasis on photography as a universal means of communication after the war mentioned above is only one hint. Towards the end of the war, when the Allied victory was foreseeable, major photographic periodicals remarkably often emphasized the connection between photography and humanity. For example, in November 1944, the editor of *Popular Photography* commented on the liberation of France and stated that now 'Human Dignity' was 'winning its battle'. That, in his opinion, had a general 'meaning to photography', because as a consequence '[n]o photograph that you or I can take can be without human meaning'.[22]

Autobiographical accounts by most influential photographers described especially the liberation of concentration camps as an unprecedented challenge that constituted a defining moment for their further photographic work. Three well-known examples may show that they served as a significant occasion for fundamental reflection on their work, although the tangible consequences they drew differed. Margaret Bourke-White, who stated that Buchenwald to her had been 'more than the mind could grasp', took pictures, but was only able to do so by working in 'self-imposed stupor' 'with a veil over [her] mind'.[23] Robert Capa simply refused to take any pictures while the concentration camps in his perception were 'swarming with photographers'.[24] George Rodger, a cofounder of *Magnum Photos,* drew the most radical consequences from his experiences in Belsen. At the end of August 1944, he wrote in his diary: 'The horror I found was too great to comprehend, but I had to try and show it in my photographs. As it was an example of man's inhumanity to man that the world had to know. I was not proud of my pictures, and I vowed never to cover another war.'[25] Some others – like Capa – always stayed war photographers and covered one humanitarian crisis after another. Nevertheless, they did so in a particular way. As one striking characteristic of their coverage, they avoided images of unmitigated cruelty.

Basic Visual Patterns and Photographic Approaches

Given the fact that many influential photographers to this day are considered to take a humanist approach – e.g. Sebastião Salgado[26] – it seems helpful to take a closer look at the 'common ground' of their visual languages beyond that aspect. What did humanity look like through their lenses and how did they technically approach their subjects? There is a set of common, very typical patterns and photographic approaches for this visual language, which may well be the most influential strategy for picturing humanity in the twentieth century. As a starting point, it may suffice to take a general look at the oeuvres of quintessential representatives. Existing research already offers clues regarding basic visual patterns by the example of French street photographers – particularly Robert Doisneau and Henri Cartier-Bresson.[27]

The fundamental characteristic of the approach may even sound superfluous: humanist photography focused on humans. Cartier-Bresson gave a concise and memorable definition of this most important 'sujet' of his photography: 'l'homme, l'homme et sa vie si courte, si frêle, si menacée'.[28] He also stated that while a 'subject' for photography could be found in 'all that takes place in the world', the 'little, human detail can become a leitmotiv'.[29] The framing of such details (most of the time) was everyday life, primarily in urban spaces (Paris was regarded as exemplary). It was obviously crucial for a typical humanist photograph to depict a recognizable place. Soft-focus images with blurred backgrounds (characteristic of pictorialism) were intentionally avoided.

The prevalent themes were family life, playing children,[30] love, dance and leisure. Social inequality was represented at times, but frequently with a humorous touch. Ironic juxtapositions were an important stylistic means in general, of which Elliott Erwitt was a particularly skilled user.[31] Outsiders and flamboyant personalities were present – 'clochards' and 'marginal people' were core elements of the visual repertoire.[32] So hardship was not excluded, but it hardly occurred in a forthright manner. The photography especially of some of *Magnum Photos'* later founders – Robert Capa, George Rodger and David 'Chim' Seymour – before and during the Second World War seems at first sight to challenge this last attribution. For example, Capa's images of the Spanish Civil War, especially the iconic and much-discussed dying loyalist soldier, even showed the exact moment of death. Therefore, this particular kind of war photography constitutes a special case. Nevertheless, even Capa's controversial and certainly radical pictures were never simple representations of 'naked' cruelty. Beyond that, they complied with a number of requirements of paradigmatic humanist street photography.

First among these 'essentials' is the photographer's *claim* to represent an authentic scene. This means that posing was more than frowned upon. Yet more often than not, the *actual* credibility of many images is in fact doubtful. The authenticity of Capa's 'Dying Soldier' has been disputed repeatedly.[33] Robert Doisneau's endlessly reproduced 'Le Baiser de l'hôtel de ville' is another famous example of a staged setting. The list could be easily expanded. Yet, all these more or less famous 'fakes' do not abrogate the first basic rule for humanist photographs: the impression of being not staged was indispensable. Henri Cartier-Bresson objected to 'stage-management' as 'cheating'.[34] To him and other humanist photographers, the appeal of authenticity seemed to be even more important than the actual technical quality of their images, especially sharpness. He is often quoted for having said that 'sharpness' was overrated and 'a bourgeois concept'.[35] He repudiated this 'obsession' and questioned the possibility of 'get[ting] to closer grips with reality' by a 'trompe l'œil' technique (aiming to deceive the eye by creating the illusion of actually seeing reality). On the other hand, he also did not take to 'photographic anecdotes with an intentional unsharpness' with the intention of appearing particularly 'artistic'.[36] The statement can be read as a demarcation of both straight photography and pictorialism. Beyond this artistic self-positioning, the presence of occasional in-motion blurriness or even a slightly missed focus may also be interpreted as a visual strategy to represent authenticity.

Authenticity in the humanist visual repertoire is closely linked to another important concept that was also popularized by Cartier-Bresson: the 'Decisive Moment'. Koral Ward pointed out in his dissertation that this moment was devised to be a 'narrative climax':[37] a moment making visible a whole story at first glance; a single picture as 'a whole story in itself'.[38] The strolling photographer had to recognize these moments and capture them. Paradoxically, this spontaneous approach was frequently accompanied by carefully composed images. In the introduction to his landmark monograph, entitled *The Decisive Moment* in English, Cartier-Bresson elaborated on this concept.[39] In the wake of Cartier-Bresson's success, the concept gained popularity after the monograph was published in 1952. The concept implied that there was a certain moment making human identity visible within a condensed narrative. In some iconic street photographs, these narratives cumulated in a single image. However, especially in journalistic contexts and monographs, photographers and editors often produced photo essays that placed images in a sentence- or text-like order. As, for instance, the work of Elliott Erwitt shows, these stories could be dramatic, romantic and humorous at the same time.[40]

The work of the humanist photographers furthermore bespeaks a particular interest in apparent expressions of emotions. As Carl Sandburg put it: 'Often faces speak what words can never say.'[41] Closely linked to the awareness for facial expressions was a special attention for glances and especially eye contact. They represented interaction in a very graphic way. Interaction and communication were *the* focal points of the visual strategy. One option that was frequently used was an intense look into the camera, which turned street photography into a special kind of portraiture. Cartier-Bresson decidedly aimed to capture the most 'fugitive and transitory' facial expressions to reflect the personality of a subject. He pointed out that besides psychology and camera position, the 'decisive moment' was one of the 'principal factors in the making of a good portrait'.[42] Another common alternative to a straight look into the camera was the exchange of glances among those being photographed. In that context, one frequently used technique was to position the camera at eye level with the subject, or even below. Robert Doisneau mastered this aesthetic means in his images of playing children on the outskirts and in the simple 'quartiers' of Paris.[43] Still, eye contact was only one representation of (particularly) nonverbal interaction: to picture kissing, hugging, dancing and playing served a similar aim.

To make this kind of interaction visible, the photographers had to get at 'close range'.[44] The unassigned but famous words of Robert Capa sharpen it: 'If your pictures aren't good enough you're not close enough.'[45] The popularity of 'standard' lenses with a focal length of 35mm or 50mm among street photographers required them to get physically close to their subjects in the streets. As a result, the involvement of the photographers became visible in the images.

Cartier-Bresson described how he nonetheless tried to evade the impression of unrest and aggressiveness, for example, by avoiding the use of a flash and working with available light. He illustrated that he tried to get 'in unison with [the] movement [of the subject] as though it' was 'a presentiment of the way in which life itself unfolds'. Within that movement, he asserted, there was a moment 'in which the elements in motion are in balance'. Besides the notion of balance, he employed the metaphors of 'organic coordination' and 'rhythm', which reflected his practical way of tiptoeing as unobtrusively as possible around his subjects in the streets.[46]

The Family of Man

The 'essentials' of humanist photography also shaped one particularly prominent manifestation of the 'Gaze' that has to be dealt with in detail: *The Family of Man*. Without doubt, this exhibition was its most condensed expression and gave rise to elaborate reflections about the approach as a whole. It was at the New York Museum of Modern Art (MoMA) in 1955 and has been well researched, as has its subsequent journey around the world.[47] Many features of the exhibition will already be familiar after the general inspection of humanist photography.

The curator, Luxembourg-born photographer Edward Steichen, tried to represent the diversity of humankind and the variety of human practices, while at the same time identifying what unified humankind. His basic assumption was a universal comprehensibility of photographic images. Before and after the exhibition, Steichen elucidated his thoughts on the 'potentialities of photography' as a universal language and thus clearly matched Ansel Adams' expectations from 1944. As 'a visual means of mass communication', Steichen stated, photography had 'become a force, and stands without a peer'.[48] Similar assumptions about the ability of photography to reach beyond 'language barriers', 'oceans and continents' to 'communicate the realities of life' can be found in many accounts by photographers' reflections on their own medium. The eminent photographer and educator Berenice Abbott put this into a pithy motto in her popular introduction to photography: '[T]he eye knows no nation.'[49] Steichen's exhibition at MoMA became the foremost manifestation of this idea. With more than 500 pictures by photographers from eighty-six countries, the exhibition was truly global in its scope. By 1964, it had reached more than nine million people in dozens of countries, becoming the figurehead of visual approaches focusing on universal humanity – for epigones as much as for critics.

The universal potentials of photography were highly valued by the organizers and the curator. Strikingly, they were not confident enough of the intelligibility of the exhibition's message to dispense with the written word altogether; thematically related groups of images were always combined with short philosophical, religious or literary quotes, sayings and aphorisms from all around the world. Most statements assumed general qualities of humankind or touched alleged universal aspects of the human condition. This juxtaposition of images and words showed how closely concepts of humanity, human rights and humanitarianism were intertwined not only semantically but also visually. An image of the United Nations Assembly, framed by a quote from its charter concerning the 'faith in fundamental human rights', was included.[50] One of the stated aims of the exhibition was to stimulate 'thinking concerning the problems of the human community, and inspiring humanitarian feelings by presenting the unifying elements common to man and thus promoting friendship and peace among all nations and races'.[51]

What did the visual counterpart to this broad semantic field look like? As the title of the exhibition implied, representations of family life were of great importance: love, courtship, marriage, pregnancy, babies and children. Other core areas were images of everyday and leisure activities. Play, music, festivities and dance, religious as well as other spiritual practices were on display. It is easy to recognize a rather conventional repertoire of anthropological constants in this choice of predominant motifs. Humanist photography represented experiences that were supposedly *familiar* to all people – with the aim of presenting 'the unifying elements common to man'. Hard work, self-doubt and loneliness were also shown – famine, revolt, upheaval, even lynching. Nonetheless, a vision of human goodness prevailed. This vision directly correlated with (and at the same time juxtaposed to) the cruelties of the Nazi regime: a quotation from the diary of Anne Frank framed a passage with images that broached the issue of adolescence in different cultures: 'I still believe that people are really good at heart.'[52] Steichen consciously chose this optimistic bias. He had tried a negative approach in exhibitions before and had presented hard images of war, but had to concede that this had failed strategically – it did not influence the spectators in the way he wanted to. He also discarded the idea of curating an exhibition on human rights because he suspected that this topic had already become 'international political football' by that time.[53]

Summing up the combination of photographic essentials of humanist photography, the basic assumptions of *The Family of Man* and the prevailing themes described so far, they translate into a basic visual concept of humanity that was supposed to be universally understandable: humanity becomes visible in condensed narrations of recognizable everyday situations. The spectator encounters them at close range, frequently even at eye-level, while being pushed into personal, often emotional, interactions.

The Humanist Vision in Photojournalism and Travelogues by the 'Concerned Photographer'

The typical visual elements of the Human Gaze gained presence in popular photo books and in the booming weekly illustrated magazines like *Life, Paris Match,*

Stern and *Picture Post,* to name just a few in different countries. Their enormous thirst for 'human interest' photography was an important precondition for the broad diffusion of the Human Gaze.[54] This development has convincingly been described a 'humanist vision' in photojournalism, especially for the 1950s.[55] Since the interwar years, small 35mm cameras had made a 'new picture-story format' possible, which, for example, in Germany was promoted particularly by the Hungarian editor Stefan Lorant, who had popularized unposed 'candid shooting' to show people 'as they really are' at the *Berliner Illustrirte Zeitung* and the *Münchner Illustrierte Presse* as early as the mid 1920s.[56] In the United States, *Life* from the late 1930s popularized this characteristic approach.[57] Other magazines around the world emulated the typical style more or less quickly.[58] It offered striking compatibilities with humanist photography. As Margaret Bourke-White described it in retrospect, *Life* was committed to 'tell[ing] the news in pictures' from its first issue in 1936. This meant that it aimed to narrate and condense stories through photographic images – and humans were frequently in focus. Bourke-White, who did not even articulate a particular humanist self-conception, nonetheless stated in her autobiography that her photographic work for *Life* was all about helping to 'interpret human situations by showing the larger world into which people fitted'.[59]

There was not only compatibility between *Life's* way of telling stories visually and the humanist photographic approach. Already the late 1940s saw photographic longtime projects of illustrated magazines that antedated *The Family of Man* conceptually. An important predecessor (probably even a creative inspiration for Steichen) was John G. Morris. The editor of the influential *Ladies' Home Journal* sent *Magnum* photographers around the world in 1948 to capture the everyday life of twelve families in as many countries. The title of the story was: '"People are People the World Over'. Twelve Countries, Three Races and Five Religious Faiths. They Speak Eleven Languages.'[60] That story was in many respects typical of journalistic implementations of the humanist approach: an affinity to extensive travelling and a tendency to produce elaborate photo essays.

The claim to capture even the most complex stories visually frequently led to long series of photographs. Cartier-Bresson stated that even in photojournalism, a 'single picture' *could* be 'a whole story in itself', but he conceded that 'this rarely happens'.[61] The tendency to produce long series of pictures to capture the whole story often caused conflicts between editors and photographers.[62] Sometimes it even led to serious problems. W. Eugene Smith, a highly praised war photographer and surely a prime exponent of the long 'humanistic photographic essay',[63] was the most dramatic example of passionate involvement and sometimes self-destructive excesses. In 1955, after a conflict-laden time at *Life* and during his temporary affiliation with *Magnum,* he got a three-week-assignment to produce photographs for a book edited by Stefan Lorant on the occasion of Pittsburgh's bicentennial. Smith could not be held off staying for a year. He took about 16,000 photographs.[64]

This was an extreme example. Yet, the ambition to use photography as a language to encompass complex phenomena often led to long visual 'texts'. Photographers aspired to publish monographic editions of their work on a specific topic. Moreover, many of those named so far gained attention doing so.[65]

Strikingly often, their books were autobiographical travelogues. Travelling was a crucial part of the photographer's work and before the backdrop of humanist universalism, this also had a symbolic dimension: photographers travelled the world to capture the commonalities of humankind. Against the backdrop of the incipient Cold War, this message took on a political meaning. Nonetheless, most of the photographers explicitly distanced themselves from politics and asserted the neutrality of their coverage. Photobooks on journeys through 'hot spots' of the Cold War became hugely popular. Capa and Cartier-Bresson teamed up with intellectuals and writers for spectacular accounts of China and Russia.[66] The hardly accessible Eastern Bloc held particular fascination in the light of their own assertion that there 'had been no camera coverage of the Soviet Union by an American for many years' before Capa and John Steinbeck entered Russia in 1947.[67] Consistent with the universal message, the books were presented in a demonstratively apolitical manner. Steinbeck stated in the explication of his project with Capa: 'Russian politics are important just as ours are, but there must be the great other side there, just as there is here. There must be a private life of the Russian People, and that we could not read about because no one wrote about it, and no one photographed it.'[68] Capa's images that accompanied the text strongly resembled the humanist visual repertoire. As Steinbeck remarked in his introductory words, the photos showed 'everyday-life': people holding their children, people playing and dancing, working and eating.[69] The simple words Steinbeck used to summarize their investigation at the end of the *Russian Journal* also mirrored the basic assumptions of the humanist approach: 'We found, as we had suspected, that the Russian people are people, and, as with other people, that they are very nice.'[70] Cartier-Bresson's images of China (1948–49), for which Jean-Paul Sartre wrote an introduction in the French edition, and those of the Soviet Union from 1954 presented a very similar visual repertoire.[71] They featured in *Life* and were praised for 'show[ing] the Russians as intensely human beings'.[72]

The connectivity to discourses and intellectual statements on the Cold War can be understood as another important precondition for the spread of the Human Gaze, especially in the 1950s. The examples also allude to an additional characteristic feature: there was a tendency to include biographical and often autobiographical passages in the publications. They make it possible to trace the discursive construction of the 'humanist photographer'. Not only in the monographs but also in magazine articles, the textual framing of the photographs was frequently shaped by this specific social figure: a passionate, occasionally audacious, and more often heroic[73] photographer supplying the world with pictures that communicated humanity. In *Life,* for example, prominent photojournalists like Carl Mydans and the photographic staff were frequently mentioned in articles. Cartier-Bresson's name and his coverage of Moscow during the Cold War even made it to the cover.[74]

In the magazines, in the autobiographical passages of their features, but also in comments of prominent writers like Steinbeck, downright legends of 'humanist photographers' were created.[75] The magazines were not the only actors making use of their prominent photographic staff for marketing. Agencies, particularly *Magnum Photos,* strategically employed the social figure of the 'humanist photographer'. The leading figures of the agency even invented a generic term: 'The Concerned Photographer'. In particular, Cornell Capa, the brother of Robert, worked hard to perpetuate the legend of the outstanding humanist with a camera. His work on the 'myth' of *Magnum*[76] was manifested in a 'memorial fund' for his brother, 'to promote the understanding and appreciation of photography as a medium for revealing the human condition'. The fund as much as a series of exhibitions and photo books traded under the name 'The Concerned Photographer'.[77] In that context, Cornell Capa was probably the one who continued to publish the most extensive assumptions on the potentials of photography until the 1970s. In doing so, he frequently alluded to Robert Capa and opened up analogies to religious history. Introducing a volume he edited on Jerusalem, he considered photography 'the most logical place to make a statement on the human condition'. Whereas once 'the message – in several versions – came from there in *words*; it seems fitting that the new message now emanate from there in photographic images – the universal language of the twentieth century'.[78]

The popularity and connectivity of such constructions of humanist photographers should be noted as another key condition for the success of the Human Gaze. The social figure obviously had a market value – *he* (the construction unmistakably had a male connotation) stood for commitment, sometimes heroism and even recklessness; the reports from his adventurous and often exotic travels supported the claims for authenticity on which the illustrated magazines based their relevance. Thereby the photographers themselves became part of media representation.

The Trickle Down of the Human Gaze

The diffusion of the Human Gaze went significantly beyond the figureheads and beyond the prestigious illustrated magazines named so far. An unmistakable sign hinting at the popularization of the respective visual means was the emergence of the relevant visual and technical repertoire in photographic 'how to' literature. A first type of literature showing the diffusion was handbooks for aspiring *professional* journalists. A revealing example is the introduction to *Press Photography* by Robert B. Rhode and Floyd H. McCall. At the time, Rhode was Associate Professor of Journalism at the University of Colorado, while McCall was chief photographer at the *Denver Post*. Already on the first pages, they praised the photographer's ability to capture the 'full range of human experience'.[79] The rest of the introduction showed the authors' familiarity with communication theories, but was also perfectly in tune with Steichen's assumptions on photography as a 'the most universal of all languages'. By not having to rely on 'abstract symbols' and 'words', it was supposed to be more directly understandable: 'it is a medium, exceptional for its universality when used properly . . . in the sense that photographs are not "foreign" to anyone, no matter what his native tongue'.[80] In their opinion, the 'effectiveness of photography as a universal language' had 'never been better demonstrated' than by '*Life* and *Look* magazines' during the Second World War. They described the typical search for 'the storytelling shot, or series of shots that can be arranged in a picture story or picture essay' and presented various crucial techniques. Among them was working with available light, i.e. without a flash, all with the aim to capture 'the complexities of human relationships'.[81]

This shows that basic characteristics of the Human Gaze had made their way past *Magnum* and *Rapho* into 'everyday' photojournalism. Methodologically, it is hard to judge on the diffusion of the humanist approach among *amateur* photographers in detail. But there is evidence that not only professionals followed in the footsteps of *The Family of Man,* Cartier-Bresson, Capa and others. A useful hint is the recent discovery of the body of work by the solitary amateur Vivian Maier. The eccentric full-time nanny secretly produced a broad oeuvre throughout the 1950s and 1960s in the streets of (not only) American cities. Her style was complex and cannot be reduced to humanist photography. Many of her pitiless images of adults seem to stem from a darker, partially even anti-humanist tradition of street photography.[82] However, her images of children are strikingly reminiscent of Cartier-Bresson and Doisneau.[83]

We are not even dependent on such fortuitous discoveries. The figureheads themselves, including Edward Steichen, encouraged amateurs to follow their trails. Already in 1947 at a meeting of the Photographic Society of America (PSA), visited by amateurs from the United States, Canada and Mexico, he urged them to focus on nothing but humanity: 'Let's photograph humanity . . . Let's stop quibbling about whether it's going to be a pictorial or a documentary. Let's forget the interminable talk about points of interest and "S" curves.'[84] Different journals – e.g. *Popular Photography* – aimed to decipher and teach elements of the typical visual language. The periodical literature also hints at activities by amateur photo clubs that emulated the humanist approach and strove to recreate something like *The Family of Man,* albeit in a local setting.[85] Additionally, there also was a 'how to' literature for *amateurs.* It taught many of the techniques and approaches discussed above to novices. A rich and comprehensive example for the diffusion of the described characteristics was the 1953 edition of Berenice Abbott's *New Guide to Better Photography.* In her profound introduction, she pleaded to bring 'human beings' 'into the picture' and praised the ability of photography to transcend 'language barriers'. In her view, photography should (and could) be a 'broad humanistic art, as wide as the world of human thought and action'.[86]

Other 'self-help' books taught prospective photographers how to capture the 'human spark' on film. They learned not only about the visual language and concepts, but also received precise instruction on the technical approach and the essential gear. A telling example is a handbook for owners of the German Leica camera published as early as 1938, which taught readers how to tell 'simple human stories' by using compact, fast, wide-aperture lenses without flash and to avoid missing the decisive motives during the 'critical moments' of changing the lens.[87] It comes as no surprise that a publication on the use of the Leica cameras discussed all these technical aspects. The famous brand and its celebrated range-finder cameras cannot be separated from the discourses on and the social practice of visualizing humanity through photography. The small and lightweight camera was an important precondition of this photographic approach and became a myth in its own right.[88]

Humanitarian Photography

A last and very important precondition of the institutionalization and diffusion of the 'Gaze' is the field of humanit*arian* photography in a narrower sense. Not only does the thematic scope of the volume at hand suggest taking a closer look at the visual repertoires of humanitarian campaigns, but scholars from various disciplines have also emphasized how much the humanitarian narrative as well as the 'human rights culture' was characteristic especially of the 'post-Holocaust age'.[89] Visualizations were crucial to a narrative that aimed at a universal form of collectivization, which can be described as the globalization of compassion.[90] The ongoing specialized research on the history of humanitarian photography already gives insights into the imagery of campaigns by many humanitarian organizations, especially regarding concepts and visualizations of cruelty.[91] Yet it does not give many clues for tracking down the images and underlying concepts of humanity. To understand and explain the broad diffusion of the Human Gaze, it also seems crucial to understand its compatibility with the 'humanitarian narrative'.

A prominent humanitarian postwar project of UNESCO, to pick just one case, shows that campaigns not only focused on suffering and cruelty but also displayed humanity. The 'official' aim of *The Family of Man* represents well the main objective of humanitarian campaigns as well: to inspire 'humanitarian feelings by presenting the unifying elements common to man'.[92] The globalization of compassion was dependent on a means to visualize common elements of humankind. Looking at the respective visual strategies after the war quickly brings the network of early *Magnum* photographers into view again. One particularly telling case was the 1949 project 'Children of Europe' by *Magnum* cofounder David Seymour, whose work is an exemplary representation of the principles of the Human Gaze as described above.[93] He documented the life and suffering of children all over postwar Europe. The published images contained many elements of the humanist visual repertoire: children in everyday situations, the appearance of authenticity not staged, the characteristic eye contact, the motifs of dance and play – to name just a few.[94] Not surprisingly, an image from Seymour's UNESCO campaign also appeared in *The Family of Man* a few years later: Italian children dancing in circles holding hands – in front of ruins.[95] Seymour made the misery of Europe's children visible and the after-effects of cruelty were one of the main themes of the volume. However, the visual strategy aimed at something else: Seymour's images mainly show that those affected by unprecedented cruelty were human beings in need of solidarity.

To be clear, the visual representation of 'naked' cruelty (e.g. devastation, mutilation and corpses) is a relevant element of humanitarian imagery, one that was frequently employed throughout the twentieth century. Nevertheless, a hybrid form was of even greater relevance, at least for the immediate postwar era. An exemplar of this form is the war photography of Robert Capa and others: suffering, death and cruelty were presented within the campaigns and coverage. Yet as a visual pattern, they only worked in contrast to humanity, which was shown simultaneously. These representations have a history of their own and draw upon the visual repertoire of the Human Gaze.

Criticism of the 'Gaze'

Recapitulating all these contexts and means of diffusion of the 'Gaze' in the after-war years may sound like a straight success story. At first sight, it may seem hard to criticize visual approaches that aimed at global understanding and a humanitarian spirit at all. What could be bad about understanding and solidarity between all humankind? On closer examination, *The Family of Man* in 1955 was already the '[h]ighpoint of twentieth-century photographic humanism'.[96] The middle of the century offered a particularly dynamic and ambivalent constellation. On the one hand, the optimism that images of humanity were able to bridge inequality and even political antagonism were never more pronounced than in the mid 1950s. On the other hand, *The Family of Man* and its intellectual reception also marked a discursive shift. The belief in the potentials of the visual and the criticism of the respective views coexisted from that time onwards and were polarized in intellectual debates as well as being embodied in subsequent exhibitions. Although the confident basic argument of *The Family of Man* was and continues to be repeated in other contexts,[97] some basic a priorities of the exhibition's concept were criticized immediately in 1955. A particularly influential critique came from Roland Barthes, who deconstructed the implicit 'Adamism' and suspected that this 'myth' ultimately served to stabilize and justify social inequality.[98]

The most fundamental criticism focused directly on the basic assumptions of the exhibition: some contemporaries perceived Steichen's approach as neither universal nor apolitical. It even seems plausible that the high compatibility of the visual approach with 'Western' and 'modernist' ideologies in the Cold War was an important precondition of its success. At the same time, in the eyes of critical contemporaries, the exhibition's universal humanity was dominated not only by Christian imagery, but also by the 'bourgeois' nuclear family.[99] Consciously or not, Steichen's search for a pancultural core of humanity implied a specific master narrative of Western modernity.[100]

Even some younger artists whose images were in the exhibition criticized the 'benevolent, sentimentalized view of humanity'.[101] Susan Sontag later sharpened that criticism. Her work on photography from the 1970s took the exhibition as an important argumentative starting point. She systematically historicized the photographic 'humanism' of the 1950s and highlighted that, seventeen years after *The Family of Man,* another photo exhibition attracted masses to the MoMA. However, the message it seemed to convey was very different: a retrospective of the work of Diane Arbus, who had died in 1971, decidedly opposed the assumption that humanity was 'one'. Arbus' photography dealt with social outsiders or 'freaks', as she referred to them, and she radically undermined prevalent aesthetic preferences like those of humanist photography. In her famous book-length essay *On Photography,* Sontag proclaimed: 'The Arbus photographs convey the anti-humanist message, which people of good will in the 1970s are eager to be troubled by, just as they wished, in the 1950s, to be consoled an distracted by sentimental humanism.'[102] The early criticism of the Human Gaze was thus sharpened and systematized in the 1970s. The posthumous success of Arbus, whose work was showcased in 1972 at the Venice Biennial, may be considered proof of the popularity of anti-humanist visual languages. Furthermore, the 1970s mark a very practical shift in media history that can only be alluded to here: although it still produced a huge amount of 'iconic' photographs and much-discussed press photographs, the Vietnam War was the first global media event in which photography lost significant ground to television.[103] In addition, the heydays of illustrated magazines like *Life* had ended.

Persistence and Further Diffusion

All this may indicate a gradual decline of the Human Gaze. At the same time, it is easy to find evidence of broad optimism towards the unifying potentials of photography as a 'world language'.[104] Beyond intellectual debates and regardless of the intellectual and artistic countermovements, it lived on in other communicative spaces and was sometimes even radicalized. One example has already been discussed above – Cornell Capa's work on the 'myth' of the 'Concerned Photographer'. It also lived on in the efforts of publishers and museum curators.

One example for an influential publisher with a strong interest in photography and an affinity to humanist approaches was Dumont in Germany.[105] Also in the Federal Republic of Germany (and some other European countries), a project that strongly resembled *The Family of Man* was pursued from the mid 1960s to the 1970s under the title *Weltausstellung der Photographie* (World Exhibition of Photography).[106] In the exhibitions and in the catalogues, the photos were organized in chapters and arranged in a sentence-like order. The whole project was based on an understanding of photography as a universal language, but it was not universally admired. Its curator, Karl Pawek, was sharply criticized. The weekly *Der Spiegel* called the project a 'pretentious panopticon' – '*Family of Man* with a dash of *Mondo Cane*' (an Italian pseudo-documentary released in 1962, assembling scenes of cruelty and depravity for shock effect). Still, the magazine had to concede that the catalogue was a 'bestseller'.[107]

In the GDR, an exhibition entitled *Vom Glück des Menschen* (*On the Happiness of People*) emulated and simultaneously criticized *The Family of Man* (and the *Weltausstellung*) in 1967. Unsurprisingly, here the kind of family presented as an ideal of humanity was far from 'bourgeois': It was 'a socialist family of man', and socialism appeared as the crucial precondition for a truly humane world.[108]

The list of manifestations of the 'Gaze' since the 1970s could be prolonged and differentiated. To conclude, I will only hint at one last dimension of its diffusion that went further – not only in order of time but also space. As described above, the Human Gaze was accused of being Western and modernist. The fact that some humanist photographers permanently circled the world for their work did not exempt them from these framings. Although references to the Western origins were always sustained, the 'Gaze' also partially detached itself from that framing until the late twentieth century. There has on the one hand been a profound critique of Western stereotyping of Africa and the inherent 'decontextualizing' of suffering through humanist approaches in photography (as opposed to 'pluralist photography').[109] On the other hand, there are hints at creative adaptions of the 'Gaze' and humanist aesthetics in various 'non-Western' framings, e.g. in South Africa (already since the 1950s)[110] or Japan.[111] A particularly illustrative example may be the Indian photographer Raghubir Singh, who consciously adapted the Human Gaze to pursue postcolonial concerns.[112] As he explained in 1998,[113] he felt a special affinity for the flexibility and agility of Cartier-Bresson's characteristic way of taking pictures. He defined the latter as a countermodel to the colonial photographer, who staged his own imaginations of India in front of tripods and heavy monorail cameras. In this open-eyed search for 'decisive moments' in a foreign culture, Singh recognized in Cartier-Bresson's work the exact opposite of such colonial approaches.

At the same time, Singh transformed the visual language by adapting it in a certain way: he combined it with traditions of Indian miniature painting – which were eminently colourful.[114] By contrast, colour photography was scorned among serious 'Western' photographers until the late 1960s (and for many even beyond that time). This last characteristic of the Human Gaze, which has not been dealt with, lost its axiomatic character later in the century: images of humanity, which for a long time were exclusively black and white, gained colour. This was not only due to technical reasons, but also had a symbolic dimension, as Singh's reflections show. It would be an overestimation of Singh's influence on humanist photography in general to make him alone responsible for the increased importance of colour. Western artists and street photographers like Saul Leiter, Helen Levitt, William Eggleston and Fred Herzog had begun to pioneer colour photography in the 1960s and certainly in Leiter's even earlier. Nevertheless, to this day, it seems that the 'Colours of India' inspire photographers, who feel committed to the humanist tradition. This becomes most obvious when we finally look at one of the most prominent contemporary representatives: *Magnum*'s Steve McCurry. He gained much of his prestige by the unique use of colour in his coverage of humanitarian crises and everyday life in Asia, though he is also notable for his landscapes. Before his first and defining trip to India, he had made himself familiar with the work of Cartier-Bresson and Bourke-White, who had produced some of the most prominent photographic accounts on India in black and white. Unlike them, he travelled to India in 1978 with a suitcase containing 250 rolls of Kodachrome colour film.[115] For him and many other photographers, India and its cultural traditions has since then formed an important space of experience for 'serious' humanist photographers using colour.

To conclude, it was possible to produce evidence for a significant 'rise' of the Human Gaze after the Second World War. In the immediate postwar years, a qualitatively new link between humanity and visual representation was established. The visual repertoire of universal humanity received particular attention in the 1940s and 1950s, and *The Family of Man* certainly contributed to this attention significantly. Nevertheless, it is also unquestionable that the respective visual patterns derived from older photographic traditions. After *The Family of Man* and throughout the rest of the century, a characteristic coexistence of sharp criticism and persistence of the Human Gaze evolved. It continues to shape our perception of humanity. At the same time, we have to note that the 'rise and fall' of humanist approaches in humanit*arian* photography throughout the twentieth century still has to be fully traced – particularly in its relation to representations of cruelty. It will be rewarding to examine shifts in the prevalence of either 'shocking' images of cruelty or images of humanity aiming to represent the underlying unity of humankind. While the latter probably dominated the 1940s and 1950s, the Vietnam War produced a huge number of images of cruelty. Whether, for instance, the representation of the Biafra famine or other humanitarian crises by the media led to effects of 'oversaturation' with images of cruelty and suffering remains to be examined. Particular attention should be paid to the Rwandan genocide as a defining moment that had similar effects on the photographers involved[116] to the coverage of German concentration camps at the end of the Second World War.

Figure 6.1. Children were a common motif of the classic French photographie humaniste. Robert Doisneau frequently captured them at eye level, playing in everyday situations in recognizable urban (in this case suburban) settings. This image was entitled 'L'enfant papillon' ('The Butterfly Child') and taken in Saint-Denis in 1945. It was frequently reprinted, e.g. in J.-C. Gautrand, *Robert Doisneau. 1912–1994* (Cologne: Taschen, 2003), 53. Photo by Robert Doisneau. Gamma Rapho archives.

Figure 6.2. Henri Cartier-Bresson also frequently took the characteristic pictures of children. In his work on the Soviet Union, he contrasted the portraits of Lenin, Stalin and other politicians with a typical scene from a young pioneer camp near Moscow in 1954. It also was printed in *Life*: Anonymous, The People of Russia, *Life* 38(3) (17 January 1955), 25. Photo by Henri Cartier-Bresson. Magnum Photos/Agentur Focus.

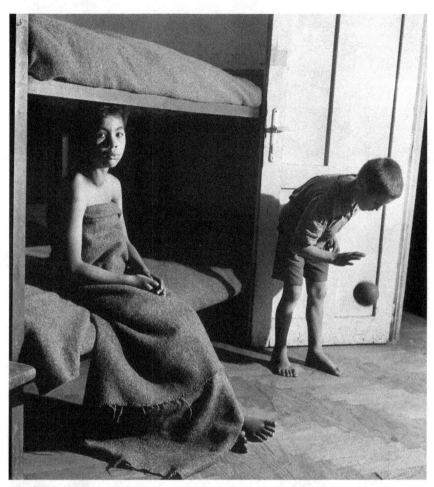

Figure 6.3. This image was taken by David Seymour in Hungary in 1948 as part of his UNESCO project 'Children of Europe'. It brought together multiple characteristics of the humanist approach: children, viewed from below in a rather close distance, an intensive eye-contact and the motive of play. We see two children in a detention room at a police station. The two boys were found in the streets in need of care. It was printed in David Seymour, *Children of Europe* (Paris: UNESCO, 1949), 28. The image paradigmatically shows the combined display of calamity and humanity, typical of the humanist visual strategy in humanitarian contexts. Photo by David Seymour. Magnum Photos/Agentur Focus.

Tobias Weidner is a research assistant at Georg-August-University Göttingen and teaches nineteenth and twentieth-century history. His current project focuses on photographic representations of 'humanity' since the 1940s. He holds a PhD in History from Bielefeld University and wrote a dissertation on the relation of German medical men and politics in the long nineteenth century. His research interests include visual history, the cultural history of politics, historical semantics and the theory of history. His recent monographs are *Die Geschichte des Politischen in der Diskussion* (2012) and *Die unpolitische Profession: Deutsche Mediziner im 'langen' 19. Jahrhundert* (2012).

Notes

1. R. Eichberg, 'Will Rogers, Jr. – Congressman with a Camera', *Popular Photography* 5 (1943), 34–35, 70–71.
2. Ibid., 34, 70f.
3. For biographical notes, see: Anonymous. 'Rogers, William Vann, Jr.', *Biographical Directory of the United States Congress,* Retrieved 22 August 2018 from http://bioguide.congress.gov/scripts/biodisplay.pl?index=R000406.
4. See, for example, R. Graf and C. Goschler, *Europäische Zeitgeschichte seit 1945* (Berlin: Akademie Verlag, 2010), especially 151–53. P. Gödde, 'Globale Kulturen', in A. Iriye and J. Osterhammel (eds), *Geschichte der Welt 1945 bis heute: Die globalisierte Welt* (Munich: C.H. Beck, 2013), 535–670; S.-L. Hoffmann (ed.), *Human Rights in the Twentieth Century* (Cambridge: Cambridge University Press, 2011); recently J. Eckel, *Die Ambivalenz des Guten: Menschenrechte in der internationalen Politik seit den 1940ern* (Göttingen: Vandenhoeck & Ruprecht, 2014); L. Wildenthal and S.-L. Hoffmann, *The Language of Human Rights in West Germany* (Philadelphia: University of Pennsylvania Press, 2012).
5. See J. Paulmann (ed.) *Dilemmas of Humanitarian Aid in the Twentieth Century* (Oxford: Oxford University Press, 2016); M.N. Barnett, *Empire of Humanity: A History of Humanitarianism* (Ithaca: Cornell University Press, 2011); and R. Brown and R. Ashby Wilson (eds), *Humanitarianism and Suffering: The Mobilization of Empathy* (Cambridge: Cambridge University Press, 2009).
6. Ideals of humanism gained great importance in German intellectual debates and networks. See S.A. Forner, 'Für eine demokratische Erneuerung Deutschlands: Kommunikationsprozesse und Deutungsmuster engagierter Demokraten nach 1945', *Geschichte und Gesellschaft* 33(2) (2007), 228–57. In addition, immediately after the war, German literary debates focused on the reception of Goethe and the 'correct' understanding of humanism: H. Saner, 'Existenzielle Aneignung und historisches Verstehen: Zur Debatte Jaspers-Curtius um die Goethe-Rezeption', in B. Weidmann (ed.), *Existenz in Kommunikation: Zur philosophischen Ethik von Karl Jaspers* (Würzburg: Königshausen u. Neumann, 2005), 151–66, at 151.
7. See e.g. the main definitions in the *Oxford Advanced Learner's Dictionary,* 7th ed. (Oxford: Oxford University Press 1992), 608. All these layers of meaning (and many more) occur simultaneously even in individual uses of the term. Indistinct semantic demarcations to the related concepts named above and further pejorative collocations (hardly found in dictionaries) complicate the case even more.

8. A brilliant example of conceptual history of *Humanität* and similar *Grundbegriffe*, especially in the eighteenth and nineteenth centuries, is H.E. Bödeker, 'Menschheit, Humanität, Humanismus', in O. Brunner, W. Conze and R. Koselleck (eds), *Geschichtliche Grundbegriffe: Historisches Lexikon zur politisch-sozialen Sprache in Deutschland* (Stuttgart: Klett-Cotta, 1982), vol. 3, 1063–128.

9. See J. Paulmann, 'Humanity – Humanitarian Reason – Imperial Humanitarianism. European Concepts in Practice', in F. Klose and M. Thulin (eds), *Humanity: A History of European Concepts in Practice from the Sixteenth Century to the Present* (Göttingen: Vandenhoeck & Ruprecht, 2017), 287–311.

10. For recent reflections on 'Conceptual History beyond Language', see M. Pernau and I. Rajamani, 'Emotional Translations: Conceptual History beyond Language', *History and Theory* 55 (2016), 46–65. I would like to thank them and the participants of their Berlin workshop in December 2015 for their advice. I would also like to thank Sascha Schießl for his help with the manuscript and Annette Vowinckel for important hints.

11. Foucault's 'medical gaze' and its modification by visual historians in the 'tourist gaze' inspired this approach. See M. Foucault, *The Birth of the Clinic: An Archaeology of Medical Perception* (London: Tavistock, 1973); C. Pagenstecher, 'Reisekataloge und Urlaubsalben: Zur Visual History des touristischen Blicks', in G. Paul (ed.), *Visual History: Ein Studienbuch* (Göttingen: Vandenhoeck & Ruprecht, 2006), 169–87.

12. See W. Steinmetz, 'New Perspectives on the Study of Language and Power in the Short Twentieth Century', in W. Steinmetz (ed.), *Political Languages in the Age of Extremes* (Oxford: Oxford University Press, 2011), 3–51.

13. A. Adams, 'A Personal Credo', *American Annual of Photography* 58 (1944), 7–16, cited by N. Lyons (ed.), *Photographers on Photography* (Englewood Cliffs, NJ: Prentice Hall, 1966), 25–26.

14. But he gained prominence well after his death in 1927 and owes much of this to Berenice Abbott. She had bought his estate, published a book on him in 1964 and sold his pictures to the Museum of Modern Art in 1969. See B. Abbott, *The World of Atget* (New York: Horizon Press, 1964).

15. C.H. Cookman, *American Photojournalism: Motivations and Meanings* (Evanston, IL: Northwestern University Press, 2009), 224.

16. See e.g. K. Acker, *Dorothea Lange* (Philadelphia: Chelsea House Publishers, 2004). But as far as I can see, this *ex post* denomination dates back to the 1970s. See H. O'Neal, *A Vision Shared: A Classic Portrait of America and its People, 1935–1943* (New York: St Martin's Press, 1976), 75–144.

17. Some of the FSA photographs – two of them by Lange – were included in *The Family of Man* (see below). See A. Böger, *People's Lives, Public Images: The New Deal Documentary Aesthetic* (Tübingen: Narr, 2001), 172. Also, the tendency of documentary photography to transcend one medium and go beyond 'words alone', 'to see, know and feel the details of life, to feel oneself part of some other's experience', antedate an approach that was condensed and reflected in *The Family of Man*. This is the interpretation given by Warren Susman: W. Susman, 'The Thirties', in Stanley Coben and Lorman Ratner (eds), *The Development of an American Culture* (Englewood Cliffs, NJ: Prentice Hall, 1970), 179–218, as cited by Böger, *People's Lives,* 42.

18. The prominent reflections on the *photographie humaniste* by figureheads of the French 'movement' cited by Thézy – especially Cartier-Bresson – also have their origins in the postwar period. See M. de Thézy and C. Nori, *La photographie humaniste: 1930–1960 : Histoire d'un mouvement en France* (Paris: Contrejour, 1992), especially 15 and 16.

19. J.-C. Gautrand, *Paris mon Amour* (Cologne: Taschen, 2014), 18.
20. It had been drafted between 1946 and 1948 – 'precisely the Period when Magnum was in the making'. C. Chéroux, 'Magnum Manifesto', in C. Chéroux and C. Bouveresse (eds), *Magnum Manifesto* (London: Thames & Hudson, 2017), 8–17, at 14.
21. How broadly photojournalists and especially war photographers conveyed humanitarian and humanist values within their work ethic is concisely described in the recent comprehensive study on the history of photographers in the twentieth century by A. Vowinckel, *Agenten der Bilder: Fotografisches Handeln im 20. Jahrhundert* (Göttingen: Wallstein, 2016), 82–88.
22. J.R. Whiting, 'Editorial', *Popular Photography* 15(5) (1944), 16.
23. M. Bourke-White, *Portrait of Myself* (New York: Simon & Schuster, 1963), 259f.
24. R. Capa, *Slightly Out of Focus* (New York: Holt, 1947) (as quoted in the reprint – New York: Modern Library 2001, 226).
25. G. Rodger, 'Paris, August 31, 1944', as quoted by A. Holzherr and I. Siben (eds), *On the Road 1940–1949: From the Diaries of a Photographer and Adventurer* (Ostfildern: Hatje Cantz, 2009), 37f.
26. See, for example, the introduction by Christian Caujolle in C. Caujolle, *Sebastião Salgado* (Heidelberg: Wachter, 2006), n.p.
27. The work of the latter will frequently serve as an exemplar of the humanist approach for two reasons: he was already regarded and analysed as a crucial exponent of humanist photography by contemporaries, and he provided reflections on the character of his own photographic work.
28. D. Masclet, 'Un reporter . . . Henri Cartier-Bresson, interview de Daniel Masclet', *Photo-Monde* 7 (1951), 28, as quoted by de Thézy and Nori, *La photographie humaniste*, 15.
29. H. Cartier-Bresson, *The Decisive Moment* (New York: Simon & Schuster, 1952), cited by N. Lyons (ed.), *Photographers on Photography* (Englewood Cliffs, NJ: Prentice Hall, 1966), 45. For the following characterizations, see especially: P. Hamilton, 'A Poetry of the Streets? Documenting Frenchness in an Era of Reconstruction: Humanist Photography 1935–1960', *French Literature Series* XXVII (2001), 177–217.
30. As an example, see the photograph 'L'enfant papillon' ('The Butterfly Child') by Robert Doisneau at the end of this chapter (Figure 6.1).
31. See e.g. D. Haberstich, 'Elliott Erwitt', in L. Warren (ed.), *Encyclopedia of Twentieth-Century Photography* (London: Routledge, 2005), 451–52.
32. Hamilton, 'A Poetry of the Streets?', 205.
33. See H.-M. Koetzle, 'Robert Capa: Spanischer Loyalist', in H.-M. Koetzle (ed.), *Photo Icons: Die Geschichte hinter den Bildern* (Cologne: Taschen, 2012), 178–87.
34. Cartier-Besson, *Decisive Moment*, 43.
35. This was an ironic comment Cartier-Bresson made when he was juxtaposed as an attracting 'opposite' with Helmut Newton for an interview – the latter being best known for ultimate sharpness in his carefully staged images. D. Thomas, 'Opposites Attract: Helmut Newton Shooting Cartier-Bresson? Too Weird. But', *Newsweek* (2 June 2003), 60.
36. Cartier-Bresson, *Decisive Moment*, 50.
37. K. Ward, '"In the Blink of an Eye": An Investigation into the Concept of the "Decisive Moment" (Augenblick) as Found in Nineteenth and Twentieth Century Western Philosophy', PhD dissertation (Perth: Murdoch University, 2005), 329.
38. Cartier-Bresson, *Decisive Moment*, 43.
39. Ibid., especially 46–47.

40. A master of ironic and amusing 'snaps' is Elliott Erwitt. See the extensive anthology of his work: E. Erwitt, *Snaps* (New York: Phaidon, 2001).

41. C. Sandburg, 'Prologue', in Museum of Modern Art (ed.), *The Family of Man: The Greatest Photographic Exhibition of All Time – 503 Pictures from 68 Countries – Created by Edward Steichen for the Museum of Modern Art* (New York: Maco, 1955), 2.

42. Cartier-Bresson, *Decisive Moment*, 46f.

43. For exemplification, see the following photos by Doisneau: 'Le bidon de lait' (1946), 'Le enfant papillon' (1945), 'Les enfants de la place Hébert' (1957), 'Le saut sans corde' (1953), 'La maison de carton' (1957), 'Le prisonnier' (1956) and 'Barricades et H.L.M' (1956) to name just a few. They are accessible e.g. in J.-C. Gautrand, *Robert Doisneau: 1912–1994* (Cologne: Taschen, 2003), 52f, 124f, 126, 128f.

44. Cartier-Bresson, *Decisive Moment*, 45.

45. R. Whelan, *Robert Capa: A Biography* (New York: Knopf, 1985), 211.

46. Cartier-Bresson, *Decisive Moment*, 44–46.

47. Two examples are E.J. Sandeen, *Picturing an Exhibition: The Family of Man and 1950s America* (Albuquerque: University of New Mexico Press, 1995); and M. Berlier, 'The Family of Man: Readings of an Exhibition', in B. Brennan and H. Hardt (eds), *Picturing the Past: Media, History, and Photography* (Urbana: University of Illinois Press, 1999), 206–41.

48. See, e.g., the condensed roundup of his assumptions in E. Steichen, 'On Photography', *Daedalus* 42 (1960), 136–37.

49. See e.g. B. Abbott, *New Guide to Better Photography*, revised ed. (New York: Crown, 1953), 12.

50. Museum of Modern Art, *The Family of Man*, 184ff.

51. This quote is taken from an investigation of reactions at the exhibition in Munich: Research Staff. Office of Public Affairs. American Embassy (ed.). 1956. *Visitors' Reactions to the 'Family of Man' Exhibit* (Series no. 2, Report – no. 225 – January 23, 1956), III.

52. Ibid., 162f.

53. E. Steichen, *Steichen: A Life in Photography* (New York: Harmony Books, 1963), 228.

54. On the importance of 'human interest' photography also in *Life,* see Abbott, *New Guide,* 35.

55. For this and the following passages, see Cookman, *American Photojournalism,* especially 223–38. Regarding the 'humanistische Bild' in photojournalism after the Second World War, see H. Knoch, 'Bewegende Momente: Dokumentarfotografie und die Politisierung der westdeutschen Öffentlichkeit vor 1968', in B. Weisbrod (ed.), *Die Politik der Öffentlichkeit – die Öffentlichkeit der Politik: Politische Medialisierung in der Geschichte der Bundesrepublik* (Wallstein: Göttingen, 2003), 97–122, especially 99–106.

56. Cookman, *Photojournalism,* 41f.

57. See e.g. K. Adatt, *Picture Perfect: Life in the Age of the Photo Op* (Princeton: Princeton University Press, 2008), 47.

58. For the influence of *Life* and 'Human Interest Photography', especially on German photojournalism, see B. Städter, *Verwandelte Blicke: Eine Visual History von Kirche und Religion in der Bundesrepublik 1945–1980* (Frankfurt am Main: Campus, 2011), 164ff. On the general influence especially since the 1960s, see also F. Bösch, *Mediengeschichte: Vom asiatischen Buchdruck zum Fernsehen* (Frankfurt am Main: Campus, 2011), 209.

59. Bourke-White, *Portrait of Myself,* 116.

60. J.G. Morris, 'People are People the World over', *Ladies' Home Journal* (April 1948–March 1949) (12 articles). See also Cookman, *American Photojournalism,* 226; and R. Miller,

Magnum. Fifty Years at the Front Line of History: The Story of the Legendary Photo Agency (New York: Grove Press, 1997), 56f.

61. Cartier-Bresson, *Decisive Moment,* 43.
62. See the many examples in Miller, *Magnum.*
63. See the now posthumously published 'Big Book' he had planned in the 1960s as a retrospective of his own work: W.E. Smith, *The Big Book,* K. Martinez, W. Johnson and J. Berger (eds) (Austin: University of Texas Press, 2013).
64. See Miller, *Magnum,* 138ff. The 'core' of the enormous body of work was published in 2003: S. Stephenson, A. Trachtenberg and W.W. Norton (eds), *Dream Street: W. Eugene Smith's Pittsburgh Project* (New York: Norton & Co, 2001).
65. Praise and attention did not always mean huge commercial success. For example, Cartier-Bresson's *Decisive Moment* quickly became a 'bible of photography', although the initial print run was rather small and it was not reissued for a long time. See the booklet with an essay on the history of Cartier-Bresson's book by Clément Chéroux accompanying the latest edition: C. Chéroux, *The Decisive Moment: A Bible for Photographers* (Göttingen: Steidl, 2014).
66. H. Cartier-Bresson and J.-P. Sartre, *D'une Chine à l'autre* (Paris: Delpire, 1954); J. Steinbeck, *A Russian Journal: With Pictures by Robert Capa* (New York: Viking Press, 1948).
67. Steinbeck, *Russian Journal,* 5. In 1941, Margaret Bourke-White had had the chance to photograph Moscow just before the German army invaded. See Anonymous, 'A *Life* Photographer Looks at Moscow a Week before the Nazi Invasion Began: Pictures by Margaret Bourke-White', *Life* 11(6) (11 August 1941), 17–27. In 1947, *Life* presented a set of pictures by Thomas D. McAvoy presenting the cultural life of Moscow: Anonymous, 'Spring Comes to Moscow', *Life* 22(15) (14 April 1947), 31–39.
68. Steinbeck, *Russian Journal,* 4.
69. They clearly outnumbered images of landscapes, buildings or technical infrastructures.
70. Steinbeck, *Russian Journal,* 220.
71. See, for example, the characteristic display of street scenes, dance, everyday activities of families and exceptionally often children in the German version: H. Cartier-Bresson, *China gestern und heute* (Düsseldorf: Rauch, 1955), e.g. 1–25, 34f, 70, 80, 114–17, 126, 128, 135. As an example from Russia, see Figure 6.2 at the end of this chapter.
72. Anonymous, 'The People of Russia: Part One: Moscow. Photographed by Henri-Cartier-Bresson', *Life* 38(3) (17 January 1955), 15–30, at 16.
73. See e.g. the comments on Robert Capa in the broad coverage of the 'Landings in Normandy', *Life* 16 (25) (9 June 1944), 25–37.
74. See the cover of: *Life* 38 (3) (17 January 1955).
75. For example, Steinbeck described a dialogue with the Russian consul general in New York who proposed to employ a Russian photographer for the 'Journal' project: 'And I replied, "But you have no Capas"'. Steinbeck, *Russian Journal,* 5.
76. Scholars have already taken up the 'myth': M. Christen and A. Holzer, 'Mythos Magnum: Die Geschichte einer legendären Fotoagentur', *Mittelweg* 36(5) (2007), 53–80.
77. See e.g. the exhibition catalogue C. Capa (ed.), *The Concerned Photographer: The Photographs of Werner Bischof, Robert Capa, David Seymour ('Chim'), André Kertész, Leonard Freed, Dan Weiner* (New York: Grossman, 1968). The myth of humanist photography is still being updated: the 'W. Eugene Smith Grant in Humanistic Photography' was founded in 1979 to 'seek out and encourage . . . independent voices' in photography, who, like Smith 'demonstrated a belief in the human spirit and the ability of humanity to rise above the immense destruction it had sown'. It is still awarded. See http://smithfund

.org/smith-legacy and http://smithfund.org/humanistic-photography (accessed 27 August 2018).

78. C. Capa, *Jerusalem: City of Mankind* (New York: Grossman, 1974), 10.

79. R.B. Rhode and F.H. McCall, *Press Photography: Reporting with a Camera* (New York: Macmillan, 1961), 1.

80. Ibid., 2ff.

81. Ibid., 27–29, 113, 138, 200. The authors also elaborated on different traditions of photography. Among them was also the documentary movement of the interwar years, which they partially praised, but also delimited from due to its mere 'concentration on human misery'; ibid., 29.

82. She has been compared to Diane Arbus, Robert Frank, Garry Winogrand or even Weegee. See e.g. T. Castle, 'New Art', *Harper's Magazine* (2015). Retrieved 22 August 2018 from harpers.org/archive/2015/02/new-art/?single=1. On the anti-humanist countermovement and especially on Arbus, see below.

83. See e.g. J. Maloof (ed.), *Vivian Maier, Street Photographer* (New York: Powerhouse, 2011), 14, 15 and 19.

84. Quoted in F. Fenner, Jr., 'Candid Shots', *Popular Photography* 20(1) (1947), 40.

85. P. Mozesson, 'San Francisco Weekend', *Popular Photography* 38(3) (1956), 60–63, 122–26. See the subheading on 60: 'San Francisco photographers Create Their Own "Family of Man".'

86. Abbott, *New Guide*, 8, 12, 18.

87. W.D. Morgan and H.M. Lester, *The Leica Manual: A Manual for the Amateur and Professional Covering the Field of Photography with the Leica Camera* (New York: Morgan & Lester, 1938), 521.

88. Many photographers commented on this aspect by themselves. See e.g. Cartier-Bresson, *Decisive Moment*, 42; Rodger, as quoted by Holzherr and Siben (eds), *On the Road*, 12. The use of Leicas by Capa and David 'Chim' Seymour during the coverage of wars was already emphasized in 1944. See J.R. Whiting, 'Editorial', *Popular Photography* 15(5) (1944), 16.

89. For example, Thomas Laqueur claimed that: 'We are, in fact, more likely today to have sympathy for, and even to do something to alleviate, the suffering of people . . . distant from ourselves . . . than were men and women three centuries ago.' T.W. Laqueur, 'Mourning, Pity, and the Work of Narrative in the Making of "Humanity"', in R. Ashby Wilson and R.D. Brown (eds), *Humanitarianism and Suffering: The Mobilization of Empathy* (Cambridge: Cambridge University Press, 2009), 31–57, at 32.

90. Sociologists emphasized that this specific form of empathy and compassion was closely linked to visualizations of human suffering. See A. Poferl, 'Problematisierungswissen und die Konstitution von Globalität', in H.-G. Soeffner (ed.), *Transnationale Vergesellschaftungen: Verhandlungen des 35. Kongresses der Deutschen Gesellschaft für Soziologie in Frankfurt am Main 2010* (Wiesbaden: Springer VS, 2010), 619–32, at 626.

91. See especially the recent work H. Fehrenbach and D. Rodogno (eds), *Humanitarian Photography: A History* (Cambridge: Cambridge University Press, 2015).

92. See above. Quote: Research Staff, *Visitors' Reactions*, III.

93. See e.g. T. Beck. 2005. *David Seymour (Chim)* (London: Phaidon Press), 19f.

94. David Seymour, *Children of Europe*. Paris: UNESCO, 1949. As an example, see Figure 6.3 at the end of this chapter.

95. Museum of Modern Art, *The Family of Man*, 94.

96. Cookman, *American Photojournalism*, 225.

97. After its 'journey' around the world, the exhibition finally found a permanent home in the castle of Clervaux in Luxembourg in 1994. In 2003, it was added to the 'Memory of the World Register' by UNESCO. After restoration works between 2010 and 2013, it was reopened.

98. R. Barthes, 'The Great Family of Man', in R. Barthes (ed.), *Mythologies: The Complete Edition*, trans. R. Howard (New York: Hill and Wang, 2012 [1957]), 196–99, at 199.

99. For a summary of the critique, see e.g. Berlier, 'The Family of Man', 221ff.

100. On the hypothesis that in the exhibition 'American modernity . . . was projected both nationally and globally, as the way of life natural to the "Family of Man"', see T. Smith, *Making the Modern: Industry, Art, and Design in America* (Chicago: University of Chicago Press, 1993), 350.

101. See especially P. Bosworth, *Diane Arbus: eine Biographie* (Munich: Schirmer-Mosel, 1984), 143–49, especially 146. Decided photographic countermovements like the so-called 'New York School', Robert Frank, Diane Arbus and others distanced themselves from the exhibition. Criticism of sentimentalism had been an important element of anti-humanist arguments since the nineteenth century. This means that humanist approaches in photography and humanism in general were subject to similar patterns of critique.

102. See Sandeen, *Picturing an Exhibition*, 176. The essays 'On Photography' were published between 1973 and 1977 in the *New York Review of Books*. Reprinted in S. Sontag, *Essays of the 1960s and 70s* (New York: Library of America 2013). For the quote, see S. Sontag, *On Photography* (Harmondsworth: Penguin, 1979), 32f.

103. With a focus on *Magnum*, see Miller, *Magnum*, especially the chapter 'End of the Glory Days' (252ff).

104. This development recalls another ambivalence that shaped the history of photography: the belief in the ability of photography to picture reality. It spread following the invention of photographic techniques in the nineteenth century, but was gradually undermined by intellectuals. Nonetheless, the 'belief' lived on in popular discourses.

105. See K. Thomas, *DuMont: Literatur und Kunst: Eine Verlagsgeschichte 1956 bis 2005* (Cologne: Dumont, 2006). For references to *The Family of Man* see 26, 28, 38; on collaborations with Cartier-Bresson, see 53.

106. As an example, see K. Pawek, *Weltausstellung der Photographie: 555 Photos von 264 Photographen aus 30 Ländern zu dem Thema: Was ist der Mensch?* (Hamburg: Nannen, 1964). The first catalogue was published in 1964 under the title *Was ist der Mensch? (What is Man?)*. Follow-up were titles like *Die Frau (The Woman)* and *Unterwegs zum Paradies (On the Way to Paradise)*.

107. Anonymous, 'Weltausstellung der Photographie', *Der Spiegel* (35) (1965), 95 (translated by the author).

108. S. Goodrum, 'A Socialist Family of Man: Rita Maahs and Karl-Eduard von Schnitzler's Exhibition *Vom Glück des Menschen*', *Zeithistorische Forschungen* 12(2) (2015), 370–82. Retrieved 22 August 2018 from http://www.zeithistorische-forschungen.de/2-2015/id=5245. See also Vowinckel, *Agenten der Bilder*, 85f.

109. R. Bleiker and A. Kay, 'Representing HIV/AIDS in Africa: Pluralist Photography and Local Empowerment', *International Studies Quarterly* 51(1) (2007), 139–63.

110. D. Newbury, 'Johannesburg Lunch-Hour 1951–1963: The Emergence and Development of the Humanist Photographic Essay in Drum Magazine', *Journalism Studies* 8(4) (2007), 584–94.

111. A. Tucker, K. Iizawa and N. Kinoshita, *The History of Japanese Photography* (New Haven: Yale University Press, 2003) (in association with the Museum of Fine Arts), e.g. 339.

112. He even embraced its 'modernist' dimension to save spirituality from 'postmodern' de-
constructions through the humanist approach. See A. Freedman, 'On the Ganges Side of
Modernism: Raghubir Singh, Amitav Ghosh, and the Postcolonial Modern', in L. Doyle
and L. A. Winkiel (eds), *Geomodernisms: Race, Modernism, Modernity* (Bloomington:
Indiana University Press, 2005), 114–29.
113. See R. Singh, 'Introduction', in *River of Colour: the India of Raghubir Singh* (London:
Phaidon, 2000), 9–17, especially 13.
114. See e.g. Freedman, 'On the Ganges Side', 118f.
115. R. Lowry, 'See India through Steve McCurry's Lens', *Time Lightbox* (18 November
2015). Retrieved 22 August 2018 from http://www.time.com/4102163/see-india-
through-steve-mccurrys-lens. Just recently, his images of India were brought together in
an exhibition by the Rubin Museum of Art in New York and the International Center
of Photography. See the description on the homepage of the Museum: 'Steve McCurry:
India (Exhibition 18 November 2015 – 4 April 2016)'. Retrieved 22 August 2018 from
http://rubinmuseum.org/events/exhibitions/steve-mccurry-india.
116. For example, this is documented for Luc Delahaye. See E. Roskis, 'A Genocide without
Images: White Film Noirs', in A. Thompson (ed.), *The Media and the Rwanda Genocide*
(London: Pluto Press, 2007), 238–41, at 241. Following his experiences in Rwanda,
Sebastião Salgado has mainly turned to landscape photography. See e.g. M. Bogre, *Pho-
tography as Activism: Images for Social Change* (Waltham, MA: Focal Press, 2012), 67.

Bibliography

Abbott, B. *New Guide to Better Photography*, revised ed. New York: Crown, 1953.
———. *The World of Atget*. New York: Horizon Press, 1964.
Acker, K. *Dorothea Lange*. Philadelphia: Chelsea House Publishers, 2004.
Adatt, K. *Picture Perfect: Life in the Age of the Photo Op*. Princeton: Princeton University Press,
2008.
Barnett, M.N. *Empire of Humanity: A History of Humanitarianism*. Ithaca: Cornell University
Press, 2011.
Barthes, R. 'The Great Family of Man', in R. Barthes (ed.), *Mythologies: The Complete Edition*.
trans. R. Howard (New York: Hill and Wang, 2012 [1957]), 196–99.
Berlier, M. 'The Family of Man: Readings of an Exhibition', in B. Brennan and H. Hardt (eds),
Picturing the Past: Media, History, and Photography (Urbana: University of Illinois Press,
1999), 206–41.
Bleiker, R., and A. Kay. 'Representing HIV/AIDS in Africa: Pluralist Photography and Local
Empowerment'. *International Studies Quarterly* 51(1) (2007), 139–63.
Bödeker, H.E. 'Menschheit, Humanität, Humanismus', in O. Brunner, W. Conze and R.
Koselleck (eds), *Geschichtliche Grundbegriffe: Historisches Lexikon zur politisch-sozialen
Sprache in Deutschland* (Stuttgart: Klett-Cotta, 1982), 1063–128.
Böger, A. *People's Lives, Public Images: The New Deal Documentary Aesthetic*. Tübingen: Narr,
2001.
Bogre, M. *Photography as Activism: Images for Social Change*. Waltham, MA: Focal Press, 2012.
Bösch, F. *Mediengeschichte: Vom asiatischen Buchdruck zum Fernsehen*. Frankfurt am Main:
Campus, 2011.
Bosworth, P. *Diane Arbus: eine Biographie*. Munich: Schirmer-Mosel, 1984.

Bourke-White, M. *Portrait of Myself*. New York: Simon & Schuster, 1963.

Brown, R., and R. Ashby Wilson (eds). *Humanitarianism and Suffering: The Mobilization of Empathy*. Cambridge: Cambridge University Press, 2009.

Capa, C. *Jerusalem: City of Mankind*. New York: Grossman, 1974.

Capa, R. *Slightly out of Focus*. New York: Holt, 1947.

———. (ed.). *The concerned photographer: The photographs of Werner Bischof, Robert Capa, David Seymour ('Chim'), André Kertész, Leonard Freed, Dan Weiner*. New York: Grossman, 1968.

Cartier-Bresson, H. *The Decisive Moment*. New York: Simon & Schuster, 1952.

———. *China gestern und heute*. Düsseldorf: Rauch, 1955.

Cartier-Bresson, H., and J.-P. Sartre. *D'une Chine à l'autre*. Paris: Delpire, 1954.

Caujolle, C. *Sebastião Salgado*. Heidelberg: Wachter, 2006.

Chéroux, C. *The Decisive Moment: A Bible for Photographers*. Göttingen: Steidl, 2014.

———. 'Magnum Manifesto', in C. Chéroux and C. Bouveresse (eds), *Magnum Manifesto* (London: Thames & Hudson, 2017), 8–17.

Christen, M., and A. Holzer. 'Mythos Magnum: Die Geschichte einer legendären Fotoagentur'. *Mittelweg* 36(5) (2007), 53–80.

Cookman, C.H. *American Photojournalism: Motivations and Meanings*. Evanston, IL: Northwestern University Press, 2009.

De Thézy, M., and C. Nori. *La photographie humaniste: 1930–1960. Histoire d'un mouvement en France*. Paris: Contrejour, 1992.

Eckel, J. *Die Ambivalenz des Guten: Menschenrechte in der internationalen Politik seit den 1940ern*. Göttingen: Vandenhoeck & Ruprecht, 2014.

Erwitt, E. *Snaps*. London: Phaidon, 2001.

Fehrenbach, H., and D. Rodogno (eds). *Humanitarian Photography: A History*. Cambridge: Cambridge University Press, 2015.

Forner, S.A. 'Für eine demokratische Erneuerung Deutschlands: Kommunikationsprozesse und Deutungsmuster engagierter Demokraten nach 1945'. *Geschichte und Gesellschaft* 33(2) (2007), 228–57.

Foucault, M. *The Birth of the Clinic: An Archaeology of Medical Perception*. London: Tavistock, 1973.

Freedman, A. 'On the Ganges Side of Modernism: Raghubir Singh, Amitav Ghosh, and the Postcolonial Modern', in L. Doyle and L. A. Winkiel (eds), *Geomodernisms: Race, Modernism, Modernity* (Bloomington: Indiana University Press, 2005), 114–29.

Gautrand, J.-C. *Robert Doisneau: 1912–1994*. Cologne: Taschen, 2003.

———. *Paris mon Amour*. Cologne: Taschen, 2014.

Gödde, P. 'Globale Kulturen', in A. Iriye and J. Osterhammel (eds), *Geschichte der Welt 1945 bis heute: Die globalisierte Welt* (Munich: C.H. Beck, 2013), 535–670.

Goodrum, S. 'A Socialist Family of Man: Rita Maahs: and Karl-Eduard von Schnitzler's Exhibition *Vom Glück des Menschen*'. *Zeithistorische Forschungen* 12(2) (2015), 370–82. Retrieved 22 August 2018 from http://www.zeithistorische-forschungen.de/2-2015/id=5245.

Graf, R., and C. Goschler. *Europäische Zeitgeschichte seit 1945*. Berlin: Akademie Verlag, 2010.

Haberstich, D. 'Elliott Erwitt', in L. Warren (ed.), *Encyclopedia of Twentieth-Century Photography* (London: Routledge, 2005), 451–52.

Hamilton, P. 'A Poetry of the Streets? Documenting Frenchness in an Era of Reconstruction. Humanist Photography 1935–1960'. *French Literature Series* XXVII (2001), 177–217.

Hoffmann, S.-L. (ed.). *Human Rights in the Twentieth Century.* Cambridge: Cambridge University Press, 2011.

Holzherr, A., and I. Siben (eds). *On the Road 1940–1949: From the Diaries of a Photographer and Adventurer.* Ostfildern: Hatje Cantz, 2009.

Knoch, H. 'Bewegende Momente: Dokumentarfotografie und die Politisierung der westdeutschen Öffentlichkeit vor 1968', in B. Weisbrod (ed.), *Die Politik der Öffentlichkeit – die Öffentlichkeit der Politik: Politische Medialisierung in der Geschichte der Bundesrepublik* (Wallstein: Göttingen, 2003), 97–122.

Koetzle, H.-M. 'Robert Capa: Spanischer Loyalist', in H.-M. Koetzle (ed.), *Photo Icons: Die Geschichte hinter den Bildern* (Cologne: Taschen, 2012), 178–87.

Laqueur, T.W. 'Mourning, Pity, and the Work of Narrative in the Making of "Humanity"', in R. Ashby Wilson and R.D. Brown (eds), *Humanitarianism and Suffering: The Mobilization of Empathy* (Cambridge: Cambridge University Press, 2009), 31–57.

Lyons, N. (ed.). *Photographers on Photography.* Englewood Cliffs, NJ: Prentice Hall, 1966.

Maloof, J. (ed.). *Vivian Maier, Street Photographer.* New York: Powerhouse, 2011.

Miller, R. *Magnum. Fifty Years at the Front Line of History: The Story of the Legendary Photo Agency.* New York: Grove Press, 1997.

Morgan, W.D., and H.M. Lester. *The Leica Manual: A Manual for the Amateur and Professional Covering the Field of Photography with the Leica Camera.* New York: Morgan & Lester, 1938.

Museum of Modern Art (ed.), *The Family of Man: The Greatest Photographic Exhibition of All Time – 503 pictures from 68 Countries – Created by Edward Steichen for the Museum of Modern Art.* New York: Maco, 1955.

Newbury, D. 'Johannesburg Lunch-Hour 1951–1963: The Emergence and Development of the Humanist Photographic Essay in Drum Magazine'. *Journalism Studies* 8(4) (2007), 584–94.

O'Neal, H. *A Vision Shared: A Classic Portrait of America and its People, 1935–1943.* New York: St Martin's Press, 1976.

Oxford Advanced Learner's Dictionary, 7th ed. Oxford: Oxford University Press, 1992.

Pagenstecher, C. 'Reisekataloge und Urlaubsalben: Zur Visual History des touristischen Blicks', in G. Paul (ed.), *Visual History: Ein Studienbuch* (Göttingen: Vandenhoeck & Ruprecht, 2006), 169–87.

Paulmann, J. 'Humanity – Humanitarian Reason – Imperial Humanitarianism. European Concepts in Practice', in F. Klose and M. Thulin (eds), *Humanity: A History of European Concepts in Practice from the Sixteenth Century to the Present* (Göttingen: Vandenhoeck & Ruprecht, 2017), 287–311.

———. (ed.). *Dilemmas of Humanitarian Aid in the Twentieth Century.* Oxford: Oxford University Press, 2016.

Pawek, K. *Weltausstellung der Photographie: 555 Photos von 264 Photographen aus 30 Ländern zu dem Thema: Was ist der Mensch?* Hamburg: Nannen, 1964.

Pernau, M., and I. Rajamani. 'Emotional Translations: Conceptual History beyond Language'. *History and Theory* 55 (2016), 46–65.

Poferl, A. 'Problematisierungswissen und die Konstitution von Globalität', in H.-G. Soeffner (ed.), *Transnationale Vergesellschaftungen: Verhandlungen des 35. Kongresses der Deutschen Gesellschaft für Soziologie in Frankfurt am Main 2010* (Wiesbaden: Springer VS, 2010), 619–32.

Rhode, R.B., and F.H. McCall. *Press Photography: Reporting with a Camera.* New York: Macmillan, 1961.

Roskis, E. 'A Genocide without Images: White Film Noirs', in A. Thompson (ed.), *The Media and the Rwanda Genocide* (London: Pluto Press, 2007), 238–41.

Sandeen, E.J. *Picturing an Exhibition: The Family of Man and 1950s America.* Albuquerque: University of New Mexico Press, 1995.

Saner, H. 'Existenzielle Aneignung und historisches Verstehen: Zur Debatte Jaspers-Curtius um die Goethe-Rezeption', in B. Weidmann (ed.), *Existenz in Kommunikation: Zur philosophischen Ethik von Karl Jaspers* (Würzburg: Königshausen u. Neumann, 2005), 151–66.

Singh, R. 'Introduction', in *River of Colour: The India of Raghubir Singh* (London: Phaidon, 2000), 9–17.

Smith, T. *Making the Modern: Industry, Art, and Design in America.* Chicago: University of Chicago Press, 1993.

Smith, W.E. *The Big Book,* K. Martinez, W. Johnson and J. Berger (eds). Austin: University of Texas Press, 2013.

Sontag, S. *On Photography.* Harmondsworth: Penguin, 1979.

Städter, B. *Verwandelte Blicke: Eine Visual History von Kirche und Religion in der Bundesrepublik 1945–1980.* Frankfurt am Main: Campus, 2011.

Steichen, E. *Steichen: A Life in Photography.* New York: Harmony Books, 1963.

Steinbeck, J. *A Russian Journal: With Pictures by Robert Capa.* New York: Viking Press, 1948.

Steinmetz, W. 'New Perspectives on the Study of Language and Power in the Short Twentieth Century', in W. Steinmetz (ed.), *Political Languages in the Age of Extremes* (Oxford: Oxford University Press, 2011), 3–51.

Stephenson, S., A. Trachtenberg and W.W. Norton (eds). *Dream Street: W. Eugene Smith's Pittsburgh Project.* New York: Norton & Co., 2001.

Susman, W. 'The Thirties', in S. Coben and L. Ratner (eds), *The Development of an American Culture* (Englewood Cliffs, NJ: Prentice Hall, 1970), 179–218.

Thomas, K. *DuMont: Literatur und Kunst. Eine Verlagsgeschichte 1956 bis 2005.* Cologne: Dumont, 2006.

Tucker, A., K. Iizawa and N. Kinoshita. *The History of Japanese Photography.* New Haven: Yale University Press, 2003.

Vowinckel, A. *Agenten der Bilder: Fotografisches Handeln im 20. Jahrhundert.* Göttingen: Wallstein, 2016.

Ward, K. '"In the Blink of an Eye": An Investigation into the Concept of the "Decisive Moment" (Augenblick) as Found in Nineteenth and Twentieth Century Western Philosophy'. PhD dissertation. Perth: Murdoch University, 2005.

Whelan, R. *Robert Capa: A Biography.* New York: Knopf, 1985.

Wildenthal, L., and S.-L. Hoffmann. *The Language of Human Rights in West Germany.* Philadelphia: University of Pennsylvania Press, 2012.

Part II

Humanitarian Media Regimes

7

On Fishing in Other People's Ponds

The Freedom from Hunger Campaign,
International Fundraising and the Ethics of NGO Publicity

Heike Wieters

> Those who attempt to ground the obligation to provide aid to those suffering far away
> on the basis of face-to face situations use examples in which only two forms of action
> are envisaged: paying and speaking . . . Both possibilities presuppose the existence
> of a chain of intermediaries between the spectator and the unfortunate.[1]
> —Luc Boltanski, 1999

There are various ways in which modern humanitarianism is connected to the media. Humanitarian agenda setting, nongovernmental organization (NGO) practice and *témoignage* are today almost always accompanied by sophisticated publicity strategies.[2] Making human suffering visible, spreading the word, getting pictures and films to go 'viral' and organizing fundraising events via radio, television, telephone or online platforms have all become central components of humanitarian activity and awareness campaigns.[3] This means that every modern humanitarian organization or NGO has at least one dedicated PR department today that facilitates and promotes its role as the above-mentioned 'intermediary' between the suffering person and the potential donor. Picturing the plight of others in a humanitarian fundraising campaign is no longer an intuitive or immediate thing; it is embedded in a tight semantic web, or a communication strategy, and has to be contextualized and put into perspective in order to achieve an actual financial response. To this end, external firms and professional media analysts often provide additional expertise and specialized services; for example, they analyse new fundraising strategies or conduct polls into potential campaign slogans and donor preferences.[4] Hence, publicity has become a kind of currency helping to define both concrete organizational as well as abstract ethical humanitarian goals of NGOs.[5]

Where there is a currency and thus a market, there are always stakeholders and groups trying to pursue their interests. Hence, some regulation is usually sought. Humanitarian fundraising and PR are fields in which there are by now various explicit and implicit rules as well as a number of institutionalized checks and balances. Since at least the mid nineteenth century, both governmental and nongovernmental bodies have assessed the legitimacy and adequacy of NGO fundraising techniques along with the proper use of their solicited funds.[6] In addition, most humanitarian organizations analyse both their partners' and competitors' media strategies in order to learn and innovate.

For the United States at least, it is safe to say that fundraising activities by private humanitarian organizations have been systematically professionalized and institutionalized since the 1850s.[7] Alongside government controls of private humanitarian campaigning and fundraising (particularly important during the two World Wars and the interwar and postwar years), American humanitarian NGOs institutionalized increasingly elaborate mechanisms of self-regulation throughout the second half of the twentieth century.[8] By the 1950s, most large American humanitarian nonprofits, among them CARE, the American Friends Service Committee, the YMCA, Catholic Relief Services, Lutheran World Relief, the American Jewish Joint Distribution Committee and Church World Service, were members of the *American Council of Voluntary Agencies for Foreign Service* (ACVAFS). This umbrella organization had been founded in 1942 and began to establish basic joint PR rules and best practices for NGOs soon afterwards in order to authorize 'bona fide activities, prevent the unstable and racketeering type of organization which frequently springs up after a war, give positive guidance to new interested groups as to what is being done to be recognized, help channel within groups things or programs that might overlap or duplicate effort at a great expense'.[9] Throughout the 1950s, most agencies committed themselves to codified ethical fundraising principles and became subscribers of private 'watchdog' organizations such as the National Information Bureau (NIB), which rated their performance in order to provide donors with better information on their charities of choice.[10] These principles urged ethical promotion as well as sound fundraising practices, meaning that neither payment of commissions for fundraising or mailing of unordered merchandise nor 'general telephone solicitation of the public' was allowed, and that slogans and pictures used in PR had to be decent and truthful.[11]

While the institutional patterns and existing rules were fairly stable at the local level by the late 1950s, albeit certainly not without conflict, the rules and norms at the international level were not yet settled. With the establishment of the United Nations system and its specialized agencies such as the Food and Agricultural Organization (FAO), UNICEF during the 1940s and the United Nations Development Program and the World Food Program throughout the 1960s, new international players were on the rise that cut across existing fundraising arrangement at the local or national level. Mostly financed by governments directly and exclusively, some UN agencies, such as UNICEF or the FAO, became increasingly keen to use private resources for their campaigns as well. However, such appeals to the American public were thoroughly disapproved of by private American NGOs, which were unwilling to allow direct international solicitation of donations in the United States. This chapter takes a closer look at the conflict-laden negotiations about the legitimacy of international fundraising campaigns on American soil that came to the fore in the context of the Freedom from Hunger campaign (initiated by the FAO). I will take a closer look at varying ideas surrounding the claim of 'legitimate' access of relief organizations to the American public and then at the diverse institutional mindsets that differentiated the fundraising strategies of private NGOs and international organizations. New light is thereby shed on the evolution of the 'mechanics' of international humanitarian campaigning at the beginning of the 1960s.[12]

The Contested Right to Enlist the Public

In June 1963, the First World Food Congress took place in Washington DC. Officially convened and sponsored by the FAO, the international gathering was a globally publicized milestone in surveying and confronting the so-called 'World Food Problem' and in making hunger prevention and food aid distribution an international policy issue. The President of the United States, John F. Kennedy, gave the opening speech. Boasting with optimism regarding humanity's ability to 'outlaw and banish hunger', Kennedy announced: 'We have the ability, we have the means, and we have the capacity to eliminate hunger from the face of the earth. We only need the will.'[13] The next day, his quotation hit the front page of almost every major international newspaper. The inaugural message at the international gathering was certainly bold and florid in its wording, characteristic of a new era: if previous attempts to ban hunger on a global scale had mostly conceived (yet failed to implement) a systematic approach, the World Food Congress in Washington DC aimed at the heart of new international realities. All speakers acknowledged the fact that hunger as a global threat would have to be confronted by a coalition of already existing international actors, not by another new, yet-to-be-established institution.[14] This new approach to international hunger relief was also mirrored by the conference's participants. Apart from large delegations of government representatives and dozens of officials from international organizations, hundreds of high-ranking executives from voluntary groups and NGOs were present. These groups (mainly from the United States, Europe, Canada and Australia, but also a couple of groups from Asia and Latin America) used the gathering in Washington DC as a forum and networking opportunity. NGO members had worked tirelessly for months in order to turn the official FAO event into a real 'people-to-people'[15] congress at which 'the food problems of the world [could be addressed and] solved' by a broad coalition of civic, governmental and international groups.[16] In doing so, these NGOs ensured that solving the 'World Food Problem' was no longer the sole responsibility of governments and international organizations, but an essential part of a shared global private-public agenda.

Five years earlier, very few people would have anticipated such cooperation among the roughly 1,300 conference participants from over 100 countries. When FAO Director-General Binay R. Sen first came up with a plan for a Word Food Congress in the late 1950s[17], his ideas were met with great reservation by U.S. diplomats in particular. Having started his career as Indian relief commissioner during the Bengal famine in the early 1940s, Sen was keen to use the powers vested in his office as the new FAO Director-General (1956–67) to make hunger prevention a central policy issue of the FAO.[18] However, the organization's incremental shift from a data-gathering organization focusing on agriculture in the broadest sense to an active player in the field of global hunger prevention was not universally acclaimed. Given that U.S. President Dwight D. Eisenhower's policy focus for the 1960s was clearly on 'promoting trade rather than providing higher levels of aid', the President and his entourage were far from happy with the FAO's overall impact on the Western development agenda.[19] Given that the FAO's budget depended on government sponsorship, Sen's plea for a large congress aimed at pushing global hunger into the limelight of international attention created a headwind and was met with strong budgetary refutations.[20] However, instead of quietly burying his plan, Sen opted for another strategy. He and his coworkers decided to push forward with a concept for a large global grassroots campaign called Freedom from Hunger (FFH), which was intended to be carried out by a broad coalition of UN bodies, governments and – most importantly – private groups.[21] From the early 1960s onwards, he started contacting NGOs all over the world to persuade them to join the five-year campaign that aimed at making hunger history.[22] These private sector initiatives were, in the majority, much more open to the FFH campaign than government delegations. Civic groups in Great Britain and Canada were particularly easily persuaded to join the world-wide drive against hunger and malnutrition. These private charities, clubs and NGOs soon launched an impressive network of local and national fundraising initiatives that contributed greatly to the FAO-led campaign, both in terms of raising awareness for global food issues and in terms of donations that fed into FFH projects or directly into the FAO budget.[23]

In the United States, however, the FFH campaign was confronted with significant reservations at first. This led to its much later adoption by NGOs than in other industrialized countries. This was mainly for two reasons: first of all, direct relations between NGOs in the United States and United Nations (UN) organizations were not very elaborate by the early 1960s. Despite the fact that many private American groups had taken a great interest in setting up the UN system in the 1940s, few attempts at closer cooperation had been made afterwards.[24] Apart from limited field coordination with United Nations Relief and Rehabilitation Administration (UNRRA in the immediate postwar period, a few encounters with the UN Civil Assistance Corps Korea, and sporadic liaisons with select UNICEF and FAO representatives, few American NGOs had invested much time in developing close working relationships with UN bodies.[25] However, this indifference had been mutual. Despite a number of affirmative UN statements regarding the general inclusion of so-called nongovernmental groups into FAO or UN committees throughout the 1950s, few real offers of integration had been made to voluntary agencies.[26] In fact, for most of the postwar period, the preference in the UN system had been to keep these civic groups at arm's length. Neatly organized by official categories and a standardized classification system, NGOs were not allowed to speak or intervene with these groups and were only permitted to silently attend select meetings.[27] This very limited form of representation in the UN system had only limited appeal, particularly for the large operational agencies that needed to maximize publicity and wanted to be taken seriously as humanitarian experts and highly professional international food aid providers.[28] Hence, even if American NGOs were interested in the FAO's first major move to proactively enlist voluntary agencies, they did not necessarily share Sen's enthusiastic impression that FFH was instrumental in bringing 'out the NGOs from their hitherto confined 'Consultative Status' . . . [as] somewhat distant and detached observers of the world' into the status of active participants in global affairs and international politics.[29]

The second reason for the somewhat rocky path towards joint FAO–NGO collaboration in the United States was the fact that Binay Sen started his approach with a veritable faux pas, as far as the largest and most traditional American humanitarian NGOs were concerned. While Sen's overall idea of a global movement against hunger had at first been enthusiastically welcomed by the agencies in the American Council of Voluntary Agencies, his official appeal to civic groups in April 1960 aroused general irritation. This was mainly due to the fact that he chose U.S. government channels and the American media to publish an open letter in order to win over grassroots groups and NGOs for a joint campaign.[30] Undoubtedly intended as a generous invitation to reach the maximum number of American organizations possible, Sen's broad public appeal was seen as sidelining more traditional food relief agencies. NGOs such as CARE, Catholic Relief Services, Lutheran World Relief, Church World Service and the Quakers had by this point been active in the field of hunger prevention and relief for decades. They had delivered millions of tons of food aid to Europe during and after the Second World War, and had continued, or rather extended, their service to hungry civilians in non-European countries afterwards.[31] Given their impressive track record and professional experience, these NGOs were now clearly irritated by the fact that Sen effectively disregarded their significant role in food relief by immediately going public without consulting them beforehand.[32]

Contemporaries could have interpreted Sen's faux pas as a communicative oversight or a diplomatic gaffe, revealing his inexperience with the local American NGO hierarchy. Instead, Sen's open call for partners raised a bright red flag among the American agencies, suggesting that he inadvertently touched upon a highly sensitive matter underlying the ostensible problem: from the perspective of the American Council of Voluntary Agencies, FAO's open invitation to the FFH campaign was proof that the international organization was actively trying to solicit funds from the American public in an attempt to counter its desperate financial situation.[33] However, this was a clear violation of a decade-long tacit agreement of noninterference amongst international organizations in any national fundraising issues.[34] While most American NGOs, and certainly the American Council, entertained pragmatic administrative relations with UN agencies and believed cooperation to be important, they still held the view that UN agencies should be financed by governments only. As Joseph Chamberlain of the American Council of Voluntary Agencies put it: 'In the United States it is generally recognized that supplying basic relief needs is the responsibility of government [while] the role of the voluntary agencies is to provide supplementary and demonstrative services.'[35] From the perspective of the American NGOs, international organizations as inter-governmental bodies lacked fundamental qualities such as proximity to different parts of society or traditional ties to a constituency, and thus were deficient in true support of a community and democratic legitimacy. American voluntary agencies as domestic players, in turn, possessed both democratic backing and traditional personal bonds to their long-standing supporters and donors.[36] Fundraising for charitable purposes was seen as a field in which trust and the everyday demonstration of ethical responsibility and accountability played an eminent role. Given that trust is most easily established and maintained in close relationships, the agencies felt that it was precisely their standing as local voluntary organizations that gave them trustworthiness, and therefore created the ethical legitimacy to act on behalf of their constituents as intermediaries between the American public and any beneficiaries overseas.[37] It was against this backdrop that the voluntary agencies were clearly alarmed about the FAO's intrusion into their territory. In order not to establish a precedent, the American Council reacted immediately by passing a resolution declaring that 'any effort in the United States of the intergovernmental and United Nations Specialized Agencies to finance their activities otherwise than through government appropriation produces confusion and disrupts the understanding of the proper relationship between' the two parties.[38] The Council argued that in the long run, any violation of these 'long established' patterns would out of necessity 'affect adversely public support by Congressional appropriations'.[39] It thus underscored that it would not tolerate any open campaign by the FAO to raise funds in the United States.

Negotiating a Mode of Cooperation

While the American Council persevered with diplomacy together with a frank but friendly reminder that there were rules governing international fundraising and publicity activities, several of the Council's member agencies were less moderate. There were rumours circulating about the FAO's intention in meddling with established American food aid distribution schemes and its attempt to monopolize hunger relief projects.[40] CARE's management – being particularly active in the distribution of government sponsored surplus food abroad – reacted with a particular furore to the FAO's direct mobilization of the American public for the FFH campaign. Claiming that the FAO's intrusion was a hostile act that directly threatened the NGO's own legitimate fundraising activities and its privileged access to U.S. agricultural surplus, CARE's executive director, Richard Reuter, eventually went so far as to charge the FAO officials of finally discovering that 'the American public [was] a gold mine they should tap'.[41] Against this backdrop of direct competition, Reuter was determined that all private agencies in the American Council should reject the FFH campaign and refuse to cooperate with the FAO altogether.

However, this was a problem of closing the stable door after the horse had bolted. With his public appeal in 1960, Sen and his colleagues had created a precedent. Countless private American organizations outside the American Council – from school projects to women's and community clubs – were beginning to subscribe to the initiative.[42] The FFH campaign resonated well with rising global concern about the 'World Food Problem'. As a topic, it linked issues such as global soil degradation, alleged 'overpopulation', and the realization that hunger and malnutrition were still a severe everyday threat to millions of people in 'developing countries'.[43] In addition, Sen had obviously hit a nerve by asking everyone, no matter how professional or experienced, to be part of a global campaign that aimed at abolishing hunger within a five-year window. This necessitated some kind of compromise. In an attempt to reconcile agencies such as CARE, which threatened to leave the American Council if no joint position against the FAO was found, and those agencies that had already accepted that there was no longer any way to stop the campaign, members of the American Council met several times in 1960 and 1961. It was only after a number of personal meetings among all chief executives that the dust settled and CARE could finally be persuaded that FFH was 'not a governmental or intergovernmental or UN campaign but . . . a *citizen* undertaking'.[44]

The eventual solution hints at the long-established patterns of public–private cooperation in charitable matters in the United States.[45] Starting in October 1960, agency representatives met almost weekly with U.S. diplomats from the Department of Agriculture, the White House and American FAO representatives from the FFH campaign. Officially reasserting – but thereafter gradually softening their position on fundraising of UN bodies in the United States – the private agencies made it clear that any future campaign would, out of necessity, have to include the American NGOs as major players. Government officials, in turn, assured agencies of their support and respect, and emphasized that the presidential Thanksgiving address would 'as usual . . . give proper stress to voluntary agency services overseas'.[46] Thus, both sides decided to develop a common position and to move towards the formation of a United States citizen committee.

In the course of 1961/1962, this committee, along with a new foundation, was eventually established to coordinate the American branch of the FFH campaign. Headed by James G. Patton (National Farmers' Union) and President Truman, the Freedom from Hunger Foundation (FFHF) relied on a wide array of popular representatives who possessed deep roots in U.S. political, agricultural and philanthropic affairs. Representatives from all major American voluntary agencies were invited and sworn in to the foundation's board.[47] Realizing that further resistance to the FFH campaign would be futile, as there was little prospect of turning things around, even ardent critics finally decided to play along. Murray Lincoln, CARE's former president and leader of the Nationwide Insurance Company, took on a post as trustee in the new FFH foundation, and his right-hand man (and CARE founding father) Wallace Campbell was promoted to the position of Patton's assistant.[48] This way, a steady flow of information and more equal representation of voluntary agency interests within the American FFH context could be assured. The agencies were thus able to ensure that the foundation's functions were limited to the following: 'publicize and promote FFH, stimulate organizations, businesses, and so forth to undertake special projects for the foundation – but not a full-fledged public fund raising campaign – and to take responsibility for the forthcoming World Food Conference'.[49]

With strong NGO representation on the American FFHF board, a viable compromise was found. What remained an issue was the question of financing. CARE, for instance, was reluctant to divert any funds or donations to the foundation. On various occasions, the agency underscored that every cent of CARE's income was 'badly need[ed] for our own campaign'.[50] While the foundation was, at times, successful in playing the agencies against each other in order to channel funds its way, there was basic agreement among the large NGOs in the American Council that the FFHF was neither entitled to funding by the large operational agencies, nor should there be any official projects run by the foundation overseas.[51] On the contrary, the NGOs underscored repeatedly that the FFHF had to refrain from becoming operational at all.[52]

The FFHF thus developed into an administrative network and a publicity hub that connected diverse types of grassroots activities and fundraisers (such as sponsored hunger marches or charity dinner parties) and granted permission to use the FFH logo within the United States. This latter permission was especially useful for the large NGOs that eventually obtained permission to establish proper NGO-run FFH projects abroad. These individual projects enabled the agencies to solicit donations under the FFH banner and to administer and use these donations in their 'own' NGO-led food aid projects. In addition, it transpired rather quickly that the larger agencies with their own public relations departments and mailing lists, together with very strong ties to major newspapers and magazines, had a strategic advantage over the smaller or newly formed initiatives in using FFH publicity for their own purposes. Given that the FFH campaign received generous government funding and additional support from the Advertising Council – a semi-public public relations network fostering 'American' projects and image campaigns[53] – these agencies were able to build on the momentum that the global campaign created. A CARE public relations specialist remarked that CARE had 'everything to gain' in taking part in the FFH publicity programme, as CARE would get 'top billing with an alphabetical listing', resulting in 'an extra push for our Food Crusade and perhaps to some extent our Christmas card program'.[54]

Hence, CARE, as well as several other agencies in the American Council, decided to profit from the public focus on hunger prevention created by FFH and successfully channelled media attention and additional donations towards their own projects.[55] Instead of subscribing to open conflict, the American voluntary agencies eventually opted for a strategic bargain: they successfully took 'advantage of the campaign as much as possible'[56] through their clout as major American overseas voluntary agencies. They thus turned FFH into an opportunity to spread the word that the American NGOs were at the heart of events – both in the United States and on the international 'stage'.

Conclusion

Despite initial difficulties and rivalries, the FFH campaign turned out to be a milestone in international cooperation in the field of hunger prevention. While the goal of ending hunger worldwide was certainly not achieved, the overall campaign was still a leap forward: the 'humanitarian international', which had been formed in the wake of the two World Wars, was now reconfiguring itself under the pressures and demands of modern hunger prevention strategies.[57] By the mid 1960s, internationally active NGOs and grassroots groups had successfully positioned themselves not only as new partners but also as competitors of governments and international organizations in the field of global food policy. They claimed to have a say in humanitarian hunger prevention and they had demonstrated that they were highly resourceful in mobilizing public support and donor dollars for a global campaign. Furthermore, they had been successful in utilizing the FAO-led campaign by linking it with local institutions, traditions and conventions. After having expressed collective opposition to the FAO's attempt to sideline large and traditional American NGOs with FFH, the American Council of Voluntary Agencies and its members were successful in claiming that direct solicitation of funds and public communication of humanitarian issues in the United States was their prerogative as voluntary agencies. The NGOs were able to point to their special qualities as ethically accountable local players and ensured that no international fundraising be allowed without their consent and involvement.

On the other hand, FFH was a success story for the FAO as well. The global campaign demonstrated the effectiveness of IO fundraising within an international context and underscored the FAO's ability to enlist governmental and nongovernmental players alike. Despite the fact that FFH's goal of actually ending hunger could not be achieved, the campaign was prolonged and integrated into the UN programme of the first UN Decade of Development.[58] This mixed approach put the FAO into a leading position as *the* international player addressing the 'World Food Problem' – at least in the short run.[59] As a result of the campaign, the FAO was able to convince its member states that massive (almost tenfold) budget increases were in order.[60]

While the FAO's cooperation with private players in the campaign was generally successful, the FAO had to learn to respect different (national) charitable traditions and institutional settings. In the United States, cooperation between NGOs, government players and the FAO was eventually organized by the newly established local American FFHF. This body came to work as some kind of hub between the private, governmental and intergovernmental levels, and managed to include the FAO into already established patterns of public–private cooperation in the United States. By institutionalizing and facilitating new modes of cooperation, communication and exchange of best practices between grassroots organizations, traditional NGOs, governments and international organizations, the foundation developed into a paragon that exerted large influence on the direction and institutional setup of future global campaigning in humanitarian affairs.

Heike Wieters holds a Ph.D. in history and works as a postdoctoral researcher at the Department of History at Humboldt-Universität zu Berlin. Since 2013 she has been the coleader of a research group on the transformation of welfare institutions in Europe (Saisir l'Europe). Her PhD dissertation dealt with the humanitarian NGO CARE and its development from an organization focusing on postwar relief to an international humanitarian player providing development aid. She has written several articles and book chapters on the history of NGOs; a monograph on the history of CARE (1945–80) was published in 2017. Her current project deals with the transformation of private and public welfare institutions, as well as with changing perceptions of risk and social security after 1945, therefore linking the history of humanitarianism with debates about welfare in industrialized countries.

Notes

1. L. Boltanski, *Distant Suffering: Morality, Media and Politics* (Cambridge: Cambridge University Press, 1999), 17.
2. P. Redfield, 'A Less Modest Witness: Collective Advocacy and Motivated Truth in a Medical Humanitarian Movement', *American Ethnologist* 33(1) (2006), 3–26.
3. M. Lindenberg and C. Bryant, *Going Global: Transforming Relief and Development NGOs* (Bloomfield, CT: Kumarian Press, 2011), 177f; R. Read, B. Taithe and R. Mac Ginty, 'Data Hubris? Humanitarian Information Systems and the Mirage of Technology', *Third World Quarterly* 37(8) (2016), 1314–31.

4. K. Waters, 'Influencing the Message: The Role of Catholic Missionaries in Media Coverage of the Nigerian Civil War', *Catholic Historical Review* 90(4) (2004), 697–718; for the German context, see S. Baringhorst, *Politik als Kampagne: Zur medialen Erzeugung von Solidarität* (Opladen: Westdt. Verl. 1998); R. Auts, *Opferstock und Sammelbüchse: Die Spendenkampagnen der freien Wohlfahrtspflege vom Ersten Weltkrieg bis in die sechziger Jahre* (Paderborn: Schöningh, 2001); G. Lingelbach, 'Die Entwicklung des Spendenmarktes in der Bundesrepublik Deutschland: Von der staatlichen Regulierung zur medialen Lenkung', *Geschichte und Gesellschaft* 33(1) (2007), 127–57.
5. T. Büthe, S. Major and A. de Mello e Souza, 'The Politics of Private Foreign Aid: Humanitarian Principles, Economic Development Objectives, and Organizational Interests in NGO Private Aid Allocation', *International Organization* 66(4) (2012), 571–607.
6. S. Roddy, J.-M. Strange and B. Taithe, 'The Charity-Mongers of Modern Babylon: Bureaucracy, Scandal, and the Transformation of the Philanthropic Marketplace, c.1870–1912', *Journal of British Studies* 54(1) (2015), 118–37.
7. S.M. Cutlip, *Public Relations History: From the 17th to the 20th Century: The Antecedents* (Hillsdale, NJ: Erlbaum, 1995), 252–78; B.R. Hopkins, *Charity under Siege: Government Regulation of Fund-raising* (New York: Wiley, 1980).
8. A.C. Ringland, *The Organization of Voluntary Foreign Aid. 1939–1953* (Washington DC: Department of State Bulletin, 15 March 1954); M. Curti, *American Philanthropy Abroad: A History* (New Brunswick, NJ: Rutgers University Press, 1963), 432f.
9. ACVAFS, Box 5, ACVAFS MECM 26 September1945; See E.C. Reiss. *The American Council of Voluntary Agencies for Foreign Service, ACVAFS: Four Monographs* (New York: self-published, 1985), vol. 1, 10–80; R.M. McCleary, *Global Compassion: Private Voluntary Organizations and U.S. Foreign Policy since 1939* (Oxford: Oxford University Press, 2009), 51–53.
10. J.E. Silvergleid, 'Effects of Watchdog Organizations on the Social Capital Market', *New Directions for Philanthropic Fundraising* 41(1) (2003), 7–26; B.R. Hopkins, *The Law of Fundraising* (Hoboken, NJ: John Wiley, 2009), Chapter 9; on the NIB, see H. Wieters, *Showered with Kindness? The NGO CARE and Food Relief from America, 1945–1980* (Manchester: Manchester University Press, 2017), 122–30.
11. CARE, Box 73, NIB 'Basic Standards in Philanthropy' for the year 1955.
12. M.H. Geyer and J. Paulmann, 'Introduction: The Mechanics of Internationalism', in J. Paulmann and M.H. Geyer (eds), *The Mechanics of Internationalism: Culture, Society and Politics from the 1840s to the First World War* (Oxford: Oxford University Press, 2001), 1–25, at 22–23.
13. J.F. Kennedy, Remarks to World Food Congress delegates, 4 June 1963, JFK, Papers of John F. Kennedy, Presidential Papers, President's Office Files, (Digital Identifier JFKPOF-044-034), 4f. Retrieved 22 August 2018 from http://www.jfklibrary.org/Asset-Viewer/Archives/JFKPOF-044-034.aspx.
14. R. Jachertz and A. Nützenadel, 'Coping with Hunger? Visions of a Global Food System, 1930–1960', *Journal of Global History* 6(1) (2011), 99–119.
15. Frank Goffio to Lyle Webster, Secretary General WFC, 23 May 1963, CARE, Box 78. See also D.J. Shaw, *World Food Security: A History since 1945* (Basingstoke: Palgrave Macmillan, 2007), 82.
16. MECM Mar. 27, 1963, CARE, Box 1171.
17. The campaign was officially announced in 1960, but planning for the international campaign had already started by mid 1958; see FFHC Background Papers, Draft proposal

Project for a Free the World From Hunger Year, 16 July 1958, FAO, RG 12, Sec 4, B-067 B15.

18. Shaw, *World Food Security*, 77.

19. Staple, *Birth of Development*, 109.

20. A.L.S. Staples, *The Birth of Development: How the World Bank, Food and Agriculture Organization, and World Health Organization Changed the World, 1945–1965* (Kent, OH: Kent State University Press, 2007), 106–9.

21. Shaw, *World Food Security*, 77–84; FFH was approved at the FAO's tenth session in 1959, in resolution 13/1959.

22. FAO Information Sheet, Freedom from Hunger Campaign, 22 April 1960 (received by the American Council on 15 September 1960), ACVAFS, Box 59.

23. For Canada, see, for instance: M.J. Bunch, 'All Roads Lead to Rome: Canada, the Freedom from Hunger Campaign, and the Rise of NGOs, 1960–1980' (UWSpace, 2007). Retrieved 22 August 2018 from http://hdl.handle.net/10012/3134; interestingly enough, CARE of Canada was involved in the Canadian mobilization of the FFH campaign (at 196f).

24. See D.B. Robins, *Experiment in Democracy: The Story of U.S. Citizen Organizations in Forging the Charter of the United Nations* (New York: Parkside Press, 1971), 88–89; see also E. Borgwardt, *A New Deal for the World: America's Vision for Human Rights* (Cambridge, MA: Harvard University Press, 2007).

25. MBDM 17 October 1951, CARE, Box 1170. On the cooperation with UNRRA, see, for example, S. Salvatici, 'Professionals of Humanitarianism: UNRRA Relief Officers in Post-War Europe', in J. Paulmann (ed.), *Dilemmas of Humanitarian Aid in the Twentieth Century* (Oxford: Oxford University Press, 2015), 235–59.

26. Relations with organizations other than UN family 1947–58, Memo concerning Relations with Non-governmental Organizations, (Orbenya), undated [1950?], FAO, RG 001,1 Series D 14,

27. P. Chiang, *Non-governmental Organizations at the United Nations: Identity, Role, and Function* (New York: Praeger, 1981), 85–102.

28. F.W. Stoecker, *NGOs und die UNO: Die Einbindung von Nichtregierungsorganisationen (NGOs) in die Strukturen der Vereinten Nationen* (Frankfurt am Main: Peter Lang, 2000), 64–67.

29. B.R. Sen, *Towards a Newer World* (Dublin: Tycooly International Publishing, 1982), 280.

30. Charlotte E. Owen (ACVAFS) to George McGovern (Food for Peace), 10 March 1961, CARE, Box 31; announcement of Freedom from Hunger Campaign, 22 April 1960, ACVAFS, Box 50.

31. H. Wieters, 'The World's Hungry: American NGOs and New Private Partnerships after WWI', *Contemporanea. Rivista di storia dell'800 e del '900*, 18(3) (2015), 349–66.

32. MBDM, 26 October 1960, CARE, Box 1171.

33. Staples, *Birth of Development*, 106f.

34. Letter, from Joseph Chamberlain (ACVAFS) to Arthur Ringland (Department of State), 25 February 1947, cited in Reiss, *The American Council*, vol. I, 78.

35. Letter, from Joseph Chamberlain (ACVAFS) to Arthur Ringland (Department of State), 25 February 1947, cited in Reiss, *The American Council*, vol. I, 78.

36. ACVAFS paper, 'The Continuing Challenge of American Abundance', 15 November 1956, ACVAFS, Box 5.

37. Working Paper International Conference on 'Development Aid of Private Organizations', 20–25 November 1963, ACVAFS, Box 14. Regarding the importance of trust and cred-

ibility for non-profit fundraising, see, for instance, H.B. Hansmann, 'The Role of Non-profit Enterprise', *Yale Law Journal* 89(5) (1980), 835–901; T.R. Tyler, 'Why Do People Rely on Others?', in K. Cook (ed.), *Trust in Society* (New York: Russell Sage Foundation, 2001), 285–303; see also U. Frevert, 'Vertrauen - Eine historische Spurensuche', in U. Frevert (ed.), *Vertrauen: Historische Annäherungen* (Göttingen: Vandenhoeck & Ruprecht, 2003), 7–66; and the classical text by M. Granovetter, 'Economic Action and Social Structure: The Problem of Social Embeddedness', *American Journal of Sociology* 91(3) (1985), 481–510.

38. Minutes of Meeting, 9 February 1960 and 11 April 1960, ACVAFS, Box 8; see also ACVAFS position paper on solicitation of voluntary contributions by intergovernmental and United Nations agencies, approved by the board of directors, 18 May 1960, Box 14.

39. Minutes of Meeting, 9 February 1960 and 11 April 1960, ACVAFS, Box 8.

40. Executive Committee Meeting, 30 November 1960, ACVAFS, Box 8.

41. Richard Reuter to Sheri Eberhart, 14 December 1961, CARE, Box 31.

42. Charlotte Owen, Executive Director ACVAFS to all members of the executive committee, Subject Freedom from Hunger Campaign – USA participation, 17 November 1960; draft memo 'expected participation by non-governmental organizations in the Freedom from Hunger Campaign', 23 March 1960, ACVAFS, Box 50; FAO, RG 12, Box 2, folder 7.

43. On the prehistory of the 'World Food Problem', see N. Cullather, *The Hungry World: America's Cold War Battle against Poverty in Asia* (Cambridge, MA: Harvard University Press, 2010), 11–42; see also the contemporary study by the President's Science Advisory Committee, *The World Food Problem: Vol I. Report of the Panel on the World Food Supply* (Washington DC: US Government Printing Office, May 1967); C.B. Baker, 'U.S. Perspectives on World Food Problems', *Illinois Agricultural Economics* 17(2) (1922), 1–6.

44. Charlotte Owen (ACVAFS) to Bishop Edward E. Swanstrom (CRS), 17 July 1961, ACVAFS, Box 29. Emphasis in original.

45. P.D. Hall, 'A Historical Overview of Philanthropy, Voluntary Associations, and Nonprofit Organizations in the United States 1600–2000', in W.W. Powell and R. Steinberg (eds), *The Nonprofit Sector: A Research Handbook* (New Haven: Yale University Press, 2006), 32–65; see also L.M. Salamon, 'Government-Nonprofit Relations in International Perspective', in E.T. Boris and C.E. Steuerle (eds), *Nonprofits and Government: Collaboration and Conflict* (Washington DC: Urban Institute Press, 2006), 329–67.

46. Charlotte Owen, Executive Director ACVAFS to all members of the executive committee, Subject Freedom from Hunger Campaign – USA participation, 17 November 1960, ACVAFS, Box 59.

47. Confidential report on Freedom from Hunger Foundation [presumably written or at least forwarded by Wallace Campbell], 4 October 1962, CARE, Box 73.

48. Wallace Campbell (Assistant to the President of FFH Foundation) to James Lambie (CARE), 6 May 1963, CARE, Box 78.

49. Wallace Campbell to Murray Lincoln, 22 January 1962, CARE, Box 31.

50. Letter, from Fran Goffio to James G. Patten, 19 August 1963, CARE, Box 31.

51. Letter, from James G. Patten to CARE, AJJDC and CRS asking for a 10,000 $ Grant for administrative campaign costs, 26 May 1964, CARE, Box 31; see also the negative reply by AJJDC (4 June 1964), CARE (5 June 1964) and CRS (9 June 1964).

52. Undated Memorandum to: Affiliates of the Foundation (FFH Foundation Inc.), CARE, Inc [1964], CARE Box 31, undated Memorandum to: Affiliates of the Foundation (FFH Foundation Inc.), CARE, Inc [1964].

53. R. Griffith, 'The Selling of America: The Advertising Council and American Politics, 1942–1960', *Business History Review* 57(3) (1983), 388–412; see also D.L. Lykins, *From Total War to Total Diplomacy: The Advertising Council and the Construction of the Cold War Consensus* (Westport, CT: Praeger, 2003).
54. Harry J. Cooper to Richard Reuter, 18 June 1962, CARE, Box 31: Subject: Ad Council program, 'Join the Freedom from Hunger Campaign'.
55. Harry W. Edwards (CARE) to Chet Huntley (NBC news), 9 January 1963, CARE, Box 31. Edwards proposed a programme on CARE's contribution to a scientific food lab in Ecuador financed by CARE FFH donations; see also excerpt from Freedom from Hunger Foundation executive committee meeting, 27 June 1962.
56. MECM 27 February 1963, CARE, Box 1171.
57. M.N. Barnett, *Empire of Humanity: A History of Humanitarianism* (Ithaca, NY: Cornell University Press, 2011), 97–106.
58. M. Cépède, 'The Fight against Hunger: Its History on the International Agenda', *Food Policy* 9(4) (1984), 282–90, at 286.
59. Shaw, *World Food Security*, 83f.
60. The FAO's budget increase more than tenfold between 1958 and 1967, from less than $7 million to roughly $83 million; see Staples, *Birth of Development*, 120.

Bibliography

Auts, R. *Opferstock und Sammelbüchse: Die Spendenkampagnen der freien Wohlfahrtspflege vom Ersten Weltkrieg bis in die sechziger Jahre*. Paderborn: Schöningh, 2001.
Baringhorst, S. *Politik als Kampagne: Zur medialen Erzeugung von Solidarität*. Opladen: Westdt. Verl., 1998.
Barnett, M.N. *Empire of Humanity: A History of Humanitarianism*. Ithaca, NY: Cornell University Press, 2011.
Boltanski, L. *Distant Suffering: Morality, Media and Politics*. Cambridge: Cambridge University Press, 1999).
Borgwardt, E. *A New Deal for the World: America's Vision for Human Rights*. Cambridge, MA: Harvard University Press, 2007.
Bunch, M.J. 'All Roads Lead to Rome: Canada, the Freedom from Hunger Campaign, and the Rise of NGOs, 1960–1980'. UWSpace, 2007. Retrieved 22 August 2018 from http://hdl .handle.net/10012/3134.
Büthe, T., S. Major and A. de Mello e Souza. 'The Politics of Private Foreign Aid: Humanitarian Principles, Economic Development Objectives, and Organizational Interests in NGO Private Aid Allocation'. *International Organization* 66(4) (2012), 571–607.
Cépède, M. 'The Fight against Hunger: Its History on the International Agenda'. *Food Policy* 9(4) (1984), 282–90.
Chiang, P. *Non-governmental Organizations at the United Nations: Identity, Role, and Function*. New York: Praeger, 1981.
Cullather, N. *The Hungry World: America's Cold War Battle against Poverty in Asia*. Cambridge, MA: Harvard University Press, 2010.
Curti, M. *American Philanthropy Abroad: A History*. New Brunswick, NJ: Rutgers University Press, 1963.
Cutlip, S.M. *Public Relations History: From the 17th to the 20th Century: The Antecedents*. Hillsdale, NJ: Erlbaum, 1995.

Frevert, U. 'Vertrauen: Eine historische Spurensuche', in U. Frevert (ed.), *Vertrauen: Historische Annäherungen* (Göttingen: Vandenhoeck & Ruprecht, 2003), 7–66.

Geyer, M.H., and J. Paulmann. 'Introduction: The Mechanics of Internationalism', in J. Paulmann and M.H. Geyer (eds), *The Mechanics of Internationalism: Culture, Society and Politics from the 1840s to the First World War* (Oxford: Oxford University Press, 2001), 1–25.

Granovetter, M. 'Economic Action and Social Structure: The Problem of Social Embeddedness'. *American Journal of Sociology* 91(3) (1985), 481–510.

Griffith, R. 'The Selling of America: The Advertising Council and American Politics, 1942–1960'. *Business History Review* 57(3) (1983), 388–412.

Hall, P.D. 'A Historical Overview of Philanthropy, Voluntary Associations, and Nonprofit Organizations in the United States 1600–2000', in W.W. Powell and R. Steinberg (eds), *The Nonprofit Sector: A Research Handbook* (New Haven: Yale University Press, 2006), 32–65.

Hansmann, H.B. 'The Role of Nonprofit Enterprise'. *Yale Law Journal* 89(5) (1980), 835–901.

Hopkins, B.R. *Charity under Siege: Government Regulation of Fundraising*. New York: Wiley, 1980.

———. *The Law of Fundraising*. Hoboken, NJ: John Wiley, 2009.

Jachertz, R., and A. Nützenadel. 'Coping with Hunger? Visions of a Global Food System, 1930–1960'. *Journal of Global History* 6(1) (2011), 99–119.

Lindenberg, M., and C. Bryant. *Going Global: Transforming Relief and Development NGOs*. Bloomfield, CT: Kumarian Press, 2011.

Lingelbach, G. 'Die Entwicklung des Spendenmarktes in der Bundesrepublik Deutschland: Von der staatlichen Regulierung zur medialen Lenkung'. *Geschichte und Gesellschaft* 33(1) (2007), 127–57.

Lykins, D.L. *From Total War to Total Diplomacy: The Advertising Council and the Construction of the Cold War Consensus*. Westport, CT: Praeger, 2003.

McCleary, R.M. *Global Compassion: Private Voluntary Organizations and U.S. Foreign Policy since 1939*. Oxford: Oxford University Press, 2009.

Read, R., B. Taithe and R. Mac Ginty. 'Data Hubris? Humanitarian Information Systems and the Mirage of Technology'. *Third World Quarterly* 37(8) (2016), 1314–31.

Redfield. P. 'A Less Modest Witness: Collective Advocacy and Motivated Truth in a Medical Humanitarian Movement'. *American Ethnologist* 33(1) (2006), 3–26.

Reiss, E.C. *The American Council of Voluntary Agencies for Foreign Service, ACVAFS: Four Monographs*. New York: self-published, 1985.

Ringland, A.C. *The Organization of Voluntary Foreign Aid: 1939–1953*. Washington DC: Department of State Bulletin, 15 March 1954.

Robins, D.B. *Experiment in Democracy: The Story of U.S. Citizen Organizations in Forging the Charter of the United Nations*. New York: Parkside Press, 1971.

Roddy, S., J.-M. Strange and B. Taithe. 'The Charity-Mongers of Modern Babylon: Bureaucracy, Scandal, and the Transformation of the Philanthropic Marketplace, c.1870–1912'. *Journal of British Studies* 54(1) (2015), 118–37.

Salamon. L.M. 'Government-Nonprofit Relations in International Perspective', in E.T. Boris and C.E. Steuerle (eds), *Nonprofits and Government: Collaboration and Conflict* (Washington DC: Urban Institute Press, 2006), 329–67.

Salvatici, S. 'Professionals of Humanitarianism: UNRRA Relief Officers in Post-War Europe', in J. Paulmann (ed.), *Dilemmas of Humanitarian Aid in the Twentieth Century* (Oxford: Oxford University Press, 2015), 235–59.

Sen, B.R. *Towards a Newer World.* Dublin: Tycooly International Publishing, 1982.

Shaw, D.J. *World Food Security: A History since 1945.* Basingstoke: Palgrave Macmillan, 2007.

Silvergleid, J.E. 'Effects of Watchdog Organizations on the Social Capital Market'. *New Directions for Philanthropic Fundraising* 41(1) (2003), 7–26.

Staples, A.L.S. *The Birth of Development: How the World Bank, Food and Agriculture Organization, and World Health Organization Changed the World, 1945–1965.* Kent, OH: Kent State University Press, 2007.

Stoecker, F.W. *NGOs und die UNO: Die Einbindung von Nichtregierungsorganisationen (NGOs) in die Strukturen der Vereinten Nationen.* Frankfurt am Main: Peter Lang, 2000.

Tyler, T.R. 'Why Do People Rely on Others?', in K. Cook (ed.), *Trust in Society* (New York: Russell Sage Foundation, 2001), 285–303.

Waters, K. 'Influencing the Message: The Role of Catholic Missionaries in Media Coverage of the Nigerian Civil War'. *Catholic Historical Review* 90(4) (2004), 697–718.

Wieters, H. 'The World's Hungry: American NGOs and New Private Partnerships after WWI'. *Contemporanea. Rivista di storia dell'800 e del '900,* 18(3) (2015), 349–66.

———. *Showered with Kindness? The NGO CARE and Food Relief from America, 1945–1980.* Manchester: Manchester University Press, 2017.

8
Advocacy Strategies of Western Humanitarian NGOs from the 1960s to the 1990s

Valérie Gorin

Introduction: The Shifting Definition of Advocacy

Influenced by the culture of human rights campaigning, advocacy has emerged as a policy in Western international NGOs since the 1960s.[1] Reactivating the political–humanitarian division of the aid organizations' identities, advocacy has now become a specific category of humanitarian communication, both public and operational. There is, however, a knowledge gap between advocacy as a practice and academic research. Although scholarly works and practical guidelines on humanitarian advocacy have increased over the last fifteen years, only a few studies tackle the history of its practices. The interest from humanitarian practitioners in particular is linked to the Darfur crisis[2] and the increased number of attacks on humanitarian operations, the shrinking of the humanitarian space, the difficulties of accessing and protecting civilian populations and the professionalization of the humanitarian sector.[3]

The surge in the literature on advocacy shows major divergences and different practices on 'whom to lobby' (institutions, authorities or individuals), 'what to lobby on' (policies, ideologies or emergency issues) or 'how to lobby' (at the macro- or the micro-levels).[4] Therefore, advocacy is an umbrella term that represents 'activism ... undertaken to influence stakeholders so that tangible changes can be obtained for the benefit of an affected population'[5] or, more generally, all communication activities aiming to influence not only decision-makers (authorities, parties at war, populations, corporations) but also systems and ideas.

A semantic confusion remains about different words used as synonyms, or 'interchangeable terms',[6] for advocacy: testimony, (eye)witness, campaigning, to speak out, to make public claims, to advocate, to call attention, to raise awareness, to denounce. However, all of these communication activities have been used as, or are parts of, public campaigns from humanitarian agencies, which aim to improve policies or to question misuses of aid.

Earlier advocacy campaigns were initially rooted in the search for justice in the late nineteenth and early twentieth centuries, when missionaries and non-governmental organizations (NGOs) such as the Save the Children Fund (SCF) used pictures and movies as visual evidence of abuses, grounded in the belief that 'seeing is believing'.[7] But it was not before the 1960s that British NGOs opened their first 'advocacy units' to fight poverty and hunger and promote children's rights; the concept of advocacy has since gained more political attention in the 1970s with the birth of Médecins Sans Frontières (MSF). The mythological split of French doctors from the International Committee of the Red Cross (ICRC) during the Biafra War, and the 'media buzz' on which MSF would later build its reputation, marked a turning point in the history of advocacy in the later twentieth century because it fulfilled what has since been regarded as an efficient advocacy campaign.

As we will see in this chapter, this has favoured two types of advocacy between the 1960s and the 1990s, emblematic of two different 'schools of humanitarianism': the British and the French.[8] The first case studies explored hereinafter focus on educational advocacy, developed by British NGOs such as SCF or Oxfam in the 1960s and 1970s, and intended to impose a transformative agenda based on solidarity and equality. It seeks to create awareness and thereby attempts 'to alter the ways in which power, resources, and ideas are created, consumed, and distributed at global level, so that people and their organisations in the South have a more realistic chance of controlling their own development'.[9] Educational advocacy tends to be deployed through public mobilization, with either authorities, civil society or communities. The second case studies exposed in this chapter highlight the rise of political advocacy in the 1970s and 1980s. Because it aims at limiting obstacles to assistance and increasing the protection of civilians in emergency settings, it targets states, governments and armed groups in priority, through speaking-out strategies such as 'persuasion' or 'denunciation'.[10] Representative of MSF's identity, which sees the humanitarian worker as a witness whose duty is to provide testimony, political advocacy is also a form of 'humanitaire à la française'[11] that sets MSF apart from all previous humanitarian initiatives.

British Expertise: The Educational Advocacy of Save the Children and Oxfam

Starting from the 1960s onwards, particularly through the growing ideology of 'Third Worldism', NGOs turned to a human rights-based approach, in the sense of the nineteenth-century early reformists, to confront discriminatory practices in development cooperation and to move the legitimacy of their action into the sphere of political decision-making. The Freedom from Hunger Campaign (FFHC) and later the Baby Milk Campaign (BMC) are illustrative of how British NGOs, such as SCF and Oxfam, developed a rights-based approach for more equality between the North and the South through transnational advocacy collaborations. While remaining sometimes quite amateur in their media strategies, these campaigns also questioned the fear of strong political engagement from British NGOs and to what extent they challenged governments' duties when doing public advocacy.

Save the Children and the FFHC

The Food and Agricultural Organization (FAO) launched the FFHC in 1960. Its main goal was to 'alert public opinion to the growing danger of world-wide hunger and malnutrition . . . [to open] public debate . . . [and to] challeng[e] the leaders of the nations to new thinking'[12] through a series of international events, notably the World Food Congress in Washington DC in June 1963. To ensure international resonance of the campaign, a number of international NGOs were asked to participate: SCF, Oxfam, Christian Aid, War on Want and Inter-Church Aid among others. No specific media agenda was set up; each NGO developed communications on its own.

SCF agreed to join the campaign on the basis of advocating for the right for food in developing countries, as embodied in the Declaration of the Rights of the Child: 'The child that is hungry must be fed' (Article 2). During its first meeting on 21 November 1961, the SCF special subcommittee decided to 'concentrate on the education of the local people in the better use of foods' through projects that should be 'conducted on a small scale'. Interestingly, SCF chose to use a traditional, early-twentieth-century media approach with local activities and without any coordinated national media action. The subcommittee also agreed to limit political risks as much as possible, fearing rejection from countries in which it did not seek the government's approval. Special promotional material was created for the campaign, including films on the contexts where SCF worked (Jordan, East Africa and the West Indies).[13] Together with its press and publicity units, SCF started its awareness campaign by working closely with mayors from major cities and suburbs.

After the first World Food Congress, SCF's subcommittee met in November 1963 to re-evaluate its participation within the project. Its members feared that campaigning was indeed too political and beyond its scope: 'The Fund had no role in this and should not become part of such a great machine . . . the campaign was best left to Governments.'[14] Nevertheless, the Congress successfully pushed the United Nations (UN) General Assembly to adopt a resolution on men's rights for food in the 'Draft Covenant on Economic, Social and Cultural Rights', in

December 1963. A 'world campaign against hunger, disease and ignorance' was proposed and several communication perspectives were emphasized, including the need to keep the pressure on influential political and economic stakeholders through lobbying activities and larger coordinated media actions. SCF therefore decided to continue the campaign until 1970, with a strong commitment to its educational role towards public opinion.

Throughout the campaign, SCF failed to build strong ties with the media. The NGO admitted in July 1962 that 'the launching of the campaign was lamentable as regards the Press . . . the headlines and the impact on the man in the street was almost nil . . . Our Projects are not a good story'.[15] They remained hesitant in using mass media, preferring instead specialized journals or their own bulletins, for example, the *World's Children* magazine.[16] The visual strategy behind the campaign had not changed since the 1920s: a negative imagery of the 'shock picture' relying on stereotyping the foreign child,[17] without offering any 'counter-hegemonic' voice to media representations of poverty.[18] SCF soon realized that isolated action is unsuccessful when trying to attract media attention. Personal contacts with the press were to be built by targeting journalists in economics or foreign affairs. The subcommittee finally managed to arrange a tour of the different UK-financed projects in Africa for journalist Fred Redman, which resulted in several articles in the *Sunday Mirror* and the *Sunday Telegraph* in 1970.

Apart from lobbying, SCF also participated in a joint action program, the 'Youth against Hunger' movement, together with the other British aid organizations involved in the FFHC. A particular aspect of this movement was to raise awareness of the social, political and economic situation of hunger in developing countries and the inequalities it engendered by promoting the issues in the educational sector (with teachers), producing information on the matter (with publishers) and organizing public action (with voluntary and youth agencies). Highly publicized social mobilization in the street was launched across the globe between October 1965 and March 1966. The goal was to engage young people to embrace the cause of development, aid and trade, and to organize teach-ins and briefings. The academic world was especially targeted and would result in the creation of the Universities Fight for Economic Development (UNFED), including Cambridge, Keele, Oxford and Reading. Well covered by national media, such as the *Daily Mirror*, this national movement was part of a boom in voluntary service.[19]

Beyond the educational and vocational purpose of such advocacy, the 'Youth against Hunger' movement thus aimed at building a stronger sense of political involvement in the younger generations, but it did not succeed for lack of a clear strategy. NGOs seemed to be lost on how to become channels to politicize the concern. By reinforcing public opinion and mobilizing the youth and volunteers, the hope was to pass the responsibility of political action into the hands of voluntary aid: 'We have therefore to recognize that we have failed to provide an articulate enlightened public opinion on this subject. There is even a danger that the existence of voluntary organizations gives Government an excuse for inactivity.'[20]

Such international public actions were at the core of the new awareness strategy of the FFHC campaign as reframed by the FAO in January 1967. To prepare for the second World Food Congress in 1968, in which the FAO intended to implement its World Plan for Agricultural Development facing demographic growth, the media strategy was improved. The FAO put priority on publicity, information, education and discussion, and encouraged more coordinated action. As the public was not expected to influence the content of such a plan, expert groups and social leaders were specifically targeted: 'students and professors, business leaders, etc. . . . can help formulate national views on the Plan'.[21] This resulted in massive international action, such as 'Walks for Development', which occurred in major Western and African cities during the 1–3 May 1971 weekend (see Figure 8.1). These marches mobilized citizens as advocates for the South, wearing political slogans, which were attractive for media coverage. In one weekend, the FAO was able to raise about $8 million for the Third World. Three hundred and twenty walks were organized in the United States, and more than 80,000 marchers gathered in Rome to raise $200,000.[22]

This participation in more visible, political actions was not without consequences for British NGOs, especially for SCF, whose activities had always been depoliticized since its early years.[23] In the early 1960s, British charities came under scrutiny by the charity commissioners regarding their advocacy campaigning on world hunger and overseas activities, as British charity laws strictly prohibit national charities from political activity. In 1970, the commissioners warned aid

Figure 8.1. City youth marching to protest world hunger, United Kingdom, May 1971. © UK Freedom from Hunger Campaign. Photo courtesy of FAO.

charities to desist from calling on governments to change policies.[24] This strong legal boundary prevented NGOs from more aggressive and politicized media strategies. One good example was SCF's refusal to collaborate with the advocacy group Fast for World Justice (FWJ) in 1972. Adopting militant public strategies, FWJ wanted to shock consciences with people fasting to raise more media coverage on world development. FWJ wanted to petition the Prime Minister and bore a black coffin representing the Third World to No. 10 Downing Street.[25] Although SCF's public relations and press offices agreed to participate, the director of fundraising and the deputy director general both refused on the grounds that 'this is [not] the right forum for Save the Children to express views on the subject'.[26] Even though no further justification was given, the political outplay of the campaign might have certainly restrained SCF.

Oxfam and the Baby Milk Campaign

The end of the 1960s was a time of restructuring media strategies in the NGO sector, especially in the new era of satellites and transboundary television. NGOs media strategies were impacted by the inflation of the global economy, the new competition of actors in the field and, more importantly, the lessons learned from the famine in Biafra: this first televised famine epitomized the tandem rescuer-journalist in media coverage, purposely used in the Biafran political propaganda for marketing the famine as genocide.[27] This new awareness about public relations with the media is obvious in SCF's different reports evaluating their publicity techniques.[28] Incentives were given, such as contacts in press agencies, the hiring of a new advertising agency, connecting stories with the British audience, and the use of more pictures and TV training. At the beginning of the 1970s, NGOs tended to move further in the era of public educational communication by launching their own magazines. The *New Internationalist*, backed by Oxfam and Christian Aid, was thus created in 1973 as a monthly magazine on development issues. The 1960s were also an era of learning how to campaign within the legal limits imposed by British authorities. Although Oxfam was founded in October 1942 to lobby the British government to lower the Allied blockade in Greece, the NGO did not fully develop effective lobbying action at the international level before its role in the FFHC. Oxfam established a Public Affairs Unit in the mid 1970s and a Campaigns Unit in 1979, showing the steps taken in professionalizing its public actions.[29]

Transnational advocacy campaigns in the 1970s were largely influenced by the UN agenda, especially in concerted action. Nevertheless, media action was limited to traditional educational means, like leaflets, posters, local newspapers and conferences. Starting with the 'World Refugee Year' campaign in 1959–60, the UN was successful in establishing specific moments in the year to mobilize the public sphere around an issue, such as the popular 'World Days'. The United Nations Children's Fund (UNICEF), for example, which started in the 1950s with the goodwill ambassadors as advocates for children, achieved its first successful lobbying campaign by pushing the UN to adopt 1979 as the Year of the Child. During the 1980s, UNICEF's Executive Director James P. 'Jim' Grant managed to mount successfully the social mobilization of political and religious leaders, economic companies and sports and arts celebrities. He was a leader in promoting direct action to create visibility on hidden issues and persuading for action to be taken.[30]

Consequently, the BMC became a typical UN public action from 1979 to 1988, coordinated under the International Baby Food Action Network (IBFAN, including Oxfam and the World Health Organization (WHO)), but largely dominated by UNICEF. For John Clark, Oxfam's Campaign Officer and founding member of IBFAN, the BMC was seen as 'one of the most cost effective ventures in infant health care ever'.[31] Their goals were to reduce infant mortality due to infected water (needed to fill the milk bottles) and to move back to breastfeeding, therefore reducing the distribution of milk substitutes by Western producers in developing countries. The BMC was launched through a *New Internationalist* special issue in 1973. Following the steps of the FFHC in the 1960s, the international public campaign largely spread in the 1980s with the help of special committees in Britain and North America and the expertise of BBC journalist and campaigner Esther Rantzen (see Figure 8.2). Materials included special leaflets and cartoons for children. The message was clear: to make people aware of the danger involved in using baby milk and to shame manufacturing companies with their aggressive marketing strategies. The BMC managed to push the World Health Assembly to adopt the Code of Conduct on baby milk companies in 1981.

French 'Speaking out': Political Advocacy by MSF in the 1980s

Compared to the two previous decades, the 1980s saw the emergence of more political and confrontational advocacy, which assumed a strong (although generally short-term) media engagement, especially through live coverage on television. New campaigning units were opened by international NGOs, and lessons learned from public awareness and media collaborations pushed for 'an *increasing strength* of the 'NGO lobby', a more *strategic approach* to advocacy, closer *integration* of lobbying and public campaigning/education, and more attention to the use of the *media*'.[32] The impetus was the birth of MSF in 1971, which profoundly reshaped the humanitarian system by stating in its founding charter to 'act and speak out' and to 'treat and bear witness'. MSF operations remained clandestine throughout the 1970s, which was a foundational decade for the organization to build its public image of emergency doctors, but also to experiment with its 'speaking out' duty.[33]

Three episodes slowly put MSF in front of the camera differently from British NGOs, thus pushing the organization to improve its public strategies and

Figure 8.2. Journalist Esther Rantzen in Oxfam's Baby Milk campaign leaflet, 1983. MS. Oxfam, CPN/3/311 © Oxfam, photo courtesy of Oxfam (Bodleian Library).

question the limits of its political neutrality. Because MSF was not afraid of provocative media engagement, especially through public demonstration and outbursts, it participated in the emergence of three new forms of political advocacy: mobilization during the boat people crisis (1978–79), persuasion during the March on Cambodia (1980) and denunciation during the Ethiopian famine (1984–85).

The Boat People and the March on Cambodia (1978–80)

The story of the boat people is indicative of MSF's capacity to build a strategy based on sharing information and simultaneously mobilizing a strong network of decision-makers, attention-grabbers and civil society. It started on TV evening news programmes in November 1978, showing the *Hai Hong* ship wandering on the China Sea, filled with 2,500 Vietnamese refugees fleeing the brutality of the new communist regime. Forty thousand refugees had already landed on Malaysia's Pulau Bidong Island, as neighbouring countries refused to accept them.[34] Following international outrage, the French newspaper *Le Monde* published the 'Ship for Vietnam' appeal on 21 November 1978. Largely orchestrated by Bernard Kouchner, one of MSF's founding members, the appeal aimed at sending a cargo boat, named *Island of Light* (*Ile-de-Lumière*), to rescue the boat people from drowning at sea and being attacked by pirates, and offering medical support. Kouchner wanted to fund the boat through public support, but this was mainly a political campaign galvanized by French intellectuals: some influential celebrity supporters were the French intelligentsia of the old and new Left (Raymond Aron, Jean-Paul Sartre, Bernard Henry-Lévy and André Glucksmann) and movie stars (Yves Montand and Simone Signoret).

Kouchner also mobilized his network, with journalists Olivier Todd and Jean-François Revel (*L'Express*) and Gilles Bresson (*Libération*). They helped to generate a strong echo throughout the French media when the operation was launched in April 1979. However, the initiative created a strong division inside MSF. President Claude Malhuret and Dr Rony Brauman, among others, criticized the media spectacle around the personality of Kouchner because MSF advocated for anonymous and collective actions: 'The whole episode had been "mediaterized" to a degree that distorted the essence of medically and technically competent humanitarian action.'[35] The NGO was afraid of the blurring lines between the political operation and MSF, as Kouchner used the TV cameras to start advocating for the 'right to interfere'.[36] The schism was irreconcilable, and Kouchner split from MSF during its seventh General Assembly on 7 May 1979. While the campaign itself was mainly built around one activist and advocate, it taught MSF a media strategy that Brauman summarized years later in 'How to Engineer an International Event': the use of images, the originality of the event, the humanitarian mediator and the innocence of the victim.[37] Despite its opposition to Kouchner, MSF curiously used his strategy with the Cambodian refugees in 1980.

At that time, MSF's attitude shifted to accusations of the Vietnamese regime by using persuasion, a strategy that aims at convincing authorities in their own interests through private dialogue or delegations. After the collapse of the Khmer Rouge regime and the Vietnamese invasion of Cambodia in January 1979, the country was closed and rumours of famine spread through the international media. MSF still ran three medical missions in the refugee camps of Aranya-Prathet, Nam Yao and Surin, at the borders between Thailand and Cambodia. Concerns were raised again about the politicization of aid: the Vietnamese refused any humanitarian relief if not channelled by them, whereas the international community and the UN refused to recognize the new occupiers as the legitimate rulers of Cambodia, considering the invasion illegal. While UNICEF and the ICRC were focused on negotiating an agreement with the Vietnamese, Oxfam agreed to compromise and was granted access.[38] MSF refused to collaborate with the French Communist Party, which coordinated aid for Cambodia, and started an operation with its media network in France.[39] The 'March on Cambodia' was launched on 21 December 1979, with the following text published in the leftist press: 'We have to enter in Cambodia, to convince the Vietnamese occupier not to let the survivors of the Khmer Rouge genocide die . . . Five years ago, the international public opinion forced the bombings on Vietnam to cease; today, only this public opinion will force the Vietnamese to let humanitarian relief be distributed in Cambodia.'

MSF worked in coordinated action with other NGOs, such as Action against Hunger and the International Rescue Committee (IRC). Despite the critiques raised against the boat for Vietnam, the same components were at work: MSF doctors, international journalists, intellectuals, celebrities and French politicians were the marchers. This mixed group arrived at the Cambodian border on 6 February 1980. Reading a message of solidarity in French, English and Khmer, Claude Malhuret (then MSF's General Secretary) and Leo Cherne (the IRC's Chairman) expected to persuade the Vietnamese soldiers to let them come in with a humanitarian convoy (see Figure 8.3).[40] After hours of praying, singing and sitting, the group realized the futility of its action and flew back to France the next day.

Even though the results were negative, this episode interestingly reveals a naive optimism in the use of television to foster public attention and humanitarian response; it pre-dates the famous 'CNN effect' of the 1990s. However, this type of hypervisible and symbolic strategy has found its limits, as a media presence will not bypass political blockades. The initiative looks more like the militant, fashionable sit-ins of the 1960s social movements than a true advocacy strategy. During its General Assembly in March 1980, MSF decided to limit such actions, arguing that it had to undertake such a mission because 'no one else took the responsibility to do it'.[41] However, the NGO learned of a new position of public

Figure 8.3. 'March for the Survival of Cambodia'. In the picture, Dr Claude Malhuret, with Leo Cherne next to him, reports on his unsuccessful intervention towards the Bo Doi (Vietnamese soldiers). © Patrice Cotteau, photo courtesy of MSF.

agitateur and thus improved its bystander-witness role by working on medical and humanitarian evidence.

The Famine in Ethiopia

In the 1980s, MSF was still operating through 'clandestine'[42] surgical missions. It conducted missions in Eritrea and Tigre to help refugees, which would soon lead them to an extreme form of advocacy – denunciation – as the very last resort MSF could take to shame and put pressure on Ethiopian authorities by displaying publicly their reprehensible actions. After the revolution in 1974, in which overthrown Emperor Haile Selassie was replaced by Colonel Mengitsu, Ethiopia was reshaped through the model of the communist USSR. At war with the Eritrean and Tigrean provinces seeking autonomy, the Ethiopian communist regime also implemented an agricultural reorganization of collective ownership. Although famine had threatened the severely drought-affected northern provinces since 1983, the government did not grant MSF the authorization to conduct evaluation missions until February 1984. MSF started a medical programme in the Korem camp in the Wollo province, built by the Relief and Rehabilitation Commission (RRC), a government agency. Nutritional activities were held by SCF.

As the Ethiopian authorities were about to launch the tenth anniversary celebration of the regime's revolution, journalists were welcomed for the festivities, but were blocked from the crisis-affected areas by the regime, which was deliberately hiding the severity of the famine.[43] After the celebrations concluded on 3 October 1984, journalists were finally granted access to the crisis-afflicted areas; a BBC team composed of Michael Buerk and his camera operator produced a famous report on the famine on 24 October 1984, broadcast on the six o'clock news on 25 October. MSF played a role in publicizing and criticising the human-made character of the famine since the characterization began. When meeting a representative of the World Food Programme in Korem in July 1984, MSF-France Medical Coordinator Brigitte Vasset had upset the authorities by using the word 'famine'.[44] She was the only humanitarian worker interviewed in Buerk's reportage and provided medical evidence of the famine. She used her role as a witness repeatedly when meeting with political representatives or journalists in the camp. Humanitarian workers appeared sympathetic in the media in general, which were particularly fond of rescuers' images to provide first-hand accounts of the severity of the crisis.[45]

The resettlement programme worsened in November 1984 with populations from the rebellious Northern provinces being forced to relocate to the more fertile Southern and Western regions. Several organizations, such as War on Want and MSF, started protesting in the international media in December 1984;[46] in the early months of 1985, MSF further investigated the abuses against Ethiopian farmers through a series of medical-evaluation missions. MSF's Board of Directors explored different ways to handle the situation in its meeting in March 1985, facing the same dilemma the ICRC did forty years earlier when facing the Holocaust: '[To] criticise the conduct of the resettlement publicly in the media, which would involve withdrawing the teams . . . [or to] take a more pragmatic approach . . . to continue our aid and presence as witnesses to events.'[47] It is worth noting the emphasis on witnessing: although MSF clearly viewed the media as its natural allies, it decided to use more discreet pressure by pushing the UN representative in Addis Ababa.

International outrage increased in March 1985 when 50,000 people were forcefully evacuated from the Ibnet camp, which was set on fire by Ethiopian forces. Taking one step further towards denunciation, MSF, Concern (an Irish relief agency) and World Vision testified about the abuses in the media: 'As political considerations move to the fore, they [humanitarian groups] often find themselves agreeing to accept violations of their principles.'[48] MSF was reaching its breaking point, as it questioned the very roots of humanitarian action and its original links with the human rights approach. Not only did MSF consider the need to debate the political world in which it operated, but it also embodied the true advocate of reporting for those who could not: 'protest . . . constitutes a moral imperative and a moral responsibility that we must assume on our own behalf, as well as that of the people who place their trust in us and those we are reaching out to. Out of ethical concerns, as well as concern for the effectiveness of our activities, we cannot accept conditions that violate the very spirit that moves us'.[49] By implementing the practical consequences of speaking out, MSF then moved away from sensibility to endorse a humanitarian responsibility.[50]

According to its principles, the ICRC conducted an evaluation of the resettlement areas; although the report mentioned devastating conditions of life, it was sent only to the Ethiopian RRC and was not made public. Despite growing pressure from the international community, the government refused to give more access to humanitarian organizations, as it used its own feeding centres to lure the population and force them to relocate. Brauman finally evoked the possibility of leaving the country in a discussion at the British-American Press Club in Paris. Picked up by Reuters and AFP, the story was all over the American and French press: 'now that we are speaking openly about the matter, the Ethiopian government is accusing MSF of using a disinformation campaign to undermine aid efforts for the famine victims . . . If we do not speak out, and if our message to the public at large is, "Move along, there's nothing to see here", we are violating those two contracts [relief and accountability]'.[51] This further step in the political fight put the NGO in a delicate position, as Brauman did not ask his colleagues beforehand to make the statement. Not only was the precarious balance between aid and politics endangered by such accusations, but so too were the very purpose of aid – if it does more harm than good – and the possibility of carrying out missions in a neutral and protected space. Because these minimum conditions were not fulfilled,[52] MSF-France's board decided to explain its difficulties on French TV on 31 October 1985.[53]

Summarized in Brauman's words – 'If we simply ignore what we know and think, then what is the point of our existence [as MSF]?'[54] – the controversy emphasized the roles of the witness and the activist over the role of the rescuer. The risk was important, as it might position doctors as spies. On 1 November 1985, the Ethiopian RRC denied the charges, criticizing MSF for 'making more noise than miracles', calling 'for media attention through which it hopes to gain credit that is not due' and suggesting that the NGO leave.[55] Thus, a schism appeared in the humanitarian sector: on the one side, the Francophone and Anglophone media echoed MSF denunciations and presented MSF as the only NGO that dared to speak out publicly; on the other side, the UN representative for relief operations in Ethiopia completely denied the forced resettlements, while humanitarian agencies (Concern, Save the Children, Oxfam, the FAO and the World Food Programme) stood divided on the political action; they admitted to the deportations, but preferred to remain silent and use humanitarian diplomacy.[56] Interestingly, the ICRC aligned with MSF on the denunciations, although not publicly. After heated correspondence, the RRC ordered MSF to leave the country on 2 December 1985, 'in view of the politically motivated false allegations . . . and . . . refusal to follow norms and procedures established with the other NGOs'.[57] In the end, MSF grew stronger from the case. Since the political denunciations were intended more for decision makers, governments and international donors, the public continued to send money, moved by compassion.

'Liberté Sans Frontières'

The episodes from Vietnam, Cambodia and Ethiopia not only had a lasting impact on MSF in its use of the media, but also deeply questioned its ideological background. During the MSF General Assembly in May 1984, MSF decided to found a communication association focusing on Third World issues. 'Liberté sans Frontières' (LSF), or 'Freedom without Borders', was launched on 10 January 1985. Presented as neutral, the foundation was paradoxical with MSF dogma; it was, in fact, engaging in a political fight by criticizing 'Third Worldism' as another means to reproduce the hegemonic power of the North over the South with liberal ideals. LSF planned to advocate by winning public opinion through several channels: the media, the political world and the informal relays, the latter encompassing celebrities, associations and lobby groups.[58]

This foundation had three main activities: research on development, political lobbying and mobilization of public opinion on international matters, and a fundraising unit. The foundation's board was composed of MSF members and intellectuals (academics and journalists) belonging to the traditional network of the NGO. Interestingly, LSF can be seen as a political (but not neutral) advocacy satellite of MSF whose lobbying techniques aimed to an audience including Members of Parliament, journalists or opinion leaders. The foundation also planned to have more general public information: LSF public relations activities consisted of a journal, books, newsletters and even a news agency. MSF was indeed convinced of the need for more visible public mobilizations.

However, the creation of LSF again provoked a division in the movement, as MSF-Belgium did not agree with the political nature of their engagement. Greeted partly with unease and scepticism by journalists, the foundation was seen as the political arm of MSF. LSF also complicated matters in the field, as it breached MSF principles and threatened the NGO's existence; many members thought the MSF movement required a complete separation of the two institutions.[59] LSF came at a perfect time for Ethiopia, and some feared that the French section was using the famine as an excuse to enter the political arena. MSF was marginalized as the episode emphasized shifts in the aid system. It was quite obvious in the critiques of forty NGOs against MSF in Ethiopia: 'There is further the very real risk that the bad publicity stirred up by MSF will cause major aid donors to reduce both their immediate and long term aid commitments to Ethiopia in 1986.'[60] This was probably the limit of MSF's utopic dream of speaking out: that it would create a coalition among the NGOs to influence Ethiopian politics. After four years of stormy existence, LSE was dissolved on 28 April 1989 on the basis that 'if MSF has something to say, it can say it under its own name . . . It is MSF that catches the flak'.[61]

Conclusion

The case studies explored in this chapter reveal that the two schools of humanitarianism – the British model of educational development or the French model of political emergency – are not that different. They understand the need to criticize the underlying ideology of development since the 1960s: Oxfam and SCF through large public activities and MSF through its LSF utopia. However, these NGOs have chosen different paths in their media strategies. More limited by the U.K. juridical system on charity, British NGOs have expressed more shy attitudes towards using aggressive denunciations in the media, preferring coordinated public education at the national scale to change mentalities and influence generational behaviours. At the same time, SCF and Oxfam were able to professionalize their communication units during the 1970s and the 1980s for the benefit of fundraising and public campaigning. On the other hand, MSF has learned to play the role of the 'lone ranger' since the 1980s, using its public image to openly speak out on behalf of abused beneficiaries, building from case to case and relying mainly on its personal journalistic network. While revealing sometimes-amateur decisions and a lack of strategy, this attitude has since positioned MSF as one of the NGOs that does not compromise its humanitarian principles and that openly criticizes collusion of aid agencies with states. The political advocacy implemented by MSF (eyewitnessing and speaking out for the victims) is prevalent today in front of strong political impediments in the humanitarian field, but without the media sphere, it would remain a purely emotional reaction.[62] It also has its opponents, such as the ICRC, which prefers to refrain from public statements for 'humanitarian diplomacy'[63] like behind-the-door negotiations and bilateral practices, although this type of diplomacy is limited to agencies that operate at the judicial level.

NGOs thus became 'major players' in policy-making during the 1960s and 1980s. They positioned themselves as legitimate intermediaries between the two ends of the scale: addressing the root causes of poverty and misery and dealing with humanitarian needs in conflict-related issues; gathering grassroots information as well as building on the visibility, sympathy and contacts they have in the media networks. During these decades, humanitarian advocacy was suddenly seen as a promising adventure, but with the need for better guidelines. As put in the words of an MSF-France logistician in Ethiopia, advocacy came as a learning-by-doing tool, which was quite amateurish in the beginning: 'We didn't have any guidelines on advocacy, but there was a lot of direct action . . . This reflected what advocacy was like in those days; we saw horrible things, so we talked about them. We gave no thought to security or to the risk of being expelled.'[64] Therefore, by the end of the 1980s, advocacy strategies of the Western humanitarian sector provided mixed results, especially in the development sector. NGOs failed to promote alternatives to neoliberal approaches to development aid, to develop a strong advocacy strategy and to evaluate the impact and effectiveness of their previous campaigns; they have achieved limited results because of a lack of more coordinated activities in building alliances, for example, with other social movements like women, trade unions or environmentalists.[65]

Before Ethiopia, the Biafra famine played a pivotal role in showing the politicization of aid and making the NGOs more aware of their use of media and propaganda, and their relations with journalists. After Ethiopia, humanitarian advocacy shifted from amateurism to professionalism, with improvements in lobbying techniques towards political and economic stakeholders, and by opening the advocacy networks to more participative and representative actions from Southern actors.[66] Yet it was the Nazi horrors of the Second World War and the guilty silence of the ICRC at the time that raised the fundamental question lying at the core of any humanitarian advocacy initiative: is it possible for agencies to remain bystanders? Can they talk? Can they really change attitudes, policies or governments? Issuing public statements sometimes does not have any effect or can completely jeopardize the aims of an organization, its image or its access to a population. The genocide in Rwanda in 1994 tragically showed that speaking out has not resolved the dilemma of how to stop abuses and use the media with maximum leverage effect: 'The problem is simply that this generally amounts to nothing more than calling on someone else to do something.'[67] Sharing information with the public, speaking out or lobbying are different steps to be taken, but it clearly shows that humanitarian organizations and the media are just lonely players if the states do not fulfil their political responsibilities.

Valérie Gorin is a senior lecturer and researcher at the Center for Education and Research in Humanitarian Action (CERAH), a joint center of the University of Geneva and the Graduate Institute. She is in charge of the programmes in history of humanitarianism and humanitarian communication. She holds a Ph.D. in communication and media sciences, which focused on the photojournalistic coverage of humanitarian crises in American and French news magazines from the 1960s to the 1990s. She has written several articles about the uses and evolution of photojournalism and documentary photography in humanitarian settings, from the late nineteenth century to the recent development of amateur photography. Her areas of research relate to the history of humanitarian crises in the twentieth century, crisis reporting, photojournalism and amateur photography, visual culture of suffering, (eye)witnessing and advocacy strategies in humanitarian settings.

Notes

1. K. Davies, 'Continuity, Change and Contest: Meanings of "Humanitarian" from the "Religion of Humanity" to the Kosovo War', in *HPG Working Paper* (London: ODI), 11–16.
2. The civil war in Darfur (Western Sudan) began in February 2003, with rebel groups opposing the government of Sudan, which was accused of ethnic cleansing, crimes against humanity and forced displacement against non-Arab populations. Most humanitarian

organizations faced important dilemmas in this highly politicized environment. Many preferred to remain silent in order to gain access to affected populations, before advocating on civilian insecurity in 2004, therefore challenging the humanitarian principle of neutrality. For more information, see S. O'Callaghan, 'Humanitarian Advocacy in Darfur: The Challenge of Neutrality', in *HPG Policy Brief* (London: ODI, 2007); M. Haeri, 'Saving Darfur: Does Advocacy Help or Hinder Conflict Resolution?', *Praxis* 23 (2008), 33-46.

3. V. Pupavac, 'The Politics of Emergency and the Demise of the Developing State: Problems for Humanitarian Advocacy', *Development in Practice* 16(3–4) (2006), 255-69; M. Labonte and A. Edgerton, 'Towards a Typology of Humanitarian Access Denial', *Third World Quarterly* 34(1) (2013), 39-57; J. Servaes and P. Malikhao, 'Advocacy Communication for Peacebuilding', *Development in Practice* 22(2) (2012), 229-43.

4. C. Dolan, 'British Development NGOs and Advocacy in the 1990s', in M. Edwards and D. Hulme (eds), *Making a Difference: NGOs and Development in a Changing World* (London: Earthscan, 1992), 203-10, at 206.

5. K. Bridges, 'Between Aid and Politics: Diagnosing the Challenge of Humanitarian Advocacy in Politically Complex Environments – The Case of Darfur, Sudan', *Third World Quarterly* 31(8) (2010), 1251-69, at 1252.

6. M. DuBois, 'Civilian Protection and Humanitarian Advocacy: Strategies and (False?) Dilemmas', *Humanitarian Exchange Magazine* 39 (2008), 12-15, at 12.

7. V. Gorin, 'L'enfance comme figure compassionnelle : étude transversale de l'iconographie de la famine aux dix-neuvième et vingtième siècles', *European Review of History* 22(6) (2015), 940–62; S. Sliwinski, *Human Rights in Camera* (Chicago: University of Chicago Press, 2011); L. Torchin, 'Ravished Armenia: Visual Media, Humanitarian Advocacy, and the Formation of Witnessing Publics', *American Anthropologist* 108(1) (2006), 214–20.

8. P. Ryfman, 'Vers une "Ecole française" d'analyse de l'humanitaire ?', *Revue internationale et stratégique* 3(47) (2002), 133–44.

9. M. Edwards, 'Does the Doormat Influence the Boot? Critical Thoughts on UK NGOs and International Advocacy', *Development in Practice* 3(3) (1993), 163-75, at 164.

10. H. Slim and A. Bonwick, *Protection: An ALNAP Guide for Humanitarian Agencies* (London: ODI, 2005), 79-87.

11. MSF, 'Entretien avec Rony Brauman', *L'ENA Mensuel* (1995), 1–6.

12. FAO, 'Freedom from Hunger Campaign: 1967-1968-1969', January 1967. All SCF documents come from the SCF archives on microfilms. See Save the Children Fund Archive. *Western Aid and the Global Economy: Cumulative Guide. Reels 1–101* (London: Primary Source Microfilm and Thomson Gale).

13. SCF, 'Minutes of the First Meeting of the Special Sub-Committee', 21 November 1961.

14. SCF, 'Minutes of the Ninth Meeting of the Special Sub-Committee', 6 November 1963.

15. SCF, 'Minutes of the Fourth Meeting of the Special Sub-Committee', 18 July 1962.

16. For example, in SCF's *World's Children* magazine.

17. V. Gorin, '"Millions of Children in Deadly Peril": utilisation des photographies d'enfants affamés par le Save the Children Fund pendant l'entre-deux guerres', *Itinera*, supplement of *Revue suisse d'histoire* 37 (2014), 95–112.

18. N. Dogra, '"Reading NGOs Visually": Implications of Visual Images for NGO Management', *Journal of International Development* 19(2) (2007), 161-71, at 169.

19. J. Sheard, 'From Lady Bountiful to Active Citizen: Volunteering and the Voluntary Sector', in J. Smith et al. (eds), *An Introduction to the Voluntary Sector* (London: Routledge, 1995), 114–27, at 116.

20. Youth against Hunger, 'UK programme', 1967–68.
21. FAO, 'Freedom from Hunger Campaign: 1967-1968-1969', January 1967.
22. FAO Press release, 'This was the Walk That was', May 1971.
23. K. Freeman, *If Any Man Build: The History of the Save the Children Fund* (London: Hodder & Stoughton, 1965).
24. For a good analysis of the inquiry by the Charity Commission between 1962 and 1965, see M. Black, *A Cause for Our Times: Oxfam - the First 50 years* (Oxford: Oxfam Professional, 1992), 85–107.
25. Fast for World Justice, 'Projected Programme and Organization', August 1972.
26. SCF Director of Fund Raising, 'Memorandum on Fast for World Justice', 11 September 1972.
27. R. Doron, 'Marketing Genocide: Biafran Propaganda Strategies during the Nigerian Civil War, 1967–70', *Journal of Genocide Research* 16(2–3) (2014), 227–46.
28. SCF, 'Trends in Fund Raising and Organizational Development', May 1970; SCF, 'Memorandum to All Honorary Press and Publicity Officers and Other UK Branch Officers from the SCF Press Officer', July 1970; SCF, 'Review of the Public Relations Programme for 1971', 3 January 1972.
29. The 'Public Affairs Unit' carried out research to provide evidence in health-related issues before public campaigning, while the 'Campaigns Unit' was in charge of all campaigning activities within Oxfam. The two later integrated the 'Public Affairs and Communications Services (PACS) Division' established in the 1990s, which then changed its name to the 'Campaigns and Policy Division' in the 2000s. See the 'Introduction' of the online 'Catalogue of the Oxfam Archives: Campaigns' created in 2015 by the Bodleian Library (University of Oxford). Retrieved 22 August 2018 from http://www.bodley.ox.ac.uk/dept/scwmss/wmss/online/modern/oxfam/oxfam-cpn.html#introduction. See also D. Bryer and J. Magrath, 'New Dimensions of Global Advocacy', *Nonprofit and Voluntary Sector Quarterly* 28(4) (1999), 168–77, at 173.
30. UNICEF, *1946–2006: Sixty Years for Children* (New York: United Nations Children's Fund, 2006), 4–21; M. Black, *Children First: The Story of UNICEF, Past and Present* (Oxford: Oxford University Press, 1996), 1–32.
31. J. Clark, 'Policy Influence, Lobbying and Advocacy', in M. Edwards and D. Hulme (eds), *Making a Difference: NGOs and Development in a Changing World* (London: Earthscan, 1992), 191–202, at 198.
32. Clark, 'Policy Influence, Lobbying and Advocacy', 198.
33. M. Givoni, 'Humanitarian Dilemmas, Concern for Others, and Care of the Self: The Case of Médecins sans Frontières', in J. Paulmann (ed.), *Dilemmas of Humanitarian Aid in the Twentieth Century* (Oxford: Oxford University Press, 2016), 371–92.
34. M. Pugh, 'Drowning Not Waving: Boat People and Humanitarianism at Sea', *Journal of Refugee Studies* 17(1) (2004), 50-69.
35. R. Fox, *Doctors without Borders: Humanitarian Quests, Impossible Dreams of Médecins Sans Frontières* (Baltimore: Johns Hopkins University Press, 2014), 47.
36. A. Vallaeys, *Médecins sans frontières : la biographie* (Paris: Fayard, 2004).
37. R. Brauman, 'When Suffering Makes a Good Story', in F. Jean (ed.), *Life, Death and Aid* (London: Routledge, 1993), 149–58, at 150.
38. Black, *A Cause for Our Times*, 224–28.
39. *Le Nouvel Observateur, Libération, L'Express* and *Le Monde*.
40. See the TV footage of JA2, 8 pm and IT1, 8 pm, on 7 February 1980. A similar performance was undertaken by a group of activists during the crises in East Pakistan at the

beginning of the 1970s; F. Hannig, 'Negotiating Humanitarianism and Politics: Operation Omega's Border Breaching Missions during the East Pakistan Crisis of 1971', in Paulmann, *Dilemmas*, 329–43.

41. MSF-France, 'Annual Report of the 1980 General Assembly', 28 March 1980. All MSF documents are published online on MSF's speaking-out case studies: http://speakingout .msf.org/en/famine-and-forced-relocations-in-ethiopia/reference-materials (accessed 22 August 2018).

42. MSF used to run clandestine missions (small mobile medical units illegally crossing the borders and working in complete isolation) since the Soviet invasion of Afghanistan. See P. Redfield, *Life in Crisis: The Ethical Journey of Doctors without Borders* (Berkeley: University of California Press, 2013), 61 and 76.

43. F. Jean, *Du bon usage de la famine* (Paris: MSF, 1986), 31.

44. MSF and L. Binet, *Famine and Forced Relocations in Ethiopia* (Paris: MSF, 2005), 14.

45. S. Franks, *Reporting Disasters: Famine, Aid, Politics and the Media* (London: Hurst, 2013), 133–60.

46. Newspapers and magazines, such as *The Times,* the *Herald Tribune, Le Monde* and *Time,* interviewed the two NGOs.

47. MSF-France, 'Summary of the Meeting of the Board of Directors', 24 March 1985.

48. P. Haski, 'Ethiopie: évacuation forcée de 60'000 réfugiés', *Libération* (3 May 1985). See also 'Aider les victimes et se taire' in the same newspaper; and B. Harden, 'Force Evacuation in Ethiopia Confirmed by Relief Workers', *Washington Post* (2 May 1985).

49. MSF-France, 'Annual Report of the 1985 General Assembly', May 1985.

50. M. Givoni, 'Beyond the Humanitarian/Political Divide: Witnessing and the Making of Humanitarian Ethics', *Journal of Human Rights* 10(1) (2011), 55–75.

51. 'Interview with Rony Brauman, President of MSF: 'MSF will leave Ethiopia if . . .', *La Croix* (1 November 1985).

52. MSF-France, 'Summary of the Board Meeting', 28 October 1985.

53. Antenne 2, 'Interview with Dr. Claude Malhuret', *Midi 2*, 31 October 1985.

54. MSF and Binet, *Famine and Forced Relocations in Ethiopia,* 61.

55. RRC Ethiopia, 'Press Statement', 24 October 1985.

56. MSF-France, 'Summary of the Board Meeting', 25 November 1985

57. Letter from RRC to Bertrand Desmoulins, Coordinator, MSF-France, 2 December 1985.

58. LSF, 'Introductory Materials', January 1985.

59. MSF team mission in Chad, 'Open Letter to the Management and Membership of MSF', 10 February 1985; Director, President and Board of Directors to the members of MSF-Belgium, 'MSF and LSF: Incompatible – A Summary of the Analysis', 12 March 1985.

60. 'CRDA Member's Statement on Resettlement', 18 December 1985.

61. MSF-France, 'Summary of the Board Meeting Council', 28 April 1989.

62. D. Fassin, 'The Humanitarian Politics of Testimony: Subjectification through Trauma in the Israeli-Palestinian Conflict', *Cultural Anthropology* 23(3) (2008), 531–58.

63. L. Minear and H. Smith (eds), *Humanitarian Diplomacy: Practitioners and Their Craft* (Tokyo: UN University Press, 2006).

64. MSF and Binet, *Famine and Forced Relocations in Ethiopia,* 82.

65. I. Anderson, 'Northern NGO Advocacy: Perceptions, Reality, and the Challenge', *Development in Practice* 10(3–4) (2000), 445–52.

66. L. Minear, 'The Other Missions of NGOs: Education and Advocacy', *World Development* 15 (1987), 201–11.

67. J. Kellenberger, 'Speaking out or Remaining Silent in Humanitarian Work', *International Review of the Red Cross* 86(855) (2004), 593–609, at 602.

Bibliography

Anderson, I. 'Northern NGO Advocacy: Perceptions, Reality, and the Challenge'. *Development in Practice* 10(3–4) (2000), 445–52.

Black, M. *A Cause for Our Times: Oxfam - the First 50 Years.* Oxford: Oxfam Professional, 1992.

———. *Children First: The Story of UNICEF, Past and Present.* Oxford: Oxford University Press, 1996.

Brauman, R. 1993. 'When Suffering Makes a Good Story', in F. Jean (ed.), *Life, Death and Aid* (London: Routledge, 1993), 149–58.

Bridges, K. 'Between Aid and Politics: Diagnosing the Challenge of Humanitarian Advocacy in Politically Complex Environments – The Case of Darfur, Sudan'. *Third World Quarterly* 31(8) (2010), 1251–69.

Bryer, D., and J. Magrath. 'New Dimensions of Global Advocacy'. *Nonprofit and Voluntary Sector Quarterly* 28(4) (1999), 168–77.

Clark, J. 'Policy Influence, Lobbying and Advocacy', in M. Edwards and D. Hulme (eds), *Making a Difference: NGOs and Development in a Changing World* (London: Earthscan, 1992), 191–202.

Davies, K. 'Continuity, Change and Contest: Meanings of "Humanitarian" from the "Religion of Humanity" to the Kosovo War', in *HPG Working Paper* (London: ODI, 2012), 11–16.

Dogra, N. '"Reading NGOs Visually": Implications of Visual Images for NGO Management'. *Journal of International Development* 19(2) (2007), 161–71.

Dolan, C. 'British Development NGOs and Advocacy in the 1990s', in M. Edwards and D. Hulme (eds), *Making a Difference: NGOs and Development in a Changing World* (London: Earthscan, 1992), 203–10.

Doron, R. 'Marketing Genocide: Biafran Propaganda Strategies during the Nigerian Civil War, 1967–70'. *Journal of Genocide Research* 16(2–3) (2014), 227–46.

DuBois, M. 'Civilian Protection and Humanitarian Advocacy: Strategies and (False?) Dilemmas'. *Humanitarian Exchange Magazine* 39 (2008), 12–15.

Edwards, M. 'Does the Doormat Influence the Boot? Critical Thoughts on UK NGOs and International Advocacy'. *Development in Practice* 3(3) (1993), 163–75.

Fassin, D. 'The Humanitarian Politics of Testimony: Subjectification through Trauma in the Israeli-Palestinian Conflict'. *Cultural Anthropology* 23(3) (2008), 531–58.

Fox, R. *Doctors without Borders: Humanitarian Quests, Impossible Dreams of Médecins Sans Frontières.* Baltimore: Johns Hopkins University Press, 2014.

Franks, S. *Reporting Disasters: Famine, Aid, Politics and the Media.* London: Hurst, 2013.

Freeman, K. *If Any Man Build: The History of the Save the Children Fund.* London: Hodder & Stoughton, 1965.

Givoni, M. 'Beyond the Humanitarian/Political Divide: Witnessing and the Making of Humanitarian Ethics'. *Journal of Human Rights* 10(1) (2011), 55–75.

———. 'Humanitarian Dilemmas, Concern for Others, and Care of the Self: The Case of Médecins sans Frontières', in J. Paulmann (ed.), *Dilemmas of Humanitarian Aid in the Twentieth Century* (Oxford: Oxford University Press, 2016), 371–92.

Gorin, V. '"Millions of Children in Deadly Peril": utilisation des photographies d'enfants affamés par le Save the Children Fund pendant l'entre-deux guerres'. *Itinera,* supplement of *Revue suisse d'histoire* 37 (2014), 95–112.

———. 'L'enfance comme figure compassionnelle : étude transversale de l'iconographie de la famine aux dix-neuvième et vingtième siècles'. *European Review of History* 22(6) (2015), 940–62.

Haeri, M. 'Saving Darfur: Does Advocacy Help or Hinder Conflict Resolution?' *Praxis* 23 (2008), 33–46.

Hannig, F. 'Negotiating Humanitarianism and Politics: Operation Omega's Border Breaching Missions during the East Pakistan Crisis of 1971', in J. Paulmann (ed.), *Dilemmas of Humanitarian Aid in the Twentieth Century* (Oxford: Oxford University Press, 2016), 329–43.

Harden, B. 'Force Evacuation in Ethiopia Confirmed by Relief Workers'. *Washington Post* (2 May 1985).

Haski, P. 'Ethiopie: évacuation forcée de 60'000 réfugiés'. *Libération* (3 May 1985).

Jean, F. *Du bon usage de la famine.* Paris: MSF, 1986.

Kellenberger, J. 'Speaking out or Remaining Silent in Humanitarian Work'. *International Review of the Red Cross* 86(855) (2004), 593–609.

Labonte, M., and A. Edgerton. 'Towards a Typology of Humanitarian Access Denial'. *Third World Quarterly* 34(1) (2013), 39–57.

Minear, L. 'The Other Missions of NGOs: Education and Advocacy'. *World Development* 15 (1987), 201–11.

Minear, L., and H. Smith (eds). *Humanitarian Diplomacy: Practitioners and Their Craft.* Tokyo: UN University Press, 2006.

MSF, and L Binet. *Famine and Forced Relocations in Ethiopia.* Paris: MSF, 2005.

O'Callaghan, S. 'Humanitarian Advocacy in Darfur: The Challenge of Neutrality', in *HPG Policy Brief* (London: ODI, 2007).

Pugh, M. 'Drowning Not Waving: Boat People and Humanitarianism at Sea'. *Journal of Refugee Studies* 17(1) (2004), 50–69.

Pupavac, V. 'The Politics of Emergency and the Demise of the Developing State: Problems for Humanitarian Advocacy'. *Development in Practice* 16(3–4) (2006), 255–69.

Redfield, P. *Life in Crisis: The Ethical Journey of Doctors without Borders.* Berkeley: University of California Press, 2013.

Ryfman, P. 'Vers une "Ecole française" d'analyse de l'humanitaire ?' *Revue internationale et stratégique* 3(47) (2002), 133–44.

Servaes, J., and P. Malikhao. 'Advocacy Communication for Peacebuilding'. *Development in Practice* 22(2) (2012), 229–43.

Sheard, J. 'From Lady Bountiful to Active Citizen: Volunteering and the Voluntary Sector', in J. Smith et al. (eds), *An Introduction to the Voluntary Sector* (London: Routledge, 1995), 114–27.

Slim, H., and A. Bonwick. *Protection: An ALNAP Guide for Humanitarian Agencies.* London: ODI, 2005.

Sliwinski, S. *Human Rights in Camera.* Chicago: University of Chicago Press, 2011.

Torchin, L. 'Ravished Armenia: Visual Media, Humanitarian Advocacy, and the Formation of Witnessing Publics'. *American Anthropologist* 108(1) (2006), 214–20.

UNICEF. *1946–2006: Sixty Years for Children.* New York: United Nations Children's Fund, 2006.

Vallaeys, A. *Médecins sans frontières : la biographie.* Paris: Fayard, 2004.

9

Humanitarianism and Revolution

*Samed, the Palestine Red Crescent Society
and the Work of Liberation*

Ilana Feldman

From the perspective of the early twenty-first century, the years of the Palestinian 'revolution' (*al-thawra*) appear as a future-past and as a future-lost. Material reminders of the (at least temporary) defeat of Palestinian national aspirations can be found across the Palestinian landscape, in both absence and ruination. In sharp contrast to the years (1969–1982) when the Palestine Liberation Organization (PLO) was based in Lebanon, controlled the refugee camps and organized Palestinian military, economic and social activity under the banner of 'the revolution' and with the aim of liberating Palestine, today Palestinians in Lebanon confront numerous restrictions on economic opportunity and a political leadership that seems to have no capacity to move a national agenda forward.[1] The anthropologist Diana Allan describes camp residents as 'refugees not only of "the catastrophe" (*al-Nakba*) – their 1948 expulsion from their homes in Palestine – but of *al-thawra*'.[2]

The fate of key institutions of the revolution highlights both absence and ruination. Absent are the workshops of Samed (the Palestinian Martyrs Society), the economic institution of the PLO. These workshops used to employ large numbers of camp residents. In the current circumstances where employment opportunities are severely constrained, the absence of this PLO-based economy is sorely felt. When residents of camps like Burj al-Barajneh, in the southern suburbs of Beirut, recall the camp's past, they often gesture fleetingly to 'over there', where the workshops used to be. In ruination are other buildings, such as the 'Gaza hospital',[3] in the Sabra and Shatila refugee camps. The hospital was a premier installation of another PLO institution, the Palestine Red Crescent Society (PRCS). It provided healthcare to Palestinians and Lebanese, free of charge. During the Sabra and Shatila massacres as well as during the War of the Camps, the hospital was a key space to treat the wounded and was targeted by combatants. With the medical facility ultimately destroyed, in the years since it has become a 'gathering', one of the informal, unrecognized, spaces of refugee life.[4]

Keeping these outcomes in mind, this chapter looks back to the time before this ruination to explore the landscape of possibility that institutions like Samed and the PRCS both represented and enabled. It focuses on Lebanon, which, prior to the departure of the PLO in 1982, was the centre of 'the revolution'.[5] But both Samed and the PRCS operated, unevenly, across the spaces of Palestinian exile and, in the case of Samed, also had a global reach, with workshops and collaborations in other allied states (particularly in Africa). Both Samed and the PRCS still exist, the latter more vibrantly than the former. The Oslo Accords in 1993 and 1995 marked the substantive death knell of Samed (already much diminished), a process insightfully described by Raja Khalidi.[6] The PRCS runs hospitals and clinics inside and outside Palestine, providing important health services in these locales.

I turn to Samed and the PRCS to consider how a national liberation movement takes up humanitarian concerns: both humanitarianism defied and humanitarianism enacted. As objects of analysis, Samed and the PRCS can be approached in a variety of ways – as economic, political and social bodies. In thinking about their humanitarian intersections, I am specifically interested in the question of how a liberation organization that was dedicated to ending displacement and resolving dispossession engaged the humanitarian question in its quest for a different future. Much of the scholarship on humanitarianism, whether anthropological or otherwise, begins by thinking about humanitarianism as a form of foreign or international intervention into a situation of suffering.[7] And this is very often the case. But humanitarian action is not only a response to 'distant suffering';[8] it also involves local actors in a variety of ways.[9] International organizations hire 'local staff' to help provide aid to suffering compatriots.[10] In the Palestinian case, the vast majority of humanitarian workers are themselves Palestinian refugees – 95 per cent of United Nations Relief and Works Agency (UNRWA) staff are refugees[11] – and so occupy the dual position of aid provider and recipient. In addition to locals working for international humanitarian organizations, local (and national) organizations themselves engage in humanitarian activity; Samed and the PRCS are examples of this.[12] In thinking about these instances of national aid, I investigate the intersection of revolution and humanitarianism in their work.

The publications of Samed and the PRCS – *Samed al-Iqtisadi* and *Balsam* – are my primary sources and objects of analysis. In publishing journals that explained their mission and trumpeted their work, Samed and the PRCS participated in a wider humanitarian media field. Media are a crucial part of the humanitarian enterprise generally, being used to draw public attention to suffering and to generate donations.[13] The articles in the Samed and PRCS journals identified the organization's place within the broader humanitarian field, at times claiming identity with the larger apparatus and at times claiming distinction from it. Media was also a crucial part of the Palestinian revolution. *Samed al-Iqtisadi* and *Balsam* were part of a broader PLO-supported media landscape that included newspapers, radio and film production. All this media served to proclaim and propagate the PLO, the Palestinian revolution, and the institutions of that revolution. The audience of Arabic-language journals such as *Samed al-Iqtisadi* and *Balsam* was both Palestinians and other sympathetic Arabs. Their contents, obviously, are neither 'objective' records of this work nor primarily 'subjective' accounts of recipient or worker experiences, though both journals do include such accounts. They served a propaganda purpose. Not only do they showcase the efforts and successes of these institutions, they highlight their effects on Palestinian participants. The journals also served the revolution in another way. They include research articles on the Palestinian economic, social and health condition, and thus provide information and analysis for planners and activists. Both continue to publish, but my focus is on issues from the 1970s and 1980s. I read them principally for their articulation of the vision and purpose of Samed and the PRCS.

At the Intersection of Revolution and Humanitarianism

Palestinian refugees have been recipients of humanitarian assistance of various kinds since their displacement in 1948. UNRWA, established in 1950 to replace the multiple volunteer organizations that delivered United Nations (UN) aid for the previous two years, works across five fields: Jordan, Syria, Lebanon, West Bank and the Gaza Strip. In each of these areas, multiple other humanitarian organizations are also working. UNRWA is the only international organization that operates across this full breadth, but it is not the only institution that has such a comprehensive presence. The PLO, and its institutions, has also operated in every place where Palestinian communities live. The capacity of the organization to operate has often been constrained – and sometimes nearly wholly stopped – by host country policies. Nonetheless, this institutional reach is very significant in connecting Palestinians dispersed across multiple countries and in providing important services.

From 1970, when the PLO moved its base of operations to Lebanon from Jordan in the wake of Black September, until 1982, when the organization was forced out of the country after Israel's invasion, Lebanon was the centre of both Palestinian resistance and Palestinian institutions.[14] The Palestinian scholar Yezid Sayigh notes the wide range of services provided to Palestinians by PLO-affiliated institutions and argues that, as important as these were, 'providing vital services and support in the Palestinian exile has not been the main driving force and achievement of Palestinian institution-building. More significant have been the political implications of institutionalisation . . . [the PLO] is the organised expression of Palestinian national identity'.[15] As institutions of the revolution, Samed and the PRCS described their purpose as providing support for the national struggle. Both organizations saw their efforts to change Palestinian lives as part of the work of liberation: liberating Palestinians even before the liberation of Palestine. In so doing, they operated at the intersection of humanitarianism and revolution in related, but also distinct ways.

Broadly, Samed can be described as pursuing an alternative to living with aid indefinitely through what can be called 'revolutionary development'. It ran workshops in a number of refugee camps, producing furniture, clothing and other goods, and always described its activities as a key part of the Palestinian revolution. Precisely through providing employment and contributing to a vibrant camp economy, it created opportunities to let people leave behind the need for humanitarian aid. Income generation was considered revolutionary work: to help create self-sufficiency and economic self-determination. In 1981, the foreign affairs journalist Robin Wright reported in the *Christian Science Monitor* that 'with 6,500 full-time employees, and another 4,000 part time, the revolutionary group ranks as one of the largest employers in Lebanon'.[16] She quotes from a Samed booklet that describes its aims as being 'to create the nucleus for a Palestinian revolutionary economy, to develop economic self-sufficiency for the revolutionary and the masses, and to lay the foundation for the economic structure of the future Palestinian soviet'. In addition to its industrial activities, Samed had a film production department and, beginning in 1978, published the monthly journal.[17]

The PRCS, no less revolutionary in orientation, pursued a humanitarian politics that both operated according to the classic terms of humanitarian relief (about which see below) and enabled the emergence of a revolutionary persona (dignified, steadfast and committed to struggle). Since 2006, the PRCS has been a full member of the International Federation of Red Cross and Red Crescent Societies through a negotiation that also admitted the Israeli Magen David Adom society to full membership.[18] It described its work in the terms of this international movement from its establishment. Its 1968 founding charter states that 'the society's system is based on the Geneva conventions and the principles of the international Red Crescent and Red Cross'.[19] The PRCS engaged in humanitarian politics not by challenging the parameters of the humanitarian mandate or by shading into human rights or development work, but precisely by seeing classic humanitarian labour as a means of supporting and promoting the Palestinian revolutionary character.[20] Both Samed and the PRCS tried to defend and transform Palestinian people and Palestinian society. They were building the nation's institutions before the nation-state returned. The journals of both organizations were key instruments in this project, showcasing the achievements of these national institutions and showing Palestinians (and other supporters) how they could both participate in and benefit from the struggle.

Humanitarianism for the Revolution

The PRCS was founded in Jordan in 1968 and its first clinic was established in the Marka refugee camp. When the PLO departed to Lebanon after Black September, the focus of its institutional work also shifted, though the PRCS operated – and still operates – across the geography of Palestinian displacement. While UNRWA provided primary medical care to refugees across its area of operations, with clinics in each of the refugee camps, the PRCS joined this medical landscape, in part as a humanitarian response to inadequacies in the humanitarian system. As the historian Rashid Khalidi noted about the growth of PLO-sponsored services in the mid 1980s, 'as UNRWA services declined due to budgetary reasons, and as the social fabric of Lebanon deteriorated (in large measure-but not entirely-due to the conflict over the Palestinian presence there), a larger and larger burden was thrust on the PLO. Its services thus grew in response to needs rather than as a result of any preconceived plan. They also had to grow in great haste'.[21] The PRCS journal also noted not so much that the growth of services was ad hoc, but that the organization took on care in areas where UNRWA failed: 'UNRWA services are few and are insufficient. The UNRWA clinics are incapable of meeting the demand.'[22]

Humanitarian services are often deployed when states are incapable of or uninterested in meeting the needs of populations. In this case, PRCS services filled a gap in the services being offered by an international humanitarian institution, and they did so in the name of the Palestinian nation and its future state. The PRCS did not identify its humanitarian activity as being in any way in tension or at odds with its revolutionary contributions. As the PLO representative put it, addressing a PRCS conference in 1977: 'It is a mistake to imagine that the Palestinian people's struggle . . . is limited to the armed struggle. The humanitarian struggle of the Palestinian revolution is conducted alongside the armed struggle. And this humanitarian struggle is best represented by the PRCS.'[23] Revolutionary humanitarian work included providing health and social services to Palestinians, offering rehabilitation services for those wounded in war, whether civilians or fighters, and training a medical cadre to serve the people. What did it mean to the PRCS to be pursuing humanitarianism *for* the revolution? As I have already suggested, it meant several things: a commitment to working according to internationally accepted humanitarian principles, serving as a voice for Palestinians to the international humanitarian community, and building up the Palestinian spirit of dignity and steadfastness. The journal trumpeted all these efforts.

The fate of the Gaza hospital in Beirut highlights the dual struggles of revolution and assistance. The hospital began as a small clinic and developed into a premier medical establishment, serving both Palestinian and Lebanese patients.

A report in the PRCS journal – which since 1982 has had the title *Balsam* – from 1984 noted:

> The Gaza medical complex was one of the most important centers of steadfastness during the Zionist war. It helped Beirut remain steadfast despite the barbaric shelling. Work did not stop . . . The medical team and volunteers proved their role in the struggle. Everyone worked hard despite the power outages, lack of water, and the siege. The complex itself was shelled several times.[24]

The hospital survived the Israeli invasion with its functions intact, but it did not make it through the War of the Camps.[25] With the hospital's equipment destroyed and the building heavily damaged, its personnel were distributed to other medical centres. Reflecting on the trajectory of events, the PRCS Lebanon director stated that:

> the strike that hit the Gaza hospital at the beginning of the camps war was harsh but was not fatal. We had a 25 million Liras loss and the psychological losses are incalculable. But the employees, including the administrators, the doctors and others were stronger than the tragedy. This is not new to us. The first principle of the Society is not to look behind us but to learn from our experiences.[26]

One lesson that the PRCS took from the destruction of the Gaza hospital was the need for medical self-sufficiency in each camp:

> The lessons learned from the camps war and interest in the Palestinian individual are behind the new work plan of the PRCS that aspires for self-sufficiency in the camp by building a complete hospital in every camp. This is to avoid the suffering of the Shatila camp during the camps war. The life of 21 of the murdered in the camp would have been saved if they had good medical services.[27]

The attacks on 'different Palestinian hospitals, schools, and Samed facilities' were identified by the journal as 'policies intended to eliminate Palestinian steadfastness'. But, even as the Gaza hospital was never restored, 'the society built a hospital in Shatila after the camps war to meet the needs of the residents of Sabra and Shatila after the occupation of the Gaza hospital and the siege. The employees at the hospital are hardworking and experienced. What the hospital offers is heroic'.

The journal also highlighted the value that Palestinians saw in the PRCS institutions. As with national, or nationalist, media in many contexts, it served a dual purpose of displaying how the community felt about the PRCS (and the revolution more generally) and inculcating a sense of how they *should* feel and act. The pages of *Balsam* showcased interviews with patients who praised the quality of care and identified its revolutionary contribution. Some patients, while offered free services due to their poverty, 'insisted on paying as a donation to support the hospital'.[28] Students training in the PRCS's medical programmes described their work as personally valuable and nationally important. In 1977, a student in a PRCS nursing school insisted that people participated in these programs 'not only for the certificate [*shahada*], but because of our belief in our people's right to life and dignity'. She described how they were being trained 'not to discriminate in their work and to continue in humanitarian service for the victims of racist, Zionist aggression among our people'.[29] A nurse in the Gaza hospital urged 'every young woman who believes in the Palestinian people's right to life and freedom to join the PRCS . . . to have confidence in ourselves'. These quotes suggest that it was not just – and sometimes not even primarily – recipients of PRCS assistance whose dignity was enhanced, but at least equally that of the staff themselves. With its coverage, *Balsam* made a case for the value to individuals of participating in the national struggle.

Along with these Palestine-specific discussions, in its descriptions of its humanitarian endeavours, the journal highlighted that the PRCS followed the key principles of international humanitarian work – impartiality being central among them – and that it had a place in the international humanitarian system; that it was, in other words, a member of what Michael Barnett and Peter Walker have called 'the humanitarian club'.[30] It was, the journal indicated in 1978, committed to 'providing services to all those in need, without discrimination or favoritism'.[31] Describing the work in one of its hospitals in Damascus, the journal noted in 1975 that:

> The activities of the PRCS are not limited to providing treatment and medicine for the Palestinian people, but instead, its hospitals and clinics are open day and night for the sons of the Arab Umma from various countries. Because it feels that the humanitarian message was abandoned by others, its work is dedicated to every person in need of treatment and medication. It does not refuse any person who knocks on its door. It embraces, sponsors, and rejuvenates with vigor, vitality and hope.[32]

And from Lebanon in April of the same year – after the first outbreak of violence that marked the start of the civil war – the journal reprinted an article from *An-Nahhar* entitled 'The Roles of the Lebanese Red Cross and the PRCS: They Rose above the Conflict and Soothed All Wounds' that described this impartiality of assistance:

> Medical staff from the Crescent mobilized from the first moment to help all the wounded and without discrimination. Red Crescent hospitals were receiving wounded day and night, sometimes above their capacity, and for this purpose they emptied the corridors. They did not reject any wounded person regardless of their background . . . The medical team consisted of Lebanese and Palestinian volunteers who stayed at the hospital for four days.[33]

The repeated underscoring of the centrality of internationally accepted humanitarian principles in PRCS practice made a claim about the character not only of this organization, but also of the Palestinian people and Palestinian revolution more generally. Reflecting in 1978 on ten years of work, the journal summed up the work of the PRCS, saying that it represented the 'humanitarian [or human] face of the revolution (*wujh al-insani lil-thawra*)'.[34]

In doing so, it not only engaged with the Palestinian masses (*jamahir*), but also 'brought the voice of the right of Palestinians [haq al-Filastini] to various international forums' such as the World Health Organization, the International Committee of the Red Cross (ICRC) and international peacekeepers.[35] The journal regularly trumpeted its international connections. And it made Palestinian suffering visible. It also underscored the difference between the Palestinian commitment to international community and law, and Israeli disregard of these things. In 1979, the journal wrote: 'The series of Israeli horrors increases daily, episode-after-episode, increasing its hellish campaign without deterrent or sanction, without following custom, law, or international conventions . . . as Israel kills, the PRCS heals the wounded and tends to the needy, offering its services in each and every one of its centers.'[36]

Reflecting on the PRCS experience during the Israeli occupation of Lebanon, *Balsam* described its diverse efforts:

> During this war, the PRCS employed all its capabilities. It treated the wounded and assisted the displaced. Its humanitarian and revolutionary message expanded to include mobilizing international public opinion regarding the events in Lebanon and coordinating effective positions with different international humanitarian institutions to expose the fascist practices of the Zionist entity . . . The activities of the society at the international level had great returns as seen in the Arab and foreign medical delegations that came to Lebanon to participate in easing the miseries of the war and in the position of the international and humanitarian organizations condemning the barbarism of the Zionist enemy.[37]

The PRCS served as a conduit to make the Palestinian case in the international arena. It made Palestinian suffering known to these audiences. And, through the commitment to humanitarian principles I have described above, it claimed a place in the international community not just as victims, but also as members committed to 'custom, law, [and] international conventions'.

To the extent that the PRCS pushed at the limits of the humanitarian imaginary, it was not by challenging the nature of that work, but in how it thought about its effects. To put it perhaps overly schematically, the PRCS saw the life-saving work of medical humanitarianism as not merely about 'survival', but as essentially about dignity. The anthropologist Peter Redfield describes survival as the 'perpetually temporary outcome' that makes humanitarianism 'troubling work' for its practitioners.[38] Redfield notes that humanitarian organizations like Doctors Without Borders, the subject of his research, believe dignity to be a humanitarian virtue and a basic requirement of humanity, but that the demands of supporting human survival mean that dignity has to remain a 'secondary consideration' in their work. For the PRCS, on the other hand, the humanitarian labour of its medical practitioners *and* the receipt of medical care by its recipients were seen as being fundamentally about promoting Palestinian dignity and enabling the possibility of unleashing the full potential of the community and its component parts. Rather than being 'undignified', the messy and uncomfortable 'facts of survival'[39] were presented by the PRCS as essentially revolutionary.

Revolutionary Development

With the experience of repeated assault and siege, the PRCS identified 'medical self-sufficiency' as a necessity for each camp. For Samed, the Palestinian Martyrs Society, the self-sufficiency at issue in its revolutionary development was economic. And, as noted above, Samed's work was part of an effort to break out of the confines of a 'life lived in relief'. The articles in its journal *Samed al-Iqtisadi* include descriptions of different workshops, interviews with Samed workers and analyses of the projects. And they also provide a clear statement of the way in which leaders and participants in the organization understood the endeavour. The pages of the journal allow us to explore how this effort to develop a 'revolutionary economy' that operated as a refusal of humanitarian dynamics, particularly of the hierarchies and paternalism that went along with this practice.

I describe Samed's efforts as humanitarianism *defied* not because it represented a wholesale rejection of the idea of humanitarian action; on the contrary, Samed often described its work in humanitarian terms. A reflection in the journal about the impact of Samed's presence in the camps in northern Lebanon makes the humanitarian need for income clear:

> The Palestinian camps in the north lacked many basics of life. They were limited to the work of the UNRWA, which offered primary services. The Lebanese authorities did not offer any services. Thus, the Palestinians felt oppressed because of being treated as unwanted foreigners . . . The Palestinian has to get a work permit, which is very difficult, even though the Palestinians actively participated in building the Lebanese economy in construction, agriculture and industry. If a Palestinian gets a job, he does not enjoy his full rights, including his salary and social and health security although he has to pay part of his salary to the insurance fund.[40]

Samed clearly defined its workshops and interventions as humanitarian in orientation and effect: '[Samed] has become the main job provider for the Palestinians in Lebanon. 70 percent of the Palestinian workforce works in Palestinian revolutionary institutions, which confirms the depth of the belonging to the revolution among Palestinians. At the same time, this percentage reflects the difficulties of finding a suitable job.'[41] Rather, Samed (and here I make a distinction between Samed and the PRCS) was part of a challenge to narrow definitions of 'proper' humanitarian activity. Debates about the limits of humanitarian jurisdiction are endemic to the field and often centre around questions of whether there are fundamental differences between humanitarianism, development and human rights, as well as the place of 'politics' in the humanitarian world. Doctors Without Borders represents one end of the spectrum in the debate about distinction – generally seeking to do no infrastructure building and to imagine its stay as temporary (even though it has a long-term presence in many places). CARE, on the other hand, carries out both relief and development work and describes all its efforts as humanitarian.

Samed defied humanitarian limits in this sense – expanding the definition of humanitarianism beyond relief. And it also defied humanitarianism precisely by seeking to move people beyond relief without 'settling' them in exile. Those who know something about Palestinian politics – and about the politics surrounding Palestinians in the countries of exile – will know how strongly the *idea* of resettlement (*tawtin*) without resolution is rejected (even if in practice many refugees are settled where they are). From Samed's perspective, economic self-sufficiency was revolutionary, nationalist, *political* activity.

And this brings me to Samed's other defiance. Its work took place on the ground of an intersecting set of hierarchical systems: of humanitarianism *and* capitalism. An article recounting conversations with workers in a tailoring workshop in the Burj Shamali camp in south Lebanon highlighted this multiplicity of targets. One of the workers, Fatima Mezyan, contrasted Samed's workshops with ordinary 'commercial institutions' who only care about 'material gains'.[42] Samed was founded as an institution to improve the condition of the Palestinian people: 'The work then has humanitarian and nationalist motivations.' She then went on to talk about the conditions of labour in the workshop: 'We do not feel that we are employees. We own the work. The work is not for our sake; it is for the revolution and the revolution is for the people.' Samed's aim was to make Palestinians self-sufficient not simply as individuals, but as a collective and as a nation: to refuse hierarchies of humanitarian assistance *and* capitalist labour by creating alternative possibilities.

The journal includes many personal accounts that seem intended to convey the success of this project, not yet in liberating Palestine, but in transforming Palestinians. In providing these accounts, the journal did not simply bear witness to this transformation, but also participated in it. As a testament to this effect, the interview with Fatima included a question about whether she read the journal. Yes, she did, she answered: 'I always read the journal, especially the interviews in the workshops and the news and activities of Samed workers. I hope the journal continues to enable the workers to express their ideas because there are many talents among our workers.'[43] Fatima was thus a conduit for the journal's claim to be a conduit for the transforming voice of the Palestinian people.

An account by a painter (the arts being another area supported by Samed) described her transformation from a life defined by the 'struggle for life and a bit of bread' that began in 1948 to one where she struggled for the nation through her art.[44] Her first painting was of a humanitarian scene: children at an UNRWA school drinking ration milk. She said that she had refused to sell it to a foreigner who saw it at her exhibition because she felt he wanted to take pleasure in the pain of Palestinian lives. Rejecting this relationship was one declaration of Palestinian self-sufficiency, and a refusal of the relationships in which refugees were ensconced. She used another artist's words to describe her aims: 'I paint my wounds and the wounds of my people. I paint my hopes and the hopes of my people.' But her art was not just a form of personal expression; it was a means to change how foreigners engaged them. The article ends with a description of another exhibition in Germany and a quote from one of the guestbooks: 'I now understand why there are Palestinian fidayeen [guerrillas].' The article seems to suggest that by transforming the subjectivity and activity of Palestinian refugees, it will be possible to change the international political landscape: to move people from pity to solidarity.

Other articles in the journal describe Samed's structure and method, underscoring that the organization was established for 'the achievement of self-sufficiency regarding the needs of the revolution and the masses'.[45] In a discussion with Samed's director, Abu Ala' (Ahmad Qurei'a), he described how this revolutionary institution 'sees the human being as the most valuable means of production and the most valuable means of struggling as well'. Through this structure and this transformation in the means of production, Samed was preparing for a liberated future:

> [Samed] is an economic experience that will define the features of the society in the future ... This people has many qualifications and skills. These features are among the most important for production and economic activity. But this Palestinian expertise and individual initiatives inside and outside [of Palestine] were never allowed to integrate within a public communal project.[46]

Samed, he suggests, makes such common work possible and therefore can make it possible for Palestinians to create radically new possibilities.

In addition to generating economic opportunity, Samed engaged in a range of social service and educational activities that were meant to support the 'full' Palestinian subject. For instance, the journal celebrated the graduation of the second class of students in a Samed literacy programme by stating: 'Samed's work is not limited to production and covering the needs of the masses. It is not only concerned with hiring the workforce and spreading its workshops in all Palestinian camps. Rather, its role extends to building the human being armed with education and capabilities to fight some of the social problems caused by hijra [the 1948 displacement] and exile, especially illiteracy.'[47] Just like economic activity, social service work was accorded revolutionary value as the builder of the Palestinian struggler for the present and the Palestinian national for the future. The journal also gave significant attention to its efforts to support Palestinian women as revolutionary subjects: 'revolutionary institutions, especially Samed, gave the Palestinian woman the opportunity to work, produce and struggle and take her pioneering role in a progressive human framework'.[48]

Just as the PRCS saw itself as bringing the Palestinian message to an international audience, Samed also claimed to have:

> a great role in forming a new form of Palestinian media that resulted in highlighting the civil face of the Palestinian people ... Currently it is representing the PLO in 36 commercial exhibits through which it highlights different Palestinian cultural dimensions. The number of exhibits increasing due to the rise in support for the PLO and Samed's enthusiasm to present the civil face of the Palestinian revolution and people.[49]

The journal carried the multidimensional success of the exhibits: 'These exhibits have had political, economic and cultural effects in introducing the Palestinian heritage and leading the civil challenge against the Zionist enemy. This highlighted the social and humanitarian dimension of the Palestinian revolution.'[50] Where the PRCS addressed what it saw as a global international field (the UN and the ICRC), Samed's international focus was primarily 'third-worldist': what would now be called South–South connections: 'Since its early days, the Palestinian revolution tried to build cooperative relations with third world countries, especially in Africa and among national liberation movements.'[51] Its workshops, exhibitions and collaborations were located in countries such as Guinea-Bissou, Sudan, Somalia, Uganda and Congo. It developed agricultural projects, in part as a response to Zionist efforts to 'infiltrate some African countries under the cover of technical assistance . . . Some Arab countries offered assistance through development funds in African countries . . . The PLO moved in this direction, especially after the support demonstrated by the African countries towards the Palestinian cause and cutting relations with Israel after 1973 war'.[52] Samed, as part of the broader PLO, also pursued cooperative agreements with Hungary, the German Democratic Republic (GDR) and Cuba.

The Samed experience, like so many other Palestinian experiments in living otherwise, did not come to full fruition. When the PLO left Lebanon, its capacity to continue to support these ventures was extremely limited. Many workshops were destroyed in the war and many workers died or were dispersed. In 1985, the journal reported the results of a self-survey on the state of affairs, noting that some people were staying 'away from Samed because of fear of oppression, as being a Palestinian and getting close to Palestinian institutions have become a crime'.[53] But the article also noted that the Society was working to rebuild, to open new workshops despite the constraints and to offer employment to as many as possible. In fact, on the ground in Lebanon, Samed was never able to fully recover from the losses of war and the departure of the PLO.

Nonetheless, until the signing of the Oslo Accords, the complete turning of PLO focus to the occupied territories, and the entrance of the World Bank and its 'Washington Consensus' into this Palestinian economic landscape, Samed continued to declare a 'revolutionary responsibility'.[54] In 1990, the journal averred: 'Studying Samed means studying the development of the Palestinian people and their struggle . . . The experience of Samed documents a phase of the Palestinian economy, which is unique for a people outside of their land. It is an experience that can be a reference for liberation "revolutions" around the world. Yet, Samed remains in the experimental phase until it is moved to the homeland.'[55] The establishment of the Palestinian Authority after 1993 could perhaps have constituted the moment of bringing this economic vision to the 'homeland', but it was instead, as Raja Khalidi puts it, the moment when 'the PLO went from building a developmental state in exile to accepting a neoliberal economy under colonialism'.[56]

Conclusion: Ruination and the Work of Liberation

From today's vantage point, it is difficult to consider the PLO's institutions without being conscious of their 'ruination'. The failures of 'the revolution' and the PLO are evident. Palestinians in Lebanon, and elsewhere, suffer the effects of these failures. Diana Allan dubs camp residents in Lebanon 'refugees of the revolution', in recognition of the significance of this fact.[57] As one person in Burj al-Barajneh put it to me: 'In the past there was Samed, which provided work. They dismantled it. There were many institutions. They dismantled them. A person cannot work anymore. And there is a generation – with nothing. There is no care for this generation.'[58] And yet, the work of liberation of institutions like Samed and the PRCS contributed to an important Palestinian success: they continue to exist as a people. And their existence is internationally recognized – considerably more than it was when they were first dispossessed. So what are we to make of institutions that seem to have failed in their revolutionary aims, but that have also contributed to the sustaining of Palestinian existence – itself a revolutionary act? I cannot offer a definitive answer to this question. Indeed, grappling with the fate of Palestinian revolutionary ideals, politics and institutions is one of the tasks with which Palestinians are now urgently faced. Instead, I conclude by returning to the other part of this chapter's pair: humanitarianism.

Humanitarianism is a field filled with dilemmas and contradictions. It often seems to be defined by action in the face of unsolvable dilemmas.[59] The experience of Samed and the PRCS shed light on two challenges of this field: the concern that humanitarian aid can be an impediment to political action and resolution, and therefore may do harm to those it seeks to help; and the worry that 'nontraditional' humanitarian actors will create problems for the international humanitarian community by failing to uphold its key values and principles.[60] The ways in which Samed and the PRCS positioned themselves in relation to both politics and humanitarianism provide further perspectives on both of these questions.

As politically positioned humanitarian actors (and of course both these institutions were also something other than humanitarian actors), Samed and the PRCS challenge the view that apolitical neutrality vis-à-vis the world is always a requirement for the impartial delivery of humanitarian assistance. This conjoining of a political mission with neutral aid delivery was an especially central part of the PRCS mission and was highlighted in its self-presentation. These organizations suggest that it can be possible to address multiple needs: that humanitarian activity perhaps need not always require that providers and recipients hold the political parts of themselves wholly in abeyance. In this way, their work also addresses the concern that humanitarianism can get in the way of other, equally necessary action in the world.

Among the criticisms often raised about humanitarianism as a mode of intervention and engagement is that it can impede political action and analysis, that it can narrow the ways in which people can be understood to the category of 'victims' or 'suffering subjects', and that it produces and reproduces global (and local) hierarchies.[61] In positioning their work as 'revolutionary' humanitarianism, Samed and the PRCS offered a practice that tried to break through these limitations. They posited humanitarianism as a means of reaching the international community, not only to generate sympathy, but also to increase political solidarity. They highlighted the collective (common) character of their interventions and outcomes, as opposed to the sometimes atomizing effects of aid targeted at needy individuals. And they clearly identified their humanitarian activity as having the aim of changing people, not just saving them. In this, both institutions not only shaped the Palestinian condition, but also shifted the humanitarian terrain. In order for their humanitarian activity to have this effect, humanitarian media was vital. It was in part through journals such as *Samed al-Iqtisadi* and *Balsam* that the lessons of Palestinian revolutionary humanitarianism could circulate. Media is important to all humanitarian activity. But while much humanitarian media is meant to produce donations or intervention, revolutionary humanitarian media was intended to generate solidarity among supporters and commitment among Palestinians.

Ilana Feldman is Professor of Anthropology, History, and International Affairs at George Washington University. She is the author of *Governing Gaza: Bureaucracy, Authority, and the Work of Rule, 1917–67* (2008), *Police Encounters: Security and Surveillance in Gaza under Egyptian Rule* (2015) and *Life Lived in Relief: Humanitarian Predicaments and Palestinian Refugee Politics* (2018), and is coeditor (with Miriam Ticktin) of *In the Name of Humanity: The Government of Threat and Care* (2010).

Notes

This chapter is based on Ilana Feldman, *Life Lived in Relief: Humanitarian Predicaments and Palestinian Refugee Politics* (Oakland: University of California Press, 2018).

1. *Al-thawra* both denotes a moment in time and an institution. With the moment over, today Palestinians in Lebanon frequently refer to the PLO, and its factions, as 'the revolution'.
2. D. Allan, *Refugees of the Revolution: Experiences of Palestinian Exile* (Stanford: Stanford University Press, 2014), 3.
3. In using the term 'ruination', I reference Ann Stoler's work: A.L. Stoler (ed.), *Imperial Debris: On Ruins and Ruination* (Durham, NC: Duke University Press, 2013).
4. A. Slemrod, 'A Peek at Life in Beirut's Defunct Gaza Hospital', *Daily Star* (24 April 2013). Retrieved 22 August 2018 from http://www.dailystar.com.lb/News/Local-News/2013/Apr-24/214829-a-peek-at-life-in-beiruts-defunct-gaza-hospital.ashx.
5. C.A. Rubenberg, 'The Civilian Infrastructure of the Palestine Liberation Organization: An Analysis of the PLO in Lebanon until June 1982', *Journal of Palestine Studies* 12(3) (1983), 54–78; and R. Brynen, 'The Politics of Exile: The Palestinians in Lebanon', *Journal of Refugee Studies* 3(3) (1990), 204–27.

6. R. Khalidi, 'The Economics of Palestinian Liberation: How the PLO Went from Building a Developmental State in Exile to Accepting a Neoliberal Economy under Colonialism', *Jacobin* (15 October 2014). Retrieved 22 August 2018 from https://www.jacobinmag.com/2014/10/the-economics-of-palestinian-liberation.

7. D. Fassin and M. Pandolfi (eds), *Contemporary States of Emergency: The Politics of Military and Humanitarian Interventions* (New York: Zone Books, 2011); M. Barnett and T.G. Weiss (eds), *Humanitarianism in Question: Politics, Power, Ethics* (Cornell: Cornell University Press, 2008); M. Barnett, *Empire of Humanity: A History of Humanitarianism* (Ithaca: Cornell University Press, 2011).

8. See L. Boltanski, *Distant Suffering: Morality, Media and Politics* (Cambridge: Cambridge University Press, 1999).

9. CARE, for instance, was founded to enable Americans to send parcels (CARE packages) to people they knew in Europe (distantly, but not strangers). See I. Feldman, 'The Humanitarian Circuit: Relief Work, Development Assistance, and CARE in Gaza, 1955–1967', in E. Bornstein and P. Redfield (eds), *Forces of Compassion: Ethics and Politics of Global Humanitarianism* (Santa Fe: SAR Press, 2011), 203–26.

10. P. Redfield, 'The Unbearable Lightness of Expats: Double Binds of Humanitarian Mobility', *Cultural Anthropology* 27(2) (2012), 358–82.

11. 'Working at UNRWA'. Retrieved 22 August 2018 from http://www.unrwa.org/careers/working-unrwa.

12. J. Benthall, 'Islamic Humanitarianism in Adversarial Context. In Forces of Compassion: Humanitarianism between Ethics and Politics', in Bornstein and Redfield (eds), *Forces of Compassion*, 99–122; M.J. Petersen, 'Trajectories of transnational Muslim NGOs', *Development in Practice* 22(5–6) (2012), 763–78.

13. S. Cottle and D. Nolan, 'Global Humanitarianism and the Changing Aid-Media Field: "Everyone was Dying for Footage"', *Journalism Studies* 8(6) (2007), 862–78; P. Robinson, 'The CNN Effect Revisited', *Critical Studies in Media Communication* 22(4) (2005), 344–49.

14. R. Brynen, 'PLO Policy in Lebanon: Legacies and Lessons', *Journal of Palestine Studies* 18(2) (1989), 48–70; A. Shiblak, 'Palestinians in Lebanon and the PLO', *Journal of Refugee Studies* 10(3) (1997), 261–74.

15. Y. Sayigh, 'The Politics of Palestinian Exile', *Third World Quarterly* 9(1) (1987), 28–66, at 58.

16. R. Wright, 'PLO's Pinstripes, Money behind Fatigues and Guns', *Christian Science Monitor* (1 October 1981). Retrieved 22 August 2018 from http://www.csmonitor.com/1981/1001/100134.html.

17. Copies of this journal, *Samed Al-Iqtisadi*, are housed in the Institute for Palestine Studies library in Beirut.

18. M. McLaughlin, 'Red Cross Breaks 57-Year Israel Impasse', *UPI* (2006). Retrieved 22 August 2018 from http://www.upi.com/Business_News/Security-Industry/2006/06/22/Red-Cross-breaks-57-year-Israel-impasse/29941150991485.

19. 'The Palestine Red Crescent Society, established in 1968: The Basic Law', *Balsam* (September 1984), 82.

20. For a discussion of Red Crescent Societies more generally, see J. Benthall, 'The Red Cross and Red Crescent Movement and Islamic Societies, with Special Reference to Jordan', *British Journal of Middle Eastern Studies* 24(2) (1997), 157–77.

21. R. Khalidi, 'The Palestinians in Lebanon: Social Repercussions of Israel's Invasion', *Middle East Journal* 38(2) (1984), 255–66, at 257.

22. 'The Palestinian Camps', *Balsam* 108 (June 1984), 74.
23. *PRCS Journal* 35–36 (1977), 30.
24. 'The Gaza Medical Complex: From an Underground Garage to 10 Floors', *Balsam* 106 (April 1984), 83.
25. 'The Palestinian Hospitals after the War of the Camps', *Balsam* 124 (October 1985), 81.
26. 'The Shatila Hospital: The Myth of Birth from the Siege', *Balsam* 137 (November 1986), 70.
27. 'The Health Conditions of the Palestinians in Lebanon', *Balsam* 133 (July 1986), 68.
28. 'The Gaza Hospital, a Proud Edifice That is Open for All', *Balsam* 113–15 (November 1984–January 1985), 25.
29. 'The Palestinian Red Crescent Society Journal Meets with Successful Graduates from the Vocational Courses Program', *Journal of the Palestine Red Crescent Society* 38 (September/October 1977), 15.
30. M. Barnett and P. Walker, 'Regime Change for Humanitarian Aid: How to Make Relief More Accountable', *Foreign Affairs* 94(4) (2015), 130–41.
31. 'The Palestinian Red Crescent Society at Ten Years', *Journal of the Palestine Red Crescent Society* 52 (1978), 12.
32. 'Medical Achievement in the Jaffa Hospital in Damascus', *Journal of the Palestine Red Crescent Society* 5 (1975), 12.
33. 'The Roles of the Lebanese Red Cross and the PRCS: They Rose above the Conflict and Soothed All Wounds', *Al-Nahhar* (26 April 1975), reprinted in *Journal of the Palestine Red Crescent Society* 8 (1975), 16.
34. 'The Palestine Red Crescent Society at 10 Years', *PRCS Journal* 52 (1978), 13.
35. Ibid., 14.
36. 'PRCS Activities in the North', *The Journal* 61 (1979), 14.
37. 'The International Response to Back Steadfastness', *Balsam* 94–95(April/May 1983), 16.
38. P. Redfield, *Life in Crisis: The Ethical Journey of Doctors without Borders* (Berkeley: University of California Press, 2013), 17.
39. Ibid.
40. 'Samed Workshops in the Camps in the North', *Samed Al Iqtisadi* 4(30) (1981), 168.
41. Ibid., 159.
42. 'Inside the Martyr Abu Ali Iyad Tailoring Worskhop', *Samed* 1(7) (1978), 38.
43. Ibid.
44. 'Tamam il Akhal, I Paint the Wounds of My People: I Paint for Their Pain and Hope', *Samed Al Iqtisadi* 1(9) (1978), 48.
45. 'With Brother Abu Ala', Head of Samed', *Samed Al Iqtisadi* 1(11–12) (1978), 11.
46. Ibid., 12.
47. 'Celebrating the Graduation of the Second Class in the Eradication of Illiteracy Campaign', *Samed Al Iqtisadi* 4(25) (1981), 197.
48. 'Samed Workshops in the Camps in the North', 169.
49. 'Samed's Cultural Activities', *Samed al Iqtisasdi* 4(26) (1981), 164.
50. 'Samed 1970–1982, the Experience and the Ambitions in its 12th Year. Samed's Annual file', *Samed Al Iqtisadi* 5(36) (1982), 196.
51. Ibid.
52. Ibid.
53. 'Samed Branch in Lebanon: A Reading of the Work of the Past Two Years, 1983–4', *Samed al-Iqtisadi* 7(53) (1985), 147.

54. I. Jundi, 'Samed, a Twenty-Year Experience of Palestinian Economic Work', *Samed al-Iqtisadi*, 12(79) (1990), 19.
55. Ibid., 38.
56. Khalidi, 'Economics of Palestinian Liberation'.
57. Allan, *Refugees of the Revolution*.
58. Interview, Burj al Barajneh, 16 September 2011.
59. F. Terry, *Condemned to Repeat? The Paradox of Humanitarian Action* (Ithaca: Cornell Press, 2002); D. Kennedy, *The Dark Sides of Virtue: Reassessing International Humanitarianism* (Princeton: Princeton University Press, 2004); I. Feldman, 'The Quaker Way: Ethical Labor and Humanitarian Relief', *American Ethnologist* 34(4) (2007), 689–705.
60. Barnett and Walker, 'Regime Change for Humanitarian Aid', 130–41; M. Barnett, 'Humanitarian Governance', *Annual Review of Political Science* 16 (2013), 379–98.
61. D. Fassin, 'Humanitarianism as a Politics of Life', *Public Culture* 19(3) (2007), 499–520; I. Feldman, 'Gaza's Humanitarianism Problem', *Journal of Palestine Studies* 38(3) (2009), 22–37.

Bibliography

Allan, D. *Refugees of the Revolution: Experiences of Palestinian Exile*. Stanford: Stanford University Press, 2014.

Barnett, M. *Empire of Humanity: A History of Humanitarianism*. Ithaca: Cornell University Press, 2011.

Barnett, M. 'Humanitarian Governance'. *Annual Review of Political Science* 16 (2013), 379–98.

Barnett, M., and P. Walker. 'Regime Change for Humanitarian Aid: How to Make Relief More Accountable'. *Foreign Affairs* 94(4) (2015), 130–41.

Barnett, M., and T.G. Weiss (eds). *Humanitarianism in Question: Politics, Power, Ethics*. Cornell: Cornell University Press, 2008.

Benthall, J. 'The Red Cross and Red Crescent Movement and Islamic Societies, with Special Reference to Jordan'. *British Journal of Middle Eastern Studies* 24(2) (1997), 157–77.

———. 'Islamic Humanitarianism in Adversarial Context. In Forces of Compassion: Humanitarianism between Ethics and Politics', in E. Bornstein and P. Redfield (eds), *Forces of Compassion: Ethics and Politics of Global Humanitarianism* (Santa Fe: SAR Press, 2011), 99–122.

Boltanski, L. *Distant Suffering: Morality, Media and Politics*. Cambridge: Cambridge University Press, 1999.

Brynen, R. 'PLO Policy in Lebanon: Legacies and Lessons'. *Journal of Palestine Studies* 18(2) (1989), 48–70.

———. 'The Politics of Exile: The Palestinians in Lebanon'. *Journal of Refugee Studies* 3(3) (1990), 204–27.

Cottle, S., and D. Nolan. 'Global Humanitarianism and the Changing Aid-Media Field: "Everyone was Dying for Footage"'. *Journalism Studies* 8(6) (2007), 862–78.

Fassin, D. 'Humanitarianism as a Politics of Life'. *Public Culture* 19(3) (2007), 499–520.

Fassin, D., and M. Pandolfi (eds). *Contemporary States of Emergency: The Politics of Military and Humanitarian Interventions*. New York: Zone Books, 2011.

Feldman, I. 'The Quaker Way: Ethical Labour and Humanitarian Relief'. *American Ethnologist* 34(4) (2007), 689–705.

————. 'Gaza's Humanitarianism Problem'. *Journal of Palestine Studies* 38(3) (2009), 22–37.

————. 'The Humanitarian Circuit: Relief Work, Development Assistance, and CARE in Gaza, 1955–1967', in E. Bornstein and P. Redfield (eds), *Forces of Compassion: Ethics and Politics of Global Humanitarianism* (Santa Fe: SAR Press, 2011), 203–26.

Kennedy, D. *The Dark Sides of Virtue: Reassessing International Humanitarianism.* Princeton, N.J.: Princeton University Press, 2004.

Khalidi, R. 'The Palestinians in Lebanon: Social Repercussions of Israel's Invasion', *Middle East Journal* 38(2) (1984), 255–66.

————. 'The Economics of Palestinian Liberation: How the PLO Went from Building a Developmental State in Exile to Accepting a Neoliberal Economy under Colonialism'. *Jacobin* (15 October 2014). Retrieved 22 August 2018 from https://www.jacobinmag.com/2014/10/the-economics-of-palestinian-liberation.

Petersen, M.J. 'Trajectories of Transnational Muslim NGOs'. *Development in Practice* 22(5–6) (2012), 763–78.

Redfield, P. 'The Unbearable Lightness of Expats: Double Binds of Humanitarian Mobility'. *Cultural Anthropology* 27(2) (2012), 358–82.

————. *Life in Crisis: The Ethical Journey of Doctors without Borders.* Berkeley: University of California Press, 2013.

Robinson, P. 'The CNN Effect Revisited'. *Critical Studies in Media Communication* 22(4) (2005), 344–49.

Rubenberg, C.A. 'The Civilian Infrastructure of the Palestine Liberation Organization: An Analysis of the PLO in Lebanon until June 1982'. *Journal of Palestine Studies* 12(3) (1983), 54–78.

Sayigh, Y. 'The Politics of Palestinian Exile'. *Third World Quarterly* 9(1) (1987), 28–66.

Shiblak, A. 'Palestinians in Lebanon and the PLO'. *Journal of Refugee Studies* 10(3) (1997), 261–74.

Stoler, A.L. (ed.). *Imperial Debris: On Ruins and Ruination.* Durham, NC: Duke University Press, 2013.

Terry, F. *Condemned to Repeat? The Paradox of Humanitarian Action.* Ithaca: Cornell Press, 2002.

10

Mediatization of Disasters and Humanitarian Aid in the Federal Republic of Germany

Patrick Merziger

> The world of disaster relief has always had its cyclical fads. A major disaster unleashes popular demonstrations by concerned people anxious to help the afflicted. Journalists stand poised, pens in hand, ready to expose the ostensible strengths and weaknesses of the relief system. Wise commentators propound on the underlying causes of the disaster and the inadvertent consequences of intervention. And then it all seems to die away. The disaster and the relief response are over. The attentions of the public, the media and the experts are spent. There seems little more to say until the next disaster grips the consciousness of all those various components that comprise the disaster relief community.
> —R. Kent, 'Interpreting Disaster Relief', 1986

In this quote from 1986, Randolph Kent, at that time a humanitarian aid worker, summarized the habitual complaint that aid organizations voiced when they were reflecting on problematic currents in the relief and development field during the Cold War and after. The growing media attention was already perceived as problematic. Aid organizations in particular criticized the fast pace of news. They felt exposed, helplessly swept up by the ebbs and flows of coverage, and complained that they had to align with media logic. The audience would lose interest all too fast and the next disaster would draw journalists as sure as night follows day. Therefore, journalists would not take time to analyse who was responsible for a disaster. The media could not depict aid efforts that aimed at sustainable, slow development; instant and visible gratification was expected.[1]

However, especially in retrospect, it becomes clear that media coverage was not only an extrinsic, invasive logic but also an important and productive factor in the ascent of humanitarian nongovernmental organizations (NGO) and the growing importance of humanitarian policies in international relations.[2] Communication scholars described the pivotal role of media in steering attention to disasters in the first place[3] and detected considerable effects of media coverage on how we perceive the environment.[4] They have highlighted that media reports have been indispensable in triggering disaster relief action.[5] Humanitarian organizations have relied heavily on media reports to finance their endeavours.[6] The word is that one *New York Times* article is 'worth more disaster aid dollars than 1,500 fatalities'.[7]

The important role media played in steering relief aid collides with our notion of disasters. Disasters are generally perceived as a state of emergency. Actually, disasters in particular appear as the prototypical event in the sense of a 'total' or 'impossible' event.[8] They seem to befall us suddenly, they seem to come out of nowhere, holding nobody to account. They make a great stir, cause enormous suffering and thereby trigger a seemingly natural wish to assist the victims.[9] However, in recent years, scientific studies have also begun to question the image of disasters as 'bolts from the blue' that compel us to help inevitably. Geological studies point to a consistent distribution of negative events on a global scale. Yet, catastrophes take place only in states that cannot provide appropriate security to their people.[10] Therefore, political science rejects the notion of manmade disasters as opposed to natural disasters: 'In the late modernity, there are no more natural disasters, because catastrophization is always socially and politically mediated.'[11] Disasters put in their political and social contexts lose their sudden immediacy and their cataclysmic substantiality.

At the same time, it became more and more obvious that the seemingly natural reaction of going to the rescue has not always materialized in the same way; sometimes it has even failed to appear altogether. Germany did not engage in relief aid before 1951 when a flood hit northern Italy, whereas Great Britain and the United States have a longstanding tradition of providing aid; countries such as Sweden, Norway and Canada position themselves as 'superpowers' of humanitarianism, outdoing other countries in their relief efforts.[12] The seemingly natural response of giving aid is obviously a product of specific historical conditions.[13] Science focusing on international assistance suggested describing relief as a very specific answer to sociopolitical 'failure'.[14] Therefore, aid should be conceptualized rather as a political and deliberate action than as a compulsory reaction.

However, the media focus is on 'spectacular images' and breaking news. They prefer disaster reports rather than analysis circumstances that lead to a negative event. It favours quick solutions that produce visible successes over complex strategies that tackle deep-routed problems.[15] If disasters were described, for example, as the outcome of structural deficiencies, our response might be very different – or perhaps would fail to appear at all. This media logic became especially meaningful during the 1960s, as with the worldwide ascent of television the media acquired ever-growing influence over how countries shaped international relations.[16] During this time, foreign policy lost its monopoly over deciding where and how to help those in need. With growing media influence, a process of 'catastrophization' can be observed, i.e. the tendency to interpret negative events as 'disasters' that required immediate relief. The sociologist Craig Calhoun diagnosed an ever-growing 'emergency thinking' mindset: since the 1960s, Western societies have increasingly conceived of negative events as disasters. In Calhoun's conceptualization, a disaster is not a sudden event outside of human control, but the product of complex attribution processes.[17]

The growing number of catastrophes around the world, the attribution processes involved in their identification, the varying timelines and the fluctuating intensity of relief efforts suggest that emergencies (disaster and relief) are to some extent a construct. The notion of emergencies as constructs does not imply that the media somehow fabricate disasters where there are none. It does not deny that famines, floods, earthquakes, war and unrest have tormented hundreds of thousands and have meant death for many. Nor should the constructive approach be misunderstood as plea against relief aid. However, a constructivist perspective suggests that media play a key role in identifying disasters as such and in shaping the responses. By highlighting the processes involved in this construction, such an approach has drawn attention to the contingency of specific perceptions and their effects on actions. From this point of view, disaster relief is only one possible response to negative events and only *appears* to be the natural reaction.

In this chapter, I want to take up the suggestions of the constructivist perspective and analyse the role that media have played in producing and shaping disaster relief of the Federal Republic of Germany from the 1960s to the 1980s. This process can be described as 'mediatization of disaster relief' as the media have taken the leading role in 'constructing' disasters by describing negative events as such and thereby triggering relief. This is often conceptualized as an advancing submission under powerful media logic.[18] However, as postulated already in the concept of mediatization,[19] mediatization is not a unidirectional process but a two-way-relationship: media and aid organizations cooperated extensively in initiating relief aid and thereby established a specific mode of humanitarian aid in disaster situations that appears all too natural today.[20] By taking into account this interdependence, the approach of 'mediatization' highlights the 'productive' aspects of media coverage and the role of aid organizations rather than making media responsible for 'undesirable' developments.

In the first part of the chapter, I will scrutinize the role media has played in identifying disasters since the 1960s. I will ask how and why media, through their reporting, have contributed to the fact that many negative events have appeared as disasters. Second, I will consider the effect media coverage has had on the attempt to lend a hand to 'distant others': how has the specific presentation of negative events as disasters influenced political action and the idea and practice of humanitarian aid? In order to answer these questions, I will focus on four major disasters that stirred the Western world. They all took place between 1968 and 1985, a period that I would describe as the heyday of media influence on humanitarian aid – at least in Germany.

The Secession of Biafra: A Shift in the Relationship between Media, Foreign Policy and Humanitarian Aid

Of course, the media, especially newspapers, magazines and journals published by humanitarian organizations, covered disasters broadly and intensely well before 1968. This coverage was one of the reasons why the German government committed to humanitarian causes and relief action as early as 1951. Up to that date, Germany had not committed to helping the 'distant other', and when northern Italy was hit by a devastating flood, Germany itself was still struggling with the after-effects of the Second World War (homelessness, hunger and destruction). But the government realized the opportunity to present Germany as a 'great power of humanity'[21] that had learned its lessons and was ready, again, to taking its place in global politics. Soon a secondary effect became apparent: humanitarian aid also supported nation building from within by giving the people a common task. Therefore in the first two decades after the Second World War, politics decided where and how Germany would set out to provide aid to people in need. Thereby, the allocation of aid mainly took into account considerations regarding foreign policy, such as positive image effects, geostrategic arguments and the improvement of international relations.[22]

The Biafra famine of 1968 can be considered the first catastrophe in which the media took the leading role in the initiation of relief action in Germany. In 1967, the southeastern region of Nigeria had broken away and given itself the name 'Republic of Biafra'. A complex conflict along political, ethnic, economic, sociocultural and religious faultlines was at the root of the secessionist movement. The government of Nigeria took military action and, after several setbacks, decided to block transport routes to Biafra, thereby causing a devastating famine.[23] Up to that point, the Federal Republic of Germany had been a close ally to Nigeria. Since Nigeria had gained independence, Germany had strongly supported the new African nation. It invested in development programmes, cofinanced the construction of industrial plants and even supported Nigeria in establishing an airforce by providing planes and appointing military instructors.[24] Like the West in general, Germany insisted on the territorial integrity of the newly formed African nation-states and turned against any secessionist movement in the 1960s that challenged the colonial borders in the process of decolonization.[25]

Against this backdrop, support for Biafra seemed unlikely. Nevertheless, one of the largest relief actions soon began.[26] One important reason for this was that the media did not report a complex conflict that would have been difficult to resolve or a civil war that both sides and the international community fostered and had an interest in. Instead, the suffering of the Biafran people was depicted as a disaster, a great famine and a case of genocide for no reason.

From the outset, Biafra committed itself to bringing its cause before the public. The new state provided text and images highlighting the suffering of the Biafran people.[27] In February 1968, Biafra appointed the Swiss PR agency Mark Press to make its point of view known.[28] It founded a radio station (Radio Biafra) that broadcast propaganda and false information. On several occasions, journalists were invited to press conferences and fact-finding tours at the cost of the self-proclaimed government. In many European countries, eastern Nigerian student organizations committed themselves to alerting the public and gaining support for the Biafran cause. They printed flyers and brochures, organized demonstrations, held press conferences and wrote letters to politicians.[29]

In Germany, the availability of these disaster images intersected with a specific media situation. In the context of the '68 student movement, the established magazines faced new competitors. New forms of journalism thrived and the so-called 'sex wave' was selling. The illustrated magazine *twen* successfully launched new formats of reportage that presented social topics in an entertaining style and in a fresh-faced layout.[30] The satirical magazine *pardon* reached a circulation of nearly 300,000 copies in 1968. It established a new style of satire, featuring anti-authoritarian absurdism that was revolutionary in the German context, where up to that point satire had been a serious, meaningful business.[31] At the same time, the *St. Pauli Nachrichten* combined progressive political reports with pornography and provided another success story. The 'sex wave' also spilled into longstanding magazines such as *twen* or *Quick* and gave them a new look.[32] In this situation, the spectacular political images of the Biafran War were more than welcome. The famine made the front page of the main political magazines *Stern* and *Spiegel* several times. *Spiegel* boasted with its photos: 'For the first time genocide before the eyes of the world.'[33] The magazine altered its usual layout for multipage photo spreads. It even resorted to rare and expensive colour printing to present its images in all their spectacularity.[34]

Stern spared no efforts in presenting the crisis. The editor had prepared a typical summer issue when the first images of the Biafran disaster arrived. On short notice, he replaced the title, depicting the sailing boat *Germania,* with photos of a Biafran child suffering. Inside the issue, the photo reportage (of unknown origin) applied spectacular effects such as sharp contrast and powerful clichés. On one side, the editor printed a picture that advertised a Nigerian programme designed to provide nutrition to infants. Alongside a photo of a chubby baby, one could read the slogan 'where babies are happy and healthy'. This image was in stark contrast to one of a starving Biafran child who was sucking desperately at the breast of his emaciated mother. By the arrangement of a dying child in the arms of its mother, the photo clearly echoed the Pietà as a powerful cliché of suffering. The caption proclaimed that this ensemble represented the 'two million children and nursing mothers' who would die of hunger by the end of August if help did not arrive.[35]

Following media logic, the spectacular was pushed to the fore and the reports became polemical and challenging, partly because the government of Biafra provided the corresponding material. The magazines could effortlessly communicate the cliché of a 'disaster' and of 'innocent victims'. Any discussion of the problematic image sources would have diluted the visual appeal. The underlying causes appeared too complex – and also too boring. In this case, features assigned to catastrophes such as suddenness, groundlessness and overpowering onset clearly stem from a media logic that urges the delivery of spectacular news.

Since 1968, the disturbing notion of the 'Biafran child' has been used for decades to describe starving children, thereby echoing the lasting impression those images made. But the spectacular reports also achieved direct political effects. In the civil war, unusual congruities emerged that transcended the frontlines of the Cold War. Due to the media pressure, the Federal Republic of Germany remained ambivalent in its attitude: it did not cut ties to the central government, but supported the relief action and even provided a brand-new German Army plane that was awaiting commission.[36]

The Ethiopian Drought: Media Commits in Identifying Disasters

Still, in the case of Biafra, the impulse originated from the political sphere as the Biafran government committed itself to a public relations effort. But the media learned quickly. As early as 1973, the magazine *Stern* identified a disaster all by itself and brought 'it before the eyes of the world'. In this year, disaster relief from the United Nations for the Sahel was well underway when a German missionary wrote a letter to *Stern*. He called attention to the worsening situation in Ethiopia. *Stern* reporters were sent immediately and procured images confirming the catastrophe. But *Stern* did not leave it at that. The magazine founded a relief committee, '*Stern* Aktion "Rettet die Hungernden"', and successfully set up a donation account. The editor Henri Nannen chaired the board of trustees and recruited prominent supporters, including Hans-Dietrich Genscher, the Minister of the Interior, Walter Bargatzky, the President of the German Red Cross, Heinz-Oskar Vetter, the Chairman of the German Union Confederation, and Kurt Hansen, the CEO of Bayer AG.[37]

Soon the magazine proudly announced substantial contributions. The action had unleashed a 'wave of help', and in the first weeks it received 498,000 individual donations. By the end of 1974, the readers had donated DM 17.995 million. This '*Stern* Aktion' spent the money on supplying food and medicine, paying medical personnel, buying and distributing seeds, and constructing infrastructure such as roads and wells. At the site, the *Stern* journalists even coordinated the relief efforts and felt entitled to command the German armed forces, which provided aircraft and helicopters for relief flights.[38]

This unusual arrangement ensured a string of exclusive stories. *Stern* had taken the lead over its competitors by identifying the disaster. The photographers were able to shoot spectacular images of the first German Army helicopters and planes arriving. Such privileged access to relief aid and the victims also opened up new possibilities for reporting. For example, the magazine printed several 'before-and-after stories' depicting the miraculous recovery of the Ethiopian victims. The photographer Fred Ihrt illustrated these reports and pursued the fate of Teru Musema, among others. She was admitted in the worst condition, famished to the point of being 'skin and bones'. 'Four weeks later, the 16-year-old had already gained 14 pounds' and was now smiling at the camera again.[39] Up to that point, disaster reports were dominated by horrific images of anonymous victims, but now *Stern* was able to give them names and faces.

The magazine had successfully drawn attention to a region that had not attracted much focus before. The journalists acted against the explicit will of the Ethiopian government, which had asked them to avoid 'sensational reports on famine in the international press' as it feared that this would make obvious its failures in providing for the Ethiopian people.[40] Actually, the Ethiopian Emperor Haile Selassie I, who had determined the fate of the country since 1916, had to abdicate in the end. The reports of famine undermined public confidence in the Emperor and disloyal military factions took advantage for political gain. They spread rumours that 'the emperor and his family were living at the expense of the people and that they were a gang of rip-off merchants and cut-purses'.[41] In September 1974, the newly formed Coordinating Committee of the Armed Forces, Police, and Territorial Army (aka Derg) took control of the government and established a Socialist People's Republic. Thereby, the Federal Republic of Germany and the 'Western world' lost an important ally to the 'Eastern Bloc' in the Horn of Africa, an area of great geostrategic importance.[42]

The unwanted effects on international relations in Nigeria and in Ethiopia indicate that from now on, German foreign policy could no longer exclusively determine where and how to provide aid. The media, illustrated magazines, political magazines and later television in particular discovered that they were able to draw attention to disasters all by themselves and operating according to their own logic. Disasters and relief provided spectacular images that could increase the number of copies sold. The reports on disasters and calls to action created a positive image of media committed to the greater good of humanity. Thereby the periodicals appealed to new, young audiences that had discovered the issue of international solidarity in the course of cultural transformation through the student movement.[43]

The 'Boat People': The Emergence of New, Media-Oriented Humanitarian NGOs

The pursuit of the spectacular in the reports and the specific temporality of coverage proved to be crucial. Henceforth, the media set out to identify disasters around the world. In the following years, it became obvious that the media were not limited in how they could affect foreign policy, but also changed how the 'Western world' provided aid. In the late 1970s and the 1980s, new humanitarian NGOs emerged that set out to meet media expectations, focusing on emergencies abroad and short-term assistance.

The operation of NGOs providing aid changed greatly in Germany. Until the 1970s, the government entrusted relief aid to large welfare organizations or charities, mainly the Catholic Caritas, the Protestant Diakonisches Werk and the German Red Cross. These charities acted as an extension of German foreign policy. They aimed mainly at demonstrating their effectiveness to politics because they had to prove their eligibility for state funding, which was their main source of financing. In the German efforts to save the 'boat people', a new NGO emerged at the end of the 1970s. The organization was originally named 'Ein Schiff für Vietnam' as it followed the role model of the French 'un bateau pour le Vietnam'. It achieved prominence as Cap Anamur and is internationally known by the abbreviation GED (for German Emergency Doctors). The journalist Rupert Neudeck founded it in the process of drawing attention to the Vietnamese refugees. This organization was a product of the new attention that the issue of humanitarianism generated. At the same time, it made use of the media to enforce its own goals. GED set out to identify catastrophes by itself following their own logic of humanitarian causes.[44]

The term 'boat people' refers to Vietnamese citizens who left communist Vietnam by sea after the surrender of the U.S. ally South Vietnam in 1975. They fled the hardships of a destroyed country and the repression that the new government imposed to punish the 'traitors'. They continued fleeing for more than two decades, with at least four peaks that should have captured attention.[45] It was only in 1979 that the situation turned into a catastrophe, at least from the German perspective. Even then, the status of a disaster was disputed, as many contemporary observers regarded it as a migration movement. They highlighted that the United States had established the expectation that fleeing by boat would open a way to the West when they rescued and took in tens of thousands Vietnamese after the fall of Saigon. In addition, the Vietnamese government was accused of supporting the refugees in their flight, as it was an easy way to get rid of opposition.[46]

GED was crucial in creating the perception of disasters *as* disasters in 1979. Therefore, GED had to connect with media. The founder, Neudeck, already stood for the close link the new organization implemented. He was contributing editor for a German public radio station and had good contacts to journalists. On his fact-finding tours, he was always on the lookout for new disaster zones. At the same time, his deployments for GED delivered material for reports that in turn promoted the cause of his organization.[47] In the case of the 'boat people', GED could also rely on the prominence of its supporter Heinrich Böll; the Nobel laureate appeared at several press conferences supporting them enthusiastically.[48] Neudeck ascribed a much higher effectivity to television and especially to the support of Franz Alt, host of the popular television news magazine 'report'. Alt was struck by the fate of the Vietnamese refugees and televised a detailed and sympathetic report on the fundraiser on 24 July 1979.[49] He also decided to show the bank account number of GED, thereby violating an unwritten rule that forbade advertising by NGOs. (The person in charge at the public television station saw the principle of neutrality in reporting at risk and feared 'campaign journalism'.)[50] The success was overwhelming; within days, the donations exceeded DM 1 million.

Until then, the new NGO had planned to support the French ship *Ile de Lumière*. However, Neudeck realized that a German ship could raise further awareness and further his cause. The idea to charter a ship was born spontaneously in the aforementioned 'report' magazine. From the perspective of the media professional, Alt had demanded a visible intervention: 'Why did no German organization hit on the idea to charter a plane or a ship?'[51] On 30 July 1979, Hans Voss, the owner of a distinguished shipping company, contacted Neudeck. He had learned of the initiative through television and suggested a charter contract for the ship *Cap Anamur*. In the following weeks, the ship proved to be a central selling point and an important means of obtaining publicity for the cause, even before the relief action started. All reports printed pictures of the ship and these images emphasized the will to proceed to action. [52]

When the *Cap Anamur* set sail, its meaning for public relation increased. From the beginning, the GED invited journalists to travel on the ship in order to witness the suffering for themselves. However, producing images proved difficult at first. When the *Cap Anamur* arrived at the South China Sea, it could not find any refugees. As a last resort, the crew headed for a refugee camp located on the Anambas Islands and supported other NGOs in supplying the camp. As Neudeck reported: 'These one-and-a-half days on Anambas . . . were the big days for the two television crews. They started immediately to shoot like crazy.'[53] For now, the problem of lacking images was resolved.

However, the TV reports were not friendly and presented the endeavour as ineffective. In fact, the volunteers of GED did not rescue any refugees on their first trip. But the press and radio reported consistently positive stories about the organization.[54] The journalists outdid each other by raising the number of deaths at sea. Local sources estimated that 10 per cent of the boat crews drowned.[55] Neudeck and Böll spoke of 50 per cent without having any data to support their estimates. The magazine *Spiegel* finally increased the share of deaths to 70 per cent and quoted a diplomat who described the Vietnamese refugees as 'the Jews of the East – without Israel'.[56] Because of the journalists allowed on board, several picture stories were published depicting the plight of the people fleeing across the sea in their small sinking ships, showing the emaciated children on the boats.

The illustrated magazine *Stern* got the most spectacular images. In addition to the ship, GED chartered a helicopter to support the search. It became apparent immediately that it was not useful for that purpose, but the *Stern* photographer could still take a series of pictures from above, contrasting the small vessels and the *Cap Anamur* against the endless vastness of the South China Sea.[57] The lasting effect of the ship on the German public is indicated by the popularity of its name. At first, the volunteers had planned to rename the ship to *Port de Lumière* in honour of their French role model. However, when media and donors kept referring to it by the original name *Cap Anamur*, they kept it and even decided to rename their entire organization after the ship. To the present day, the association bears that name; its logo still shows a Vietnamese refuge boat, although the NGO is now operating worldwide and no longer provides aid by sea.

GED's orientation towards visible campaigns met the need of journalists to produce news. The ship can be seen as the very symbol of immediate, spectacular action and it was perceived as such. However, even more important than this newfound enthusiasm for public relations was GED's compliance with fundamental media policies and procedures. The media influenced the essence of the organization; the very idea that motivated the founders aligned with media logic. GED introduced so-called 'radical humanism'. It proclaimed that aid agencies should concentrate on the human being and that relieving the suffering of humans had to supersede any political concerns.[58] Thereby, GED echoed the media's tendency to personalize news and supress political and historical context.

Rupert Neudeck interviewed Heinrich Böll in a public radio interview on 7 September 1979. He asked Böll why he committed himself to the cause of GED. They also discussed how to reply to objections against their relief actions and to voices that cast doubt on the necessity to flee Vietnam. Böll elaborated: 'I think it is forgotten when faced with these considerations, disputes, controversies that people are actually drowning . . . and nobody, literally nobody, is allowed to arrogate the decision who has to drown and who should be rescued.' From his point of view, which he shared with Neudeck, it would have been deeply inhuman to bring political considerations into the discussion: 'I cannot ask anyone who drowns for his political ideology or his social status' and 'I am not going to ask if he is a socialist or a capitalist, or both, or what will become of him.'[59] In only a few sentences, Böll had summarized the basis of the 'radical humanism', which emerged in the late 1970s and informed the relief actions of GED: only the individual human counted. Political considerations had to step back when there was a life to save.

With this focus on humanism and on bare life, GED was able to push aside questions about the causes or the motives of the fleeing Vietnamese. Immediate action seemed more important than evaluating an appropriate reaction to the crisis. The volunteers assessed their ignorance regarding the contexts as their central virtue. Neudeck cited a protagonist of Albert Camus's *The Plague* as his guiding motto: 'Il faut choisir: savoir ou guérir.'[60] It was necessary to choose between knowing and acting, because too much contemplation would inhibit any impulse to come to the rescue.

In this way, 'radical humanism' brought into the public consciousness regions of the world that had remained outside the considerations of international policy or had been 'uncharted territories' in relation to humanitarian efforts.[61] The volunteers of GED also succeeded in mobilizing much broader audiences for their humanitarian cause because they stripped it of any political implications when committing to providing aid. At the same time, the reduction to pure humanism and the occlusion of context met the expectations of the media, especially the tendency of journalists to put people at the centre of their reports, to skip over complicated processes and to appeal to the reader by emotionalizing the situation. The specific conception of 'radical humanism' that reduced a complex structural crisis and 'necessarily political events' to individual suffering made it easier for the media to portray the events as a humanitarian disaster that required help without question.

GED's approach, which aligned with media expectations, proved to be successful in the 1980s. Tens of thousands were ready to fund this 'dubious association' (by the estimation of the Foreign Office)[62] that had no experience in conducting relief operations, the internal organizational structure of which was unknown and that could not disclose where the money would go. In the first year, GED collected nearly DM 6 million; by the second year, 1980, it was DM 20 million.[63] GED also put notable pressure on semi-official and longstanding charities in Germany. The German Red Cross felt forced to charter its own ship, the *Flora*. It was sent to the coasts of Vietnam to confront the impending loss of prestige caused by its inaction.[64]

GED acted as a catalyst in the field of relief and it was also part of a broader development. The big aid organizations, such as World Vision, Plan, and CARE, opened representative offices in Germany at the end of the 1970s. These offices did not initiate any action, but confined their activities to public relations, advertising and soliciting donations. Therefore, they also placed emphasis on disasters and human suffering. In Germany, GED served as a role model for new foundations such as Humedica (1979), Menschen helfen Menschen (1980), HELP – Hilfe zur Selbsthilfe e.V. (1981), Aktionsgruppe Kinder in Not (1983), Ärzte für die Dritte Welt (1983, since 2011 German Doctors) and ghana action (1983, since 2003 africa action). They focused on spectacular relief actions and relied on the simple slogan that humanity had to prevail. For example, Karlheinz Böhm founded 'Menschen helfen Menschen' onstage when he was guest on the most famous TV show *Wetten dass?* on 16 May 1981. In the 1950s, Böhm had gained lasting prominence by representing the Austrian Kaiser Franz at the side of Romy Schneider in the 'Sissi' films. On the entertainment show, he used his high profile to call on the audience to donate to the Ethiopian cause.[65] The money laid the foundation for his humanitarian NGO whose 'greatest asset' was in his own words 'my person as a media figure, as the driving force'.[66]

The Ethiopian Famine: The Effects of Media Reports on Field Work

The effects of intensifying media coverage were not restricted to aid agencies, but can also be found in the direction of humanitarian aid. When it came to choosing where and whom to help, media logic played an increasingly prominent role. Contemporary observers feared that disaster relief would no longer reflect long-term political considerations, but would instead follow a 'selective humanitarian bias'.[67] For example, GED complained that it was almost impossible to solicit donations for Chad, where the organization had been providing aid since 1980. The country was traditionally not at the centre of attention and for the German public, it was unknown territory: 'Unfortunately, *Stern* or *Spiegel* are not willing to send any journalist that could exploit our spectacular relief.'[68] In Somalia, the NGO faced the opposite problem. The country had become known for its support when, in 1977, a German police force successfully liberated German hostages whose plane had been hijacked and forced to land in Mogadishu by Palestinian terrorists. The project manager at the site warned the German crew that the enormous sums of money pouring in should not tempt them to extend relief unnecessarily.[69]

The political bias has been replaced by a humanitarian bias informed by media attention, but the effects of media coverage went further and also changed the modalities of proliferating aid at the site. This became clear in the case of the devastating famine in Ethiopia in 1984 and 1985. Aid organizations perceived this deployment as a turning point, as the massive media attention undeniably affected their onsite work. That a famine of enormous dimensions was imminent was already obvious in 1983. The UN warning system sounded the alarm. Even the socialist government, the Derg, issued warnings of the sort it had avoided at all costs in the years before as it feared that this would shed a bad light on its rule. In the autumn of 1983, the first press reports appeared.[70] However, they did not resonate, probably because they joined a whole series of drought warnings for the African continent that had been issued since 1980. The perception was common that aid would be provided following established protocols. The reports lacked the indispensable moment of suddenness and uncontrollability; the disaster did not appear to be a disaster.

This perception only changed in October 1984. In the preceding months, the Ethiopian military government had denied Western reporters access to the country. It had planned extensive celebrations of its tenth anniversary. No negative news about Ethiopia was to be spread. However, Ethiopian students abroad leaked information indicating that a severe famine was imminent. This news generated considerable interest in the United Kingdom in particular. Two broadcasting networks, the public British Broadcasting Company (BBC) and the private Independent Television (ITV), competed for spectacular news. Both sent television crews to Ethiopia immediately after re-admission of journalists. They were shocked by the misery – and both teams attempted to draw the most from the situation.

In the end, BBC reporter Michael Buerk filed his report first. The BBC broadcast his report as part of the main evening news. Therefore, the report turned out to be much shorter than the competing documentary that ITV aired later. At the same time, the BBC report was marked as something special as it ran for seven minutes and thereby broke with news conventions. Buerk focused mainly on the devastating and impressive images of hunger without giving any context or explanation. The effect of the report was overwhelming. People in the United Kingdom and other European countries felt compelled to call for action. Donations immediately started to pour in. Relief organizations hit the road, and the nations of the 'Western world' and the 'Eastern Bloc' offered help. The highlight of mobilization was the Live Aid concert that Bob Geldof organized in the summer of 1985.[71]

The effect of Buerk's TV report was closely linked to its imagery.[72] The famous comment of the speaker followed familiar patterns that the media applied to represent disasters: 'Dawn. And as the sun breaks through the piercing chill of night on the plain outside Korem, it lights up a biblical famine, now, in the twentieth century. This place, say workers here, is the closest thing to hell on earth.'[73] With the formula of the 'biblical famine' and the reference to the mythical 'hell', Buerk evoked the perception of disasters as Acts of God. He thereby obscured the political and social context; it remained unclear how this disaster could have happened and who could have been responsible. Seemingly, an unpredictable, sudden and uncontrollable plague had befallen the country that required the global community to come to its rescue.

At the same time, the images were exceptional. Until then, photojournalists had focused primarily on individual portraits of starving and suffering. The visual appeal of Buerk's report arose from the fact that there were so many people in one place. Buerk repeatedly showed crowds who had gathered in the hope of securing medical care and food. He emphasized the visual appeal of the huge scale of suffering in his comments: 'Thousands of wasted people are coming here for help. Many find only death. They flood in every day from villages hundreds of miles away, felled by hunger, driven beyond the point of desperation. Death is all around.'[74]

To be sure, the massed number of people was closely connected to the situation on site. In many cases, the aid agencies could not reach the villages located in remote areas of the Ethiopian highlands and mountains. Therefore, people had to come to the camps and dispensaries. However, these reports also made clear that this special form of humanitarian aid produced the most effective images. The pictures confirmed the overwhelming extent of the negative event and the aid agencies could prove that help was easily provided.

The practice of concentrating people in camps for the purpose of distributing food and aid immediately proved to be problematic. Disentangling people from their social structures and removing them from their land and jobs turned them into permanent aid recipients. They could no longer apply their learned knowledge in the new situation; in these camps of short-term relief, no possibilities were offered to gather new skills that could open pathways out of the situation. In addition, the camps often created problems that needed to be tackled later, since the vulnerability to epidemics grew strongly through the concentration of people. In the case of Ethiopia, the number of people in camps proved to be especially problematic. The military government took advantage and deported these people to the lowlands, executing a long-planned resettlement programme. Thousands died because they could not manage life in their new surroundings. Some observers recognize this follow-up disaster as the actual catastrophe that was ignored by the West.[75]

Many aid agencies perceived Ethiopia as a turning point, a shift away from the development approach towards short-term technical aid. Until then, the motto was: 'Give a man a fish and you feed him for a day; teach a man to fish and you feed him for a lifetime.' However, it became obvious that in terms of media coverage, such agencies had an advantage in distributing fish to many in one place instead of teaching a few people in many places to fish. These images motivated donors and verified the efficiency of the relief. Aid organizations that were willing to provide aid in this way, without regard to the political context, profited. Oxfam and Save the Children were able to double the amount of donations they attracted because of the Ethiopian disaster.[76]

Conclusion: The Mediatization of Disaster

The media played a key role in the 'catastrophization' of our perception of disasters. They proved to be important because their reports rendered aid possible in the first place by identifying disasters. Key definitions of a disaster such as suddenness, unpredictability and uncontrollability do not align with the experiences at the site, but are the outcome of a specific representation. Without doubt, the media and especially news organizations were characterized by a short attention span that valued crisp headlines over broad, in-depth analysis. Media reports cut off possible explanations for conflicts, long-term trends and relevant contexts; they concentrated on human suffering instead of political analysis. Negative events appeared as unpreventable disasters, the global community felt urged to come to the rescue even for the 'distant other', donors started sending money and rescue teams were deployed.

If a disaster is proclaimed, aid agencies must provide short-term assistance if they wish to be successful in terms of donations later on. Once a disaster is identified as such, no country can claim its national sovereignty and reject aid. In the case of Biafra, at the end of the 1960s, competition for spectacular images proved to be crucial for a broad coverage campaign that focused on the suffering of the population. In 1973, *Stern* showed that it understood this logic; the magazine launched relief itself, and earned privileged access to the victims, from which it drew exclusive pictures and reports for multiple issues. Since the late 1970s, new humanitarian NGOs emerged, which themselves promoted the identification of the disaster by supplying appropriate images. By their spectacular entrance, GED drew attention to the refugees of Southeast Asia and mobilized the German population in ways never seen before. In Ethiopia in the mid 1980s, the competition between two TV channels was crucial for the perception of the famine as a disaster.

The specific medial constellations on the part of donor countries were much more relevant than the situation at the site for determining when disasters occurred. From the perspective of affected countries, the identification of events as disasters appeared arbitrary. In their view, disasters resulted from political, cultural and social processes, and were part of longstanding structural crises. Ethiopia in particular is an example of how random the proclamation of such a disaster can appear if we take into account the situation at the site. Northern Ethiopia had been undersupplied for more than fifty years and is characterized by a weak state structure and armed conflict. Famine was always looming, but only made headlines at select moments in 1973 and 1984. At the same time, 'disasters' went unnoticed. The massive supply problem and starvation from 1980 to 1983 did not resonate at all; the masses dying after the forced relocation in 1988 did not happen in Western perception. But then again, the alleged 'Ethiopian great famine' of 2003 was triggered by reports that interpreted local supply problems as a nationwide trend.[77]

However, the media coverage not only 'produced' disasters but also affected aid and contributed to the formation of humanitarian relief. With the examples of Biafra in 1968 and Ethiopia in 1973, it became clear that media coverage for disaster reporting could supersede any political consideration about where and to whom aid should be provided. Impressive images combined with a radicalized humanitarian sentiment proved to be so powerful that any political consideration about whether or not to help would have appeared downright immoral and heartless. This 'radical humanism' was of course – despite all assurances – not apolitical; for this reason alone, it went against longstanding political alliances and destabilized allies.

The example of the 'boat people' in 1979 indicates that media coverage of disasters also affected the form and idea of humanitarian NGOs. The new type of organizations that emerged after the late 1970s was characterized by relief efforts that aligned with media expectations. These organizations no longer based their actions on complicated and controversial concepts of political solidarity, but were instead driven by humanitarian sentiment that was far more easily communicable. This conformed to the media trend towards personalizing news and focusing on the human aspects of a situation. The spectacular was pushed to the fore.

The example of Ethiopia in 1984 made it clear that relief efforts meeting media needs could be problematic in their own right. The massed gathering of people for the purpose of distribution was ideally suited to confirming a disaster on television. TV crews could effortlessly reach the site of the disaster – the camp – shoot film and take photographs of suffering people. At the same time, this concourse of people had a negative impact. It destroyed social and economic structures, and assigned the nearly insuperable role of the auxiliary receiver to many Ethiopians.

At the same time, the media's discovery of 'relief aid' as a topic opened up new possibilities for aid agencies, since these new NGOs could now draw attention to regions and causes that had not received any previously. In addition, the alignment with media logic procured a hitherto unknown autonomy from politics. The new German aid agencies could now rely on donations, thereby breaking away from state funding and its limitations – always under the condition that humanitarian NGOs provided corresponding images.

However, mediatization is not an ever-intensifying process. Since the late 1960s, media logic has frequently prevailed in Germany, but foreign politics still remains an important actor when it comes to identifying disasters. With the advent of humanitarian NGOs in Germany in the 1980s, on several occasions, the media followed the lead of these new agencies. In the 1990s, we can observe a repoliticization and a new militarization, for example, in Somalia in 1992–94. Furthermore, strong media influence seems to be closely linked to a unique media formation. The new media have introduced a multiplication of channels. Challenging the presentation of seemingly sudden news, they have made it more difficult to supress political and historical contexts, and thus it has become increasingly difficult to divide the world into 'good' and 'evil'.

In all the cases I have described above, it has to be emphasized that nothing would have happened without media coverage. The terrible suffering of the people would have gone unnoticed and the mobilization of the 'Western world' would have failed to appear. Then again, the media logic of the disaster affected humanitarian aid and relief profoundly. In the long run, we can observe a trend towards short-term assistance replacing development approaches; disasters are used to justify intervention instead of negotiating solutions at an increasing rate. The 'production' of disasters is an ambivalent process that discloses many possibilities for aid and solidarity, but its implementation does not always achieve the desired effects.

Patrick Merziger is Assistant Professor of Communication History at the University of Leipzig. He received his PhD from Freie Universität Berlin. His research interests focus on the history of popular culture and the history of humanitarianism in the twentieth century. His publications include *Nationalsozialistische Satire und Deutscher Humor. Politische Bedeutung und Öffentlichkeit populärerUnterhaltung 1931–1945* (2010) and *The Politics of Humour: Laughter, Inclusion, and Exclusion in the Twentieth Century* (coedited with with Martina Kessel, 2012). Currently he is working on a project about disaster relief provided by the Federal Republic of Germany from 1951 to 1992, on which he published in English 'The "Radical Humanism" of "Cap Anamur". 'German Emergency Doctors' in the 1980s: A Turning Point for the Idea, Practice and Policy of Humanitarian Aid'. *European Review of History* 23(1–2) (2016), 171–92.

Notes

1. Cf. also [Rupert Neudeck], radio report 'Flüchtlinge in Südostasien', [May 1981], private archive Rupert and Christel Neudeck, folder 'Komitee bis 24.11.1981, Cap Anamur 1979–1981'.
2. M. Barnett, *The International Humanitarian Order* (London: Routledge, 2010), 1–18.
3. Y. Yan and K. Bissell, 'The Sky is Falling: Predictors of News Coverage of Natural Disasters Worldwide', *Communication Research* (26 February 2015), 1–25, doi: 10.1177/0093650215573861.
4. S. Orgad, *Media Representation and the Global Imagination* (Cambridge: Polity Press, 2015), 52–80; H. Fehrenbach and D. Rodogno (eds), *Humanitarian Photography: A History* (New York: Cambridge University Press, 2015).

5. S. Cottle, 'Mediatized Disasters in the Global Age: On the Ritualization of Catastrophe', in J.C. Alexander, R. Jacobs and P. Smith (eds), *Oxford Handbook of Cultural Sociology* (Oxford: Oxford University Press, 2012), 259–83; P. Robinson, 'The Policy-Media Interaction Model: Measuring Media Power during Humanitarian Crisis', *Journal of Peace Research* 37(5) (2000), 613–35.

6. S. Cottle and D. Nolan, 'Global Humanitarianism and the Changing Aid-Media Field', *Journalism Studies* 8(6) (2007), 862–78; M. Moke and M. Rüther, 'Humanitäre Hilfe und Medien', in J. Lieser and D. Dijkzeul (eds), *Handbuch Humanitäre Hilfe* (Berlin: Springer, 2013), 171–82, at 176–78.

7. A. Cooper Drury, R.S. Olson and Douglas A. van Belle, 'The Politics of Humanitarian Aid: U.S. Foreign Disaster Assistance, 1964–1995', *Journal of Politics* 67(2) (2005), 454–73, at 470.

8. Cf. for these notions J. Baudrillard, *Das Ereignis* (Weimar: Klassik Stiftung Weimar, 2007), 6–25; J. Derrida, *Eine gewisse unmögliche Möglichkeit, vom Ereignis zu sprechen* (Berlin: Merve, 2003), 32–33.

9. For an overview over definition of disasters, cf. P.H. Schuck, 'Crisis and Catastrophe in Science, Law, and Politics', in A. Sarat and J. Lezaun (eds), *Catastrophe: Law, Politics, and the Humanitarian Impulse* (Amherst: University of Massachusetts Press, 2009), 19–59.

10. D. Strömberg, 'Natural Disasters, Economic Development, and Humanitarian Aid', *Journal of Economic Perspectives* 21(3) (2007), 199–222.

11. A. Ophir, 'The Politics of Catastrophization: Emergency and Exception', in D. Fassin and M. Pandolfi (eds), *Contemporary States of Emergency: The Politics of Military and Humanitarian Interventions* (Brooklyn, NY: Zone Books, 2010), 59–88, at 60.

12. J. Paulmann, 'Conjunctures in the History of International Humanitarian Aid during the Twentieth Century', *Humanity: An International Journal of Human Rights, Humanitarianism, and Development* 4(2) (2013), 215–38; M. Barnett, *Empire of Humanity: A History of Humanitarianism* (Ithaca: Cornell Paperbacks, 2013); P. Walker and D. Maxwell, *Shaping the Humanitarian World* (London: Routledge, 2009).

13. A.M. van der Veen, *Ideas, Interests and Foreign Aid* (Cambridge: Cambridge University Press, 2011); P. Merziger, 'Humanitäre Hilfsaktionen der Bunderepublik Deutschland (1951–1991) als Medium der Außenbeziehung: Von der Beziehungspflege zur Intervention', in A. Tischer and P. Hoeres (eds), *Medien der Außenbeziehungen von der Antike bis zur Gegenwart* (Cologne: Böhlau, 2016), 490–516.

14. N. Middleton and P. O'Keefe, 'Politics, History and Problems of Humanitarian Assistance in Sudan', *Review of African Political Economy* 33(109) (2006), 543–59, at 543–45; G. Dodds, '"This was No Act of God": Disaster, Causality, and Politics', *Risk, Hazards & Crisis in Public Policy* 6(1) (2015), 44–68, at 59–62.

15. M. Pantti, K. Wahl-Jorgensen and S. Cottle, *Disasters and the Media* (New York: Lang, 2012), 25–35; J. Benthall, *Disasters, Relief and the Media* (London: Tauris, 1993), 172–217.

16. P. Hoeres, 'Außenpolitik, Öffentlichkeit, öffentliche Meinung: Deutsche Streitfälle in den "Langen 1960er Jahren"', *Historische Zeitschrift* 291 (2010), 689–720; F. Bösch and P. Hoeres, 'Im Bann der Öffentlichkeit? Der Wandel der Außenpolitik im Medienzeitalter', in F. Bösch and P Hoeres (eds), *Außenpolitik Im Medienzeitalter: Vom späten 19. Jahrhundert bis zur Gegenwart* (Göttingen: Wallstein, 2013), 7–38; S. Kunkel, *Empire of Pictures: Global Media and the 1960s Remaking of American Foreign Policy* (New York: Berghahn Books, 2015), 166–70.

17. C. Calhoun, 'The Idea of Emergency: Humanitarian Action and Global (Dis)order', in Fassin and Pandolfi, *Contemporary States of Emergency*, 29–58.

18. Cottle and Nolan, 'Global Humanitarianism and the Changing Aid-Media Field', 873–74.

19. M. Meyen, 'Medialisierung', *Medien & Kommunikationswissenschaft* 57(1) (2009), 23–38.

20. L. Mükke, *'Journalisten der Finsternis': Akteure, Strukturen und Potenziale deutscher Afrika-Berichterstattung* (Cologne: Herbert von Halem Verlag, 2009), 256–90; L. Mükke, 'Humanitär embedded: Wie symbiotische Beziehungen zwischen Hilfsorganisationen und Medien Qualitätsjournalismus aushöhlen', in V. Lilienthal (ed.), *PR und Journalismus: Zwischen Kooperation und Konfrontation* (2011), 23–30. Retrieved 23 August 2018 from http://docplayer.org/4088691-Pr-und-journalismus-zwischen-kooperation-und-konfrontation.html.

21. H. Gebhardt, 'Hilfe!', *Stern* 26(48) (1973), 18–36, at 36.

22. Merziger, 'Humanitäre Hilfsaktionen der Bunderepublik Deutschland (1951–1991) als Medium der Außenbeziehung', 513–14.

23. L. Heerten and A.D. Moses, 'The Nigeria–Biafra War: Postcolonial Conflict and the Question of Genocide', *Journal of Genocide Research* 16(2–3) (2014), 169–203.

24. C. Eugster, 'Die Luftwaffe und der Aufbau der Nigerian Air Force (1963–1967)', in E. Birk, W. Schmidt and H. Möllers (eds), *Die Luftwaffe in der Moderne* (Essen: Mönch, 2011), 217–38.

25. Report, Nigeria an der Jahreswende 1966/67 – Rückblick und Ausblick, from Botschaft der Bundesrepublik Deutschland, Lagos to Auswärtiges Amt, 2 January 1967, PPAA, den 2. Januar 1967, PP AA, B 34, vol. 710.

26. M.-L. Desgrandchamps, 'Dealing with "Genocide": The ICRC and the UN during the Nigeria–Biafra War, 1967–70', *Journal of Genocide Research* 16(2–3) (2014), 281–97.

27. R. Doron, 'Marketing Genocide: Biafran Propaganda Strategies during the Nigerian Civil War, 1967–70', *Journal of Genocide Research* 16(2–3) (2014), 227–26.

28. G. Zieser, 'Die Propagandastrategie Biafras im Nigerianischen Bürgerkrieg (1967–1970)', *Publizistik* 16(2) (1971), 181–93.

29. PA AA, B 34, vol. 711 and 712.

30. D. Siegfried, *Time is on My Side: Konsum und Politik in der westdeutschen Jugendkultur der 60er Jahre* (Göttingen: Wallstein, 2006), 521–40.

31. O.M. Schmitt, *Die schärfsten Kritiker der Elche: Die Neue Frankfurter Schule in Wort und Strich und Bild* (Berlin: Alexander Fest, 2001), 103–23.

32. O. König, *Nacktheit. Soziale Normierung und Moral* (Opladen: Westdeutscher Verlag, 1990), 284–90.

33. 'Biafra/Völkermord/Nur beten', *Der Spiegel* 22(34) (1968), 71–76.

34. 'Afrika/Biafra/Lebendig begraben', *Der Spiegel* 22(27) (1986), 70–76.

35. 'Warten auf den Hungertod', *Stern* 21(30) (1986), 12–19.

36. 'Bundeswehr/"Transall"-Transporter/Wie ein alter Schlauch', *Der Spiegel* 23(18) (1969), 38–41; cf. also Bundesarchiv/Militärarchiv, BL 1 4874.

37. 'Hilfe! Hunderttausende verhungern, wenn wir nichts tun', *Stern* 26(48) (1973), frontispiece; H. Nannen, 'Ich bitte um Hilfe', at 17; Gebhardt, 'Hilfe!', 18–36.

38. 'Stern Aktion "Rettet die Hungernden"', *Stern* 26(51) (1973), 134; H. Nannen, 'Bilanz', *Stern* 27(52) (1974), 12.

39. P.-H. Lehmann, 'Rettung in letzter Stunde', *Stern* 27(12) (1974), 38–57.

40. Gebhardt, 'Hilfe!', 18–36.

41. 'Und das Volk schrie: " Verhaftet den Dieb!"', *Stern* 27(39) (1974), 18–28, at 25: 'Sie . . . begannen . . . mit der Verbreitung von Nachrichten, die den Kaiser und seine Familie als Bande von gerissenen Geldschneidern zu Lasten des armen Volkes spiegelten.'

42. Freedom House, *Ethiopia: The Politics of Famine* (New York: Freedom House, 1990); cf. also 'Das Ende einer Epoche', *Stern* 27(19) (1974), 55–58; 'Und das Volk schrie: "Verhaftet den Dieb!"', 18–28.

43. D. Weitbrecht, *Aufbruch in die Dritte Welt: Der Internationalismus der Studentenbewegung von 1968 in der Bundesrepublik Deutschland* (Göttingen: V&R unipress, 2012), 73–91.

44. P. Merziger, 'The "Radical Humanism" of "Cap Anamur". "German Emergency Doctors" in the 1980s: A Turning Point for the Idea, Practice and Policy of Humanitarian Aid', *European Review of History* 23(1–2) (2016), 171–92.

45. N.M. Vo, *The Vietnamese Boat People, 1954 and 1975–1992* (Jefferson, NC: McFarland & Company, 2006), 64–100.

46. W. Langlott, 'Ein Schiff gegen Vietnam: Über die "Cap Anamur"-Affäre', *Konkret* 9 (1981), 20–21; cf. also the documentation of the discussion: [various authors], 'Die Linke und Vietnam: Eine Dokumentation', in R. Neudeck (ed.), *Wie helfen wir Asien? Oder 'Ein Schiff für Vietnam'* (Reinbek bei Hamburg: Rowohlt, 1980), 165–205.

47. Cf. e.g. R. Neudeck, 'Präsident Habre steht vor dem Nichts: Nach dem Bürgerkrieg ist der Tschad ausgeblutet', *Hannoversche Allgemeine Zeitung* 261 (9 November 1982).

48. H. Böll, 'Das Jahrhundert der Flüchtlinge: Zur Einführung [Erklärung auf der Pressekonferenz am 18. April 1979]', in Neudeck (ed.), *Wie helfen wir Asien?*, 7–8.

49. R. Neudeck, 'Ein Schiff für Vietnam', in Neudeck (ed.), *Wie helfen wir Asien?*, 70–145, at 88.

50. 'Fernsehen/Reine Hände', *Der Spiegel* 34(29) (1980), 37–39; Letter, from Rupert Neudeck to Dietrich Schwarzkopf, 18 August 1980, archive Cap Anamur Deutsche Notärzte e.V., Cologne, folder 'Schiff f. Vietnam, Komitee-Archiv 1979 1'.

51. Cited after Neudeck, 'Ein Schiff für Vietnam', 95.

52. 'Deutsches Hilfsschiff auf Flüchtlingssuche', *Frankfurter Allgemeine Zeitung* 184 (10 August 1979), 3.

53. Neudeck, 'Ein Schiff für Vietnam', 109.

54. J. Körner, 'Die bittere Reise des guten Willens', *Hamburger Abendblatt* 2 (30 August 1979), 17; 'Vietnam-Flüchtlinge/Gegen die Regeln', *Der Spiegel* 33(45) (1979), 29–30; J. Boehnke, 'Die nichts mehr zu verlieren haben: Zwei Wochen auf der Cap Anamur im Vietnamesischen Meer', *Badische Zeitung Magazin* 201 (30/31 August 1980), 1–2; E. Wiedemann, 'Schwimmende Festung der Menschlichkeit?', *Der Spiegel* 35(49) (1981), 142–44.

55. B. Wain, *The Refused: The Agony of the Indochina Refugees* (New York: Simon & Schuster, 1981), 83.

56. "Die Juden des Ostens – ohne ein Israel'. SPIEGEL-Report über den Menschenhandel mit Vietnam Flüchtlingen', *Der Spiegel* 33(26) (1979), 116–24.

57. E. Follath, 'Rettet diese Schiff!', *Der Stern* 33(43) (1980), 20–31; cf. also 'Ein Schiff rettet Flüchtlinge: "Cap Anamur" im Einsatz', *Illustrierte Wochenzeitung* 29 (19 July 1980), frontispiece, 6–9 and 15; 'Sie hielten ihm ein Messer an die Kehle', *Der Spiegel* 35(43) (1981), 80.

58. H. von Hentig, 'Radikale Humanität', in R. Neudeck (ed.), *Radikale Humanität: Notärzte für die Dritte Welt* (Reinbek bei Hamburg: Rowohlt, 1986), 9–12; cf. also N. N., outline of an appeal, 3 August 1981, folder 'Komitee bis 24.11.1981 - Cap Anamur 1979–1981', private archive of Rupert and Christel Neudeck; N. N., concept paper, without date, ar-

chive Cap Anamur Deutsche Notärzte e.V., Cologne, folder 'Schiff f. Vietnam, Komitee-Archiv 1979 1'

59. 'Kritisches Tagebuch', 7. September 1979, WDR III, cited after Neudeck, *Wie helfen wir Asien?*, 186–97, 187–88: 'Nur finde ich, dass bei all diesen Überlegungen, Auseinandersetzungen, Kontroversen vergessen wird, dass es sich um Ertrinkende handelt, im buchstäblichen Sinne . . . und sich keiner, aber wirklich keiner anmaßen darf zu sagen: der muss ertrinken, der soll ertrinken, der nicht.' 'Jemand, der am Ertrinken . . . ist den frage ich nicht nach seiner politischen Einstellung, auch nicht nach seiner sozialen Herkunft.' 'Ich kann niemanden, der ertrinkt, fragen . . . ob er Sozialist ist oder Kapitalist oder beides oder was aus ihm werden wird.'

60. R. Neudeck, 'Zwischen Verzweifeln und Helfen', *Orientierung. Katholische Blätter für weltanschauliche Information* 49(4) (1985), 44–47.

61. G. Loescher, *The UNHCR and World Politics: A Perilous Path* (Oxford: Oxford University Press, 2001), 144.

62. Neudeck, 'Ein Schiff für Vietnam', 83.

63. Statement of donations 197–2010, archive Cap Anamur Deutsche Notärzte e.V., Cologne.

64. German Red Cross archive, Nr. 03312 and DRK-Präsidium Generalsekretariat, Nr. 00021. On the dispute and rivalry between Neudeck's organization and the German Red Cross, see M. Vössing, 'Competition over Aid? The German Red Cross, the Committee Cap Anamur, and the Rescue of Boat People in South-East Asia', in J. Paulmann (ed.), *Dilemmas of Humanitarian Aid in the Twentieth Century* (Oxford: Oxford University Press, 2016), 345–68.

65. K. Böhm, *Mein Weg: Erinnerungen* (Munich: Knaur, 1993), 9–27.

66. Ibid., 243

67. 'Fernsehen/Reine Hände', *Der Spiegel* 34(29) (1980), 37–39; H. von Ditfurth, 'Die mörderische Konsequenz des Mitleids', *Der Spiegel* 38(33) (1984), 85.

68. Letter, from the project manager to Rupert and Christel Neudeck, 23. October 1983, private archive Rupert and Christel Neudeck, folder 'Tschad 1983': 'Leider haben wir halt kein *Stern*- oder *Spiegel*-Team in der Nähe um solche Aktion [*sic*] publizistisch auszuschlachten.'

69. 'Vorschlag eines Konzeptes zur Arbeit im Hargeisa Hospital', September 1982, private archive Rupert and Christel Neudeck, folder 'Somalia 2. 20.7.1982. 1994'.

70. J. von Dohnanyi, 'Hungern, warten, sterben', *Stern* 36(39) (1974), 60–69.

71. S. Franks, *Reporting Disasters: Famine, Aid, Politics and the Media* (London: Hurst, 2013), 11–39 and 71–87.

72. H. Lidchi, 'Finding the Right Image: British Development NGOs and the Regulation of Imagery', in Fehrenbach and Rodogno, *Humanitarian Photography*, 275–96, at 280–81.

73. M. Buerk, 'BBC News 10/23/84' (2009). Retrieved 23 August 2018 from https://www.youtube.com/watch?v=XYOj_6OYuJc.

74. Ibid.

75. L. Binet, *Famine and Forced Relocations in Ethiopia 1984–1986* (Geneva: Médecins Sans Frontières, 2013), 66–111; A. Pankhurs, *Resettlement and Famine in Ethiopia: The Villagers' Experience* (Manchester: Manchester University Press, 1992), 23-50; G. Woldemeskel, 'The Consequences of Resettlement in Ethiopia', *African Affairs* 88(352) (1989), 359–74.

76. P. Gill, *Famine and Foreigners: Ethiopia since Live Aid* (Oxford: Oxford University Press, 2010), 45–62.

77. L. Mükke, 'Der inszenierte Hunger', *Die Zeit* 58(17) (2003), 13–16.

Bibliography

Barnett, M. *The International Humanitarian Order.* London: Routledge, 2010.

———. *Empire of Humanity: A History of Humanitarianism.* Ithaca: Cornell Paperbacks, 2013.

Baudrillard, J. *Das Ereignis.* Weimar: Klassik Stiftung Weimar, 2007.

Benthall, J. *Disasters, Relief and the Media.* London: Tauris, 1993.

Binet, L. *Famine and Forced Relocations in Ethiopia 1984–1986.* Geneva: Médecins Sans Frontières, 2013.

Böhm, K. *Mein Weg: Erinnerungen.* Munich: Knaur, 1993.

Böll, H. 'Das Jahrhundert der Flüchtlinge: Zur Einführung [Erklärung auf der Pressekonferenz am 18. April 1979]', in R. Neudeck (ed.), *Wie helfen wir Asien? Oder 'Ein Schiff für Vietnam'* (Reinbek bei Hamburg: Rowohlt, 1980), 7–8.

Bösch, F., and P. Hoeres. 2013. 'Im Bann der Öffentlichkeit? Der Wandel der Außenpolitik im Medienzeitalter', in F. Bösch and P Hoeres (eds), *Außenpolitik im Medienzeitalter: Vom späten 19. Jahrhundert bis zur Gegenwart* (Göttingen: Wallstein, 2013), 7–38.

Calhoun, C. 'The Idea of Emergency: Humanitarian Action and Global (Dis)order', in D. Fassin and M. Pandolfi (eds), *Contemporary States of Emergency: The Politics of Military and Humanitarian Interventions* (Brooklyn, NY: Zone Books, 2010), 29–58.

Cooper Drury, A., R.S. Olson and Douglas A. van Belle. 'The Politics of Humanitarian Aid: U.S. Foreign Disaster Assistance, 1964–1995'. *Journal of Politics* 67(2) (2005), 454–73.

Cottle, S. 'Mediatized Disasters in the Global Age: On the Ritualization of Catastrophe', in J.C. Alexander, R. Jacobs and P. Smith (eds), *Oxford Handbook of Cultural Sociology* (Oxford: Oxford University Press 2012), 259–83.

Cottle, S., and D. Nolan. 'Global Humanitarianism and the Changing Aid-Media Field'. *Journalism Studies* 8(6) (2007), 862–78.

Derrida, J. *Eine gewisse unmögliche Möglichkeit, vom Ereignis zu sprechen.* Berlin: Merve, 2003.

Desgrandchamps, M.-L. 'Dealing with "Genocide": The ICRC and the UN during the Nigeria–Biafra War, 1967–70'. *Journal of Genocide Research* 16(2–3) (2014), 281–97.

Dodds, G.G. '"This was No Act of God": Disaster, Causality, and Politics'. *Risk, Hazards & Crisis in Public Policy* 6(1) (2015), 44–68.

Doron, R. 'Marketing Genocide: Biafran Propaganda Strategies during the Nigerian Civil War, 1967–70'. *Journal of Genocide Research* 16(2–3) (2014), 227–46.

Eugster, C. 'Die Luftwaffe und der Aufbau der Nigerian Air Force (1963–1967)', in E. Birk, W. Schmidt and H. Möllers (eds), *Die Luftwaffe in der Moderne* (Essen: Mönch, 2011), 217–38.

Fehrenbach, H., and D. Rodogno (eds). *Humanitarian Photography: A History.* New York: Cambridge University Press, 2015.

Franks, S. *Reporting Disasters: Famine, Aid, Politics and the Media.* London: Hurst, 2013.

Freedom House. *Ethiopia: The Politics of Famine.* New York: Freedom House, 1990.

Gill, P. *Famine and Foreigners: Ethiopia since Live Aid.* Oxford: Oxford University Press, 2010.

Heerten, L., and A.D. Moses. 'The Nigeria–Biafra War: Postcolonial Conflict and the Question of Genocide'. *Journal of Genocide Research* 16(2–3) (2014), 169–203.

Hoeres, P. 'Außenpolitik, Öffentlichkeit, öffentliche Meinung: Deutsche Streitfälle in den "Langen 1960er Jahren"'. *Historische Zeitschrift* 291 (2010), 689–720.

Kent, R. 'Interpreting Disaster Relief'. *Third World Quarterly* 8(4) (1986), 1432–38.

König, O. *Nacktheit: Soziale Normierung und Moral.* Opladen: Westdeutscher Verlag, 1990.

Kunkel, S. *Empire of Pictures: Global Media and the 1960s Remaking of American Foreign Policy.* New York: Berghahn Books, 2015.

Lidchi, H. 'Finding the Right Image: British Development NGOs and the Regulation of Imagery', in H. Fehrenbach and D. Rodogno (eds), *Humanitarian Photography: A History* (New York: Cambridge University Press, 2015), 275–96.

Loescher, G. *The UNHCR and World Politics: A Perilous Path.* Oxford: Oxford University Press, 2001.

Merziger, P. 'Humanitäre Hilfsaktionen der Bunderepublik Deutschland (1951–1991) als Medium der Außenbeziehung: Von der Beziehungspflege zur Intervention', in A. Tischer and P. Hoeres (eds), *Medien der Außenbeziehungen von der Antike bis zur Gegenwart* (Cologne: Böhlau, 2016), 490–516.

———. 'The "Radical Humanism" of "Cap Anamur". "German Emergency Doctors" in the 1980s: A Turning Point for the Idea, Practice and Policy of Humanitarian Aid'. *European Review of History* 23(1–2) (2016), 171–92.

Meyen, M. 'Medialisierung'. *Medien & Kommunikationswissenschaft* 57(1) (2009), 23–38.

Middleton, N., and P. O'Keefe. 'Politics, History and Problems of Humanitarian Assistance in Sudan'. *Review of African Political Economy* 33(109) (2006), 543–59.

Moke, M., and M. Rüther. 'Humanitäre Hilfe und Medien', in J. Lieser and D. Dijkzeul (eds), *Handbuch Humanitäre Hilfe* (Berlin: Springer, 2013), 171–82.

Mükke, L. 'Der inszenierte Hunger'. *Die Zeit* 58(17) (2003), 13–16.

———. *'Journalisten der Finsternis': Akteure, Strukturen und Potenziale deutscher Afrika-Berichterstattung.* Cologne: Herbert von Halem Verlag, 2009.

———. 'Humanitär embedded: Wie symbiotische Beziehungen zwischen Hilfsorganizationen und Medien Qualitätsjournalismus aushöhlen', in V. Lilienthal (ed.), *PR und Journalismus. Zwischen Kooperation und Konfrontation* (2011), 23-30. Retrieved 23 August 2018 from http://docplayer.org/4088691-Pr-und-journalismus-zwischen-kooperation-und-konfrontation.html.

Neudeck, R. 'Ein Schiff für Vietnam', in *Wie helfen wir Asien? Oder 'Ein Schiff für Vietnam'* (Reinbek bei Hamburg: Rowohlt, 1980), 70–145.

———. 'Zwischen Verzweifeln und Helfen'. *Orientierung. Katholische Blätter für weltanschauliche Information* 49(4) (1985), 44–47.

Ophir, A. 'The Politics of Catastrophization: Emergency and Exception', in D. Fassin and M. Pandolfi (eds), *Contemporary States of Emergency: The Politics of Military and Humanitarian Interventions* (Brooklyn, NY: Zone Books, 2010), 59–88.

Orgad, S. *Media Representation and the Global Imagination.* Cambridge: Polity Press, 2015.

Pankhurst, A. *Resettlement and Famine in Ethiopia: The Villagers' Experience.* Manchester: Manchester University Press, 1992.

Pantti, M., K. Wahl-Jorgensen and S. Cottle. *Disasters and the Media.* New York: Lang, 2012.

Paulmann, J. 'Conjunctures in the History of International Humanitarian Aid during the Twentieth Century'. *Humanity: An International Journal of Human Rights, Humanitarianism, and Development* 4(2) (2013), 215–38.

Robinson, P. 'The Policy-Media Interaction Model: Measuring Media Power during Humanitarian Crisis'. *Journal of Peace Research* 37(5) (2000), 613–35.

Schmitt, O.M. *Die schärfsten Kritiker der Elche: Die Neue Frankfurter Schule in Wort und Strich und Bild.* Berlin: Alexander Fest, 2001.

Schuck, P.H. 'Crisis and Catastrophe in Science, Law, and Politics', in A. Sarat and J. Lezaun (eds), *Catastrophe: Law, Politics, and the Humanitarian Impulse* (Amherst: University of Massachusetts Press, 2009), 19–59.

Siegfried, D. *Time is on My Side: Konsum und Politik in der westdeutschen Jugendkultur der 60er Jahre.* Göttingen: Wallstein, 2006.

Strömberg, D. 'Natural Disasters, Economic Development, and Humanitarian Aid'. *Journal of Economic Perspectives* 21(3) (2007), 199–222.

Van der Veen, A.M. *Ideas, Interests and Foreign Aid.* Cambridge: Cambridge University Press, 2011.

Vo, N.M. *The Vietnamese Boat People, 1954 and 1975–1992.* Jefferson, NC: McFarland & Company, 2006.

Von Hentig, H. 'Radikale Humanität', in R. Neudeck (ed.), *Radikale Humanität: Notärzte für die Dritte Welt* (Reinbek bei Hamburg: Rowohlt, 1986), 9–12.

Vössing, M. 'Competition over Aid? The German Red Cross, the Committee Cap Anamur, and the Rescue of Boat People in South-East Asia', in J. Paulmann (ed.), *Dilemmas of Humanitarian Aid in the Twentieth Century* (Oxford: Oxford University Press, 2016), 345–68.

Wain, B. *The Refused: The Agony of the Indochina Refugees.* New York: Simon & Schuster, 1981.

Walker, P., and D. Maxwell. *Shaping the Humanitarian World.* London: Routledge, 2009.

Weitbrecht, D. *Aufbruch in die Dritte Welt: Der Internationalismus der Studentenbewegung von 1968 in der Bundesrepublik Deutschland.* Göttingen: V&R unipress, 2012.

Woldemeskel, G. 'The Consequences of Resettlement in Ethiopia'. *African Affairs* 88(352) (1989), 359–74.

Yan, Y., and K. Bissell. 'The Sky is Falling: Predictors of News Coverage of Natural Disasters Worldwide'. *Communication Research* (26 February 2015), 1–25.

Zieser, G. 'Die Propagandastrategie Biafras im Nigerianischen Bürgerkrieg (1967–1970)'. *Publizistik* 16(2) (1971), 181–93.

11

NGOs, Celebrity Humanitarianism and the Media

Negotiating Conflicting Perceptions of Aid and Development during the 'Ethiopian Famine'

Matthias Kuhnert

Scholarship regards the Ethiopian famine of the mid 1980s as a key moment in the history of Western humanitarianism. The efforts on the part of Western organizations to provide aid at the Horn of Africa have been called 'an earthquake in the humanitarian world'.[1] In particular, the depiction of the famine in the media, the unprecedented extent of public support and the emergence of so-called 'celebrity humanitarianism' had brought lasting change to humanitarian engagement. For instance, the tremendously successful fundraising efforts during the crisis brought about a huge increase in the budgets of nongovernmental organizations (NGOs).[2]

Nearly all authors agree that the larger part of the consequences of this engagement in the course of the Ethiopian famine must be interpreted critically, since they had encouraged a distorted Western view of Africa. In order to receive and maintain access to the recipients of aid, Western organizations had agreed not to publicize the Ethiopian regime's crimes, which had decisively contributed to the famine's eruption and perpetuation. Instead, Western aid workers and media spread the myth of a natural disaster.[3] Following this interpretation, a large part of scholarship devoted itself to showing up the flaws in this commitment, the standard narrative being that a Western 'humanitarian industry' had portrayed mainly starving children in order to maximize donations. Manipulative NGOs had thus drawn an inaccurate and ethically wrong image of needy and helpless Africans dependent on Western charity.[4]

This narrative does indeed point to fundamental problems with humanitarian aid. However, it makes it harder to see that contemporaries, particularly NGO activists themselves, already criticized the depiction of the famine. Stuck in the same debates as contemporary activists, scholarship has little to say about the options open to actors within NGOs in the face of enormous publicity and media attention. What, for instance, did they make of such high-profile projects as Band Aid and Live Aid? To what extent did they try to participate in or set themselves apart from them?

These processes of negotiation within the NGOs deserve a thorough analysis. To this end, I shall examine the activities of two British organizations, War on Want and Christian Aid. The two organizations may be considered representative of the humanitarian sector in Great Britain: War on Want, founded in 1951 by individuals associated with the British Labour movement, is an example of a leftist NGO. Christian Aid, founded in 1945 by the British Council of Churches, represents Christian humanitarianism.[5]

In order to approach the processes of negotiation within Christian Aid and War on Want in the face of the huge media attention to the famine in the Horn of Africa, this chapter focuses on the debates over how aid recipients were to be perceived. The question concerns not the actors' actual perceptions, but instead which views, perceptions and ascriptions staff working for the humanitarian organizations circulated internally and which ones were communicated to the public. Furthermore, attention will be paid to the negotiations over these perceptions, that is to say, the attempts on the part of both Christian Aid and War on Want to communicate their own views of the people in the affected region against the background of massive media attention towards the famine and competing representations from the media and Band Aid. Another focus will concentrate on the strategies that these humanitarian organizations developed to deal with competing perceptions in the media.

My analysis of the actions of these two NGOs in the context of the famine will proceed in three steps: a brief account of the famine's development is followed by a description of how the media reported on it and how the celebrity humanitarianism culminating in Live Aid emerged. This is followed by a discussion of how the NGOs addressed the media's interest in the Ethiopian famine, the Band Aid phenomenon that arose in its wake and the attempts by War on Want to propagate an alternative view. The third step will foreground the practical steps made by the two NGOs to cooperate with Band Aid and how certain elements of medial representation were appropriated.

The Ethiopian Famine and the Humanitarian Boom in the Media

In early 1983, the first indications of a threatening famine were felt in Ethiopia. Its origins were complex. Natural factors certainly played a part, with some regions in the north of the country lacking rainfall. Nonetheless, the crisis might possibly have been prevented. Its origins are also to be found in the Ethiopian government's misguided agricultural policy, with its reliance on collectivization, state-run farms and cash crops. However, several authors argue that the most severe blow was dealt by the Ethiopian government's military action against secessionist rebels in the north of the country. Military offensives targeted granaries, markets and provisioning stations. Moreover, the military bombarded roads and fields, bringing agricultural activity to a standstill. Finally, these military measures provoked refugee movements, exacerbating a precarious food situation. In summary, the Ethiopian government deliberately used starvation as a weapon to fight the insurgents and, in doing so, decisively contributed to the emergence of the famine. The attacks concentrated on Ethiopia's northern provinces, like Wollo and Tigray, which were the most severely affected by the famine between 1983 and 1985.[6]

Although aid organizations and a few journalists already began to warn of a disastrous famine in early 1983, the British media scarcely showed any interest. Only when the BBC found out that its competitor ITV was planning a documentary about the famine did the network instruct its South African correspondent Michael Buerk to produce a brief report as quickly as possible.[7] However, soon afterwards, the Horn of Africa seemed once more to vanish into media oblivion. Only a second report by Buerk, broadcast by the BBC as part of its main news programme on 23 October 1984, triggered a broad response throughout the media.[8]

Buerk's report was remarkable in several respects.[9] At seven minutes, it was unusually long for a report in the regular evening news. Its visual language too was exceptional. The report from the Korem refugee camp in Wollo province combined depicting individual suffering with that of mass starvation, showing thousands of emaciated bodies packed into a tight space. In doing so, the report brought home to the TV audience just how many people were affected by this catastrophe.[10] Buerk's commentary reinforced this message in terms of biblical resonance:

> Dawn, and as the sun breaks through the piercing chill of night on the plain outside Korem, it lights up a biblical famine, now, in the twentieth century. This place, say workers here, is the closest thing to hell on earth . . . Death is all around. A child, or an adult, dies every twenty minutes. Korem, an insignificant town, has become a place of grief.[11]

Alongside drastic depictions of large-scale death and suffering, Buerk gave voice to aid workers who explained that the means at their disposal were insufficient even to begin alleviating the situation.

Even today, critics still accuse Michael Buerk of not having discussed the actual reasons for the suffering in Ethiopia. Instead of condemning the Ethiopian government's military action against its own population, Buerk's use of biblical imagery had suggested that the famine was at heart a natural catastrophe that had arisen independently of human agency.[12] Moreover, Buerk and his cameraman Mohamed Amin had systematically hidden from view such indications of military conflict as were indeed present. For instance, missile launchers had been positioned on the Korem plateau surrounding the refugee camp, but they were nowhere to be seen in the BBC's report.[13]

Why did Buerk's report not draw attention to evidence of the war? It seems likely that to do otherwise would have contradicted the public definition of a humanitarian disaster. A widespread view held that humanitarian emergencies were first and foremost crises of a natural origin, which excluded war. It thus stands to reason that those responsible at the BBC might have expected not to elicit the desired response from their audience if the report had alluded to the ongoing war. This supposition is borne out by an examination of the manner in which the BBC had responded to requests from member organizations of the Disasters Emergency Committee (DEC), an umbrella group of British charitable organizations, in previous years, when it asked for the broadcaster's cooperation in asking for donations for relief efforts in other civil war zones. For instance, the BBC and the Independent Broadcasting Authority (IBA, the regulatory body at the time) responded with extreme caution to requests from Oxfam, Christian Aid and the Catholic Agency for Overseas Development (AFOD) for free airtime to solicit donations for aid to war victims in Central America. Only after lengthy discussions did the BBC yield, doing so only on the condition that no presenter employed by the BBC read the appeal. This reluctance was not limited to the BBC and the IBA. The public reaction too left a great deal to be desired in the eyes of NGOs. A mere £400,000 was gathered, a small sum for an appeal of its kind. A paper produced by Christian Aid subsequently asked whether there was a distinction, in the eyes of the public, between a genuine or 'legitimate' need as a result of natural disasters and an 'illegitimate' need caused by wars.[14]

It thus seems plausible that Michael Buerk's report on the Ethiopian famine omitted any allusion to the war on account of these socially widespread opinions and reservations. The reaction on the part of the press seems to vindicate Buerk, whose narrative of a natural disaster free from human culpability seems to have gone largely unquestioned.[15] The newspapers described the crisis as a 'drought',[16] the consequence of unusually dry weather. Buerk's version of events had thus established itself in the mainstream British media and was to determine further reporting on the famine in the press, radio and television. Buerk's report elicited a huge response. Representatives of several organizations reported that they were facing a tremendous desire to help.[17] Only days after the report was aired, the various charities had received some £5 million in donations – a record figure.[18]

The manner in which the Ethiopian famine was reported testifies to a particular form of emotionalization by which the enormous public response might be explained. The representation of seemingly boundless suffering was invariably tied to an appeal to the recipients' conscience. Although the vast majority of journalists, as already discussed, ascribed responsibility for the catastrophe to natural rather than manmade causes, they made it clear that they expected Western governments and publics to do something about it. A particularly accusatory tone was struck by *The Guardian*, which spoke of 'the famine the world refused to believe'.[19] Western governments, the paper argued, had refused to heed warnings from Ethiopia because the country's regime was Marxist. Had the West acted sooner, rather than ignoring voices from the Ethiopian government and those of international experts, the disaster could have been averted.[20]

Based on this assumption, many articles quoted experts and aid workers who stressed the importance of fast and generous help to alleviate suffering and save lives. The government and society at large were both called on to help.[21] In doing so, responsibility for putting an end to suffering was assigned to political actors and civil society in the West. This was usually accompanied by criticism that help from Britain was not enough to solve the problem.[22] Empathy was thus also generated by apportioning blame to Western governments that were not doing enough to relieve the agonies of the people in Ethiopia.[23]

All of these elements were prefigured in Michael Buerk's report, which depicted the dramatic situation in the refugee camps, portrayed them as the consequence of natural circumstances, and pointed out that the West was not sending Ethiopia enough help. Buerk's report, as it were, had done a great deal to provide a framework around which subsequent reporting on the famine could be structured.

Letters to the national newspapers give at least a hint at the reactions elicited by this kind of emotionally charged media coverage among their readership. All correspondents wrote how deeply moved they were by the dramatic images on their TV screens. 'It was appalling and unspeakably sad to see the helpless misery of thousands of our brothers and sisters dying of starvation', wrote one reader.[24] Another said: 'Like hundreds of others, I was moved to pity for the starving in Ethiopia, as shown in the excellent television news coverage of their plight.'[25] The way in which the media depicted the crisis in Ethiopia encouraged the public to express its compassion with the people in Ethiopia. Through its emotional tone, the coverage did much to set the terms in which such feelings were expressed. With the images of enormous suffering in mind, many seem to have seen it fit to express compassion and also, in some cases, outrage. From their compassion, most deduced a call to action: 'Humanity and European civilization demand immediate help on a massive scale.'[26] 'I appeal to our leaders in government and to all members of Parliament of every party to take action immediately . . . If ever there were need for the rich to share with the poor, the need is on our doorstep.'[27]

It was this very perception that paved the way for the success of Bob Geldof and his Band Aid project, as well as its follow-up, Live Aid. The rock singer appeared on the scene with a somewhat rough-and-ready claim to do something about the famine himself. The widespread mood was such that Geldof hit a nerve. To the press, Band Aid represented the polar opposite of the pop business's widely decried hedonism:

> Nothing but admiration and congratulations are due, however, to the 40 top artists, from Boy George downwards, who came together to make the famous Band Aid single 'Do They Know it's Christmas?' whose entire proceeds are wholly dedicated to the relief of famine in Africa.[28]

Observers were unanimous in praising Geldof's initiative and charitableness.[29] Geldof's scheme, which united many of the most famous performers of the day, seemed to answer the media's call to assume responsibility.

Generally speaking, the role Geldof assumed was that of a nonpolitical helper, emphasizing that it was more important to improve the situation than to take sides in the Ethiopian civil war or be unduly worried about diplomatic niceties. 'Mr Geldof said later: "The politics of the thing don't concern me. I'll shake hands with the devil on the left and the right as long as it's going to ensure that this money ends up in the mouths of the people who need it."'[30] This nonpolitical status became Band Aid's brand, and Geldof forcefully marketed it as such to the public. In doing so, the singer catered to an idea that was still popular in the media, though it had been largely dismissed by most NGOs: that humanitarian aid was something taking place beyond the political realm. Whereas organizations like Christian Aid and War on Want had for some time been arguing for a link between poverty, famine and political action, Geldof maintained an ideal of neutrality.

This insistence on the nonpolitical nature of Geldof's activism entailed a particular interpretation of the Ethiopian famine. Since he refused to engage with politics, he also largely ignored the famine's political and military causes.[31] As a result, Band Aid perpetuated the view that the famine was a natural disaster that had come about after years of drought. Band Aid thus built on the interpretation adumbrated in Michael Buerk's TV report and helped to spread it further.[32]

A close corollary of this view was to represent those affected as victims in need of help. Band Aid's implicit message was that people in the Horn of Africa were subject to natural conditions that left them exposed to recurring epic droughts. Consequently, they were also unable to do anything to change this state of affairs by themselves, but were instead dependent on Western aid. To this day, a great deal of scholarship has criticized Band Aid for spreading a paternalistic image of Africa in which starving children and emaciated bodies were the iconic representations of Africans' neediness. Band Aid had thus confronted Africans not as equal, self-determined subjects, but from a top-down perspective. Compassion was thus the principal category of perception.[33] Band Aid had therefore reinforced the discourse of compassion that was already well established among the public.

The Attempt to Correct the Perception in the Media

The kind of emotionalization performed by Band Aid and the majority of the British media was diametrically opposed to the image of people in the Global South that NGOs sought to promote by the mid 1980s. Whereas Band Aid emphasized compassion, the emotional concept propounded by War on Want and Christian Aid was centred above all on solidarity. Whereas Geldof proposed simply to offer 'help', the NGOs' message was to help people to help themselves.

Whereas War on Want and Christian Aid had, since the early 1970s, aimed to explain the manmade causes of poverty and starvation, the media overwhelmingly insisted on portraying the Ethiopian famine as a natural disaster. Whereas the NGOs almost incessantly drummed home the message that what counted was to do justice to the agency of people in the so-called 'Third World', neither the media nor Band Aid gave much indication of sharing this notion.[34] All this points to a profound discrepancy between the perceptions of British aid organizations and that of which Michael Buerk and Bob Geldof may be considered representative.

It therefore comes as no great surprise that British humanitarian NGOs found severe problems in Band Aid's approach. Even at a purely practical level, staff working for established charities like Christian Aid found Band Aid's modus operandi to be questionable, to say the least. For instance, a worker on Christian Aid's Africa desk informed colleagues of the pop philanthropist's ideas for spending all the money generated by Band Aid. One such supposed scheme was to charter ships for transporting food to the Horn of Africa, a solution that the Christian Aid staffer thought to be far from ideal: 'It seems unlikely that anything like this will happen before May/June, which will be rather late', she remarked.[35] Indeed, it was quite hard for her to say what Band Aid intended to do at all, 'as plans seem to be changing all the time'. However, criticism of Geldof and his project from NGOs went further than such practical difficulties. Representatives of Christian Aid considered Band Aid's plan to collect food for Africa in schools to be deeply flawed: 'An over-simplified solution to Africa's problems is presented ie [sic] all that is needed is food.'[36] Band Aid was further criticized for its reliance on the '"starving baby" image', which perpetuated simplistic and indeed racist stereotypes. Christian Aid found whole range of problematic implications in such an approach:

> This reinforces: a) an oversimplified understanding of the situation and of development as something we (rich, educated whites) do for them (poor, ignorant, blacks)
>
> b) a racist view of the world – we are the good whites and they are the poor blacks/all blacks are starving etc.
>
> c) the artists in LIVE AID (UK) were all white, again reinforcing racist views.
>
> . . .
>
> There is no attempt to look at the causes of the situation.

Questions of perception were thus at the heart of the criticism levelled against Band Aid. Christian Aid accused the musicians' project of spreading simplistic and paternalistic views, which might even conceal racist messages. Christian Aid was particularly critical of the emotional language in which Band Aid described the people it set out to help. According to Christian Aid's staff, the pop-philanthropists failed to display the correct attitude towards the people of Ethiopia and Africa at large. Whereas the established NGOs always maintained that the Africans were partners, working side by side with them to combat poverty and starvation, they accused Band Aid of seeking to help hierarchically subordinate people. NGO activists saw themselves facing a fundamentally different pattern of perceiving things, and they found it to be misguided. Merely to present suffering and to generate compassion in doing so was, to their mind, the wrong approach, in that it perpetuated the victimization of Africans. What Band Aid lacked, from the perspective of Christian Aid, was an emphasis on equal footing and agency. Christian Aid was far from being alone among British NGOs in voicing such criticisms. Oxfam too expressed concern about the implications of the publicity generated by Geldof's project. 'There is a very real worry that the Band Aid/Live Aid effect on public perception would be to reinforce negative and racist stereotypes of Africa and Black people generally.'[37] The Oxford-based organization was particularly critical of Band Aid's scheme to collect food in schools, arguing that 'this has the potential to set back development education considerably, in that it is reinforcing the negative and racist image of Africa being totally dependant [*sic*] on our generosity. It does nothing to raise questions about the causes of famine or challenge widely held misconceptions'. The available evidence thus suggests that the opinion that Band Aid was spreading dubious perspectives on the predicament of the 'Third World' was a commonplace among established NGOs.[38]

To counter this narrative, War on Want, for instance, sought clearly to distinguish its own interpretation of the problems in the developing world in general and the Horn of Africa in particular from that spread by the mass media and to communicate its own view. To this end, it published leaflets and brochures that were supposed to apprise the public of the underlying factors of the Ethiopian famine and of the right approaches to resolving it. War on Want made sure to place all these efforts in the context of the famine's ongoing representation in the mass media:

> Since October last year T.V. pictures of the famine in Ethiopia have unleashed an unprecedented public response . . . In the rush to send more aid little is explained about the political and economic background and the public is left with the misleading and racist impression of dependent communities unable to help themselves. War on Want believes that emergency aid can only be effective if the real causes of the famine are understood.[39]

First of all, War on Want rejected the oversimplifying explanation of the famine as the consequence of a sustained drought: 'This simple picture is far from the truth. Agricultural practices imposed in colonial times, political and military conflicts and super power interests all play a role. In Ethiopia and Eritrea these factors have combined with a vengeance.' The NGO accused the Ethiopian government of pursuing a misconceived agricultural policy. Its land reforms and the establishment of state farms had not only hampered production, but also privileged the better-off farmers over poorer peasants. In addition, the Ethiopian military's attacks on the opposed liberation fronts of Tigray and Eritrea had deliberately targeted food production and distribution in those regions. This already complicated situation had been further worsened by the involvement of the rival superpowers, the United Stated and the Soviet Union. Both had tried to bolster their position in the strategically important Horn of Africa by means of humanitarian, economic and military aid. The USSR's military involvement on the side of Ethiopian government in particular had exacerbated the Ethiopian regime's counterproductive economic policies and military aggression.

War on Want's efforts were thus directed especially at communicating the complex causes of the famine in order to counteract the simplistic, emotional version conveyed by the media. Time and again, the NGO raised the issue of the iconography used by the media and Band Aid, and tried instead to promote a different image of the region: 'For the past few weeks the media has been dominated by images of the Ethiopian and Eritrean peoples as helpless and powerless. These photos of Eritrea, taken from War on Want's files of previous years, show that a different story is possible if international understanding, solidarity and support can be maintained.'[40] Above these words, photographs were printed of men mending a tractor tire, women merrily going about their agricultural work, and children learning and playing. War on Want deployed photographs that might illustrate the merits of helping people to help themselves as a means of counterbalancing the standard depiction of Ethiopia.

Yet the NGO also adopted the dominant starving-baby iconography when it was a matter of placing it in what it held to be the correct context. For instance, one pamphlet depicted an emaciated African child, an image familiar from and typical of TV coverage of the famine. War on Want, however, gave the photo the caption 'THIS MISERY IS MAN-MADE'.[41] In doing so, the charity clearly set its own interpretation apart from that of Band Aid and the media by emphasizing that the famine was not some sort of biblical plague, but that human actors were to be held responsible for it. Inside the pamphlet, War on Want explained its own approach to aiding development. The cover's slogan – THIS MISERY IS MAN-MADE' – was answered by the exhortation 'SO WE CAN CHANGE IT!' War on Want stressed that it was entirely possible, the drought notwithstanding, to grow ample food in the affected regions themselves. What was needed to prevent the next catastrophe was for the people there to be equipped with the necessary tools and the knowhow to use them. Given a little support and the means to provide for themselves, the people in Eritrea would indeed be able to improve their situation significantly: 'We are putting our money behind the efforts of these people who fight not just to help themselves, but to help their entire community to survive, this year, next year and in the future.' The NGO wanted to make it quite clear that such help towards self-help was not a mere chartable gesture, but entailed a deeper relationship with the Horn of Africa and its inhabitants. Donations to War on Want were thus 'the building blocks to make a fairer world. And a gesture of solidarity with the poor, the hungry and the oppressed'.

War on Want's efforts were effectively a countercampaign to Band Aid and the perception of the Ethiopian famine fostered by the media. The organization tried to spread its own interpretation of the causes of the famine, the course of events and what measures were to be taken towards its alleviation. Yet the leadership of War on Want was also concerned with aid being associated with the right attitude. Humanitarian commitment was to be understood as an act of 'solidarity' between people on an equal footing rather than a compassionate gesture to the underprivileged. In doing so, War on Want activists tried to defend central aspects of their own viewpoint, like the ideas of solidarity and help to self-help, against what they took to be a misguided discourse of compassion popularized by Band Aid and the media.

What War on Want thus offered the public was an alternative form of emotional involvement. Instead of anonymous natural phenomena, the NGO identified concrete human agents as culpable for the dire state of nutrition in Ethiopia and, in doing so, presented a target for anger and indignation. The effort to ascribe responsibility for the situation to specific actors thus constituted an alternative form of empathy, one grounded in the rejection of a designated group of people and their practices. War on Want's espousal of an alternative perspective of the famine represented the most ambitious attempt on the part of an NGO to distinguish itself from Band Aid and the media, and to put forth its own views. Central to these efforts was communicating a different interpretation of the causes of the crisis, assigning clear responsibilities and, accordingly, a different stance towards the recipients of aid, one that was characterized by solidarity rather than compassion.

The aim of this campaign was to bring the question of responsibility for the famine to public attention. That it had received such scant attention meant that the crimes of the Ethiopian regime, which were so central to War on Want's interpretation, were ignored in favour of the suffering populace rather than being justly condemned. How this 'Buchenwald of the 1980s'[42] was even possible was a question that War on Want accordingly answered by pointing to the Ethiopian regime: 'They [i.e. those affected by the famine] are the victims of that government's determination to starve its own people into submission.' George Galloway, the General Secretary of War on Want at the time, deliberately used a comparison with the Nazi death camps in order to brand the suffering of people in refugee camps in Ethiopia and countries bordering it as 'the work of evil men'. Drawing on this generally recognized shorthand for evil implied a sharp rejection of the established natural disaster narrative and underscored War on Want's interpretation of the region's plight.

Adaptation and Cooperation in Light of Celebrity Humanitarianism's Overwhelming Media Influence

It almost goes without saying that War on Want's attempts to reshape public perceptions were akin to tilting at windmills. The charity's leaflets, advertisements and occasional interviews could do little to counteract the images that had come to dominate television and the print media in equal measure since Michael Buerk's report and Band Aid/Live Aid. Public discourse had evidently taken on board the discourse of compassion. An indicator of how little resonance such alternative interpretations as those propagated by War on Want met with in the population at large can be found in the donations received by Band Aid compared to other NGOs. Data compiled by the DEC for donations received for Ethiopia between April 1984 and September 1985 shows Band Aid took in a total of some £34 million over that period.[43] The established NGOs lagged far behind. Save the Children was the most successful among them, with £15.8 million, followed by Oxfam's £11.8 million. Even the DEC itself only raised a total of £15 million. Christian Aid trailed some distance behind with £4.8 million, while War on Want, which had been the most forceful in setting itself apart from Band Aid and the media, managed to raise no more than £716,000. This meant that Band Aid alone accounted for more than a third of the total of £98 million that the people of Britain had given to the Ethiopian cause.

Such figures do not, of course, offer an accurate representation of public opinion regarding the famine and its causes. However, it does seem safe to conclude that by far the larger proportion of donors felt moved by Bob Geldof's way of presenting the famine. Conversely, the figures suggest that alternative interpretations stressing the famine's complexity reached the public to a far lesser degree than the discourse of compassion promoted by Band Aid.

The NGOs themselves were well aware that their own publicity was less successful than that of Band Aid – a problem discussed by staff at Christian Aid. Even before the Live Aid concerts of the summer of 1985, the organization had to concede that it could not compete with the coverage that Geldof's project was about to receive: 'Band Aid will be getting 16 hours of live TV coverage on July 13–14 for their concerts at Wembley Stadium and the JFK Stadium in Philadelphia.'[44] The aid workers were none the wiser after the mammoth events as to what conclusions to draw. 'After Live Aid – what?'[45] was the overwhelming question. What was certain – if nothing else – was that the Band Aid phenomenon spelled changes for the entire sector. 'Yes – the world is changed',[46] as Martin Bax, Managing Director of Christian Aid, concluded.

The NGOs were thus confronted with the challenge of dealing with the altered circumstances. For its part, however, Band Aid and Geldof himself in particular also seem to have had some reservations about working with the humanitarian establishment. A memorandum from Christian Aid concluded that Band Aid was trying to find new (and better) ways to provide humanitarian assistance, implicitly accusing the other NGOs of not being effective enough.[47] Yet Band Aid could not completely avoid working with other charities, on whose expertise it depended to identify worthwhile projects and schemes towards which the vast sums generated by record and ticket sales could be put.[48] As a consequence, Geldof and his staff called several meetings with British humanitarian organizations.

At these meetings, organizations such as Christian Aid and Oxfam tried to win Band Aid's representatives over to their approach. Their idea was that the attention that Band Aid had brought to the cause should be channelled in the NGOs' interests to publicize their approach to humanitarianism and the politics of development. A Christian Aid staffer expressed the opportunities he saw in an upcoming meeting between the DEC charities and Band Aid as follows:

> Band Aid/Live Aid has brought the problems of African famine to more people's attention than years of work by the DEC agencies. Cooperating with them does not imply total endorsement of the BandAid [*sic*] approach. It is however a way of reaching a wider group of people and we should be present if there is any possibility of influencing them in development education.[49]

Christian Aid, along with other major NGOs like Oxfam and Save the Children, thus took a different approach from War on Want, which sought publicly to distance itself from Band Aid.

Attempts to influence Band Aid on a programmatic level were flanked by close cooperation on specific projects. The NGOs recommended projects that they themselves were running or with which they were in contact.[50] In doing so, their negotiators seem to have succeeded in convincing Band Aid of their views regarding the necessity of supporting particular projects. Ultimately, Band Aid agreed to put the larger part of its funds towards long-term projects of the kind favoured by NGOs over short-term relief efforts.[51] For instance, Band Aid too soon began stress the importance of 'Rehabilitation/Long Term Development'.[52]

That the NGOs, their criticism notwithstanding, cooperated with Band Aid on projects suggests that financial considerations may have played a part. At any rate, those involved at Christian Aid discussed whether it might not be preferable to claim funds from Band Aid itself before they were spent on other, less useful purposes: 'Liveaid [*sic*] has very large sums of money which could be usefully channeled to projects we are supporting / want to support. There is a risk that this money will not be used to best effect if we simply do nothing.'[53] Christian Aid's concern was that the income from record sales and tickets to the Live Aid concerts should be used to support the developmental agenda that the organization itself espoused.

Even War on Want, which was particularly emphatic in distancing itself from the mainstream media depiction of the famine, was willing to cooperate with Band Aid if doing so meant that funds could be raised for projects of its own.[54] Indirectly, War on Want even benefited considerably from the attention that Band Aid and the media had directed towards the Horn of Africa. By taking charge of consortiums in which NGOs combined their relief efforts for Eritrea and Tigray, War on Want greatly increased its budget and became a key actor in nongovernmental intervention in the region.

Aside from direct cooperation with Band Aid, the financial and media success of celebrity humanitarianism also influenced the manner in which NGOs subsequently conducted their own public relations. Both War on Want and Christian Aid tried to draw conclusions from the Band Aid phenomenon and incorporate elements of the pop-cultural presentation of humanitarian concerns into their own campaigns. Although both charities, since the 1960s, had put on concerts and solicited support from people in the public eye, such efforts were never successful on the scale of Band Aid. Only a short time after Live Aid, a Christian Aid staffer suggested future advertising in youth and pop magazines too:

> Christian Aid should be looking for other ways of making the connection between Live-Aid supporters and broader aid and development issues. We *recommend* Christian Aid advertisements, written with Live-Aid in mind, to appear in popular and music press and Time Out, etc, to tie-in with the lobby and to let everyone know that they can do more for Africa in this way.[55]

War on Want tried its own adaptations of celebrity humanitarianism. For instance, the NGO advertised concerts by Howard Jones in the pages of *Just Seventeen*, a magazine directed at teenage girls. Jones, a singer well known in the mid 1980s, had already performed at Live Aid,[56] and the promise of special appearances was intended to raise money for local healthcare workers in Eritrea and thus improve medical care in the region. Under the slogan 'You could be helping these people and Howard Jones could be playing a free concert right here', the campaign was squarely targeted at schools. Pupils and their teachers were asked to collect money for War on Want, and Howard Jones would play at the two schools that collected the most. What was striking about this campaign is that although it deployed images from Eritrea (albeit not in the Band Aid mould), the facts about the projects that were to be supported were given visibly less space than the celebrity figurehead. Unlike in War on Want's usual campaigning material, the emphasis was placed less on the charity's work on the ground than on the chance to have Howard Jones appear at one's school.

Although campaigns of this kind increased over the following years, they continued to make up a mere fraction of 'ordinary' fundraising efforts. Nonetheless, their prominence is likely to have influenced the public perception of the NGOs. Appeals supported by celebrities probably helped them reach new and broader sections of the public. However, since these campaigns gave little room to the analysis and discussion of various approaches to development policy and humanitarian aid, they appear likely to have promoted rather than corrected simplistic views of the 'Third World' – much against their authors' intentions.

Conclusion

There are *three* conclusions to be drawn from the media's reporting on the Ethiopian famine and the ways in which the NGOs dealt with it. *First*, it must be stated that Michael Buerk's TV report and the ensuing Band Aid phenomenon made no mention of key factors in the unfolding of the crisis – namely, the role of the Ethiopian regime – and in doing so promoted the simplistic account of a natural disaster. Although the West was not held responsible for having brought about the famine, it was tasked with its swift relief. Bob Geldof's Band Aid project picked up this emotional charge and demanded compassion from its audience for the people in Ethiopia in order to put a quick end to their suffering.

Second, it should be put on record that nearly all British humanitarian NGOs were uncomfortable with this form of oversimplified representation. Those in charge criticized the fact that Band Aid and the media kept silent over the famine's true causes and perpetuated the misleading natural disaster narrative. They further criticized that racist stereotypes about Africa were being spread by representing its people as needy and incapable of helping themselves. This was seen as a danger to the image that the NGOs themselves sought to lodge in the public consciousness: that of an able and self-determined Africa in need of nothing so much as help in helping itself. What was at stake, then, was the 'right' emotional attitude towards the continent, an attitude that Band Aid threatened to reverse.

Third, although this consensus was widely held, the established NGOs could not succeed in asserting their own interpretation in the public sphere against that propounded by Band Aid and the media. Once a narrative had established itself so broadly and effectively, there was apparently nothing to be done about it. Faced with Band Aid's runaway success, most other NGOs, including Christian Aid and War on Want, tried to make arrangements with Geldof's project. One such approach was to persuade Band Aid to place stronger emphasis on long-term development. Needless to say, the desire to participate in the immense attention and financial resources that Band Aid had mobilized played a part too. The different approaches to dealing with the pop charity demonstrate how uncertain the NGOs were about how to react to Band Aid's vast appeal. In this contingent situation, the established charities had to find new ways of adapting to changed circumstances.

Therefore, the interpretation held by a large number of scholars – that NGOs wilfully used simplistic interpretations about Africa in order to maximize benefits for their *humanitarian industry* – must be modified. They did have massive reservations against those simplistic perceptions and tried to correct them. However, they were confronted by a dominant discourse in the media and they found it to be nearly impossible to counteract it.

Matthias Kuhnert holds a PhD in Modern and Contemporary History. From 2012 to 2016, he worked as a researcher and lecturer at the Ludwig-Maximilians-University Munich. His research focuses on the history of nongovernmental humanitarian organizations in the aid and development sector in the post-1945 area as well as the history of emotions. In 2017 he published his PhD dissertation entitled *Humanitäre Kommunikation. Entwicklung und Emotionen bei britischen NGOs 1945–1990.*

Notes

This article is a shortened and revised translation of a chapter from my book published in 2017; translation by Joe Paul Kroll. Cf. M. Kuhnert, *Humanitäre Kommunikation: Entwicklung und Emotionen bei britischen NGOs 1945–1990* (Berlin: De Gruyter Oldenbourg, 2017), 225–61.

 1. A. de Waal, *Famine Crimes: Politics and the Disaster Relief Industry in Africa* (London: African Rights and the International African Institute, 1997), 106.

2. S. Franks, *Reporting Disasters: Famine, Aid, Politics and the Media* (London: Hurst, 2013), 5; A. Jones, 'The Disasters Emergency Committee (DEC) and the Humanitarian Industry in Britain, 1963–85', *Twentieth Century British History* 26 (2015), 573–601, at 585–86.
3. See T.R. Müller, 'The Long Shadow of Band Aid Humanitarianism: Revisiting the Dynamics between Famine and Celebrity', *Third World Quarterly* 34 (2013). 470–84; T.R. Müller, '"The Ethiopian Famine" Revisited: Band Aid and the Antipolitics of Celebrity Humanitarian Action', *Disasters* 37 (2013), 61–79. For a positive view, see F. Westley, 'Bob Geldof and Live Aid: The Affective Side of Global Social Innovation', *Human Relations* 44 (1991), 1011–36; de Waal, *Famine Crimes,* 106–32.
4. See Jones, *DEC*; Müller, '"The Ethiopian Famine" Revisited'; Franks, *Reporting Disasters.*
5. My analysis of both organizations is based on archival sources, specifically the papers of War on Want and Christian Aid kept in the library of the School of Oriental and African Studies (SOAS), London. In the following, papers from the archive of War on Want are abbreviated as WOW, while those of Christian Aid are abbreviated as CA. On these organizations and the British humanitarian sector in general, see M. Hilton et al., *Politics of Expertise: How NGOs Shaped Modern Britain* (Oxford: Oxford University Press, 2013); M. Hilton et al., 'International Aid and Development NGOs in Britain and Human Rights since 1945', *Humanity* 3 (2012), 449–72; C. Saunders, 'British Humanitarian, Aid and Development NGOs, 1949–Present', in N.J. Crowson et al. (eds), *NGOs in Contemporary Britain: Non-state Actors in Society and Politics since 1945* (Basingstoke: Palgrave Macmillan, 2009), 38–58; K. O'Sullivan, 'A "Global Nervous System": The Rise and Rise of European Humanitarian NGOs, 1945–1985', in M. Frey et al. (eds), *International Organizations and Development, 1945–1990* (Basingstoke: Palgrave Macmillan, 2014), 196–219; Kuhnert, *Humanitäre Kommunikation.*
6. On the famine's causes, see de Waal, *Famine Crimes,* 115–21.
7. Franks, *Reporting Disasters,* 20.
8. Ibid., 11–30.
9. M. Buerk, 'Famine in Ethiopia' (1984). Retrieved 5 March 2015 from http://news.bbc .co.uk/2/hi/8315248.stm.
10. Franks, *Reporting Disasters,* 34–35.
11. Buerk, 'Famine in Ethiopia'.
12. Müller, '"The Ethiopian Famine" Revisited', 66; de Waal, *Famine Crimes,* 122.
13. T. Vaux, *The Selfish Altruist: Relief Work in Famine and War* (London: Earthscan, 2001), 52.
14. The British Council of Churches. Christian Aid. Latin America and Caribbean Regional Committee, 27 April 1982. Report on Appeal for Central American Refugees of Disasters Emergency Committee. SOAS, CA4/G/4/1.
15. Articles typical of the press coverage following Buerk's report include: 'Ethiopia Losing the Battle against Starvation', *The Times* (25 October 1984); D. Cross, 'British Emergency Food Aid for Ethiopia Famine', *The Times* (25 October 1984); 'British Aid for Famine Victims', *The Times* (25 October 1984); J. MacManus, 'Boost Airlift for Food, Ethiopia Urged', *Daily Telegraph* (25 October 1984); 'More Food Aid to Be Sent to Ethiopia', *The Guardian* (25 October 1984).
16. One article that is representative of many others is: 'Ethiopia Losing the Battle against Starvation', *The Times* (25 October 1984). This article ascribes the famine to the results of a 'decade-long drought'; the Ethiopian government's wars had served merely to complicate matters.
17. Cross, 'British Emergency Food Aid for Ethiopia Famine'.

18. 'Battle to Beat Famine: Ethiopia Aid Floods in', *The Daily Telegraph* (27 October 1984).
19. M. Simmons, 'A Famine the World Refused to Believe', *The Guardian* (25 October 1984).
20. F. D'Souza, 'The Tragedy That Need Never Have Happened', *The Guardian* (26 October 1984).
21. M. Simmons, 'A Famine the World Refused to Believe', *The Guardian* (25 October 1984).
22. Ibid.
23. This tallies with Lilie Chouliaraki's observation, according to which laying blame is an important factor in generating sympathy. Without the question concerning responsibility, Chouliaraki argues, important elements of a narrative of suffering able to arouse compassion are lacking. See L. Chouliaraki, *The Spectatorship of Suffering* (London: Sage Publications, 2006), 104–5.
24. Letter to the editor from father A.J. Baxter, *The Times* (26 October 1984).
25. Letter to the editor from J. Macgregor, *Daily Telegraph* (27 October 1984).
26. Letter to the editor from C.A. Abrams, *The Times* (26 October 1984).
27. Letter to the editor from father A.J. Baxter, *The Times* (26 October 1984).
28. Clifford Longley, The Pop-Muezzin's Call to Prayer', *The Times* (24 December 1984).
29. 'A Record for Pettiness', *The Guardian* (20 December 1984).
30. '£6m Aid Promise for Ethiopia', *The Times* (5 January 1985).
31. To this day, Geldof refuses to admit that the humanitarian measures taken at the time might in any way have influenced the conflict, and denies the possibility of funds being misappropriated for military purposes. S. Franks, 'Why Bob Geldof Has Got it Wrong', *British Journalism Review* 21 (2010), 51–56.
32. Müller, 'Long Shadow', 473–75.
33. Ibid.; Müller, '"The Ethiopian Famine" Revisited', de Waal, *Famine Crimes,* 121–23.
34. For an exhaustive analysis of these images propagated by humanitarian NGOs to influence perceptions of the Global South see Kuhnert, *Humanitäre Kommunikation,* 96–161, 184–225. For a briefer summary, see Saunders, 'British Humanitarian, Aid and Development NGOs'.
35. For this and the following quotation, see Memo Mary Galvin to Area Secretaries, 22 February 1985. SOAS, CA4/A/16/7.
36. Quotations from: Memorandum Jean Harrison to All Area Staff and Contract Volunteers, Band Aid's 'Schools for Africa' Project, 3 September 1985. SOAS, CA4/A/16/7.
37. For this and the following quotation, see Letter A. Pennington (Oxfam) to other agencies, 1 August 1985. SOAS, CA4/A/16/7.
38. On the NGOs' criticism of Band Aid and the representation of the famine in the media discussed here, cf. also: Hilton et al., *Politics of Expertise,* 176–77.
39. Quotations from: leaflet, The Politics of Famine. War on Want 1985. SOAS, WOW/107/00906.
40. Images of the Poor, in *War on Want News* Winter 1984/85. SOAS, WOW/249/0248.
41. For this and the following quotation, see undated leaflet, War on Want, This Misery is Man-Made, likely 1985. SOAS, WOW/249/02485.
42. For this and the three following quotations, see George Galloway, Eye Witness Sudan, in War on Want News Spring 1985. SOAS, WOW/107/00906.
43. These figures are taken from: DEC Secretariat, Fundraising for Famine in Africa by British Public Channelled through Voluntary Relief and Development Agencies, December 1985. SOAS, CA4/A/16/6.
44. Memo John Montagu to Area Staff, Africa Section and Appeals Unit, 5 July 1985. SOAS, CA4/A/16/7.

45. Memo Paul Renshaw to Martin Bax, undated. SOAS, CA4/A/16/7.
46. Memo Martin Bax to Paul Renshaw, 17 July 1985. SOAS, CA4/A/16/7.
47. Memo John Montagu to Area Staff, Africa Section and Appeals Unit, 5 July 1985. SOAS, CA4/A/16/7.
48. Memorandum Justin Phipps to Carlisle/Jenny/Martin/John M., Live Aid, 4 September 1985. SOAS, CA4/A/16/7.
49. Ibid.
50. For instance, Christian Aid advised its partners in Africa to apply to Band Aid for funds, appearing as a mediator between the two sides. This emerges from the correspondence between Christian Aid and Band Aid. Memo Mary Galvin (Christian Aid) to Penny Jenden (Band Aid), 1 October 1985. SOAS, CA4/A/16/7.
51. This can be deduced from the minutes of talks between representatives of Band Aid and the NGOs, though the established charities continued to criticize individual PR efforts and hurried schemes on Band Aid's part. Memorandum Anna C-J to Mary/Justin/Sarah, Band Aid Meeting: 23/24 September 1985. SOAS, CA4/A/16/7.
52. Band Aid Trust/Live Aid Foundation. A Statement of General Policy, undated, likely September 1985, SOAS, CA4/A/16/7.
53. Memorandum Justin Phipps to Carlisle/Jenny/Martin/John M., Live Aid, 4 September 1985. SOAS, CA4/A/16/7.
54. For example, Band Aid was part of the Eritrea Inter Agency Consortium, which was chaired by Christian Aid. SOAS, brochure Eritrea Inter Agency Consortium. Funding Development Programmes in Eritrea in co-operation with the Eritrean Relief Association, undated, probably 1986. WOW/107/00907.
55. Memorandum Kate Philipps to Martin Bax, Live Aid, 19 July 1985. SOAS, CA4/A/16/7.
56. War on Want leaflet, 'Howard Jones', in *Just Seventeen,* undated, probably 1986. SOAS, WOW/107/00906.

Bibliography

Chouliaraki, L. *The Spectatorship of Suffering.* London: Sage, 2006.
De Waal, A. *Famine Crimes: Politics and the Disaster Relief Industry in Africa.* London: African Rights and the International African Institute, 1997.
Franks, S. 'Why Bob Geldof Has Got it Wrong'. *British Journalism Review* 21 (2010), 51–56.
———. *Reporting Disasters: Famine, Aid, Politics and the Media.* London: Hurst, 2013.
Hilton, M. et al. 'International Aid and Development NGOs in Britain and Human Rights since 1945'. *Humanity* 3 (2012), 449–72.
———. *Politics of Expertise: How NGOs Shaped Modern Britain.* Oxford: Oxford University Press, 2013.
Jones, A. 'The Disasters Emergency Committee (DEC) and the Humanitarian Industry in Britain, 1963–85'. *Twentieth Century British History* 26 (2015), 573–601.
Kuhnert, M. *Humanitäre Kommunikation: Entwicklung und Emotionen bei britischen NGOs 1945–1990.* Berlin: De Gruyter Oldenbourg, 2017.
Müller, T.R. '"The Ethiopian Famine" Revisited: Band Aid and the Antipolitics of Celebrity Humanitarian Action', *Disasters* 37 (2013), 61–79.
———. 'The Long Shadow of Band Aid Humanitarianism: Revisiting the Dynamics between Famine and Celebrity'. *Third World Quarterly* 34 (2013), 470–84.

O'Sullivan, K. 'A "Global Nervous System": The Rise and Rise of European Humanitarian NGOs, 1945–1985', in M. Frey et al. (eds), *International Organizations and Development, 1945–1990* (Basingstoke: Palgrave Macmillan, 2014), 196–219.

Saunders, C. 'British Humanitarian, Aid and Development NGOs, 1949–Present', in N.J. Crowson et al. (eds), *NGOs in Contemporary Britain: Non-state Actors in Society and Politics since 1945* (Basingstoke: Palgrave Macmillan, 2009), 38–58.

Vaux, T. *The Selfish Altruist: Relief Work in Famine and War.* London: Earthscan, 2001.

Westley, F. 'Bob Geldof and Live Aid: The Affective Side of Global Social Innovation', *Human Relations* 44 (1991), 1011–1036.

12

The Audience of Distant Suffering and the Question of (In)Action

Maria Kyriakidou

One of the most discussed and yet elusive concepts in studies of the mediation of distant suffering and humanitarian communication is the audience. Although audiences and their responses to human suffering are the ultimate target of humanitarian communication, it is only rarely that they have been empirically studied, despite the abundance of theoretical arguments and assumptions about them. This blind spot is even more surprising given the increasing prominence of the mediation of distant suffering as a field of interest in media studies, within a broader preoccupation with the moral role of media as institutions and representations in a globalized world. Despite this broader moral turn, questions of audience engagement and interpretation of media representations of suffering have hitherto received limited academic attention.

A second blind spot in the way that audiences of suffering have been approached concerns the limited ways in which their responses have been conceptualized. The relevant literature tends to discuss or even evaluate the audience with regard to two main reactions or modes of engagement, namely compassion and action. As the desired effects of humanitarian communication, these two reactions are often approached as intertwined: compassion seems to be the prerequisite of action. What ultimately underscores such an approach to audience engagement with the suffering of others is its conceptualization as a direct response to media images. The success of humanitarian communication, be it news or campaigns, is measured with regard to its immediate effect on the audience. In this context, any kind of communication that does not have a measurable or obvious effect is critiqued as a failure. In other words, a number of empirical studies or theoretical arguments about the audience of suffering tend to adopt assumptions consonant with the media effects paradigm, itself a largely discredited approach within the field of audience research.[1]

What I wish to argue here is that the audiences of mediated suffering, despite the extraordinary experience of witnessing human pain through the media,[2] should be conceptualized as locally situated actors embedded in particular national, cultural and social contexts. Their responses are therefore mediated not only by media texts as representations but also by the viewers' evaluations of these representations, as well as broader discursive frameworks of their everyday life. In this context, emotions of empathy or compassion, as well as decisions on whether to act on the suffering of others and contribute to humanitarian relief efforts, are taken within specific social and cultural contexts. These contexts are often neglected within studies of the audiences of distant suffering.

In what follows, I will further unpack this argument, drawing upon an empirical study of audiences in Greece. After discussing the relevant literature on the audience of suffering, both theoretical and empirical, I will suggest that an approach to audience engagement that goes beyond the dichotomies of compassion/denial or action/inaction allows for a more nuanced approach to the audiences as culturally and socially embedded individuals. In particular, I will illustrate how the context of reception, in this case Greece as a cultural and political landscape, is implicated in audience decisions to act upon the suffering of others.

The Audience of Suffering: Between Compassion and Apathy

Discussions on the potential of the media to mobilize audiences and enable the formation of publics that will act to alleviate suffering witnessed through the media have been often underlined by an implicit pessimism. There are two concepts that have dominated relevant debates and underscored academic work over the last couple of decades, namely those of 'compassion fatigue'[3] and 'denial'.[4]

Coined by Susan Moeller, the 'compassion fatigue' thesis assumes that the continuous flow of images of human suffering leads to the viewers' emotional overload to a point where suffering and pain become banal, impossible to instantiate any emotion and undermining any impulse for action.[5] Images of horror have become frequent in audience experience and therefore treated by viewers' as 'banal' due to their 'overfamiliarity' and 'inevitability', the argument goes.[6] Journalistic conventions and the rules of news production along with the time restraints of news bulletins allow only for a superficial presentation of news stories, including those of suffering in distant places. At the same time, it is argued, the need for audience attention favours sensationalism expressed through the mere horror of images of pain without the necessary explanations of the factors that resulted in this horrific outcome. 'Television', Moeller argues, 'is essentially a headline service.'[7] In this context, images of suffering become overly familiar, similar to one another, failing to engage the audience.

Cohen juxtaposes to this 'populist psychology thesis', as he describes it, a more sociologically nuanced argument.[8] What often happens, he opposes, is 'less compassion fatigue than compassion *avoidance*'.[9] He attributes this to a general sociology of 'denial and bystanding', the essence of which is 'the active looking away, a sense of a situation so utterly hopeless and incomprehensible that we cannot bear to think about it'.[10] Furthermore, what is at stake, Cohen argues, is the 'normalization' and 'routinization' of suffering as the loss of the potential impact of suffering due to the viewers' familiarity with it.[11] Audience engagement meets its limit 'after activating the memory trace that "this is just the sort of thing that's always happening in places like that"'.[12] This should not necessarily be translated as the viewers' loss of the sense of conventional definitions of normal and their emotional numbness towards the suffering of others, as the compassion fatigue thesis implies.

This binary conceptualization of audience reception as compassion fatigue or denial has been largely reflected in the hitherto limited number of empirical studies in the field. Interviewing audiences in Norway and Sweden on media reports of war and violence, Höijer describes the complexity of audience responses to suffering as a 'a two-sided effect of global compassion on the one hand, and ignorance and compassion fatigue on the other' expressed through 'different forms of compassion as well as different forms of indifference'.[13] Focusing on audiences of humanitarian appeals in a U.K.-based research with focus groups, Seu focuses on the issue of audience (in)action and illustrates the different ways in which people discursively distance themselves from the suffering of others and justify their unresponsiveness to human rights appeals.[14] In another more recent study in the United Kingdom, Martin Scott explores audience mediated encounters with distant suffering across a range of television programmes and describes the engagement with these encounters as characterized mostly by indifference and solitary enjoyment.[15]

Moving beyond a narrow focus on audience *reactions* to media reports and humanitarian appeals, either as merely emotional responses to specific stories or translated in terms of action and contribution to relief efforts, I would like to argue here that the mediation of distant suffering should be studied beyond the 'media text-as-trigger approach' that seems to dominate much of the discussion. Instead, audiences need to be seen as situated within an environment of different resources of knowledge about the world and the suffering of others, where the media constitute an indispensable but not the only or even the major part of this environment. In his ethnographic study of middle-class and low-income audiences in the disaster-prone Philippines, Ong illustrates how people's engagement with images of suffering, distant or proximal, is mediated by classed moralities that shape judgements about the sufferers and the media that represent them.[16] What is highlighted in this study, and often neglected in most accounts of the mediation of distant suffering, is the significant role of the cultural and social context in the ways in which people make sense of the suffering of others.

Therefore, we need to problematize the nature of the audience as mere 'respondents' or 'receivers' of media messages of distant suffering. Instead, they are participants in a mediated global civic space, where the visibility of the vulnerability of distant others may form the basis of moral relationships and solidarity across geographical and cultural borders.[17] In this context, the emotional and moral implications of watching the suffering of others need to be theorized not only in relation to responses to particular media texts, but also as a generalized experience of the audience as witnesses, rendered possible by mediated encounters with distant suffering.[18] In this context, the focus moves from viewers' relationship to particular texts to the possibilities of agency opened up by the media as resources of knowledge about the distant.[19] This agency is mediated by media representational repertoires, which are often uneven and biased in their construction of hierarchies of life that define whose misfortune matters[20] and which lives are 'grievable'.[21] These hierarchies position the viewer in different kinds of proximity and connectivity with the sufferers, constructing maximal distance with some while rendering others as worthy of engagement and commitment.[22] At the same time, however, mediation is an intertextual process insofar as 'social resources and experiences are drawn upon in the reception and interpretation of the media'.[23] This means that audience responses and modes of engagement are contingent upon not only media texts as representations but also broader discursive frameworks people draw upon to make sense of them, including their evaluations of media representations.

In what follows, I will try to illustrate the dynamic nature of audience engagement with distant suffering regarding the question of action at a distance. I will do so by drawing upon an empirical study of Greek audiences discussing news stories of disasters and human suffering. I will argue that viewers employ a variety of social and political discourses in making sense of such stories. Most importantly, the viewers' agency vis-à-vis the suffering of distant others as expressed and enacted (or not) through action at a distance should be considered not merely in relation to or as a direct response to media coverage, but also in relation to those broader discourses that frame viewers' understanding of public action and their position as public actors in the social world.

The Research Project

The discussion that follows draws upon a research project designed to explore the ways in which audiences in Greece engage with news stories of distant suffering. The study explored the way in which Greek viewers construct their moral agency vis-à-vis human suffering they witness through television news and was empirically based on focus group discussions. As the research focus was on the mediation of distant suffering, participants were questioned on their impressions of and engagement with different disasters, and their possible contributions to relevant campaigns.

Focus group discussions were employed to explore audience discourses on the premise that in the interaction of the discussion, a greater diversity of views is being expressed and common sense assumptions are being challenged and negotiated.[24] At the same time, the active construction of meanings among discussants places the focus on viewers as participants in the process of mediation. Twelve focus groups were conducted, amounting to forty-seven participants in total. The participants were selected based on purposeful sampling, in order to maximize diversity of opinions, and were recruited through the snowballing method. They varied in terms of gender, socioeconomic status and age, with the younger cohort comprising people in their twenties and the older of people in their forties and fifties. The groups were mostly homogeneous and consisted of peers, on the assumption that their existence beyond the research setting would contribute to their discussions being more illustrative of their everyday nature.[25] This purposeful sampling reflected an attempt to explore a diversity of discourses and ways of articulating agency rather than an objective of putting the differences between the audience groupings into a strict sense. In this context, the diverse discourses are approached as *collective,* namely 'mutually constructed by the social interactions among members of particular subgroups', rather than as *taxonomic,* 'distributed across the individuals within particular sociodemographic subgroups'.[26]

Discussions covered a variety of events that participants found relevant to the concepts of global disasters and distant suffering. Questions covered memories of such events, and their emotional impact, as well as the viewers' possible participation in humanitarian appeals and other forms of contributing in efforts to help suffering victims of distant disasters. The focus here will be in the different discourses viewers drew upon in discussing these issues. In particular, the chapter will discuss the question of action at a distance, which will be illustrated here as dependent not only on the media but also on broader discourses about civic action and political participation.

There were two main themes underscoring discussions about viewers' actions with regard to humanitarian appeals and contributions to relief efforts as a response to the witnessing of suffering on the media. The first was that this action was rather limited both in terms of its extent and the variety of forms it would take, as it was mostly expressed in the form of participation to telethons. The second important theme was that participants justified their inaction on the basis of two broader discourses: a generalized culture of mistrust and their sense of powerlessness in the public space.

Telethons as Media Events

The telethon has been described by Tester as a 'lengthy television broadcast', which 'asks the audience to support a specific charitable cause or to address a particular range of suffering and deprivation by pledging donations by telephone or participation in specially organized events'.[27] As a very peculiar television genre, telethons mark 'the entry of television into a fund-raising role', while suspending the routine television programming.[28] Telethons attract viewers in three ways: by giving them the sense that 'something can be done' to alleviate the suffering and misery of other people and that viewers as individuals can have an impact in this effort; by including celebrities, who in this context represent the possibility that serious causes do not necessarily entail 'introspection' and 'inwardness'; and by connecting viewers with a community of similar individuals, such as the national community.[29] However, what was evident in the focus group discussions was that, the effectiveness of telethons to motivate the viewers aside, it was the telethon as a media event organized by and with celebrities that made a bigger impression on the viewers rather than the causes for which they felt the need to donate. This can be seen in the quote below, where the telethon is identified through its organizers rather than its cause:[30]

> Irini: I made a phone call to a telethon this year.
>
> Nana: Which one?
>
> Irini: This last one, for some kids, who was it for?
>
> Nana: Do you mean the one that Menegaki presented?
>
> Kiki: I think it was on Alpha Channel, Menegaki.
>
> Irini: Yes, on Alpha.
>
> Nana: By Hope Foundation.
>
> Irini: Yes.
>
> Nana: For something anticancer.
>
> Irini: You just make a phone call and the charging amount, let's say, goes to these little kids. Just this.
>
> (Female, twenties, middle class, FG3)

The action taken by the viewer is not described as a response to a specific instance of suffering or need, but as the response to a telethon. The latter is more easily associated with its celebrity organizer ('Menegaki')[31] rather than the cause that was at the centre of its organization. The appeal is described in vague terms as 'for some kids' and 'something anticancer'. Telethons become so integrated in the appeal to act in relation to a disaster or a charitable cause in general that they ultimately overshadow the significance of the cause. This can be seen as an extreme consequence of the assimilation of modern humanitarianism to the media logic,[32] which ultimately distracts attention from the suffering itself, projecting it onto the media spectacle instead. Viewers attribute significance to their actions as a contribution to a media appeal and, in a way, a form of participation in a media event rather than as a form of action aimed at specific suffering others.

It was often the case that participants would find it hard to specify the appeals they responded to or the context of the events that the telethons were organized to contribute to; they would only remember that they did send financial help, made a phone call or sent a text message as a response to 'some' telethon.

The specificity of events and of the different appeals would fade from memory; disasters and other charity appeals would all conflate to the single category of 'telethons', as seems to be the case in the extract below:

> Dimitris: I have sent, for example, to various telethons that take place in Greece in order to help people in Ethiopia, let's say, that Mega Channel organized, I mean, telethons and stuff, or in order to build an oncologic hospital and stuff, yes, I have sent for stuff like that, not only for the Tsunami.
>
> (Male, 27, middle class, FG8)

The prominence of telethons in instigating audience contributions illustrates public action at a distance as highly contingent upon the media and their orchestrated efforts to motivate audiences towards taking action, in this case the telethons. Significant in this media orchestration is the presence of celebrities in attracting viewers to the telethon.[33] The involvement of celebrities with charity and humanitarianism has been especially widespread over the last couple of decades as part of the expansion of practices of marketing of the charity and humanitarian sector, and the simultaneous increase in strategies of branding celebrities.[34] This synergy has been advocated, on the one hand, as necessary in order to raise the profile of humanitarian campaigns and expand their reach to the mainstream public.[35] On the other hand, the use of celebrities by charities and nongovernmental organizations (NGOs) has been heavily criticized for attracting attention to some problems and away from others, glossing over structural inequalities and emphasizing the role of the privileged as benign figures and ultimately ideologically obscuring the implications of capitalism in the reproduction of the poor in the world and global crises.[36] The analysis of the focus group discussions was revealing in terms of the problematic relationship between celebrity endorsement and charity appeals. On the one hand, the participation of popular celebrities in telethons seems to attract audience interest and motivate viewers to contribute to the relief efforts. On the other hand, celebrity-led telethons are described by the viewers as media spectacles, where the spectacular deflects attention from the cause of the appeal and the sufferers.

Mediation and the Culture of Mistrust

This limited form of action aside, viewers admitted to rarely contributing to relief efforts and humanitarian appeals. Mistrust was a concept often discussed in relation to this reluctance. Participants in the focus groups would express their mistrust both in terms of the motives of the people contributing to the relief efforts and, most often, in terms of the institutions mediating between the actions of the public and the delivering of aid to the affected victims.

At the heart of such expressions of mistrust was the nature of viewers' action as selective and media-dependent. In the extract below, a young participant expresses this position against media-instigated public action:

> Simos: I just cannot understand the concept of charity. I mean, it sounds a bit . . . that we do it in order to get a key into heaven, let's say, to get rid of the guilt. That's it, this is why I am a bit negative and even more because we live in a society, which is the way it is. Which lives through television. In which everything is business, let's say. It is not something which happens because of altruism, in no way.
>
> (Male, 26, middle class, FG1)

Aware of the embedding of media-staged humanitarianism in the economics of the culture industry, viewers apply their own critical readings of telethons as expressions of modern charity and express their suspicions of humanitarianism as a whole.

In the extract below, the criticism is centred on telethons as a media spectacle from which both television channels and the participating celebrities profit:

> Gerasimos: I don't give to the telethons, because I am against the telethons, they are just a scam. They are only organized for the spectators, I am sure of this, there is no other way. And let me tell you, Stai[37] was on [television] the other day, she earns 600,000 per year, and she was talking with Lazopoulos,[38] and she said 'we should do something! What should we do? Let's do a telethon!'. Why doesn't she just say: [I give] 100,000 Euros! Since she earns 600, she can't live without 100? I am fanatically against telethons! Because it is only to show off! And then you see [on the screen]: Mrs Katina: 50 Euros, Mrs Stavroula: 2 Euros and stuff. But how do I know? Will she give it tomorrow? Because she does call, but will she go to the bank the next day? And in the end they say: 'we have gathered so many millions!'. These millions, have they really been gathered? Who gathers it? Where does it go? And who spends it? What do they spend it on?
>
> (Male, 56, middle class, FG11)

By constructing mediated charity and humanitarian appeals as media spectacles that address them as consumers and by resenting this position, viewers move away from their relationship with the people in need and focus on their relationship with the media. Mistrust in humanitarianism and its mediation therefore distances the viewer form the scene of suffering.

If scepticism towards humanitarianism and especially its transformation into a spectacle was one way in which viewers expressed their mistrust as a discursive strategy to justify their inaction, lack of trust in the way their contributions would be handled was another way. This was similar in its consequence of drawing attention away from the relationship between viewers and sufferers, and victimizing the audience as donors. In this case, however, mistrust was not expressed towards the idea of humanitarianism as sustained by the media, but towards the way audience donations are (mis)handled in their way to the victims. Suspicion was therefore targeted more specifically towards the mediators of humanitarian help, namely NGOs, governments and the organizers of the appeals, as well as local organizations such as the church. Two main arguments were supporting this suspicion: first, rumours and reports of mishandling of the funds; and, second, the apparent lack of any evident results emanating from aid pledges. Such are the arguments underlining the following discussion:

The Audience of Distant Suffering and the Question of (In)Action   289

Penelope: Even if we did send before, I have stopped now having heard that a lot of food gets rotten, a lot of medicines expire because they throw them aside, I mean, there is not a right way to transfer them.

Chrysa: A kind of co-ordination so that they arrive there!

Penelope: Today that I walked into the supermarket, there was a basket saying 'Help for Lebanon'. I didn't reach my hand to give something . . .

Chrysa: No, me neither!

Penelope: . . . because I thought, where will all these go? Will they reach their destination?

Chrysa: Because we see on television that they say that they cannot reach it . . .

(Female, forties and fifties, middle class, FG4)

This generalized culture of mistrust in political and social institutions is embedded in the broader political culture in Greece and forms a framework for understanding politics and public life.[39] Expressions of such mistrust, Demertzis argues, are part of the broader culture of political cynicism in Greece, itself discursively constructed through the articulation of a varied vocabulary of affective expressions, such as despair, detachment, sarcasm, indignation, pessimism, fatalism and irony.[40] As such, mistrust is embedded in a wider cultural vocabulary, thus enabling the rationalization of public inaction and more specifically audience inaction and unresponsiveness towards the suffering of faraway others.[41] Framed in broader cultural discourses of mistrust, scepticism towards the organizations that staged and managed humanitarian appeals was translated into rationalized detachment from distant suffering. This rationalization took place in two steps: first, the placement of responsibility on the organizations and institutions managing action at a distance; and, second, the undermining of the effectiveness of these organizations. Implicit in this line of argumentation was the lack of control of the viewers over their contributions.

Mediated Agency and Powerlessness

Expressions of mistrust in humanitarianism, and especially institutions, displaced the focus of the discussion from the relationship between spectator and sufferers to that among the viewers, the media and humanitarian agents that handle audience contributions, thus also constructing viewers as helpless in relation to controlling their contributions in the relief efforts. This expression of helplessness was embedded in broader discourses of power and viewers' perceived powerlessness in relation to the events witnessed via the media. Diamandouros places these cultural frameworks of thinking about power within the broader framework of Greek political culture and what he calls the 'underdog culture'.[42] By this he means the inward-looking, parochial outlook and insistence on tradition, which at the same time is expressive of 'a conspiratorial interpretation of events and . . . a pronounced sense of cultural inferiority towards the West'.[43] It also includes the victimization of Greece in the 'hands of mightier entities', which results in the tendency to express allegiances to 'collectivities which share a perceived "common heritage of exploitation"' by the world's powerful.[44] Expressions of powerlessness are therefore part of a cultural vocabulary of civic detachment and cynicism, characteristic of the Greek public space.[45] Such discourses minimized viewers' agency in relation to the suffering of distant others. The underlying argument of most focus group discussions was that nothing that the viewers did could ever change the situation.

Cohen and Seu have described expressions of powerlessness and mistrust as common practices of a broader sociology of denial performed through cultural commonplaces and clichés.[46] However, it is important to consider viewers' perceived lack of agency vis-à-vis distant suffering alongside the context of the broader civic culture within which they are embedded. The focus group discussions here confirm survey findings about the low levels of charitable giving in Greece. According to the World Giving Index published in 2014 by the Charities Aid Foundation, Greece scores very low among 135 nations, being ranked in 120th place.[47] The sense of viewers' powerlessness in acting at a distance is implicated with the participants' cynicism and mistrust of the institutions that render this action possible. A generalized culture of mistrust in institutions, as illustrated above, is part of the broader public culture in Greece.[48] Distance is acknowledged as prohibitive of any kind of agency here not only in terms of the actual geographical separation from the scene of suffering, but also because viewers do not trust the mediators of the aid pledges and humanitarian appeals. Furthermore, their arguments about their sense of powerlessness can be seen as part of their broader perceived lack of agency as public actors.

Arguments about viewers' powerlessness vis-à-vis distant suffering and its alleviation were not limited to the impossibility of overcoming the geographical distance, but were further expanded to express their perceived powerlessness. Conceptualizations of power expressive of the 'underdog culture' characteristic of the popular understanding of public life in Greece[49] were also implicated in participants' sense of their agency within the public space. Positioning themselves as part of the underdog class, or 'the small people',[50] viewers minimized their sense of agency as public actors. Such arguments were constructed within the focus group discussions in a variety of ways.

First, it was commonplace among viewers to juxtapose their agency to that of media celebrities and the affluent elite within discussions about contributions and donations to humanitarian appeals. In the following extract, a group of young participants make a similar point of distinguishing between the viewers as the 'common people' and the powerful and wealthy:

> Giota: I did send help, yes. You say, OK, I do help somehow. But there are other people that can give millions, thousands of Euros, why would you go and give twenty or thirty Euros that you actually need? Therefore, you say, OK, I will give one Euro, or 1.20, which is how much a text costs and you will contribute with this action.

Mary: The fact, of course, that the powerful ones, who have all the money, do not give and it's the common people that give is even more annoying. Because, OK, it's about ten people in Greece that own billions! And they don't give!

(Female, in their twenties, working class, FG7)

The women here minimize their own sense of agency and the effect of their contributions by emphasizing how limited these can be ('somehow', 'one Euro'). At the same time, they juxtapose this minimal agency to that of the 'powerful ones' who 'don't give'. It is the actions of those 'who have all the money' that could actually make an impact; however, these people remain, according to the discussants here, unresponsive to the media appeals. Therefore, viewers themselves are to be commended despite their small contributions or even justified for remaining inactive. By victimizing themselves in relation to the 'powerful', participants first shift emphasis of the discussion from their own actions vis-à-vis distant suffering towards social relations within their own community and then use these relations to justify their lack of or minimal action.

It is not only the powerful few in relation to whom viewers juxtaposed their sense of agency as public actors but also 'the system' of local institutions and political structures, which further diminishes their willingness to offer to people in need. In the following extract, a group of housewives move from a discussion about action towards distant suffering to the obstacles they face with local charities:

Litsa: I mean, the system does not help us at all! This is my conclusion! . . . If you try through the church, the church will try to take advantage of you instead of sending you to the people in need. I don't want to go through the church! . . . There are five people that do these things to show off and they use us a bit like their instruments, they use me, they step on me, and these are the people that television shows and this annoys me so much! Incredibly!

(Female, forties, FG2)

Action at a distance and action within the local community are treated in the same context under the common theme of the viewers' powerlessness when encountering the 'system'. It is this powerlessness and mistrust in the institutions that is used once more as an argumentative strategy to justify viewers' inaction vis-à-vis the suffering of others.[51] The 'system' appears to entail the 'church', celebrities (the 'five people that do these things to show off'), as well as the media ('television') that focus their attention on them. Viewers are constructed as victims of this system and ultimately as unable to offer substantial help, even if they want to.

The distinction between the 'powerful' and the 'common people' is an underlying framework for the participants' understandings of social and political life.[52] It concomitantly affects their understanding of public action and their own agency. Identifying themselves as the 'common people', viewers minimize their role as public actors. Inaction or unresponsiveness to humanitarian appeals is therefore not to be understood as merely an indifference or failure to engage with the unfortunates or as a moral failure of the process of mediation as a whole; rather, it should be considered in relation to broader cultural understandings of power and public action. Expressions of powerlessness are part of a broader repertoire of emotion underlying conceptions of public life. As such, they are entrenched within a broader emotional discourse bound up with the social and cultural context.[53]

Expectedly, such conceptualizations of power also framed viewers' understanding of their agency within the global public space. When asked whether they felt themselves to be citizens of the world, when confronted with news of global disasters, a common answer among the participants in the focus groups would be filtered through their sense of citizenship within the national community and their perceived lack of agency within the national public space, as illustrated in the following quote by a young woman:

> Giota: I have to feel as a citizen of my own country first in order to feel a citizen of the world ... If your own country does not take you into account, no matter how cynical this sounds, how will the foreigner ever take you into account? This is what I mean ... If I can't be an active member in my own country, how can I feel a citizen of the world?
>
> (Female, 23, working class, FG7)

The viewer is once more constructed as passive in relation to an impersonal system, in this case her 'own country'. It is this system that does not take her into account and does not let her 'be an active member'. Interestingly, the global is identified here with the 'foreigner', in sharp contrast to the speaker's 'own country', which makes her powerlessness towards it even greater. Evident in both the above quotes are the characteristics of the Greek civic culture as described above, embedded with discourses of cynicism, powerlessness and ultimately disengagement. Viewers' articulation of their agency vis-à-vis the distant is therefore infiltrated with discourses about their agency within the national and local communities. As their sense of political agency is framed within discourses of powerlessness, the same discourses are implicated in viewers' construction of agency as public actors in relation to distant suffering. Constructing themselves as powerless and as 'common people' in juxtaposition with the powerful and mighty, viewers discredit the effectiveness of their action and justify their passivity in general and their unresponsiveness to the relief efforts in specific.

Conclusion

This chapter has explored the question of public action as a response to reports of distant suffering by drawing upon a study of Greek audiences. It has argued that this response has to be seen not in direct relationship with the media texts, but as situated within specific contexts and understandings of public life and public action. Questions about the effectiveness of humanitarian appeals should be discussed beyond the dichotomy between viewers' donations, on the one hand, and apathy or compassion fatigue, on the other hand, as the decision by the audience to respond to an appeal or not is embedded in broader understanding of agency and public action.

First, the chapter has illustrated action at a distance as fragmentary and elusive. It is heavily dependent on the orchestration of humanitarian appeals by the media, most often telethons. What triggers public action, it was argued, is ultimately not the moral compulsion to act in the face of suffering, but the attraction to participate to the media event of the telethon. This has further illustrated the problematic relationship between the reality of the suffering at the heart of the media appeals and their staging as a spectacle through the telethon. Although telethons manage to instigate public action and motivate audiences to contribute to relief efforts, their spectacular character ends up disassociating itself from the actual cause of the suffering, deflecting viewers' attention from the people in need to the event of the telethon and the celebrities participating in it. The latter, it was argued, although useful in attracting audience attention, were also treated by viewers with irony in their role as do-gooders, which undermined their employment as public role models of charity and humanitarianism.

At the same time, aware of the criticisms of moral failure admission to inaction in the face of human suffering might raise, viewers would employ different discursive strategies to justify their unresponsiveness. These strategies were analytically distinguished here into two main discursive frameworks: first, a discourse of generalized mistrust of humanitarian action at a distance; and, second, a discourse of powerlessness that rendered viewers' action ineffective. With regard to the first argumentative strategy, participants criticized the mediation of humanitarianism as a media spectacle, discrediting the motives both of the organizers and the donors, or expressed serious suspicions about the way public donations are handled by the mediators of humanitarian pledges, be it NGOs, governments or other institutions. With regard to their positioning as public actors, viewers would construct themselves as powerless in the broader context of public and political life. Minimizing their sense of agency as actors in the public stage, participants simultaneously discredited the effectiveness of their actions vis-à-vis distant suffering.

The two argumentative strategies of powerlessness and mistrust are intrinsically intertwined, of course. Viewers do not trust the mediators of public action, since they feel they have no power of control or monitoring over them. By mistrusting institutions who have power over the situation witnessed on TV, viewers at the same time victimize themselves in relation to these institutions and stress out their own powerlessness. The argument to be made here is that viewers' sense of agency vis-à-vis the suffering of distant others as expressed and enacted (or not) through action at a distance should be considered not merely in relation to or as a direct response to the media coverage of human suffering; it should also be seen in relation to the broader discourses that surround the viewers' understanding of public action and their position as public actors in the social world. In this context, it is a limited approach to theorize viewers' unresponsiveness to humanitarian appeals and inaction vis-à-vis distant suffering as 'moral apathy',[54] 'compassion fatigue'[55]or as merely a moral failure of the media to convey the urgency of the situation. It has to be understood alongside viewers' sense of their own agency as public actors and relevant moral and political discourses that render this inaction expected, justifiable and commonsensical.

Maria Kyriakidou is Lecturer in the School of Journalism, Media and Culture at Cardiff University. Her research interests include the role of representation in globalization, cosmopolitanism, media discourses of distant suffering and audience studies. Her doctoral thesis explored the ways in which television audiences in Greece engage with news stories of distant suffering. Her current research focuses on media discourses of the eurozone crisis, as well as the coverage of the Indignados movement and the European Left. She is also Editor in Chief (with Henry Radice) and regular contributor to the blog *LSE Eurocrisis in the Press* (http://blogs.lse.ac.uk/eurocrisispress). She holds a PhD in Media and Communications from the London School of Economics (LSE) and is an associate to the Civil Society and Human Security Research Unit at the LSE.

Notes

1. D. Gauntlett, 'Ten Things Wrong with the Media "Effects" Model', in R. Dickinson, R. Harindranath and O. Linnè (eds), *Approaches to Audiences: A Reader* (London: Arnold, 1998), 120–30.
2. M. Kyriakidou, 'Media Witnessing: Exploring the Audience of Distant Suffering', *Media, Culture & Society* 37(2) (2015), 215–31.
3. S.D. Moeller, *Compassion Fatigue: How the Media Sell Disease, Famine, War and Death* (New York: Routledge, 1999).
4. S. Cohen, *States of Denial: Knowing about Atrocities and Suffering* (New York: John Wiley & Sons, 2001).
5. Moeller, *Compassion Fatigue*, 11, 13, 53.
6. K. Tester, *Moral Culture* (New York: Sage, 1997), 39.
7. Moeller, *Compassion Fatigue*, 29.
8. Cohen, *States of Denial*, 187.
9. Ibid., 193.
10. Ibid., 194.
11. Ibid., 189.
12. Ibid.
13. B. Höijer, 'The Discourse of Global Compassion: The Audience and Media Reporting of Human Suffering', *Media, Culture & Society* 26(4) (2004), 513–31, at 528.
14. I.B. Seu, '"Your Stomach Makes You Feel That You Don't Want to Know Anything about it": Desensitization, Defence Mechanisms and Rhetoric in Response to Human Rights

Abuses', *Journal of Human Rights* 2(2) (2003), 183–96; I.B. Seu, '"Doing Denial": Audience Reaction to Human Rights Appeals', *Discourse & Society* 2(2) (2010), 438–57.

15. M. Scott, 'The Mediation of Distant Suffering: An Empirical Contribution beyond Television News Texts', *Media, Culture & Society* 36(1) (2014), 3–19.

16. J.C. Ong, 'Witnessing Distant and Proximal Suffering within a Zone of Danger: Lay Moralities of Media Audiences in the Philippines', *International Communication Gazette* 77(7) (2015), 607–21.

17. R. Silverstone, *Media and Morality: On the Rise of the Mediapolis* (Cambridge: Polity Press, 2007).

18. J. Ellis, *Seeing Things: Television in the Age of Uncertainty* (London: I.B. Tauris, 2000); P. Frosh, 'Telling Presences: Witnessing, Mass Media, and the Imagined Lives of Strangers', *Critical Studies in Media Communication* 23(4) (2006), 265–84; P. Frosh, 'Phatic Morality: Television and Proper Distance', *International Journal of Cultural Studies* 14(4) (2011), 383–400; P. Frosh and A. Pinchevski (eds), *Media Witnessing: Testimony in the Age of Mass Communication* (Basingstoke: Palgrave Macmillan, 2011).

19. N. Couldry, *Listening beyond the Echoes: Media, Ethics, and Agency in an Uncertain World* (London: Paradigm Publishers, 2006).

20. L. Chouliaraki, *The Spectatorship of Suffering* (London: Sage, 2006), 189.

21. J. Butler, *Precarious Life: The Powers of Mourning and Violence* (New York: Verso, 2006), 37–38.

22. Chouliaraki, *Spectatorship of Suffering,* 187.

23. N. Fairclough, 'Discourse and Text: Linguistic and Intertextual Analysis within Discourse Analysis', *Discourse & Society* 3(2) (1992), 193–217, at 204.

24. M. Billig, *Talking of the Royal Family* (London: Routledge, 1992), 16.

25. T. Sasson, *Crime Talk: How Citizens Construct a Social Problem* (Hawthorne, NY: Aldine-Transaction, 1995), 20.

26. S.M. Livingstone, *Making Sense of Television: The Psychology of Audience Interpretation* (London: Routledge, 1998), 113.

27. K. Tester, *Compassion, Morality, and the Media* (Buckingham: Open University Press, 2001), 116.

28. E. Devereux, 'Good Causes, God's Poor and Telethon Television', *Media, Culture & Society* 18(1) (1996), 47–68, at 48.

29. Tester, *Compassion,* 118–20.

30. The discussion extract here and the ones that follow are included as illustrative examples of the focus groups discussions held as part of the broader research project discussed in the previous section. For more information on the focus group methodology as employed in the project, as well as the broader discussions on the mediation of distant suffering, see M. Kyriakidou, 'Watching the Pain of Others: Audience Discourses of Distant Suffering in Greece', PhD dissertation (London: London School of Economics and Political Science (LSE), 2011).

31. Eleni Menegaki is a popular television personality and presenter of a daily morning show in Greece.

32. S. Cottle and D. Nolan, 'Global Humanitarianism and the Changing Aid-Media Field', *Journalism Studies* 8(6) (2007), 862–78.

33. Tester, *Compassion,* 120.

34. L. Chouliaraki, *The Ironic Spectator: Solidarity in the Age of Post-humanitarianism* (Cambridge: Polity Press, 2013), 120; Cottle and Nolan, 'Global Humanitarianism', 862–78.

35. J. Littler, '"I Feel Your Pain": Cosmopolitan Charity and the Public Fashioning of the Celebrity Soul', *Social Semiotics* 18(2) (2008), 237–51, at 241.
36. Devereux, 'Good Causes'; Littler, '"I Feel Your Pain"'.
37. Elli Stai is a Greek journalist and television news presenter.
38. Lakis Lazopoulos is a popular comedian and writer of political satire.
39. G.D. Stephanidis, *Stirring the Greek Nation: Political Culture, Irredentism and Anti-Americanism in Post-war Greece, 1945–1967* (Farnham: Ashgate, 2007), 15, 66; D. Sutton, 'Poked by the "Foreign Finger" in Greece: Conspiracy Theory or the Hermeneutics of Suspicion?', in *The Usable Past: Greek Metahistories* (Lanham, MD: Lexington Books), 191–210.
40. N. Demertzis, 'Introduction to the Greek Political Culture: Theoretical and Empirical Issues', in N. Demertzis (ed.), *Greek Political Culture Today* (Athens: Oddeseas, 2008), 7–39.
41. S. Cohen and I.B. Seu, 'Knowing Enough Not to Feel Too Much: Emotional Thinking about Human Rights Appeals', in M. Bradley and P. Petro (eds), *Truth Claims: Representations and Human Rights* (New Brunswick: Rutgers University Press, 2002), 187–204.
42. N. Diamandouros, 'Politics and Culture in Greece, 1974–1991: An Interpretation', in R. Clogg (ed.), *Greece, 1981–1989: The Populist Decade* (London: Macmillan, 1993), 1–25.
43. Ibid., 18.
44. Stephanidis, *Stirring the Greek Nation,* 8.
45. N. Demertzis, 'Cynical Democracy'. Paper presented at the 8th Greek Association of Political Science Conference 'The Turn in Democratic Function: Challenges and Threats in Early 21st Century', Athens, Greece, 2008.
46. Cohen and Seu, 'Knowing Enough', 189.
47. The survey on which the Index is based explores the percentage of population giving money to charity, volunteering and helping strangers. Retrieved 25 August 2018 from https://www.cafonline.org/pdf/WorldGivingIndex28092010Print.pdf.
48. P. Kafetzis, 'Political Crisis and Political Culture: Civic Disengagement and Political Involvement. An Incompatible Relation?', in N. Demertzis (ed.), *Greek Political Culture Today* (Athens: Oddeseas, 1994), 215–52.
49. Diamandouros, 'Politics and Culture in Greece', 1–25.
50. Demertzis, 'Cynical Democracy', 7–39.
51. Demertzis, 'Cynical Democracy'.
52. Diamandouros 'Politics and Culture in Greece', 1–25; Stephanidis, *Stirring the Greek Nation,* 60, 109.
53. C. Lutz and L. Abu-Lughod, *Language and the Politics of Emotion* (Cambridge: Cambridge University Press, 1990), 1–22.
54. Seu, '"Doing Denial"', 438–57.
55. Moeller, *Compassion Fatigue.*

Bibliography

Billig, M. *Talking of the Royal Family.* London: Routledge, 1992.
Butler, J. *Precarious Life: The Powers of Mourning and Violence.* New York: Verso, 2006.
Chouliaraki, L. *The Spectatorship of Suffering.* London: Sage, 2006.

———. *The Ironic Spectator: Solidarity in the Age of Post-humanitarianism*. Cambridge: Polity Press, 2013.

Cohen, S. *States of Denial: Knowing about Atrocities and Suffering*. New York: John Wiley & Sons, 2001.

Cohen, S., and I.B. Seu. 'Knowing Enough Not to Feel Too Much: Emotional Thinking about Human Rights Appeals', in M. Bradley and P. Petro (eds), *Truth Claims: Representations and Human Rights* (New Brunswick: Rutgers University Press, 2002), 187–204.

Cottle, S., and D. Nolan. 'Global Humanitarianism and the Changing Aid-Media Field'. *Journalism Studies* 8(6) (2007), 862–78.

Couldry, N. *Listening beyond the Echoes: Media, Ethics, and Agency in an Uncertain World*. London: Paradigm Publishers, 2006.

Demertzis, N. 'Introduction to the Greek Political Culture: Theoretical and Empirical Issues', in N. Demertzis (ed.), *Greek Political Culture Today* (Athens: Oddeseas, 2008), 7–39.

Devereux, E. 'Good Causes, God's Poor and Telethon Television'. *Media, Culture & Society* 18(1) (1996), 47–68.

Diamandouros, N. 'Politics and Culture in Greece, 1974–1991: An Interpretation', in R. Clogg (ed.), *Greece, 1981–1989: The Populist Decade* (London: Macmillan, 1993), 1–25.

Ellis, J. *Seeing Things: Television in the Age of Uncertainty*. London: I.B. Tauris, 2000.

Fairclough, N. 'Discourse and Text: Linguistic and Intertextual Analysis within Discourse Analysis'. *Discourse & Society* 3(2) (1992), 193–217.

Frosh, P. 'Telling Presences: Witnessing, Mass Media, and the Imagined Lives of Strangers'. *Critical Studies in Media Communication* 23(4) (2006), 265–84.

———. 'Phatic Morality: Television and Proper Distance'. *International Journal of Cultural Studies* 14(4) (2011), 383–400.

Frosh, P., and A. Pinchevski (eds). *Media Witnessing: Testimony in the Age of Mass Communication*. Basingstoke: Palgrave Macmillan, 2011.

Gauntlett, D. 'Ten Things Wrong with the Media "Effects" Model', in R. Dickinson, R. Harindranath and O. Linnè (eds), *Approaches to Audiences: A Reader* (London: Arnold, 1998), 120–30.

Höijer, B. 'The Discourse of Global Compassion: The Audience and Media Reporting of Human Suffering'. *Media, Culture & Society*, 26(4) (2004), 513–31.

Kafetzis, P. 'Political Crisis and Political Culture: Civic Disengagement and Political Involvement. An Incompatible Relation?', in N. Demertzis (ed.), *Greek Political Culture Today* (Athens: Oddeseas, 1994), 215–52.

Kyriakidou, M. 'Watching the Pain of Others: Audience Discourses of Distant Suffering in Greece'. PhD dissertation. London: London School of Economics and Political Science (LSE), 2011.

———. 'Media Witnessing: Exploring the Audience of Distant Suffering'. *Media, Culture & Society* 37(2) (2015), 215–31.

Littler, J. '"I Feel Your Pain": Cosmopolitan Charity and the Public Fashioning of the Celebrity Soul'. *Social Semiotics* 18(2) (2008), 237–51.

Livingstone, S.M. *Making Sense of Television: The Psychology of Audience Interpretation*. London: Routledge, 1998.

Lutz, C., and L. Abu-Lughod. *Language and the Politics of Emotion*. Cambridge: Cambridge University Press, 1990.

Moeller, S.D. *Compassion Fatigue: How the Media Sell Disease, Famine, War and Death*. New York: Routledge, 1999.

Ong, J.C. 'Witnessing Distant and Proximal Suffering within a Zone of Danger: Lay Moralities of Media Audiences in the Philippines'. *International Communication Gazette* 77(7) (2015), 607–21.

Sasson, T. *Crime Talk: How Citizens Construct a Social Problem*. Hawthorne, NY: Aldine Transaction, 1995.

Scott, M. 'The Mediation of Distant Suffering: An Empirical Contribution beyond Television News Texts'. *Media, Culture & Society* 36(1) (2014), 3–19.

Seu, I.B '"Your Stomach Makes You Feel That You Don't Want to Know Anything about it": Desensitization, Defence Mechanisms and Rhetoric in Response to Human Rights Abuses'. *Journal of Human Rights* 2(2) (2003), 183–96.

———. '"Doing Denial": Audience Reaction to Human Rights Appeals'. *Discourse & Society* 2(2) (2010), 438–57.

Silverstone, R. *Media and Morality: On the Rise of the Mediapolis*. Cambridge: Polity Press, 2007.

Stephanidis, G.D. *Stirring the Greek Nation: Political Culture, Irredentism and Anti-Americanism in Post-war Greece, 1945–1967*. Farnham: Ashgate, 2007.

Sutton, D. 'Poked by the "Foreign Finger" in Greece: Conspiracy Theory or the Hermeneutics of Suspicion?', in *The Usable Past: Greek Metahistories* (Lanham, MD: Lexington Books, 2003), 191–210.

Tester, K. *Moral Culture*. New York: Sage, 1997.

———. *Compassion, Morality, and the Media*. Buckingham: Open University Press, 2001.

Index

Abbott, Berenice, 157, 162–63
Adams, Ansel, 152, 154, 157
Adenauer, Konrad, 143
Africa, 9–10, 18, 19, 20, 43, 49, 50, 52, 54, 98–99, 166, 205, 223, 233, 243, 251, 263, 268, 269–71, 275
Agency for Overseas Development (AFOD), 266
Aktionsgruppe Kinder in Not, 250
Algeria, 98–99
Allan, Diana, 222, 234
Alt, Franz, 247
American Council of Voluntary Agencies for Foreign Service (ACVAFS), 16, 186, 189, 190, 193
American Friends Service Committee (AFSC), 16, 74, 78, 137, 186
American Jewish Joint Distribution Committee, 16, 186
Amnesty International, 3
anti-Semitism, 14, 113–18
Arbeiterwohlfahrt, 137
Arbus, Diane, 15, 165, 177n101
Armenian massacres, 49
Army Film and Photography Unit (AFPU), 131
Aron, Raymond, 209
Ärzte für die Dritte Welt, 250
Asistencia Social, 79, 80
Atholl, Duchess of, 79
atrocities, 2, 12, 14, 21, 70, 107–18, 127, 144
audiences, 4, 5, 6, 7, 10, 11, 14, 20–21, 24, 49, 98, 108, 114, 116–18, 143, 224, 240, 266, 281–94
Auschwitz, 111, 113, 114, 115, 120n14, 122n29
Austria, 54, 69, 81, 130

Baby Milk Campaign, 17, 203, 206–7, 208
Balkans, 69
Balsam, 223–24, 227, 228, 229, 235
Band Aid, 19–20, 264, 267–76
Bargatzky, Walter, 245
Barthes, Roland, 15, 164
Basque Children's Committee, 13, 76, 79, 81
Bell, Bishop George, 136–37
Benthall, Jonathan, 7–9, 10
Bergen-Belsen, 109, 110, 111–12, 114, 115, 116, 128, 137, 154
Berliner Illustrirte Zeitung, 159
Bernardo, Thomas, 49, 62n43
Biafra, 18, 100, 167, 202, 206, 243–45. *See also* famine: in Biafra
Black Book: Germans Past and Present, 135
Böhm, Karlheinz, 250
Böll, Heinrich, 247–49
Boltanski, Luc, 4, 185
Bonham Carter, Violet, 137
Bonney, Mabel Thérèse, 139
Bosnian War. *See under* wars and conflicts
Bourke-White, Margaret, 128, 154, 159, 167
Brauman, Rony, 209, 213
British Broadcasting Corporation (BBC), 8, 19, 135, 137, 212, 251, 265–66
British Council of Churches, 19, 264
British Foreign Office, 78, 79, 135
British Home Office, 79
British Medical Journal, 81
British Zone of Occupation (Germany), 127–44
Brocher, Jean, 93
Brown, Isabel, 79
Buchenwald, 115, 128, 136, 154, 272
Buerk, Michael, 19, 212, 251–52, 265–68, 269, 272, 275
Buxton, Dorothy, 69

Calhoun, Craig, 242
Cambodia, 17, 209–11, 214
Campbell, Wallace, 192
Canada, 46, 162, 187, 188, 241
Cap Anamur. *See under* German Emergency
  Doctors (GED)
Capa, Cornell, 161, 165
Capa, Robert, 67, 152, 154, 155, 156, 160,
  161, 162, 164
CARE, 9, 16, 186, 189, 191, 230, 250
Caritas, 137, 247
Cartier-Bresson, Henri, 152, 155–57, 159,
  160, 161, 162, 166, 167, 169, 175n65
Catholic Church, 13, 79, 81
Catholic Fund for Overseas Development, 8
Catholic Relief Services, 16, 186, 189
Catholicism, 42, 52
Chamberlain, Joseph, 190
Cherne, Leo, 210, 211
children, 8, 12–13, 18–19, 22, 30n60,
  41–57, 68–71, 96, 97, 127, 130–33,
  136, 138–39, 163–64, 169, 170, 245,
  263
  depicted as 'deserving' or 'innocent',
    72–76, 141
  and evacuation from Spain, 79–81, 82–83
  as 'heathens', 44, 49
Children of Europe, 83, 131–32, 163–64,
  170
children's homes, 43, 45, 48, 49
China, 44, 46, 48, 50, 53, 56, 69, 128, 160
Chouliaraki, Lilie, 5–7, 11, 27n22, 56,
  278n23
Christian Aid, 8, 19–20, 203, 206, 264,
  266, 268–70, 273–76
Christianity, 4, 12, 15–16, 21, 41–42, 48,
  56, 137, 144
Church World Service, 16, 186, 189
cinema. *See under* film
Cohen, Stanley, 283, 290
Cold War. *See under* wars and conflicts
Communism, 13, 76, 79, 95, 97, 104n34,
  209, 210, 211, 247
compassion, 4–5, 8, 19, 20, 45, 128, 131,
  133, 134, 143, 163, 267, 268, 270,
  272, 273, 275, 281, 282–84
'compassion fatigue', 4, 20, 21, 27n19,
  282–83, 293–94
concentration camps, 4, 14, 22, 97, 107–18,
  128, 154, 167
Concern (Irish relief agency), 212
Congo, 93, 94, 98, 233

Congo Reform Association, 11
Co-operative, 68, 76
Cope, Alfred, 74, 85n22
Cope, Ruth, 74
cosmopolitanism, 4, 5, 24
Cottle, Simon, 9, 10
Cranborne, Viscount, 78
Crossman, Richard, 135
Cuba, 233

Dachau, 128
Daily Express, 75
Daily Herald, 131, 133, 136
Daily Mail, 81
Daily Mirror, 204
Daily Worker, 70, 74
Darfur crisis, 201, 216n2
Dear Fatherland, Rest Quietly, 128
Declaration of the Rights of the Child, 203
dehumanization, 14, 108–10, 115–16, 118
Deutsche Film-Aktiengesellschaft (DEFA),
  96
Disasters Emergency Committee (DEC),
  8, 266
Disasters, Relief and the Media, 7–9
Displaced Persons (DP) camps, 113, 128–30
Doisneau, Robert, 152, 155, 156, 162, 168
Donges, Patrick, 9
Drexler, Karl, 54
Duvanel, Charles-George, 93

Edelmann, Maurice, 134–35
Eisenhower, Dwight D., 188
Ellis, Richard, 80–81
empathy, 4, 5, 6, 97, 116, 141, 267, 272,
  282
Eritrea, 211, 270, 271, 274, 275
Erwitt, Elliott, 155, 156, 174n40
Ethiopia, 17, 19, 92, 209, 211–214, 215,
  216, 245–46, 250–53, 263–76
Europe's Children, 139

Family of Man, The, 15, 131, 146n25,
  157–58, 159, 162, 163–67
famine
  in Biafra, 167, 206, 216, 243–45
  in Cambodia, 17
  in Ethiopia, 17, 19, 209, 211–14, 216,
    245–46, 250–53, 263–76
  in Germany and Austria, 69
  in India, 11, 188
  in Russia, 74

Index

Farm Security Administration (FSA), 153
Farquhar, Esther, 74
Fast for World Justice (FWJ), 17, 206
Fehrenbach, Heide, 10–11, 41, 68
film, 13–14, 69, 90–101
films
  Car le sang coule encore!, 98–99
  Le CICR à Genève: ses activités d'après guerre (*The ICRC in Geneva: Its Post-war Activities*), 92, 95
  Le drapeau de l'humanité – The Flag of Humanity, 93
  German Concentration Camps Factual Survey, 109–10, 112, 119n5, 120n9
  Helft Helfen (*That They May Live Again*), 95–97, 100
  Inter Arma Caritas, 93, 95, 97
  Nazi Concentration Camps, 108, 120n8, 121n21
  Prisonnier de guerre (*Prisoner of War*), 92
  Le rapatriement des Coréens du Japon en République démocratique de Corée (*The Repatriation of the Koreans from Japan to the Democratic Republic of Korea*), 92
  Ein Soldat wird vermisst (*A Soldier is Missing*), 92
  S.O.S. Congo, 98
  Die Todesmühlen, 113, 115–116, 119n5, 121n21, 122n25
  Tous frères! (*All Brothers!*), 98–99
  Une Voie reste ouverte! – One Way Remains Open!, 93, 104n22
Finley, William, 74
First World Food Congress, 187
First World War. *See under* wars and conflicts
Food and Agricultural Organization (FAO), 16, 17, 186–91, 193–94, 203, 205, 213
Forbin-Janson, Charles-August-Marie-Joseph de, 44–46
France, 12, 17, 44, 52, 56, 94, 141, 207–16
Freedom from Hunger (FFH), 16–17, 187–94, 203–6
Freedom from Hunger Campaign (FFHC). *See under* Freedom from Hunger (FFH)
Friends' Service Committee (FSC), 12, 13–14, 16, 72–75, 80
Früh, Kurt, 93
Fry, Joan Mary, 75
fundraising, 8, 13, 16, 20, 22, 23, 42, 45, 48, 49–57, 72, 74–75, 94, 101, 185–94, 215, 263, 275

Galloway, George, 272
Gaza Strip. *See under* Palestine
Geldof, Bob, 19, 251, 267–70, 273, 275–76, 278n31
gender, 12, 21–22, 42, 52, 285
genocide, 12, 107, 167, 206, 210, 216, 243, 244
Genscher, Hans-Dietrich, 245
German Democratic Republic. *See under* Germany
German Emergency Doctors (GED), 247–50, 253
German Red Cross, 137, 245, 247, 250
German Standing Committee on Youth Problems, 137
Germany, 14–15, 18, 22, 48, 95–97, 107–18, 126–44, 166, 233, 241, 242–51
  German Democratic Republic, 166, 233
ghana action, 250
Glucksmann, André, 209
Gollancz, Victor, 14, 126, 135–43
Grant, James P., 207
Great Britain, 7, 8, 13, 14–15, 23, 67–83, 116, 126–44, 202–7, 215–16, 241, 264, 267, 273
Greece, 20–21, 206, 281–94
Guardian, The, 8, 75, 81, 266–67

Hansen, Kurt, 245
Hansson, Michael, 78
Hay, Lorna, 133
HELP – Hilfe zur Selbsthilfe e.V., 250
Henry-Lévy, Bernard, 209
Hepp, Josepf, 93
Hoijer, Birgitta, 283
Holy Childhood Association, 12, 44–57
Humanitarian Photography, 10–11
humanity, representations of, 15–16, 56, 82, 116, 131, 135, 137, 140–44, 151–152, 154, 157–70,
Humedica, 250

If Thine Enemy Hunger, 137
Ihrt, Fred, 245
In Darkest Germany, 139–40
Independent Broadcasting Authority (IBA), 266
Independent Television (ITV), 251, 265
Independent Television Commission, 8
Inter-Church Aid, 203
International Baby Food Action Network (IBFAN), 207

302 Index

International Commission for the Assistance of Spanish Child Refugees, 76–78
International Commission for the Care of Spanish Refugees (IC), 78
International Committee of the Red Cross (ICRC), 7, 8–9, 13–14, 16, 23, 202, 212, 213, 215, 229, 233
and film: 90–101, 138–39
International Federation of Red Cross and Red Crescent Societies, 225
International Rescue Committee (IRC), 210
ironic spectatorship, 5–7, 21
Is It Nothing to You?, 138
Italy, 52, 94, 241, 243

Japan, 92, 94, 166
Jebb, Eglantyne, 69, 138, 140
Jews, 14, 107–18, 128, 130, 135, 136, 143
Jordan, 17, 203, 224, 226
journalists, 2, 9–11, 16, 21, 23, 67, 74, 75, 82–83, 131–32, 133, 153–54, 156, 158–63, 204, 209, 212, 214, 215–16, 240–55, 266

Kennedy, John F., 187
Kent, Rudolph, 240
Khalidi, Raja, 233
Khalidi, Rashid, 226
Khmer Rouge, 210
Kindertransports, 81
Kouchner, Bernard, 17, 209–10

Labour Party (UK), 13, 72, 79, 131, 134
Ladies' Home Journal, 159
Lancet, The, 81
Lange, Dorothea, 153
League of Nations Women's Advisory Committee, 78
League of Red Cross Societies, 13, 94
Leaving Them to Their Own Fate: The Ethics of Starvation, 136
Lebanon, 18, 222–35
Ledóchowska, Maria Teresia, 52
Le Monde, 209
Liberté sans Frontières (LSF), 214–15
Life, 158, 159, 160
Lincoln, Murray, 192
Linfield, Susie, 69
Live Aid, 19, 251, 264, 267–276
Lorant, Stefan, 159
Lutheran World Relief, 16, 186, 189

Magee, Haywood, 133
Magen David Adom society, 225
Magnum (photo agency), 15, 128, 131, 140–41, 153–54, 155, 159, 161, 162, 163–64, 167
Majdanek, 111, 113, 115, 120n14
Malhuret, Claude, 209, 210, 211
Malkki, Lisa, 50–51, 82
Malteser International, 9
Manchester Guardian. See under *Guardian, The*
Manning, Leah, 74, 79
McCall, Floyd H., 161–62
McCurry, Steve, 167, 178n115
Médecins Sans Frontières (MSF), 17, 18, 101, 202, 207–216, 219n42
media
  definition of, 2–3
  and emotion, 1, 4–5, 11, 51, 53, 75–76, 135–36, 142, 156, 249–50, 266–67, 268–69, 282–84
  'regimes', 2–3, 7–10, 18–19, 23
  and suffering, 1, 10, 11, 164, 223–24, 284
  and technological change, 2, 24, 67, 69, 90, 159, 163, 206
'mediatization', 7–10, 19, 23–24, 240–55
Menschen helfen Menschen, 250
Meyer, Hans, 96
Milk for Spain fund, 76
missionaries, 2, 11, 12, 21, 42–44, 48, 49, 50, 53, 68–69, 202, 245
Moeller, Susan, 282
Montand, Yves, 209
Montgomery, Field Marshal Bernard, 137
Morris, John G. 159
Mükke, Lutz, 9–10
Münchner Illustrierte Presse, 159
Murdoch, Lydia, 49, 62n43
Museum of Modern Art (MoMA, New York), 15, 131, 157, 165
Mydans, Carl, 161

Nannen, Henri, 245
National Information Bureau (NIB), 186
National Joint Committee for Spanish Relief (NJC), 13, 68, 79
National Society for the Prevention of Cruelty to Children (NSPCC), 75
Negro Child, The, 52
Nehru, Jawaharlal, 78
Nepal, 94

Neudeck, Rupert, 247–49
New Deal, 15, 153
New Internationalist, 206, 207
New Statesman and Nation, 135
News Chronicle, 131, 132, 134, 136
Nigeria, 17–18, 100, 101, 243, 244, 246
Nigerian Civil War. *See under* wars and
  conflicts
Nobel Peace Prize, 94
Nolan, David, 9, 10
nonfraternization policies, 141
nongovernmental organizations (NGOs),
  7–10, 16, 185–94, 202, 241, 246–47,
  263–64
Norway, 78, 241, 283
Nuremberg trials, 108, 121n15, 128

Observer, The, 136
Omarska camp, 4
Ong, Jonathan Corpus, 283
Oslo Accords, 223, 233
Ottoman Empire, 49
Our Threatened Values, 137
Oxfam, 8, 17, 20, 22, 202, 203, 206–7,
  208, 210, 213, 215, 253, 266, 270,
  273, 274

Palestine, 17, 22, 94, 128, 222–35
Palestinian Liberation Organization (PLO),
  17, 222–35
Palestinian Martyrs Society (Samed), 18,
  222–35
Palestinian Red Crescent Society (PRCS),
  18, 222–35
pardon, 244
Paris Match, 158
Pathé, 93
Patton, James G., 192
Photographic Society of America (PSA), 162
photography, 4, 10–11, 15–16, 49–57,
  67–83, 126–44, 151–70
  and humanism, 152–54
  and humanitarianism, 163–64
  and the 'Human Gaze', 151–170
Picture Post, 69, 133, 134–35, 146n26, 159
pity, 4, 5, 6, 14–15, 18, 52, 126–27,
  130–35, 136, 140
Plan, 250
Poland, 93, 112, 115, 128, 129, 135
Popular Photography, 151, 154, 162
Press Photography, 161–62
Priestley, J.B., 133, 137

professionalization, 10, 11, 22, 23, 56, 68,
  186, 201, 206, 215, 216
Protestantism, 43, 49, 115, 137, 247
Pye, Edith, 78–81

Quick, 244

racism, 99–100, 141, 269–70, 276
Rantzen, Esther, 207, 208
Red Crescent, 18, 93, 222–35
Red Cross, 23, 92, 93, 95, 96, 126, 137
Redfield, Peter, 229
refugees, 6, 13, 14, 17, 18, 70, 72, 75,
  76–81, 82, 94, 129, 133, 137, 141,
  206, 209–11, 222–35, 246–50, 265,
  267
Regarding the Pain of Others, 3–5
Reich, John F., 78
Rettungshäuser. See under children's homes
Revel, Jean-François, 209
Rhode, Robert B., 161–62
RKO, 93
Rodger, George, 154, 155
Rodogno, Davide, 10–11
Rogers, William, Jr., 151–52
Rothstein, Arthur, 128
Rozario, Kevin, 11
Russell, Audrey, 80–81
Russia. *See* Union of Soviet Socialist
  Republics (USSR)

Saeger, Willi, 127
Salgado, Sebastião, 154
Salvation Army, 79, 81
Samed al-Iqtisadi, 223–24, 230, 235
Sandburg, Carl, 156
Sander, August, 127
Sartre, Jean-Paul, 160, 209
'Save Europe Now' campaign, 137–38,
  142–43
Save the Children Fund (SCF), 7, 8, 13, 17,
  20, 22, 69, 79, 131, 138, 140, 202,
  203–206, 211, 213, 215, 253, 273,
  274
Save the Children International Union
  (SCIU), 13, 68, 72, 73, 76, 79
Sayigh, Yezid, 224–25
Schiller, Friedrich, 6
Scott, Martin, 283
Second World War. *See under* wars and
  conflicts
Seidenstücker, Friedrich, 127

Selassie, Haile, 211, 246
Sen, Binay R., 16, 188, 189, 191
Seu, Irene Bruna, 283, 290
Seymour, David 'Chim', 67, 83, 131, 132, 155, 163, 164, 170
Signoret, Simone, 209
Silverstone, Roger, 24
Singh, Raghubir, 166–67
slavery, 43, 52, 53
Smith, W. Eugene, 159
Society of Friends, 13, 68, 73, 79
Solferino, Battle of, 92, 103n11
solidarity, 5, 6–7, 14, 18, 19, 42, 48, 56, 98, 100, 164, 202, 210, 232, 235, 246, 254, 268, 271, 272, 284
Somalia, 233, 250–51, 255
Sontag, Susan, 3–5, 15, 26n11, 67, 165
Soviet Union. *See* Union of Soviet Socialist Republics (USSR)
Spain, 52, 67–83
Spanish Civil War. *See under* wars and conflicts
Spanish Medical Aid, 13, 79
Spectatorship of Suffering, 5
Spiegel, Der, 166, 244, 248, 250
Stamatov, Peter, 25n2
Steichen, Edward, 15, 131, 153, 157, 158, 159, 162, 165
Steinbeck, John, 160–61, 175n75
stereotypes, 10, 14, 98, 99, 269, 270, 276
Stern, 19, 159, 244, 248, 250, 253
    and the 'Rettet die Hungernden' campaign, 245–46
St Pauli Nachrichten, 244
St Petrus Claver Sodality, 51, 52, 53
Sudan, 216n2, 233
Sunday Mirror, 204
Sunday Telegraph, 204
Sweden, 241, 283
Switzerland, 52, 93, 94
Syria, 224

Taro, Gerda, 67, 69
telethons, 20–21, 285–94
television, 5, 18–19, 20–21, 100
'Third World', 22, 233, 270
Three Guineas, 75–76
Times, The (London), 75, 80, 134
Todd, Olivier, 209
Trades Union Congress (TUC), 13, 68, 76, 79
Truman, Harry, 192

Trümmerfrauen, 141
twen, 244
Twentieth Century Fox, 93
Twitter, 23

Uganda, 233
Union of Soviet Socialist Republics (USSR), 12, 69, 74, 75, 92, 95, 104n34, 110–11, 114, 115, 133, 135, 138, 160
United Nations (UN), 7, 23, 188, 224, 245
United Nations Children's Fund (UNICEF), 16, 144, 186, 187, 189, 206–7
United Nations Educational, Scientific and Cultural Organisation (UNESCO), 15, 68, 83, 130, 143, 163–64, 170
United Nations Relief and Rehabilitation Administration (UNRRA), 11, 128–30, 136, 146n31, 188–89
United Nations Relief and Works Agency (UNRWA), 223, 224, 226, 231
United States, 16, 20, 52, 78, 94, 95, 159, 186–94, 205, 241, 247
Universal Declaration of Human Rights, 130, 143, 153
universalism, 15, 49–50, 113–18, 130–31, 140–44
Universities Fight for Economic Development (UNFED), 204

Vachon, John, 128, 129
Valera, Eamonn de, 78
Vansittart, Lord Robert, 135
Vasset, Brigitte, 212
Vetter, Heinz-Oskar, 245
victims
    categorisation of, 12–13, 82, 130, 133, 234–235
    depiction of, 3–4, 12, 13–14, 18, 68, 69–70, 72–76, 97–100
Vietnam War. *See under* wars and conflicts
Vietnamese 'boat people', 17, 209–11, 247–50, 254
Vom Glück des Menschen (*On the Happiness of People*), 166

War on Want, 19–20, 203, 212, 264, 268–76
wars and conflicts, 4
    Black September, 224, 226
    Boer War, 73
    Bosnian War, 4

Cold War, 7, 15, 19, 127, 131, 141–43, 144, 160–61, 165, 240, 245, 246
First World War, 11, 12, 13, 41, 57, 69, 91, 94, 126, 131, 138, 140
Greco-Turkish War, 92, 93
Hungarian Bolshevik Revolution, 94
Italian-Ethiopian War, 92, 103n12
Korean War, 95
Nigerian Civil War, 17, 18, 100–101
Polish-Soviet War, 94
Rwandan genocide, 167, 216
Second World War, 13, 14–15, 16, 21, 22, 82–83, 90, 91–92, 94, 95, 126, 152, 153, 155, 162, 167, 189, 216, 243
Silesian uprising, 94
Sino-Japanese War, 92, 103n12
Spanish Civil War, 12–13, 67–83, 92, 103n12, 131, 138–39, 155
Vietnam War, 165, 167
War of the Camps, 223, 227
Weltaustellung der Photographie, 166
West Bank. *See* Palestine

Weston, Edward, 151
Wilkinson, Ellen, 137
Wilson, Francesca, 74–75
Women's International League for Peace and Freedom (WILPF), 78
Woolf, Virginia, 75–76
World Aids Day, 10
World Bank, 233
World Food Congress, 16, 187, 203, 205
World Food Programme, 16, 186, 212
World Health Assembly, 207
World Health Organization (WHO), 11, 144, 207, 229
World Hunger Day, 10
'World Refugee Year' campaign, 206
World Vision, 212, 250
World's Children, 204

Yemen, 94, 100
Young Men's Christian Association (YMCA), 16, 186

Zahra, Tara, 83